Philosophy in America
Interpretive Essays
Volume II

Bruce S. Silver
University of South Florida

Nancy A. Stanlick
University of Central Florida

D1560441

PEARSON
Prentice Hall

Upper Saddle River, New Jersey, 07458

Library of Congress Cataloging-in-Publication Data

Philosophy in America: selected readings/[edited by] Nancy A. Stanlick, Bruce S. Silver.
p. cm.
Includes bibliographical references.
ISBN 0-13-183306-5

1. Philosophy, American—History. I. Stanlick, Nancy A. II. Silver, Bruce S.

B851.P49 2004
191—dc21 2002193123

VP, Editorial Director: Charlyce Jones Owen
Acquisitions Editor: Ross Miller
Assistant Editor: Wendy Yurash
Editorial Assistant: Carla Worner
AVP, Director of Production and Manufacturing: Barbara Kittle
Production Editor: Harriet Tellem
Prepress and Manufacturing Manager: Nick Sklitsis
Prepress and Manufacturing Buyer: Christina Helder
Cover Design: Jayne Conte
Composition: Preparé Inc.
Printer/Binder: RR Donnelley, Harrisonburg
Cover Printer: Phoenix Color Corp.

Copyright © 2004 by Pearson Education, Inc., Upper Saddle River, New Jersey, 07458.
All rights reserved. Printed in the United States of America. This publication is protected by Copyright and permission should be obtained from the publisher prior to any prohibited reproduction, storage in a retrieval system, or transmission in any form or by any means, electronic, mechanical, photocopying, recording, or likewise. For information regarding permission(s), write to: Rights and Permissions Department.

Pearson Education LTD.
Pearson Education Australia PTY, Limited
Pearson Education Singapore, Pte. Ltd
Pearson Education North Asia Ltd
Pearson Education, Canada, Ltd
Pearson Educación de Mexico, S.A. de C.V.
Pearson Education–Japan
Pearson Education Malaysia, Pte. Ltd

PEARSON
Prentice Hall

10 9 8 7 6 5 4 3 2 1
ISBN 0-13-183306-5

DEDICATION

To Maria, who helped me discover
"America! my new-found-land."
Bruce Silver

For Bruce Silver, my co-author, mentor, and friend.
Nancy Stanlick

Contents

Introduction

This book bears on philosophers, speculative thinkers, political activists, traditional and radical theists, deists, and skeptics whose ties to America reach from about 1720 to 2003. Some of them, like Thomas Paine and George Santayana, were not born in America. Others, including Jonathan Edwards and the members of the revolutionary generation, were English citizens at the outset and Americans only geographically. That changed with the end of the Revolutionary War and the Treaty of Paris, September 2, 1783.

These remarks remind us that an effort to deal with the history of American philosophy ought to be recast as an attempt to say something instructive about the history of philosophy in America. Such an attempt is the reason for this book. We know that some critics will ask whether there are not already enough books that deal with this history. Our answer is that many of these books begin with the pragmatists and do not give much, if any, attention to what came before them. We also know that other critics will ask why we include lawyers, revolutionaries, and presidents in a philosophical narrative and why, speaking technically, any non-American residents are given a prominent place in an American philosophical tradition.

The essays herein provide answers, but they will not please all those who want them. For example, Jonathan Edwards, who is the subject of Essay 1, willingly embraces a kind of Calvinism in retreat, but he does so for more than abstract doctrinal reasons. He is a Calvinist above all else, yet his message is frequently refined by deep and justified fears that eighteenth-century English-American colonists were, with the progressive expansion of worldly comforts, turning their backs on the true faith. A good deal of what Edwards writes is crafted to sustain Calvinism against a growing disinclination among colonists to take it seriously. Edwards would have been a Calvinist whether he had lived and preached in Scotland, England, or Geneva. But the brand of Calvinism he zealously defended was affected by the erosion of orthodoxy in Massachusetts and Connecticut.

The division of labor in this volume reflects the interests and philosophical backgrounds of the authors. Bruce Silver wrote the essays in Part I and Nancy Stanlick wrote the essays in Part II.

We can make related claims in Essay 2 about Benjamin Franklin and in Essay 4 about Ralph Waldo Emerson. At one level, that involving Franklin's earth-bound interests as against the more metaphysical concerns of Emerson, we encounter a restless man brimming with numerous interests and another man of contemplative detachment. They seem patently different from each other and, at first glance, are apparently bound together only by living in North America. On a closer reading, however, we find a connection between these celebrated giants of American history and culture. Both insisted that the best in human beings springs from their own capacities to make autonomous choices and to be unyielding in their self-reliance. And Henry David Thoreau, also a subject of Essay 4, established to his own satisfaction, after living for two years near Walden Pond, that Emerson's transcendentalism could be practiced as well as preached. The familiar picture of an American as independent, self-trusting, and self-reliant is in large measure the legacy of these three men. Each of them left a permanent stamp on a vision of human nature that is inseparable from the American psyche and soil.

In discussing the Founding Fathers in Essay 3, whose writings provided the philosophical trip-hammer for emancipation from England, we review a call to action that in some sense comes to typify American thought. After all, the greatest of the American pragmatists, who are the focus of Essay 6, refused to promote any philosophy that is inattentive to consequences, to verification in experience, and to acting deliberately in order to solve real-life problems. These three philosophers, Charles Sanders Peirce, William James, and John Dewey, were anticipated by the less well-known Chauncey Wright, whose philosophy we discuss in Essay 5. Wright and the pragmatists, no less than Franklin and the other great lights of the revolutionary era, insisted that thought has no business being estranged from constructive practice. Pragmatists, taking their lead from Darwin's brief for change and struggle, as well as from productive scientific and technological engagement in the world, produced a truly American philosophy. This was a philosophy, or perhaps a series of intimately related philosophies, that reached beyond North America into Europe. But at the core of pragmatism in all its manifestations was the reminder of an American willingness to identify remarkable goals and to work single-mindedly to realize them.

So pervasive and durable was pragmatism that into the present it continues to exercise an influence on philosophies that followed it. Josiah Royce, the Californian who reversed the migratory trend and moved east in the late nineteenth century, spent his academic life at Harvard. Royce thought of himself as a philosophical idealist and pragmatist. We find in Essay 7 that the union of these strains of thought, drawn from two distinct philosophies, led to an American idealism that was indebted to European and English antecedents but that also arose from the marrow of concerns at the center of a growing, increasingly diverse America.

One must avoid reductionism when reductionism simplifies a story beyond what it needs to tell. Nonetheless, Royce's awareness of immigrants who suffered years of prejudicial exclusion and alienation in America influenced his philosophical arguments for loyalty and unity, for inclusive communities, and for an improved urban life that should become a haven, not remain a hell, for its residents.

What about George Santayana, whose philosophy we explore in Essay 8? Despite living many years in Massachusetts as a school boy, undergraduate, and professor in the Harvard Department of Philosophy during its Golden Age, Santayana never thought of the United States as home. This is not to say that his philosophy was insulated from American sources. Santayana was indebted to the pragmatism of James and the pragmatic naturalism of Dewey. His rejection of moral absolutes and his religious skepticism are not far from Dewey's point of view. His remarks about experience and feeling are not identical to those of James and Dewey, but they are related to what these pragmatists said about the ways in which we confront and take in the world to which we belong and from which we cannot be detached. Santayana's great essay, "The Genteel Tradition in America" (1913), remains a classic account of American sensibilities and of the extent to which James's philosophy turned philosophy in America from its romantic moorings toward a willingness to face the world with "tough-minded" hopes of success.

C. I. Lewis, Willard Van Orman Quine, and Richard Rorty are important philosophers who help to define and, in Rorty's case, to redefine the character of philosophy in America from the late 1920s into the present. In Essay 9, we make a case for Lewis and Quine as the giants of the American tradition in analytic philosophy, although it may be true that no such case needs to be made. Rorty, who remains philosophically active and influential, raises questions and doubts about the future of philosophy itself. Some might argue, as others already have, that these thinkers are potent and important but that there is nothing uniquely American in what they offer. Like any other thesis or criticism, this one is easier to announce than to defend. The truth is, again, that these philosophers owe something to English and European philosophy, but that they are, like Royce and Santayana, perhaps more deeply indebted to what they admire in the pragmatists. Some of Essay 9, therefore, is an attempt to show the ways in which American analytic and post-analytic thought looks back to the pronouncements of James and Dewey.

In Essay 10, we take a step into the American past in order to move, once more, into the American present. Here we discuss women and African American thinkers whose work has still not been fully welcomed into the traditional philosophical canon. We do not attempt definitively to answer the question whether, Frederick Douglass, Susan B. Anthony, Elizabeth Cady Stanton, and Martin Luther King, Jr., are philosophers. We concede that we are pressed—even where we deal with thinkers who noncontroversially wear the epithet "philosopher"—to say just why someone counts as a philosopher. We do, however, believe that this much is indisputable: The thought and arguments of many African American and female advocates for equality and radical social change have too often been ignored by historians of philosophy in America. We try to do something about this by reviewing their arguments for an equitable society, a society that does not enslave or segregate human beings and a society that does not deny women their rights on the grounds that they are not men.

We conclude with Essay 11, in which we emphasize ethical and political theories that major American philosophers, including John Rawls and Robert Nozick, advance and defend. Rawls's *A Theory of Justice* (1971) and Nozick's *Anarchy, State and Utopia* (1974) are already classics. In them we discover two philosophers, at the height of their powers, exploring a range of issues that reach from the late twentieth century to at least as far back as John Locke and Immanuel Kant. Readers can decide for themselves whether Rawls, Nozick, and other figures in this chapter—such as Michael Sandel in his criticism of traditional liberalism and Virginia Held in her feminist critique of liberalism and communitarianism—are simply significant American philosophers or significant American philosophers whose philosophies are distinctly American.

We have tried hard not to force any of these philosophers, speculative thinkers, and political activists to pass through any predetermined conceptual hoops. If we have discovered anything in our research for this book, it is that there is no distinct set of themes and problems that first set the tone and then determine the direction of philosophical thought in America. To be sure, some philosophical ideas and prepossessions emerge and endure longer than others. Historians still talk about the intellectual underpinnings of the rugged American individual, about the clash between radical nonconformists and communitarians, about the ties between philosophical theory and practical transactions with the world, and about the opposed values of rural and urban life. But the durability of certain ideas and debates is not unique to America's intellectual tradition. Of course we hope that our readers will find in these pages something instructive about American philosophical activity. That what they find may not in every case typify what we call "American" is less important to us than that they find something that is enlightening and provocative.

No single volume can please everyone. Some readers will detect omissions and will wonder why we include certain thinkers at the expense of others. This is reasonable and inevitable in a selected study that cannot attempt to take in the complete history of philosophy in America. We have tried to strike a judicious balance between figures who are clearly too important to omit and others who find a place because we believe that their ideas deserve more attention than they have received. We hope, of course, that we have succeeded, and that we have written a book that will be valuable to students, educators, and recreational readers.

One truism is never trivial: The authors of any book do only part of their job. There is so much else that others do to turn ideas for a book into a book. We are indebted to more people than we can name. Two of them are Ross Miller, the acquisitions editor for Prentice Hall who accepted our proposal and took a chance on us, and Wendy Yurash, the assistant editor at Prentice Hall who patiently helped us through every step of the process and lifted our spirits with her enthusiasm and encouragement. Another is Harriet Tellem, senior production editor, whose knowledge and patience provided an intense short course in all that goes into putting together a finished, readable product.

We are indebted to the following reviewers who told us what we must do to turn an acceptable manuscript into something better: John R. Shook, Oklahoma State University; Scott Barlett, Southern Methodist University; and Kenneth Stikkers, Southern Illinois University, Carbondale. Many thanks to copy editor Karen Verde, who found errors and stylistic lapses that we had missed. We thank Elithea Whittaker of the University of South Florida Department of Philosophy for her interest in this project; her own background in publishing provided information and guidance that was more valuable to us than she can know. We are also grateful to Stephen Turner of the University of South Florida Department of Philosophy for his insights into communitarianism, to Shelley Park of the University of Central Florida Department of Philosophy for her discussions of feminist theory, and to Charles Guignon for helping us to sharpen our focus on the writings of Richard Rorty. We thank Jennifer Pumo of the University of Central Florida, who began to help us assemble a manuscript before there was a manuscript. And special thanks to Eileen Kahl who prepared the index.

In spite of all the help, support, and encouragement, we are responsible for whatever errors and infelicities remain. At the end of our project, we hope that these are modest and that our readers can profit from our excursion into the history of philosophy in America.

Part I
American Metaphysics and Epistemology

Essay 1
Jonathan Edwards: Philosophy Takes Hold

Jonathan Edwards was born in East Windsor, Connecticut, on October 5, 1703. Against all odds he was the only son of ten children born to Timothy and Esther Edwards. Schooled at home until he entered Yale College in 1716, the young Edwards exhibited intellectual promise very early. His adolescent and collegiate writings plainly indicate that he was at home in the sciences, whether he was attending to the behavior of spiders or pondering the nature of light and colors. As an undergraduate at Yale, Edwards knew something about Isaac Newton's *Opticks* (1704), either from having studied it himself or through second-hand acquaintance.[1] This knowledge, which is remarkable for a teenager, is evident in his short essay "Of the Rainbow."[2]

Having graduated from Yale in 1720, Edwards spent two years preparing himself for the clergy and took a post at a Scottish Presbyterian church in New York City in 1722. He stayed in New York for a year and in April 1723 returned to Yale, where he earned an M.A. degree and then served as a tutor for about two years. On November 21, 1726, he was invited to Northampton, Massachusetts, to serve as assistant pastor to the aging and distinguished Solomon Stoddard. Ordained on February 15, 1727, and married to the seventeen-year-old Sarah Pierpoint in July, Edwards became a father in 1728 and would remain at the ecclesiastical helm in Northampton until 1750, when a congregation, weary of his rigid requirements for church membership dismissed him.

Edwards left Northampton and settled in Stockbridge, Massachusetts, where he served as pastor and missionary to the Houssatunnuck Indians. Here, when he found time away from his formal responsibilities, he wrote *Freedom of the Will* (1758) and *The Nature of True Virtue*, posthumously published in 1765. The former, a classic in American philosophy, secures Edwards's reputation as an American philosopher of the highest order. The second, although less searching or original, shows the continuity between Edwards's moral thought and the English ethical tradition that he inherited and passed on to his successors.

Edwards's career and life were cut short by his decision in 1757 to accept the presidency of the College of New Jersey (later renamed Princeton). With reluctance he accepted the position and took office in January 1758. To protect himself from an outbreak of smallpox in Princeton and its surroundings, Edwards had himself inoculated. Either the serum or the needle used for the inoculation was tainted, and Edwards died of an infection on March 22, 1758. [3]

Edwards's life was relatively brief, but the list of his sermons, miscellaneous writings, and published works is not. It is, therefore, useful to approach Edwards by concentrating on selected, representative writings. The objective is to choose writings that exhibit the marrow of Edwards's philosophy and speculative thought.

"The Spider Letter" (October 31, 1723): Natural Philosophy as Natural Religion

This brief letter[4] illustrates two coexisting manifestations of Edwards's thinking as he came to maturity in the thinly populated Connecticut Valley, which was in many places still a wilderness far removed from urban centers like Boston and New York.[5] In or near Windsor, Connecticut, Edwards observed and recorded the behavior of tree ("flying") spiders and tied their activity to his already deep religious prepossessions. His observations are careful; the conclusions he draws from them are doubtful.

In a few pages, Edwards describes the way these spiders spin their webs, use what they have spun to advance from branch to branch and from tree to tree, and finally end their lives in the sea: ". . . it must necessarily be that almost all aerial insects, and spiders which live upon them and are made up of them, are at the end of the year swept away into the sea and buried in the ocean, and leave nothing behind them but their eggs for a new stock the next year."[6]

One can give Edwards high marks for his meticulous attention to nature's clockwork and cyclical rhythms. Until the conclusion of this piece of natural history, even Darwinians, who would have to wait more than another 140 years to have their say in America, could approve this account of the way that individuals within a species blindly perish but thereby permit the species itself to survive.[7] Edwards, no more than Mather, can forego an opportunity to draw a pious conclusion from careful scientific observations.

So after five pages of description and explanation that would satisfy any field naturalist, whose empirical commitments require evidence to verify this account of the "flying spider," there is a shift. Religious hypotheses and moralizing overawe strict science. We find "evidence" of God's wisdom "in providing of the spider with that wonderful liquor with which their bottle tail is filled" that enables them to cast their webs as they fly through the trees. More remarkable is the reason to celebrate God's "exuberant goodness" because he has "not only provided for all the necessities, but also for the pleasure and recreation of all sorts of creatures, even the insects."[8] Still, Edwards recognizes that too much emphasis on the pleasures of flight can hide a fatal fact, but a fact that also testifies to God's providence: The spiders' rapturous march, as we have already been told, is a death march. Nevertheless, in death, as in life, God's guiding hand is always present. In his wisdom God clears the air of decaying and poisonous pollutants by so designing the world that spiders and the insects that sustain them settle at the bottom of the ocean where they are harmless. Moreover, God's foresight establishes a balance between what is necessary for the species of spiders to survive and to keep it from expanding beyond nature's tolerances: "The wisdom of the Creator is also admirable in so nicely and mathematically adjusting their plastic nature, that notwithstanding their destruction . . . , they do not decrease and so . . . come to nothing; and in so adjusting their destruction to their multiplication they do neither increase, but . . . there is always an equal number of them."[9]

Obviously, a Darwinian or scientifically inclined skeptic will object that Edwards draws an illicit conclusion from what is otherwise a careful inspection of the phenomena. Such a skeptic will object that nothing Edwards describes actually points beyond itself to a wise creator and that nature's balance is explained better by the struggle for survival, natural selection, organic variation, and geological time—the components that Darwinians require—to account for biological phenomena like those Edwards attempts to explain.[10]

For the callow Edwards, as for Edwards as a mature philosopher and theologian, nature's adjustment, variety, and beauty point beyond themselves to their all-knowing, all-powerful, transcendent cause. Nature, that is, the wilderness that looms so prominently in American philosophy and culture, is a *vestigium Dei*. As such, it reminds Edwards, as he intends it to remind his readers, of the divine presence that shines through and illuminates the natural order: "It is allowed that God does purposely make and order one thing to be an agreeableness and harmony with another."[11]

There is nothing novel in Edwards's belief that nature is a kind of theophany that symbolically, as well as in the adjustment of means to ends, testifies to the presence and activity of God. Newton, to take the most prominent example of the scientific and philosophical giants whom Edwards studied at Yale, links the extraordinary science in the *Opticks* to his own version of the design argument for the creation of the world "by the Counsel of an intelligent Agent."[12] At the other end of the eighteenth century, William Bartram, the Quaker Philadelphia naturalist, wrote romantically and scientifically in his *Travels* (1791) that the "world, as a glorious apartment of the boundless palace of the sovereign Creator, is furnished with an infinite variety of animated scenes, inexplicably and beautifully pleasing, equally free to the inspection and enjoyment of all his creatures."[13]

Edwards's lack of originality in his statement of the design argument is not the issue. More important is the strength of his beliefs and their continuity throughout his life and career. Doubts never intrude. No crises induce him to rethink or revise his Christian calling. No debates with his congregation in Northampton or disagreements with fellow clergymen over church government affect his Calvinism. Commenting on Edwards's lecture delivered in Boston to other ministers on July 8, 1731, Perry Miller says, "Edwards put the pure doctrine without the slightest mitigation."[14] What was the doctrine that stood at the center of his religious being and life-long convictions? It is disarmingly simple and a bit unsettling even for Puritan divines who were trying by the early decades of the eighteenth century to soften the contours of the God they worshipped and make more palatable the stiff requirements of their faith.[15] Everything and everyone—the world, men and women, animals, bodies in motion and at rest—depends absolutely and at every moment upon God for existence and persistence.

When, for example, Edwards wishes by a route other than nature's design to prove that the God he worships is surely a God who exists, he appeals and adds to a blend of idealism whose ingredients were available to him from John Locke's great *An Essay Concerning Human Understanding* (1690) and possibly Bishop George Berkeley's *A Treatise Concerning the Principles of Human Knowledge* (1710) or *Three Dialogues between Hylas and Philonous* (1713).[16] Arguing loosely and elliptically on the basis of an idealistic extension of Locke that neither primary qualities of bodies (figure, number, motion, and rest), nor their secondary qualities (color, texture, taste, odor, hot and cold) have extramental reality, Edwards insists that resistance too exists only in what is actually being resisted. From this he infers, making doubtful leaps and taking questionable steps, that resistance is nothing but the power to resist and that a power, as nothing but potentiality of some kind, lacks independent existence. His conclusion, therefore, is inescapable: The world of bodies in space is an *ideal* world that subsists in God's mind, and its contents and laws of deployment depend absolutely upon God's support and providence.[17]

When the difficult and doubtful arguments are put aside, this much is clear: Edwards—young and middle-aged, before and after Yale, minister and missionary—saw in black and white the relation between his God and the world. Whether in its intricacy and beauty or in its order and lawful regularity, the world certifies its *dependence* and, as an undeniable consequence, the existence of a wise, powerful First Cause that brought everything else into being and that alone maintains its existence. Its laws, which were Newton's great discovery, are those God freely chooses and imposes.[18] Its contents exist only at God's pleasure: "That God does, by his immediate power, *uphold* every created substance in being, will be manifest, if we consider, that their present existence is a *dependent* existence, and therefore is an *effect*, and must have some *cause*."[19] This relation of artifact to maker, of dependent to sustainer is, once more, at the core of Edwards's philosophy and theology. Autonomy, an indisputable value to philosophers who define and celebrate the Enlightenment, belongs only to God.[20] Edwards makes no compromises. Nothing else, not one creature of the universe, is autonomous. This, more than anything else, is inseparable from Edwards's insistence upon the absolute sovereignty of God. So Sang Hyun Lee stresses the obvious: "Supremely important for him was the principle of God's absolute sovereignty in all aspects of reality, both the material and the spiritual."[21]

So far, whether looking at design throughout the world or to resistant bodies in motion and at rest, our emphasis has been on material and animal beings. What, then, of spiritual reality and God's relation to men and women who, unique among all creatures, can admire his power and cosmic artistry? The answer is direct and uncompromising.

"Sinners in the Hands of an Angry God" (1741): The Absolute Sovereignty of a Calvinist God

There is no question that "Sinners in the Hands of an Angry God" is Edwards's most famous sermon, indeed, his most famous work. If students of American history, literature, and culture know nothing else about Edwards, they are at least likely to know about the grim message of this sermon. Miller says that in Enfield, Connecticut, July 8, 1741, "Edwards delivered the one work by which, if he be remembered at all, he is likely to be known forever."

Preached during that extraordinary period of intense revivalism known as the Great Awakening, "fire and brimstone" describe its content more than Edwards's oratory,[22] although an eyewitness account testifies that among the congregation, "there were moanings and cryings, until the shrieks became so 'amazing' that Edwards (his eyes fixed on the bell rope) had to pause."[23] What is it that makes "Sinners in the Hands of an Angry God" canonical and what is its argument?

Stripped to the bone, the message is duplex and is as pure a statement of New England Calvinism as one is ever likely to find. *First*, every man and woman, boy and girl is a fallen sinner. There are no exceptions. As sinners we deserve nothing from God and have no reason to expect his mercy. This is the human condition and it has been so ever since the father and mother of us all disobeyed God and were evicted from Eden. "Sin is the ruin and misery of the soul; it is destructive in its nature. . . . The corruption of the heart of man is a thing that is immoderate and boundless in its fury."[24] The sermon resonates with relentless accounts of our loathsomeness before God. Once more we encounter Edwards's interest in spiders, but the tone could not be further removed from what we find in "The Spider Letter": "The God that holds you over the pit of hell, much as one holds a spider, or some loathsome insect over the fire, abhors you, and is dreadfully provoked; his wrath towards you burns like fire; he looks upon you as worthy of nothing else, but to be cast into the fire . . . ; you are ten thousand times so abominable in his eyes as the most hateful venomous serpent is in ours."[25]

Not only are we corrupt and offensive to our creator, but we are also a blemish on the rest of his creation.[26] "Were it not that so is the sovereign pleasure of God, the earth would not bear you one moment; for your are a burden to it; *the creation groans with you; the creature is made subject to the bondage of your corruption.*"[27] Descriptions of the dignity and goodness of human beings, often fashionable among moralists of the Enlightenment, are polite but not well founded. The case for Edwards is unambiguous: Hell, whose "fiery pit" and torments are beyond anything that we can conceive, is where each of us belongs and where the majority of us will spend unbearable eternity.[28] Only the few who repent their sins and who benefit from gratuitous grace will stand forever at the right-hand side of God. They are no less sinful than their condemned brothers and sisters; they are, however, forgiven and purified to a degree that God allows them—through his generosity, not through their merit—to take their places in Heaven.[29]

This brings us to a *second* component in the message of this great, frightening sermon. As all men and women are sinners whose wills have been forever darkened and, as we will see, weakened by their corrupt natures, they are absolutely impotent to secure their own salvation or election. There is nothing surprising in this. Calvinism was rooted in New England. But there is more to being a creature than corruption. As human beings are dependent, so too, of course, they are impotent. Whatever they receive, from their continued existence on the planet to their unwarranted salvation, depends upon the gratuitous will of the God they should worship and fear. In short, the dependence of human beings, like that of the universe of bodies in motion, stands in stark contrast to the autonomy, conserving power, and sovereignty of a creator who redeems only a few of them: "you are thus in the hands of an angry God; 'tis nothing but his mere pleasure that keeps you from being this moment swallowed up in everlasting destruction."[30]

There is, moreover, no mistaking the asymmetry between the being of a creature and that of God. God owes nothing. We, on the other hand, owe him everything. Edwards has no patience with the "new" breed of New England Puritans who conceived their God as contractually bound (obligated by a covenant between him and them) to save those who have striven to lead the good Christian life and to purge their sins. The differences between our being alive or dead, between sharing the ineffable joys of Heaven and enduring the inconceivable pains of Hell, depend solely upon God's "*sovereign* pleasure, his arbitrary will, restrained by no obligation" and upon "the uncovenanted unobliged forbearances of an incensed God."[31]

The argument of "Sinners in the Hands of an Angry God" is no different from that in less well-known sermons like "The Future Punishment of the Wicked Unavoidable and Intolerable" (1741). Here too the "wicked" includes everyone to whom God has not extended his saving grace; here too the journey for most of us is a straight line from birth to damnation, and here too "weakness" and "dependence" apply to creatures as "great" and "mighty power" apply only to God:

> What art thou in the hands of the great God, who made heaven and earth by speaking a word? What are thou, when dealt with by his strength, which manages all this vast universe . . . and, when the fixed time shall come, will shake all to pieces?—There are other beings a thousand times stronger than thou . . . But how little are they in the hands of the great God . . . ; they are nothing and less than nothing in the hands of an angry God, as will appear at the day of judgment.[32]

To take Edwards seriously, and many New Englanders must have as they listened to his sermons and were mesmerized by his appeal to their emotions, is to confront the fragility of life itself. Perhaps Perry Miller was not exaggerating when he summarized the effects of Edwards's sermons and his place in the Great Awakening: "He overthrew the kind of religious philosophy that had dominated Western Europe since the fall of Rome, the system wherein there was always . . . an ascertainable basis for human safety. Now there was none. . . . Edwards' preaching was America's sudden leap into modernity."[33]

We are, therefore, as a condition of our finitude and hubris, weak and corrupt. Celebrations of dignity and self-reliance belong to a later age in American philosophy and to later essays in this study. But there is another theme that enters through the back door and is almost as much at home in the texts of Edwards's overheated Northampton and Enfield sermons as in Revolutionary Philadelphia and Boston. This theme is revealed when Edwards stresses the infinity of God and the finitude of mankind: "The greatest earthly potentates, in their greatest majesty and strength . . . , are but feeble despicable worms of the dust, in comparison of the great and almighty Creator and King of heaven and earth. . . . All the kings of the earth before God are as grasshoppers, they are nothing and less than nothing."[34] Again, "The Future Punishment of the Wicked Unavoidable and Intolerable," poses this rhetorical question: "Art thou such a fool as to think that the great King of heaven and earth, before whom all other kings are so many grasshoppers, will not vindicate his kingly Majesty on such contemptuous rebels as thou art?"[35]

From God's perspective, all human beings are *equal*. In the Calvinist tradition that Edwards tries to preserve against the tide of change and worldliness, affirming this kind of equality is not new. The Old and New Testament stress the manner and extent to which all of us are equal in God's eyes. The rich have no better chance than the poor to inherit the kingdom of heaven. The infinite chasm which distinguishes a perfect, autonomous God from radically dependent, imperfect creatures announces that from the divine perspective, there is nothing in the way of excellence or superiority that distinguishes one man or woman from another. This means the equality in question is not that of superiority, not that of merit or opportunity. When one adds, as Edwards does at every turn, that all human beings are unfathomably removed from God by their sinfulness, as well as their finitude, any inclination to revel in universal equality, an equality in finitude and depravity, evaporates.

Obviously, then, there is neither the temptation nor justification to think of Edwards as a social and political reformer. He was not. He admits that his approach to life, like that toward his faith and calling, is conservative and rigid. And like other comfortable members of his class, he had slaves to help manage his large family.[36] Equality before God does not translate into equality among men or into equal treatment under the laws that govern and restrain men. Edwards would have found no reason to revise the opening sentence of John Winthrop's *A Model of Christian Charity* (1630): "God Almighty in his most holy and wise providence, hath so disposed of the condition of mankind, as in all times some must be rich, some poor, some high and eminent in power and dignity, others mean and in subjection."[37]

Why, if his attitudes are neither novel nor reformist, is there any need to call attention to Edwards's remarks on equality? A first answer is obvious. Any effort to piece together Edwards's philosophy ought to include what illuminates it. Knowing that and why Edwards believes all human beings are in one sense equal helps us to understand his philosophy and thus helps us to satisfy our aims. There is also a second answer that is more interesting than the first but that must await fuller attention until a discussion of Ralph Waldo Emerson's Transcendentalism. This much need not, however, be postponed. After Edwards describes all human beings as indistinguishable when judged against their maker, the distance is not so great as one might at first think between a Calvinist equality of wretchedness and an Emersonian equality of dignity. The key is equality itself. Once Edwards identifies it as a staple of his stern religious doctrine, it does not fade or go away. And even as a subset of sinners is transformed by God's mercy, so too the lamentable equality of all Edwards's sinners is to be transmuted into a vigorous, admirable equality that is inseparable from Emerson's account of what constitutes human dignity and genius. This transmutation of the value and character of equality is, as we will see in the essay on New England Transcendentalism, as remarkable as the transformation of wicked sinners into righteous saints.

A Treatise Concerning Religious Affections (1746): Special Faculties for Extra-special Knowledge

Religious Affections and its companion piece "A Divine and Supernatural Light," preached in Northampton in 1734, are less well-known than "Sinners in the Hands of an Angry God." But fame is not all that matters. As the focus of this essay is to learn something about Edwards's philosophy, part of that effort is to discover how he answers, in his book and sermon, the question, "What is the nature of true religion?"[38] His answer is, "True religion, in great part, consists in holy affections," a declaration that helps to situate Edwards within an enduring expression of the American philosophical tradition and in a manifestation of the Enlightenment that he does not reject.[39] As is so often the case in philosophy, the answer to a question invites another question, and this case is no exception. What does his answer mean?

After Edwards borrows and modifies a Lockean distinction between two powers of the mind, which for him are *understanding* that discerns and judges and the *will* through which the mind is moved toward or from the things that it views, he tries to explain what he means by "true religion": ". . . true religion consists, in a great measure, in *vigorous and lively actings of the inclination and will of the soul, or the fervent exercises of the heart.*"[40] This is not altogether transparent. Fortunately, there is enough clarity in *Religious Affections* to provide some answers.

A truly religious person, a Calvinist saint who has been saved through God's grace, is obviously different from people who have not been saved because they have not received the gift of grace. The difference between the saint and the unredeemed sinner is extreme. The sinner remains a natural, tainted man or woman; the saint is "converted" into a supernatural being: ". . . those gracious influences which the saints are subject of, and the effects of God's Spirit which they experience, are entirely above nature, altogether of a different kind from anything that men find within themselves by nature, or only in the exercise of natural principles. . . . And this is what I mean by supernatural, when I say, that gracious affections are from those influences that are supernatural."[41]

The gift that the saint receives from God, which God withholds from others, is a special "sense of the heart."[42] In this context "heart" does not refer to an organ but to a capacity or faculty that is the seat of special ideas and affections. It denotes what the "Light" of "A Divine and Supernatural Light" denotes.[43] The sanctified man or woman, as a beneficiary of God's grace,[44] has a capacity to receive and to understand ideas that are never present to the five conventional senses or to ordinary human understanding:

> [I]t follows that the mind has an entirely new kind of perception or sensation . . . , which is in its whole nature different from any former kinds of sensation of the mind . . . ; and something is perceived by a true saint, in this exercise of the sense of the mind, in spiritual and divine things, as entirely diverse from anything that is perceived in them, by natural men, as the sweet taste of honey is diverse from the ideas men get of honey by looking on it, and feeling of it.[45]

A genuinely religious man or woman has not received a new soul, mind or will; rather God has transformed the understanding and will in such a way that a saint understands and wills in a new and spiritual manner.[46]

Saints sense and understand directly the loveliness of God and the Holy Spirit. But what a saint senses and understands is clear and intelligible only to the saint.[47] "Thus there is a difference between having an opinion that God is holy and gracious, and having a sense of the loveliness and beauty of that holiness and grace. . . . There is a wide difference between mere speculative, rational judging anything to be excellent, and having a sense of its sweetness, and beauty. The former rests only in the head, speculation only is concerned in it; but the heart is concerned in the latter."[48] Because this is the character of unmediated understanding and perception of the heart, there is no possibility of confusing the saint's knowledge with that of the learned interpreter of scripture.[49] Instead, as we have seen, the sanctified human being, made supernatural through the "divine light," knows that he or she is "spiritually enlightened" by religious knowledge which bears its own "kind of intuitive and immediate evidence."[50]

Here, in Edwards's intuitionism and anti-intellectualism, we encounter more foreshadowing of American philosophy to come. For Edwards it is not the intellectually elect, the educated "fit and few," who are best equipped to arrive at knowledge that matters absolutely. We will see that the same is true for Emerson, a Harvard graduate, and Jefferson, founder of the University of Virginia and champion of an enlightened, literate public. For Edwards, as for the New England Transcendentalists, knowing that which counts most depends upon metaphysical intuition, not upon being able to bring chains of inferences to their conclusions. But this is, once again, getting ahead of ourselves insofar as there remains some unfinished business with respect to *Religious Affections*.

Having a sense of the heart and acting on it are related but distinct. The truly religious man or woman who, having this preternatural sense and thereby having ideas of God's beauty and holiness that natural human beings "know" only by description, is also drawn to God as the object of his or her inclination. The saint *wills* or wishes to revel in the company of the Creator.[51] When one possesses this remarkable sixth sense, the knowledge it provides generates desire and action. There is, in short, nothing passive or restrained about the sanctified human being whose true love is also his Maker.[52] This is why Edwards says of those who are genuinely religious, we find "lively actings of the inclination and will" and the equally "fervent exercises of the heart." For Edwards and presumably for those he managed to "wake," the phrase "passive zealot" is oxymoronic: "The things of religion are so great, that there can be no suitableness in the exercise of our hearts, to their nature and importance, unless they be lively and powerful. *In nothing, is vigor in the actings of our inclinations so requisite, as in religion; and in nothing is lukewarmness so odious.*"[53]

If it is fair to think of Edwards as a mystic when he talks about a sense that perceives spiritual qualities which never appear among the qualities on which our conventional five senses bear, it is no less fair to notice that Edwards acknowledges some strain when the issue is *evidence* that someone is actually sanctified. He lists a variety of "things" that are not signs someone is a saint: (i) the strength of religious emotions, (ii) bodily effects, (iii) an augmented knowledge of Scripture, and (iv) the joy that follows a (possible) conversion.[54] Evidence in favor of being sanctified and religious comes in two varieties. There is the *inner* evidence that enables saints to know that they are redeemed and transformed, as we have already discussed, that is, consciousness of a "spiritual sense" by which a saint alone directly apprehends "the divine glory, and excellency of God."[55] The unconverted sinner has as little idea of these divine properties as a person has of beauty who has never "looked on Beauty bare." As Edwards puts it, "there is a difference between believing that a person is beautiful, and having a sense of his beauty. The former may be obtained by hearsay, but the latter only by seeing the countenance."[56]

The problem with this account of internal evidence is, as Locke and David Hume argued in their important criticisms of religious enthusiasts, the obvious difference between the propositions "I am persuaded that *p* is true" and "*p* is true." Enthusiasts, however, have no grasp of this difference. Their private persuasion is the imprimatur that they are certain, but subjective convictions that they are among the elect, no matter how intense, are not evidence, at least not for Locke: ". . . it is not the strength of our private perswasion within our selves, that can warrant it to be a light . . . from Heaven: Nothing can do that but the written Word of GOD without us, or that Standard of Reason which is common to us with all Men."[57] Hume is as skeptical as Locke. Referring to enthusiasts in the throes of their convictions, Hume writes: "Hence arise raptures, transports, and surprising flights of fancy; and confidence and presumption still increasing, these raptures, being altogether unaccountable . . . are attributed to the immediate inspiration of that Divine Being who is the object of devotion."[58]

Locke and Hume have put their fingers on a problem. In the absence of verification, beliefs are nothing but beliefs. Appealing to inner convictions that one is privileged and thus sees directly what others cannot see is very far from providing evidence that a conviction is justified. Claims to have a private access or conduit to truth or to properties of transexperiential reality inevitably wake doubts and suspicions in those who are said to lack the required sense or capacity for special intuitions. Locke so disparages this attitude that in the end he says of those who see themselves as spiritually set apart from others, "they are sure, because they are sure: and their Perswasions are right, only because they are strong in them."[59]

There is also the problem of *outer* or external evidence. Here the question shifts to the perspective of an outsider, an observer who wants evidence that a purported saint is one and is not merely a charlatan or self-deluded enthusiast.

What, in short, is the evidence that someone I know or to whom I have been introduced is sanctified? Edwards answers by listing three criteria: (i) behavior that answers to "Christian rules," (ii) attention toward practicing Christian behavior above all other concerns in this life, and (iii) acting as Christian constantly, from the moment of conversion to the end of life itself.[60] These criteria are separately necessary and jointly sufficient to satisfy any reasonable person that someone else is religious in the only sense that counts. They are the practices that serve as the outward indicia of inner sanctification, and Edwards believes that they are the most that one can reasonably request if one seeks evidence that someone else is a true Christian.[61]

If a critic or skeptic is dissatisfied with this kind and degree of evidence, Edwards has nothing else to say. To demand more evidence when one wants objective validation of an inaccessible interior state of the mind and heart is to demand more than the case permits: "Now from all that has been said, I think it to be abundantly manifest, that Christian practice is the most proper evidence of the gracious sincerity of professors, to themselves and others."[62] Obviously, the persistent critic can claim with justification that outward behavior need not indicate inner states or motives. Soren Kierkegaard, the great nineteenth-century Danish philosopher, says that a profoundly Christian "knight of faith" acts and "looks just like a tax-gatherer . . . , he belongs altogether to the world, no *petit bourgeois* belongs to it more."[63] On the other side, one can play the part of a Christian saint and not be one. Edwards knows as much but can take the argument no further. For him, when all is said and evaluated, the best available evidence for him that *S* is a saint is that *S* behaves as he expects a saint to behave.

Finally, before leaving this section, a cautionary reminder about Edwards's treatment of equality is appropriate. One might be tempted, in light of the equality announced in "Sinners in the Hands of an Angry God" and the anti-intellectual strains in *Religious Affections*, to object that Edwards does not really believe all human beings are equal from God's point of view. After all, he says saints are spiritually superior to natural men and women. Yes, Edwards makes this claim, but the objection to it might be misplaced.

Those who are sanctified and elevated through God's grace, thereby made superior, are *a fortiori* no longer ordinary men and women. Edwards is emphatic about this.[64] As transformed and thereby equipped with supernatural perceptions, which in turn depend upon a supernatural sense, Edwards describes beings who, as creatures, are not gods, but who are also not merely human. Where they fit on the chain of being is hard to say, although Edwards provides a hint when he talks about God's free gift of "spiritual wisdom" in those who receive it: ". . . there is no gift or benefit that is in itself so nearly related to the divine nature, there is nothing the creature receives that is so much of God, of his nature, so much a participation of the Deity that it is a kind of emanation of God's beauty, and is related to God as the light is to the sun."[65] The gift, whether we call it a "sense of the heart" or a "divine light," produces a class of beings who are literally, not metaphorically, *extra*ordinary. That they are different from merely human beings is a result of their being made something more and better. This is what true religion or saintliness is about for Edwards. That is why he can consistently claim, given the thesis of *Religious Affections*, that all *human* beings are equal in God's sight but that saints are superior, not equal, to those who are simply human and thus are not included within the circle of the chosen.

Enquiry into Freedom of the Will (1754): A Case for the Compatibility of Determinism and Personal Responsibility

If one were to rank Edwards's writings in terms of their philosophical value, not their influence, *Freedom of the Will* would surely take pride of place. It must be included on a relatively short list of truly great American books.[66] Unfortunately, because of its difficulty and occasional obscurity, *Freedom of the Will* gets less attention than it deserves. Here too a selective survey of philosophy in America does not permit an exhaustive analysis of Edwards's own careful treatment of the two questions that dominate this classic work: (1) are human beings free or determined in the choices they make, and (2) if they are determined, can they be held justly responsible for their choices? These are, of course, questions that philosophers and theologians have been asking since at least St. Augustine's *De Libero Arbitro* (circa 400 C.E.), and Edwards's own answers to (1) and (2) find some precedents in Hobbes's and Locke's treatment of the same questions.[67]

Attending, then, only to the salient points of Edwards's discussion, we can begin with his answer to (1), which is that human beings *are* determined in the choices they make. Edwards believes—and in this he is close to Locke—the dispute that question (1) expresses is largely the product of a needless obscurity that theologians and philosophers generate and then labor in vain to eliminate. So Edwards believes that a key step is to simplify the debate. The will, far from being some free-standing metaphysical entity that has an autonomous life of its own, is "that by which the mind chooses anything. The faculty of the will is that . . . power . . . of mind by which it is capable of choosing: an act of will is the same as an act of choosing or choice."[68] What this comes to, in still simpler terms, is that the *will* is, or designates, a person's power to choose; *willing* is nothing but choosing, and an *act of will* is a choice.

So if the question in (1) is whether one's power to choose is determined, resulting in a choice that is also determined, the answer is not only an unqualified *yes*, but Edwards also defines the precise cause or that which determines the will to choose what it chooses: "it is that *motive*, which, as it stands in the view of the mind, is the *strongest*, that *determines the will*."[69] By "motive" Edwards understands whatever induces or causes the choosing agent to choose as he or she does. The proximate cause, therefore, that induces someone to choose x over y or y over z is the prevailing motive; hence to say that the will is determined is just to say that the will is caused by the motive that prevails to choose what it chooses, but with two qualifications. (i) The agent must be conscious of the motive; "for what is wholly unperceived . . . can't affect the mind at all," and (ii) the strongest or prevailing motive is what the agent perceives or considers *good* or *best* among available options: "*And therefore it must be true, in some sense, that the will always is as the greatest apparent good is.*"[70]

Up to this point, Edwards's analysis of determinism is logically independent of his Calvinism. He is espousing and defending a determinism that requires what determinism of any variety requires, namely that every event, including every event called a "choice," has a cause. "That whatsoever begins to be, which before was not, must have a cause why it then begins to exist, seems to be the first dictate of common and natural sense which God hath implanted in the minds of all mankind. . . ." As a result, "it is indeed as repugnant to reason, to suppose that an act of will should come into existence without a cause, as to suppose the human soul, or an angel, or . . . the whole universe should come into existence without a cause."[71] Edwards, taking the position of a "necessitarian," insists not only that every event must have a causal antecedent but that there is a necessary connection between a cause and its effect.[72] Again, this causal axiom holds whether one talks about the change that a body in motion causes in another body at rest or about motives and the choices they cause agents to make: "*Moral necessity* may be as absolute, as *natural necessity*. That is, the effect may be as perfectly connected with its moral cause, as a naturally necessary effect is with its natural cause."[73]

Edwards's religious convictions enter *Freedom of the Will* when he talks about what *ultimately*, not proximately, determines everything that occurs, *viz.*, God's foreknowledge (omniscience) of all that exists and all that happens, has happened, and will happen. The argument itself is far easier to state than it is to solve, but Edwards, unlike philosophers who link free will to moral and religious responsibility, has no interest in solving it. He puts the case very simply: because God, as omniscient, "has a certain and infallible prescience of the acts of the will of moral agents . . . , it follows from hence, that these events are *necessary*, with a necessity or connection or consequence."[74] If, that is, God knows infallibly and completely everything, then all that he knows cannot but be or occur; otherwise God's knowledge would be defective or incomplete, and this is impossible. If, however, God knows or foreknows unerringly and completely all that occurs, including that cluster of occurrences called "human choices," those choices must necessarily occur as God knows them; hence they could not have been otherwise. Given this species of what philosophers call "logical determinism," every choice we make is rigidly determined and could not have been made differently.[75]

Beyond divine foreknowledge, there is also the Calvinist doctrine of foreordination. As sovereign, God predetermines, as well as foreknows, all that will happen. Nothing can threaten this basic ingredient of traditional Calvinism. But if human beings could choose freely, hence contingently, they—along with God—would have a say in the emergence and outcome of events: "For if men do have free will . . . , then the Calvinist doctrine of Divine predetermination must be false."[76] But no matter how much this appeals to those who speak for the value of self-reliance and autonomy, there is no room in Edwards's Calvinist doctrine for a softened, or mistaken, view of what God knows and does. The alternative is that well-intentioned Christians, the Arminians to whom Edwards refers pejoratively throughout *Freedom of the Will*, are mistaken and must be corrected. Arminian Protestants, English and Dutch followers of the early seventeenth-century reformed Calvinist Jacobus Arminius, believed in free will and denied divine predetermination.[77]

What, now, about question (2)? If our choices are rigidly determined, both by God's omniscience and omnipotence and by the strongest prevailing motive, can we be morally, religiously, or legally responsible for them? The intuitive answer is no, but Edwards insists that the correct answer, once we understand the only mitigating qualifications for denying responsibility, is yes. Edwards declares and defends his position by pointing out that there are different ways of talking about key words in the debate between philosophical libertarians (defenders of the reality of free will) and determinists. When philosophers and theologians, figuratively wearing their philosophical gowns and clerical vestments, talk about "necessity" and "impossibility," they have in mind the facts to which we have already alluded: There is a firm and fixed necessity between causes and effects; every event must have a cause, and God foreknows and preordains every existence and every occurrence.[78] But when ordinary men and women, or philosophers and theologians when they are not concentrating on their "official" practices and capacities, use these words ("necessity," "impossibility," and "irresistibility"), they employ them in a very different way. In conventional contexts,

> A thing is said to be *necessary*, when we can't help it, let us do what we will. So anything is said to be *impossible* to us, when we would do it, or would have it brought to pass, and endeavour it . . . ; but all our desires and endeavours are, or would be vain. And that is said to be *irresistible*, which overcomes all our opposition, resistance, and endeavour to the contrary. And we are to be said *unable* to do a thing, when our supposable desires and endeavours to do it are insufficient.[79]

The point is in actual circumstances that require taking or denying responsibility for our actions and choices, we hold others responsible for what they do if and only if *they do what they choose to do*, and the same criterion applies to us. Choices—no matter how we make them—that are neither *constrained* nor *restrained* or, more generally, that are *unimpeded*, are choices for which agents are justly accountable.[80] In Edwards's view of the matter, this is the only appropriate answer to (2).

What separates Edwards from once well-known Arminians like Whitby and Taylor is that where he requires only a single condition in terms of which to assign blame or to offer praise, they require two conditions. Morton White states the difference with economy: "They claimed that a man's past action was free if and only if *two* conditions were satisfied: firstly, that he did as he chose to do; and, secondly, that his *choice* was free in a sense which, according to Edwards, varied from one Arminian text to another."[81] In other words, Edwards, unlike his theological adversaries, unties the Gordian knot that seems to disallow compatibility between determinism and responsible choice. He does this by appealing to common sense.[82] How?

In ordinary and routine cases that call for moral, legal or religious judgments, Edwards insists that we hold people responsible for their choices and consequences of those choices only if they were able to implement what they chose. A lifeguard who chooses to save a drowning victim and fails because the powerful tides frustrate his efforts is not morally or legally culpable. He chose to do his duty but was restrained by the forces of nature from doing it. A woman who chooses to report an assault on her friend, but is constrained not to by the attacker's threats against her children, is guiltless because of her unsettling circumstances. These are two cases in which reasonable men and women, who are not doctors of divinity or philosophers, say "He or she could not have done otherwise or acted differently. Each is blameless, although the consequences of their impeded choices are unfortunate."

Suppose, however, we take exactly the same circumstances but replace action with inaction. The lifeguard makes no attempt to save the hapless victim and the woman both fails to report the felony and admits that she has no regrets about not doing so. We ask them to explain the inertia that led in each case to these undesirable consequences. The lifeguard says that the nature and unfolding of events is such that he was *necessarily* determined, even fated, to sit in his chair while the swimmer eventually drowned, and this is all he says. The woman makes her case for inaction on the grounds that the character of the universe is such that there is no way, that it was *impossible*, for her to have done otherwise. She too has nothing more to add. No one, whether an Arminian libertarian or a Calvinist determinist, accepts these excuses as mitigating blame or responsibility. Edwards, in an appeal to the ordinary acceptation of the vocabulary that we all use in assigning blame and assessing responsibility, writes:

> The plain and obvious meaning of the words *freedom* and *liberty*, in common speech, is *power*, *opportunity*, or *advantage, that any one has, to do* as he pleases. Or in other words, his being free from hindrance or impediment in the way of doing, or conducting in any respect, as he wills. And contrary to liberty, whatever name we call that by, is a person's being hindered or unable to conduct as he will, or being necessitated to do otherwise. . . . Let the person come by his volition or choice how he will, yet, if he is able, and there is nothing in the way to hinder his pursuing and executing his will, the man is fully and perfectly free, according to the primary and common notion of freedom.[83]

The key phrase is "the primary and common notion of freedom." Philosophers and divines will continue to debate the subtleties and puzzles that surround questions of free will and determinism. People of good sense know when to praise and when to blame other people, or to censure themselves, for their choices. This appeal to the sturdy common sense of practical people is at the marrow of Edwards's solution to the problem of responsibility. Rarefied discussions that few people grasp and that even fewer indulge have no bearing on how we judge conduct. More than metaphysical and theological disputes, what matters to Edwards is how we make these judgments.

The message, beyond the specific content of Edwards's answers to questions (1) and (2) as they shape *Freedom of the Will*, is akin to that in *Religious Affections* and "A Divine and Supernatural Light." In his most philosophically searching and analytical work, Edwards maintains the same position he expresses during the intensely emotional period of the Great Awakening: the voices of ordinary people are the first, best, and final arbiters of problems that religious and secular sages cannot resolve. Untutored men and women to whom he preached in the Connecticut Valley and whom he tried to "wake," as well as the even more rustic settlers in Stockbridge, knew why to praise or chide a person's choices and how to assess human behavior.[84]

Nonetheless, it took Edwards's intellectual efforts, not the intuitions of his converts and parishioners, to try to lay bare the flaws in the Arminian doctrine of free will. Whether the Arminians understood by "free will," a will from which choices arise (a) contingently, (b) indifferently, or (c) through its own self-determination, Edwards had replies. The notion that (a) choices could somehow arise contingently or uncaused from an unfettered will is senseless on its face. Apart from standing in direct opposition to the principle that every occurrence has a cause, Edwards believes that talk of a causeless choice is inconsistent with itself. "If any should imagine, there is something in the sort of event that renders it possible for it to come into existence without a cause; and should say, that the free acts of the will are existences of an exceeding different nature from other things," they are refuting themselves; "for they would be giving an account of some ground of the existence of a thing, when at the same time they would maintain there is no ground of its existence."[85] In other words, according to Edwards, to say of some choice *c* "*c* occurs without a cause" amounts to saying, "There is some cause that accounts for the causelessness of *c*." And thus the Arminians betray the claim that they make if they really mean that some choices are free insofar as they are uncaused.[86]

The shortcomings of Edwards's criticism of (a) are duplex. First, it has the look of what logicians call a "straw man" argument; that is, the argument attacks a position that no one or almost no one holds. Few philosophical libertarians characterize free choices as uncaused, and few would want to grant that there are any. We expect Paul to react in a certain way to some state of affairs and Mary to act in some other way. Why? Because the uniformity of our experience leads us to anticipate certain choices based upon what we already know of their character. If choices sprang *ex nihilo* and thus unpredictably from the agents who make them, our ability to deal with human beings would, in every context, be frustrated. So in criticizing this species of Arminian, Edwards was taking aim at a species that is not extinct but at one that has probably never appeared.

The second flaw in Edwards's criticism of this rendering of a free will is his mistaken assumption that there must be a cause for the causelessness of *c*. There is no warrant for this complaint. He is wrong to say that because *c* is uncaused there must be a cause for its being uncaused. Edwards confuses causes with reasons. There may be reasons that some events occur without causes and therefore belong to a class of events that are in this sense different from other events, but their belonging to a class of events that is uncaused is not itself a cause of their being uncaused. A correct description of *e* as causeless does not, contrary to what Edwards seems to think, make this description the cause of uncaused *c*.

What about (b) the Arminian notion that some choices are free insofar as they are generated (b) from an indifferent will, that is, from a will that is not moved by a motive of any kind? "A great argument for self-determining power, is the supposed experience we universally have of an ability to determine our wills, in cases where no prevailing motive is presented: the will (as is supposed) has its choice to make between two or more things, that are perfectly equal in view of the mind; and the will is apparently altogether indifferent."[87] Edwards says that this state of affairs is impossible insofar as choices are always products of the strongest prevailing motive.[88] In other words, having already defined an actual choice as the consequence of the strongest motive, it follows for Edwards that no deliberate choice can be a product of an indifferent will.[89] The problem is, of course, that Edwards's criticism presumes the point in question. If, after all, "*S* chose *a* over *b*" means "*S*'s preference for *a* was stronger than his preference for *b*," then the choice was not made in a state of indifference.[90] Arminians and non-Arminians like John Locke, to whom Edwards objects obliquely, simply disagree with Edwards's or with any other determinist's entry-level assumption that all our choices are determined. Indeterminists need not, as a consequence, be impressed by his argument that the phrase "indifferent choice" is contradictory.[91]

Finally, Edwards must dispense with the position that is most dear to Arminians and to others who insist upon free will, namely (c) that human beings have a self-determined will. This is, as the epithet "self-determined" suggests, a will that is not determined by anything outside itself. As appealing as this is to religious and secular patrons of self-reliance, for Edwards it too is flawed. But his criticism of this variation on the libertarian theme is more compelling than what he says against (a) or (b). Apart from objecting to the Arminians' persistent, misguided attempts to reify the will—to treat it as an agent itself instead of a power that we attribute to agents—there is a straightforward misstep in (c), which Edwards brings to the surface by asking what anyone could mean by describing the will as "self-determined." As he puts it, ". . . if the will determines all its own free acts, then every free act of choice is determined by a preceeding act of choice, choosing that act. And if that preceeding act of the will or choice be also a free act, then by these principles, in this act too, the will is self-determined."[92] Either, therefore, we have an endless, infinite regress of free choices, which is philosophically intolerable and does nothing to advance the Arminian view of free choice, or we have a first choice in the series that, because it is not the product of a prior free choice, is not a self-determined free choice: "but if the first act in the train, determining and fixing the rest, be not free, none of them all can be free."[93]

Here, if not against (a) and (b), Edwards's criticism of (c) cuts deep. In direct terms, it says what Edwards believes: The Arminians' insistence upon a liberated will is easier to demand than to defend. When they or any other indeterminists are pressed to supply content for uplifting and familiar phrases like "self-reliance," "self-determination," and "free will," they come up short. In the end, Edwards believes that Arminians have nothing to offer but vacuous language and thinly veiled threats to the sovereignty and freedom that belong to God alone.

Conclusion

When we read *Freedom of the Will* in conjunction with works that range from the early "Spider Letter" to the sermons for which Edwards is best remembered, we find hints that what is true of America's first significant philosopher may be true of American philosophy that comes after him. There is no feature or set of characteristics in terms of which to define or classify American philosophy as rationalist, empiricist, idealist, analytical, mystical, or romantic. It is closer to a patchwork or crazy quilt in which themes and trends appear but are for a time modified, suppressed, or displaced by quite different trends and themes. In this respect philosophy in America is not so different from American architecture, painting, and literature. It sometimes borrows from English and European antecedents just as it sometimes strikes out on its own, looking for new ideas to address the character of a new land and nation. In many ways Jonathan Edwards, from his first steps as a young idealist to the mature analyst at work on *Freedom of the Will*, sets the table for what is to come, and in subsequent essays we will see similarities, influences, and repudiations of what one of America's great thinkers left for other thinkers to ponder.

NOTES

1. For some idea of what and whom Edwards might have read and studied during his undergraduate days at the new and developing Yale College, see Bruce Kuklick, *Churchmen and Philosophers: From Jonathan Edwards to John Dewey* (New Haven, 1985), 15–19.
2. See *Works of Jonathan Edwards: Scientific and Philosophical Writings*, ed. Wallace E. Anderson (New Haven, 1980), 42–7, 296–301; hereafter abbreviated as *Scientific and Philosophical Writings*.
3. For this and more on Edwards's life, see Perry Miller, *Jonathan Edwards* (New York, 1949); Morton White, *Science and Sentiment in America* (New York, 1972), ch. 2; Elizabeth Flower and Murray G. Murphey, *A History of Philosophy in America* (2 vols., New York, 1977), I, ch. 3; and *A Jonathan Edwards Reader*, ed. John E. Smith, Harry S. Stout, and Kenneth P. Minkema (New Haven, 1995), vii–xxxix.
4. This is a letter to Paul Dudley, justice of the Massachusetts Superior Court and member of the Royal Society of London. *Scientific and Philosophical Writings*, 151–2.
5. In this context, see Perry Miller's *Errand into the Wilderness* (Cambridge, Mass., 1956), 17–18.
6. *Scientific and Philosophical Writings*, 168.
7. *Darwin: Texts and Commentary*, ed. Philip Appleman, 3rd edition (New York, 2001), 67–81.
8. *Scientific and Philosophical Writings*, 167.
9. Ibid. 168–9.
10. For the most important philosophical criticism of arguments akin to those that Edwards makes, i.e., the various "Design Arguments" that were so prominent throughout the seventeenth, eighteenth, and early nineteenth centuries, see David Hume's posthumously published *Dialogues Concerning Natural Religion* (1779), in Hume, *Dialogues and Natural History of Religion*, ed. and intro. J. C. A. Gaskins (Oxford, 1993), 3–130. For clear statements of the Darwinian alternative to intelligent design and to nature as a product of any antecedent plan or purpose, see Charles Darwin, *The Origin of Species* (London, 1859), chapter XIV, in *Darwin*, 164–74. See also Richard Dawkins, *The Blind Watchmaker: Why the Evidence of Evolution Reveals a Universe without Design* (New York, 1987), 5; and Daniel C. Dennett, *Darwin's Dangerous Idea: Evolution and the Meanings of Life* (New York, 1995), 59–60.
11. From *Images of Divine Things* (1728), in *A Jonathan Edwards Reader*, 16.
12. *Opticks*, 4th edition (1704), intro. Edmund Whittaker (New York, 1952), 402. See also the still useful discussion of amalgams of natural science and natural religion throughout the seventeenth century, in C. E. Raven, *John Ray, Naturalist* (Cambridge, England, 1950), 452–78.
13. *The Travels of William Bartram, Naturalist Edition*, ed. Francis Harper, reprint (Athens, Georgia, 1998), lvi.
14. *Jonathan Edwards*, 30.
15. For the manner in which Edwards's severe Calvinism was at odds with the more elastic Puritan theology of eighteenth-century New England, see ibid. 71–99.

16. *Churchmen and Philosophers*, 16–19. Perry Miller says that Edwards never studied Berkeley, but to Norman Fiering it seems likely that he was acquainted with Berkeley's thought. See Fiering's *Jonathan Edwards's Moral Thought and Its British Context* (Chapel Hill, 1981), 35–40.
17. This is a highly condensed rendering of what Edwards writes in his confused collection of topics drawn together in *The Mind* (1723). *Scientific and Philosophical Writings*, 332–9, 343–4, 350–5, 376–80.
18. *Jonathan Edwards*, 71–4.
19. *A Jonathan Edwards Reader*, 239.
20. See, for example, the pamphlet "What Is Enlightenment?" in Immanuel Kant's *Foundations of the Metaphysics of Morals,* trans. and intro. Lewis White Beck (Indianapolis, 1959), 85–92.
21. *The Philosophical Theology of Jonathan Edwards*, expanded edition (Princeton, 1988), 47–8.
22. For White's analysis of the physics of this sermon, see *Science and Sentiment in America*, 31–2. It is possible that in this regard White was influenced by Miller's discussion of Newton's influence in Colonial America. *Jonathan Edwards*, 71–4, 82–96. For a brief discussion of Edwards's part in the Great Awakening, see Sydney E. Ahlstrom, *A Religious History of the American People* (New Haven, 1972), 101–4. See also Leon Chai, *Jonathan Edwards and the Limits of Enlightenment Philosophy* (Oxford, 1998), 22, 127, notes 1–2. For a fuller and searching commentary on the revivalism that blew through New England in the 1740s and for Edwards's place in it, as well as that of the mesmerizing English preacher George Whitefield, see *Jonathan Edwards*, 133–63, and E. H. Davidson, *Jonathan Edwards, the Narrative of a Puritan Mind* (Cambridge, Mass., 1968), 58.
23. Jonathan Edwards, 145.
24. *The Works of President Edwards* (10 vols., London, 1817), reprint (New York, 1968), VI, 453. This edition includes works that are not yet available in the Yale edition.
25. Ibid. 458.
26. Ibid.
27. Ibid. 456.
28. Ibid. 455.
29. Ibid. 463–4.
30. Ibid. 457.
31. Ibid. 451, 455. Miller develops his classic account of the covenantal theology, which separates Edwards's Calvinism from the more flexible New England Puritans with whom he could not agree. *Errand into the Wilderness*, 57–79.
32. *Jonathan Edwards: Representative Selections*, ed. C. H. Faust and T. H. Johnson, revised edition (New York, 1962), 150–51.
33. *Jonathan Edwards*, 147.
34. *A Jonathan Edwards Reader*, 98–9.
35. *Jonathan Edwards: Representative Selections*, 149.
36. *A Jonathan Edwards Reader*, xxxiv, 296–7, 309–10.
37. *Puritan Political Ideas: 1558–1794*, ed. Edmund S. Morgan (Indianapolis, 1965), 76; spelling revised.
38. *Works of Jonathan Edwards: Religious Affections*, ed. John E. Smith (New Haven, 1959), 84; hereafter abbreviated as *Religious Affections*.
39. Ibid. 95. Miller thinks that the approach, if not the content, that Edwards takes in *Religious Affections*, shows his debt to Locke, a patron sage of the Enlightenment. *Jonathan Edwards*, 180–95.
40. *Religious Affections*, 99; emphasis added, and *An Essay Concerning Human Understanding*, Bk. II, ch. xxi, sections 1–2.
41. *Religious Affections*, 205.
42. *The Works of President Edwards*, VIII, 12.
43. Ibid. 9; *Religious Affections*, 102.
44. *The Works of President Edwards*, VIII, 12–13.
45. *Religious Affections*, 205–6.

46. Ibid. 206.
47. *The Works of President Edwards,* VIII 18–19; *Religious Affections,* 94.
48. *The Works of President Edwards,* VIII, 9.
49. *A Jonathan Edwards Reader,* 124.
50. *The Works of President Edwards,* VIII, 10.
51. *Religious Affections,* 98–100.
52. *A Faithful Narrative of the Surprising Work of God* (1737), case studies of conversions and intense (even fatal) religious experience, is largely Edwards's account of changes that occur in young people who believe they are among the newly elect. *Works of Jonathan Edwards: The Great Awakening,* ed. C. C. Goen, 144–211.
53. *Religious Affections,* 99–100, 102; emphasis added.
54. Ibid. 127–45.
55. *The Works of President Edwards,* VIII, 19.
56. Ibid. 9.
57. *An Essay Concerning Human Understanding,* IV, xix, 16. For White's discussion of Edwards and Locke on religious enthusiasts, see *Science and Sentiment in America,* 26–9, 51–3.
58. David Hume, "Of Superstition and Enthusiasm," in *Essays: Moral, Political and Literary,* ed. E. F. Miller (Indianapolis, 1985), 74.
59. *An Essay Concerning Human Understanding,* IV, xix, 9.
60. *Religious Affections,* 383–4.
61. Ibid. 409–10.
62. Ibid. 443.
63. Soren Kierkegaard, *Fear and Trembling* (1843), trans. Alastair Hannay (London, 1985), 68.
64. *Religious Affections,* 205.
65. *The Works of President Edwards,* VIII, 17.
66. See Miller's glowing account in *Jonathan Edwards,* 251.
67. See Hobbes's *Leviathan,* I, vi, 53; viii, 27; xxi, 2, 4, and his debate with Bishop Bramhall. *The English Works of Thomas Hobbes,* ed. W. Molesworth (11 vols., London, 1839–45), IV, 229–78.
68. *Works of Jonathan Edwards: Enquiry into Freedom of the Will,* ed. Paul Ramsey (New Haven, 1957), 137; hereafter abbreviated as *Enquiry into Freedom of the Will.* See also Flower and Murphey, *A History of Philosophy in America,* I, 169–70.
69. *Enquiry into Freedom of the Will,* 141; emphasis added.
70. Ibid. 142; emphasis added.
71. Ibid. 181, 185.
72. Ibid. 153.
73. *Enquiry into Freedom of the Will,* 157; emphasis added.
74. Ibid. 257.
75. For a brief statement of the problem, as the eighteenth-century religious libertarians called "Arminians" conceived it, see Miller's *Jonathan Edwards,* 122–3.
76. Quoted from the introduction to *Freedom of the Will,* ed. Arnold S. Kaufman and William F. Frankena (Indianapolis, 1969), xii. See also *Jonathan Edwards,* 110, 115, and Edwards's reiteration of his own Calvinism at the conclusion of *Enquiry into Freedom of the Will,* 430–39.
77. John Taylor and Daniel Whitby are notable Arminians. For a commentary on what Edwards was facing in an era that was increasingly weary of doctrinaire Calvinism, see Conrad Cherry, *The Theology of Jonathan Edwards: A Reappraisal* (New York, 1966), 186–215.
78. *Enquiry into Freedom of the Will,* 149–55.
79. Ibid. 150.
80. Ibid. 163–7.
81. *Science and Sentiment in America,* 37.
82. According to Kaufman and Frankena "The Compatibility Thesis" is the position that "determinism, in any plausible sense and of any plausible sort, is compatible, logically and morally, with moral responsibility, hence with the occurrence of sinful acts." *Freedom of the Will,* xvi.

83. *Enquiry into Freedom of the Will*, 163. See also Locke's similar treatment of restraint and constraint, a similarity Edwards acknowledges (33), in *An Essay Concerning Human Understanding*, II, xxi, 24–7.
84. Besides a small population of Houssatunnuck Indians, there was a still smaller congregation of white settlers. *Jonathan Edwards*, 247–8.
85. *Enquiry into Freedom of the Will*, 184–5.
86. Here I follow closely White's analysis of Edwards's criticisms of the Arminian position, in *Science and Sentiment in America*, 39–42.
87. *Enquiry into Freedom of the Will*, 195.
88. Ibid. 196–8.
89. Apparently, Edwards has specifically in mind the distinguished English Arminian Isaac Watts and his brief for indeterminate choice in *Essay on the Freedom of the Will*. See *Enquiry into Freedom of the Will*, 195–6.
90. For White's criticism of Edwards's treatment of an indifferent will, see *Science and Sentiment in America*, 42–5.
91. *Enquiry into Freedom of the Will*, 209–10, and *An Essay Concerning Human Understanding*, II, xxi, 52.
92. *Enquiry into Freedom of the Will*, 172.
93. Ibid.

Essay 2
Benjamin Franklin: Self-made Man and Man-made Self

Benjamin Franklin (1706–1790), possibly more than any other American, epitomizes the upwardly mobile man or woman and the values that make mobility possible. Born in Boston without a pedigree, he attended school until he was twelve. He was apprenticed to his half-brother as a printer but in 1723 moved to Philadelphia in search of more profitable opportunities. There too he worked as a printer and made friends who encouraged him to open his own printing shop. In 1724 Franklin crossed the Atlantic and, without any significant funds or connections, briefly practiced his trade in London. Back in Philadelphia by 1726, business was good enough that in 1729 he could begin publishing his own newspaper *The Pennsylvania Gazette*, which was followed by the very successful *Poor Richard's Almanac* (1733–1758).

In 1731 Franklin established America's first circulating library and in 1744 the American Philosophical Society, an endowed society that functions into the present for the advancement of theoretical and practical knowledge. At age forty-two, the industrious Franklin was financially comfortable and retired from commerce. For the balance of his long life he indulged longstanding interests in education and public service. His educational ideas led to founding an academy that would become the University of Pennsylvania. His concerns for the colonies included a Plan of Union at the Albany Conference (an abortive attempt in 1754 to unite the colonies for defensive purposes) and an appearance before the English House of Commons (1766) to oppose the Stamp Act (1765). During the Revolution, he served in the Second Continental Congress (1775–1776) and as minister to France. When hostilities had ended, he was a member of the delegation that negotiated the Treaty of Paris and thus an end to the Revolutionary War (1783). Finally, only three years before his death, he took part in the deliberations of the Constitutional Convention (1787).[1]

Then there is the scientific Franklin. His inventions—the Pennsylvania stove, lightning rod, bifocal eyeglasses, and the glass harmonica—are enduring reminders that he was eager to make life comfortable, safe, and pleasant. His electrical experiments, together with letters on a unified theory of electricity, are reminders that Franklin was more than a gentleman virtuoso. He was *the* scientific giant of Colonial America, a member of the prestigious Royal Society of London, and one of a handful of great eighteenth-century scientists. William Pitt the Elder said of Franklin that "all Europe held [him] in high Estimation for [his] Knowledge and Wisdom, and ranked [him] with our Boyles and Newtons."[2] Pitt's comments are exaggerated, but they show that Franklin, more than any other colonial American, had won fame and international admiration. His reputation alone showed England and Europe that something more than colonists' complaints and natural resources came from the "unripe side" of the Empire.

The Autobiography, 1771–1789: A Self-made Man

Because Franklin was so much a man of action, we might tend to forget that he was also a man of letters. But apart from *The Autobiography* and the bromides we quote from *Poor Richard's Almanack,* he wrote countless letters, plans, proposals, pamphlets, and articles. If, therefore, we are to find anything that entitles us to think of Franklin as philosophical, it will have to be among these. So, for example, a letter on Christian piety might address what we now call philosophy of religion. A letter on the value of industry could include a philosophy for living well. Trying to pin down Franklin's philosophy is also complicated by the question: What do we mean by "philosopher"? Insofar as philosophers and nonphilosophers alike have been wrestling with this question from antiquity into the present, it would be presumptuous to try to answer it here. If Plato is right when he says a philosopher is a lover of wisdom and Marx is correct when he says that the job of the philosopher is not only to know the world but also to improve it, then Franklin is philosophical enough for our purposes.

There is no better place to begin searching for Franklin's philosophical ideas than *The Autobiography*. Although Franklin wrote *The Autobiography* late in life, the text itself begins with a brief account of what he knew of his English ancestors and ends with his activities in 1759–1760, a full thirty years before his death. Some critics complain that an abbreviated narrative is the least serious flaw one encounters in this American classic. Leonard Labaree, whose edition of Franklin's works is the standard against which all others are judged, writes: "The autobiography also reflects the limitations of its times. Most of the literature of Georgian England lacked spiritual quality; Milton and Donne had gone before and Wordsworth and Coleridge were yet to come."[3] To find autobiographical writing in the eighteenth century that "plumb[s] the depths of the soul," one can read Jean Jacques Rousseau's *Confessions* (1781) and not *The Autobiography*, which, compared to Rousseau's intense prose, "seems reserved, impersonal, even artful."[4]

That Rousseau tried to look deep into his soul and to lay bare his fears and passions is not surprising. He was, after all, an early romantic who emphasized his feelings, often those that were unsettling, and had deep reservations about the value of cool, calculating reason. Franklin was no romantic. It is partly the rationality and restraint of *The Autobiography*, coupled with the belief in self-reliance, that so vexed D. H. Lawrence:

> Why then did Benjamin set up this dummy of a perfect citizen as a pattern to America? Of course, he did it in perfect good faith . . . He thought it simply was the true ideal. But what we *think* we do is not very important. We never really know what we are doing. Either we are materialistic engines, like Benjamin, or we move in the gesture of creation, from our deepest self, usually unconscious.[5]

Why do Lawrence and those who follow his lead disparage Franklin's rendering of himself? The obvious answer is that they have expectations about what an autobiography should be and do. Lawrence's presumption seems to be that if an account of one's life is not punctuated with angst, guilt, and wrenching regrets, it must be superficial. This attitude is unfair to Franklin and to the autobiographical genre in general.[6]

It is true that Franklin's autobiographical project is not meant to discover a self that underpins the events, choices, and ideas that he mentions in *The Autobiography,* and it is probably no less true that many philosophers think that the search for a self is one of the philosopher's fundamental missions. There is no doubt that the admonition "Know thyself" is one of the most persistent imperatives in Western philosophical literature. Franklin too was eager to know himself and to pass on what he found, first to his son and then to a larger audience. But for him this effort is as much about *making* as it is about *discovering* the man who is the subject of his account. What, then, are some of the events and activities that serve as background for understanding the man that Franklin made of himself?

We read in the first part of *The Autobiography* that Josiah Franklin "married young, and carried his Wife with three Children unto New England, about 1682. . . . By the same Wife he had 4 Children more born there, and by a second Wife ten more, in all 17 . . . I was the youngest Son and the youngest Child but two, and was born in Boston, N. England."[7] Franklin tells us that before being apprenticed as a printer, he worked for his father making candles but that he longed for a life at sea.[8] Franklin's father worked hard, and from him Franklin acquired the habits of industry and diligence. Because his father cared less about what he ate than about instructive conversation, Franklin came to be concerned more with "what was good, just, and prudent in the Conduct of Life" than with the cultivation of a fine palate.[9] Since his father had a collection of books, many dealing with religious disputes, Franklin developed a taste for reading and for thinking about controversial issues—not only in religion but also about whether women are men's equals and should be entitled, as he believed, to an education. Entering into an exchange of letters with a friend with whom he disagreed, sometimes Franklin worked hard to improve his vocabulary and writing.[10] He realized early that fluency is not merely ornamental; it adds strength to any argument.

Franklin's interest in reading exposed him to disciplines as diverse as arithmetic and moral philosophy and also to ideas as unusual, at least for a young boy, as the good sense of vegetarianism. The diversity of opinions and convictions that he encountered in reading and conversation persuaded him that one is better served by diffidence than by dogmatism. He decided, therefore, to express himself without using "the Words, *Certainly, undoubtedly,* or any others that give the Air of Positiveness to an Opinion; but rather say, I conceive, or I apprehend a Thing to be so or so, It appears to me . . . , or it is so if I am not mistaken."[11] All of these habits and choices stayed with Franklin when he became a printer in Philadelphia and when he acquired new and intimate friends, including "Sir William Keith Governor of the Province" and Deborah Read, to whom Franklin was married from 1730 until her death in 1774.[12]

Because Franklin's curiosity reached beyond his books and past the shores of North America and because he thought there might be richer opportunities for printers in London than in Philadelphia, he sailed for England in November 1724 and did not return to Philadelphia until October 1726. Before age twenty, Franklin had met Bernard Mandeville, author of the cynical but widely read *Fable of the Bees* (1714), and had done some modest business with Hans Sloane, whose collection of natural wonders and artifacts would later form the initial collection of the British Museum (1754).[13]

With each passing year, the young Franklin grew more successful in commerce. He also found time to establish, with some of his acquaintances, "A Club for mutual Improvement, which we call'd the Junto." The club met on Friday evenings. Its rules, which Franklin drafted, "requir'd that every Member in his Turn should produce one or more Queries on any Point of Morals, Politics or Natural Philosophy, to be discuss'd by the Company, and once in three Months produce and read an Essay of his own Writing on any Subject he pleased."[14]

In the years between establishing the Junto and retiring from commerce (1727–1748), Franklin also began publishing *Poor Richard's Almanack* (1735), became postmaster of Philadelphia (1737), invented the Pennsylvania (Franklin) stove (1739–1740), published the proposal that served as the principles for the American Philosophical Society (1743), and began writing about his experiments with electricity (1747).[15] He had done all of this and more at the halfway point in his life, and there was much more to come.

The tone of *The Autobiography*, after this first installment, is chiefly concerned with the affairs of Franklin's external life: "The one important exception is in Part Two, where he included a description of his project for attaining 'moral perfection' . . . With this exception, the last three parts reveal little of the inner man; the 'private Franklin' virtually disappears as he becomes more and more the public figure, concerned with civic and political affairs and with his scientific pursuits."[16] This is one of the reasons that Franklin's critics are turned aside by *The Autobiography*; for even the relatively more personal opening installment barely touches what Labaree calls the "inner man." So, once again, there is the question whether, apart from its style and importance to history, one can say anything significant about a philosophical Franklin who lurks within the interstices of this account of himself. The answer is yes.

There is the celebrated list of thirteen virtues: 1. Temperance, 2. Silence, 3. Order, 4. Resolution, 5. Frugality, 6. Industry, 7. Sincerity, 8. Justice, 9. Moderation, 10. Cleanliness, 11. Tranquility, 12. Chastity, and 13. Humility.[17] But a list alone does not instill virtuous behavior. One requires a plan of action. "I determined to give a Week's strict Attention to each of the Virtues successively. Thus in the first week my great Guard was to avoid even the least Offense against Temperance, leaving the other Virtues to their ordinary Chance, only marking every Evening the Faults of the Day." After thirteen weeks, this catalogue of virtues began by degrees, with order being the most difficult to cultivate, to take hold in his daily conduct. Each one became habitual to such a lasting degree that Franklin could write: "And it may be well my Posterity should be informed, that to this little Artifice, with the Blessing of God, their ancestor ow'd the constant Felicity of Life down to his 79th Year in which this is written."[18]

One can, of course, criticize Franklin's approach to the acquisition of virtuous habits as banal, mechanical, calculating, and uninspired, or one can point out, as Labaree does, that Franklin is in excellent philosophical company insofar as Aristotle's *Nicomachean Ethics* also provides a list of virtues and explains how they can become habitual.[19] Without passing judgment on the virtues Franklin wished to cultivate, we can also note that what he does is not very different from what one finds in Epictetus, the Stoic philosopher (circa 60–117 A.D.) whose *Enchiridion* presents a list of virtues that may help the Stoic sage to live and enjoy the virtuous life. The *Enchiridion* is a "how-to" book, and so is *The Autobiography*.[20] We may malign Epictetus's philosophy as facile and thin; we might do the same with Franklin's program for cultivating beneficial virtues and values. But if Epictetus was a philosopher—and he was—then so too is Franklin.

The problem, once more, is that critics, Lawrence and others, have their own prepossessions about what any autobiography ought to address, and when it fails to meet these expectations, critics insist that the effort at self-disclosure is a vacant failure. Mitchell Breitwieser, who believes that Lawrence "is still the best reader of the *Autobiography*," says Lawrence's basic objection is that "Franklin's clarity disavows any essential relation with the dense complexity of the person in which it originates by making that complexity into the object of its calculations."[21] Whether Franklin produces an uplifting or disappointing description of his own life therefore has everything to do with what a reader wants and expects from him, and whether his formulaic treatment of virtues and the cultivation of habits is good philosophy is equally a matter of taste and expectations. To someone who is already industrious or who wishes to be, Franklin's admonition "Lose no time. Be always employed in something useful. Cut off all unnecessary actions" will be good advice and part of a constructive philosophy of life. For someone in debt, resolving to "make no expense but to do good to others or yourself; i.e., waste nothing," is also good advice and can be a point of departure for a literally and figuratively richer philosophy of living well.[22]

What emerges overall from the philosophy embedded in *The Autobiography* is an emphasis on ideas and values that are in some way *useful*. So, to take a single instance, Franklin writes that when he was only fifteen he began to entertain doubts about the truth of revealed (Christian) religion. These doubts were fortified, not eliminated, by some books he read that criticized eighteenth-century freethinkers who believed that the existence, benevolence, and wisdom of God are validated by reason, not faith, and who were convinced by reason and experience that the revealed books of the Bible are fabrications. Yet when Franklin reflected on some of his own conduct and on that of his friends, he "began to suspect that this Doctrine [deism], *tho' it might be true, was not very useful*."[23]

Franklin means that although the supposed "facts" of revelation are doubtful, the content of revelation often has moral utility: "Revelation had indeed no weight with me as such; but I entertain'd an Opinion, that tho' certain Actions might not be bad *because* they were forbidden by it, or good *because* it commanded them; yet probably those Actions might be forbidden *because* they were bad for us, or commanded *because* they were good for us, in their own Natures, all the Circumstances of things considered."[24] And several pages later, Franklin reaffirms "that vicious Actions are not hurtful because they are forbidden, but forbidden because they are hurtful, the Nature of Man alone consider'd. That it was therefore every one's Interest to be virtuous, who wish'd to be happy even in this World."[25] These are not deep introspective insights. They are Franklin's discoveries in his own outward experience that Christianity, whether true or false, has practical advantages for promoting individual and public good. He has found that in more cases than not, virtue here and now is its own reward; therefore, he is better off (happier) for practicing Christian virtues than neglecting them in favor of short-term indulgence and vice. This is also the message of the "Two Dialogues between Horatio and Philocles," which Franklin did not write but whose message he so firmly approved that he printed both "Dialogues" in the *Pennsylvania Gazette*.[26]

As Daniel Howe puts it, "Franklin believed that the core of Christian belief consisted of a few short affirmations. Beyond that, religions justified themselves by their contributions to temporal human welfare, and should be judged accordingly."[27] And in the last year of his life, when Ezra Stiles asked to know something about Franklin's religion, he wrote in his reply of March 9, 1790: "I believe in one God, Creator of the Universe. That he governs it by his Providence. That he ought to be worshipped. That the most acceptable Service we render to him is doing good to his other Children. That the soul of Man is immortal, and will be treated with Justice in another life respecting its Conduct in this. These I take to be the fundamental Principles of all sound Religion. . . ."[28]

So what can we make of the content of *The Autobiography*, apart from its recitation of facts that run the gamut from Franklin's "strong Inclination for the Sea" as a ten-year-old apprentice to his efforts at fifty-one to resolve a taxation dispute between the Pennsylvania Assembly and Pennsylvania's English Proprietors?[29] Perhaps an acceptable answer is that it is at base a record or chronicle of Franklin's most remarkable invention, *himself*. That is, after all, the recurrent and most prominent feature that ties together the assortment of episodes *in* Franklin's account of his life. Franklin does not try to penetrate beyond the perimeters to the elusive self or soul that Lawrence calls "*a dark forest*," a reality so opaque and mysterious "*that my known self will never be more than a little clearing in the forest*."[30] Apart from his belief "That the Soul is immortal," Franklin is disinclined to make philosophical claims about the nature of the soul or, if it is are the same thing, the self.

Franklin's reluctance to speculate about what constitutes him essentially, or about whether a self explains the kind of man he is, makes sense. Notoriously, the problems in philosophical psychology—especially laying bare a substantial ego that unifies our experiences—are so difficult and metaphysical that Locke, whom Franklin read, chose instead to explain who he is in terms of the continuity of consciousness or memory. The person "Locke" is what John Locke recalls about his experiences, and the substantial self that mysteriously, even inexplicably, unifies his recollections is inaccessible.[31] And David Hume, whom Franklin met and who was his slightly younger contemporary, insisted that searching for a self that is different from one's own impressions, ideas, memory traces, and feelings is a species of philosophical indulgence that ends in frustration.[32]

Franklin, the pragmatist and inventor, had no use for philosophical speculations that rarely bear any fruit. "In recalling the period of youthful rebellion in his

Autobiography, Franklin chose to depict it with a chronicle of practical action rather than through intellectual debate."[33] Inventing oneself does not always satisfy speculative metaphysicians and literary critics, but their concerns are not Franklin's. The central issues with any of Franklin's inventions, whether it is the lightning rod, the Pennsylvania fireplace, or the man named "Ben Franklin," is what good they will do and what profit they will generate. That profit need not be financial. In fact Franklin thought he should freely share the benefits of his inventions so that they would be available to anyone who could use them.[34]

What sort of invention is Benjamin Franklin? Taking the raw materials out of which any human being is constructed, he fashions himself into different boys (printers), young men (entrepreneurs and publishers), and middle-aged men (scientists and statesmen). Each is the artifact of a particular time, place, and need—a need for a calling, for greater comfort, for time to indulge his curiosity, for a more orderly and systematic life, for the skills required to serve a social good. There is no stasis. Franklin reinvents and refines himself as requirements and interests demand that he do so. Unlike his ancestors and members of his immediate family, Franklin will not tie himself to a fixed station or vocation. That he chooses paths different from those his father would have chosen for him is not a manifestation of defiance or an expression of a rebellious, angry young man. It is Franklin's announcement that he will better serve himself if he does something different from his ancestors and does it where opportunities for him are likely to be greater, so beginning in Philadelphia rather than Boston, he makes himself into something other than what tradition dictates.[35]

In twenty-first-century America, there is nothing surprising about leaving home and trying to find opportunities elsewhere. But to a callow youth in early eighteenth-century America, leaving home and family protection for an uncertain life was at least extraordinary, if not unprecedented. If Joyce Appleby has it right, the mobility that we now take for granted is a phenomenon rooted in social, economic, and religious changes that did not really take hold until after the Revolution.[36] Franklin is again ahead of his time.

Franklin himself hints at the connection between his passion for inventing and his philosophy of human nature when he writes that in America, where titles and one's noble origins are unimportant or at least much less important than in Europe, "people do not inquire concerning a Stranger, *What is he*? But, *What can he do*?"[37] The same applies to a novel invention (making the appropriate substitution of "*it*" for "*he*"). What can Franklin's Long Arm do? *It* can safely remove and replace books on high shelves. What can the glass harmonica do? *It* can produce tones that are "incomparably sweet beyond those of any other" musical instrument.[38] Of course one can ask about any of Franklin's other inventions, "What is it?" But more important is whether it can do something worth doing. When the invention is a self-made man, it can do many worthwhile things and, when the self-made man is Franklin, it can do things that have not been done before. Throughout *The Autobiography*, the implicit question is "What can *I* do?" Franklin's answer is "almost anything I wish to do if I am prepared to work hard enough to see the task to completion." Franklin can do what others before him did not do because, apart from his own remarkable talents, he is not fettered by an indenture to the past, nor denied opportunities because his ancestry is undistinguished. Aware of these advantages, Franklin writes that Americans believe "God Almighty is himself a Mechanic, the greatest in the Univers [*sic*]; *and he is respected and admired more for the Variety, Ingenuity, and Utility of his Handyworks, than for the Antiquity of his Family*."[39]

But just as Franklin's inventions need thought to come into being and maintenance to discharge their functions, so too does Franklin as a self-made man. The celebrated virtues at the philosophical center of *The Autobiography* are individually necessary and perhaps jointly sufficient to make Franklin and to keep him functioning productively. Still, as with anything else that one invents, the pride of invention must never interfere with the recognition that the new device can always be improved: "But on the whole, tho' I never arrived at the Perfection I had been so ambitious of obtaining, but fell far short of it, yet I was by the Endeavour a better and happier Man than I otherwise should have been, if I had not attempted it."[40] Franklin, both within and outside the scope of *The Autobiography*, engineers several revisions of himself.

This interpretation of Franklin as an inventor can easily lead to a misreading of *The Autobiography*. Although Breitwieser does not explicitly characterize Benjamin Franklin as Franklin's own invention, he does interpret the book as a kind of picaresque in which one temporary self is devised only to be sloughed off by another and that, in its turn, by yet another. In short, he sees Franklin exercising his freedom so liberally that he never permits himself to be an enduring self. "Franklin first realistically develops a character option, then identifies it as a potential captivation of his free mobility, then avoids it, and defines his character by contrast with it. As the list of these roads not taken grows longer, the reader's expectation of a definition of what Franklin's character *is* is diminished . . ."[41] This criticism might be too severe.

Franklin understood the difference between scientific theory and discovery on the one hand and invention on the other. His work in electricity is instructive in this regard and also in regard to criticisms that *The Autobiography* lacks depth or substance. I. B. Cohen quotes and paraphrases the great historian Carl Becker who "concludes that science 'was after all the *one* mistress' to whom Franklin '*gave himself without reserve and served neither from a sense of duty nor for any practical purpose*'."[42] If Becker is correct, and Cohen thinks he is, *The Autobiography* differs in its character and mission from Franklin's scientific writings. Because *The Autobiography* is a self-help manual that guides its readers by giving them an example to follow, one should not indict Franklin because it does not do what his letters on electricity do, that is, probe theoretically into the nature of its subject.[43] In *The Autobiography* it is enough to show the assorted steps Franklin took and the devices he employed since his book is supposed to say something like "These are the things that I did, and this is the plan I adopted. If your aim, like mine, is to be a self-reliant, self-made man or woman (although Franklin knew that opportunities for women were far less numerous and far more restricted), try to follow my lead."

In short, the difference between Franklin's science and his account of himself is that the former is about discoveries and the theories that can explain them; the latter is about making a man, but not just any man. It is about making a man who is solvent, capable, and engaging, a man who can, if he wishes, enjoy the time, leisure, and resources to indulge a life of the mind and to work for the improvement of society. Franklin does not, therefore, come across in *The Autobiography* as one of the limited Americans whom Alexis de Tocqueville describes in his classic *Democracy in America* (1835–1840): "The first thing that strikes one in the United States is the countless multitude of those who seek to escape their original condition, and the second is the small number of great ambitions that reveal themselves in the midst of this universal motion of ambition. There are no Americans who do not show themselves to be consumed by the desire to rise; but one sees almost none who appear to nourish very vast hopes, nor to aim very high."[44]

Franklin escaped his "original condition," and if he was not "consumed by the desire to rise," he was at least striving to move beyond the limitations of his birth. But he is outside the set of Americans who do not "aim very high." We can think of Franklin as frugal, industrious, and zealous in order to advance financially. *The Autobiography* and his fragmentary "Plan of Conduct" confirm what we think: "1. It is necessary for me to be extremely frugal for some time, till I have paid what I owe . . . 3. To apply myself industriously to whatever business I take in hand, and not divert my mind from my business by any foolish project of growing suddenly rich; for industry and patience are the surest means of plenty."[45] But this is merely a prologue to the life of great plans, statesmanship, and political activity that Franklin's industriousness, thrift and, yes, acquisitiveness enabled him to pursue. Hard work and its ethic had served their purposes. "He himself . . . quit work at the age of forty-two, once he had acquired a sufficient fortune. The remainder of his life he devoted to science and public service—gentlemanly pursuits which, in the eighteenth century, did not count as work."[46] Tocqueville notwithstanding, Franklin, more than anyone else of his generation, was internationally emblematic of the rare American who aimed very high indeed.

"Queries to be ask'd the Junto," 1732: A Life Worth Living

What, then, does Franklin do with the invention called "Franklin"? Does he devote it to making money and to advising others, as he does in "The Instructor, or Young Man's Best Companion" (1748), how they too can prosper in the world of bank accounts, ledgers and commodities? ". . . the Way to Wealth, if you desire it, is as plain as the Way to the Market, It depends chiefly on two Words, INDUSTRY and FRUGALITY: i.e. Waste neither Time nor Money, but make the best use of both."[47] Does Franklin spend his leisure composing pamphlets like "The Way to Wealth" (1757), which uses some of his best-known aphorisms to promote the cultivation of calculating, debt-free capitalists and enshrines what Max Weber calls the "content of the Puritan worldly asceticism, only without the religious basis, which by Franklin's time had died away"?[48] The answer in each case is no. To think of Franklin as at base a marketplace man whose best advice is about acquiring and maintaining personal wealth or about using one's time as a busy craftsman uses his tools, is to mistake some of his recommendations for the *whole* of his program for living well. A picture of Franklin solely in terms of acquiring and saving is as unfair as it is partial. By now it should be clear that there is far more to this remarkable man than capitalist bromides and secular parables.

Among other things, Franklin invents and refines himself in such a way that he stands the best possible chance for securing the happiness that human beings desire as an end in itself. One of the questions that Franklin proposed for the meetings of the Junto is what philosophers have been asking and answering since, and no doubt before, Socrates addressed the matter that Plato recounts in the *Apology* (circa 396 B.C.). Franklin puts it in his own way: "Wherein consists the Happiness of a rational Creature? In having a Sound Mind and a healthy Body, a Sufficiency of the Necessaries and Conveniences of Life, together with the Favour of God, and the Love of Mankind. What do you mean by a sound Mind? A Faculty of reasoning justly and truly in searching after [and] discovering such Truths as relate to my Happiness."[49]

Franklin answers the first part of his question by echoing the view of Epicurus (342–270 B.C.), who held that the highest good for a human being, pleasure and the absence of pain, amounts to "the health of the body and the freedom of the soul from disturbance."[50] And Aristotle, more than two thousand years before Franklin, agreed that a happy man must have (i) external goods, so that he is not distracted by material wants, and (ii) the love of friends, "since man is a political creature and one whose nature is to live with others."[51] Furthermore, Franklin was far from the first and by no means the last to share Aristotle's conviction that human happiness is ultimately and essentially connected to the search for truth and understanding. Aristotle writes that the excellent employment of one's reason, what he calls *theoria* (contemplation), perfects what is uniquely *human* in human nature, namely, reason: "Happiness extends . . . just so far as contemplation does, and those to whom contemplation more fully belongs are more truly happy, not accidentally, but in virtue of the contemplation; for this is in itself precious. Happiness, therefore, must be some form of contemplation."[52]

With just this much background, we can see that Franklin's treatment of happiness is not original. Like Socrates, Plato, and Aristotle, Franklin is a rationalist in the broadest sense of the term. Like them, he too assumed that if by nature we are rational, it follows that reasoning well and enjoying the fruits of rationality ought to make us happy. So, once more, even though Franklin is not the author of the "Two Dialogues between Philocles and Horatio," he vigorously promotes its central, generally Aristotelian message: The "happiness or chief good" for all creatures "consists in acting up to their chief faculty, or that faculty which distinguishes them from all creatures of a different species. The chief faculty in a man is his reason; and consequently his chief good, or that which may be justly called his good; consists not merely in action, but in *reasonable action*."[53]

Moreover, Franklin was himself an active apologist for his own attitudes toward reasoning well. This advice goes far beyond reminders that "A penny saved is two pence clear" and "Haste makes waste." Whether drafting plans for the American Philosophical Society to increase "the conveniences or pleasures of life," proposing a Pennsylvania Academy to educate talented young men and thereby secure "the surest Foundation of the Happiness both of private Families and of Commonwealths," explaining in "Observations Concerning the Increase of Mankind" (1751) the mathematics of making room for a growing number of colonists,[54] or corresponding with the British botanist Peter Collinson about "electric fluid,"[55]

Franklin was endlessly reasoning at the highest registers. Franklin, no less than Aristotle in his descriptions of citizens in an ideal state, insisted that authentic happiness is the yield of a mind that is engaged in fruitful thought. Knowledge, then, is power. Franklin agreed with Francis Bacon about that, but it is also the source of the inexhaustible joy that Franklin indulged and promoted at every available opportunity.

If Franklin had any regrets that tainted his happiness, they were that the moral "sciences" that should make us better had not advanced to the level of the natural sciences that make us wiser and our lives more commodious. He expresses his disappointment in a letter (February 8, 1780) to his friend Joseph Priestly (1733–1804), the English chemist who emigrated to Philadelphia in 1804:

> "O that moral Science were in a fair a way of Improvement, that Men would cease to be Wolves to one another, and that human Beings would at length learn what they now improperly call Humanity."[56]

And two years later (June 7, 1782), he laments to Priestly that "Men I find to be a Sort of Beings very badly constructed, as they are generally more easily provok'd than reconcil'd, more disposed to do Mischief to each other than to make Reparation."[57]

These remarks are not evidence that late in life Franklin had become morose and cynical. They are actually continuous with concerns that characterize the ethical center of *The Autobiography*.[58] He believed that it was easier to alter inert matter than to change the minds of men. For Franklin this is no less a fact than that the atmosphere is electrically charged or that vibrating glasses can be made to produce sounds of varying pitch. Just as natural scientists can, with dedication and effort, dress the world to human advantage, so too men and women, with even more dedication and effort, can learn the fundamental precepts of the moral life and can employ a method for producing such a life. This is, after all, what Franklin addressed and managed as a young man when he labored to make abstract virtues and values into his own virtuous and valuable habits. But this task requires more resolve and perseverance than that of the earnest physicist who wishes to know more about the properties and uses of electrified particles of matter. Whether most human beings are prepared to commit themselves to the effort at moral improvement and to see their commitment to completion is a question for psychologists and social scientists. Franklin's letters show that he had doubts and hopes. The tone and content of his "Proposals Relating to the Education of Youth in Pennsylvania" make clear that his hopes overawed his doubts: Well-endowed minds produce citizens who not only find their own happiness but who strive to serve others in a manner that turns individual happiness and goodness into shared, public commodities.

Franklin's Legacy

A ten-year-old candle maker and a forty-two-year-old retiree, a grammar school dropout and founder of the University of Pennsylvania, a printer's apprentice and a best-selling author, a curious naturalist and a world-class scientist, a friend of

English loyalists and elder statesman of the American Revolution: Benjamin Franklin was all of these and more. He was a superstar before there were superstars, a man who was internationally recognized before the world knew about Washington and Jefferson.[59] He was an admired sage in a young country that generally did not admire sages. In the history of British America and of the United States of America, there has never been another figure quite like him.

But just as Franklin stands apart from all the other Americans who came before and after him, he also embodies what was for so long the accepted image of the American at his best. Over two hundred years ago, J. Hector St. John de Crèvecoeur wrote, with more perception than Tocqueville: "The American is a new man, who acts upon new principles; he must therefore entertain new ideas, and form new opinions. From involuntary idleness, servile dependence, penury, and useless labour, he has passed the toils of a very different nature, rewarded by ample subsistence.—This is an American."[60] This is also Benjamin Franklin.

We have encountered a few of Franklin's critics. There are others. We can add to the list the New England transcendentalist Theodore Parker (1810–1860) who complained, "Franklin thinks, investigates, theorizes, invents, but never does he dream."[61] This kind of indictment is unfair. After all, not every dream passes neatly through some preconceived ethereal hoop. One could claim against Parker, as well as others for whom he speaks, that a diplomat who hopes against all odds to make peace with a powerful enemy or a scientist who develops a radical theory about the electrified atmosphere is no less a dreamer than other-worldly poets and metaphysicians. There were, after all, dreams, imagination, and poetry in the theory and investigations that led to Newton's *Opticks* and *Principia*; otherwise we might wonder why Alexander Pope, unofficial poet of England's Augustan Age, wrote "Nature and Nature's laws lay hid in night; God said, 'Let Newton be!' and all was light."[62]

In the final analysis, of course, Franklin does not require any apologists. His place in American history, science, and culture is secure. When we think Americans are, or ought to be, self-reliant; when we admonish children and grandchildren to work hard in order to make something of themselves and the society of which they are a part; when we say that, far from being preformed to fill a particular niche, we are free to shape our own destinies, we are echoing the famous Philadelphian whose boundless optimism made these ideas and possibilities part of the American creed.[63]

Anyone is entitled, like Max Weber, to criticize Franklin either for advocating virtues that are adopted from his commercial and nominally Protestant background or, a bit more charitably, for being an optimist whose visions of self-reliance and individual initiative cannot take hold in a country and world two hundred fifty years removed from *The Autobiography* and *Poor Richard's Almanack.* Even Labaree, who prized Franklin's wisdom enough to spend his own scholarly life making it accessible, acknowledges that in

> a rapidly rising population, together with an ever more intricate technology, the consequent increase in areas where collective, even mass, action seems necessary, and a decline in the willingness and ability of individuals to manage their own destinies sometimes makes the emphasis on self-reliance in

> the autobiography appear woefully old-fashioned. In the United States and other highly developed countries . . . , Franklin's devotion to business and his advice to cultivate the simple virtues no longer seem to capture the imagination as they once did.[64]

There is no doubt that opinions will continue to vary and debates about Franklin's importance, especially as a moralist and thinker, will persist. The same is true for all other men and women who preside as giants over their times.

The point of this essay is not, however, to evaluate Franklin as a philosopher, scientist, businessman, and statesman. It is rather to bring into sharper relief a Founding Father who, whether inadvertently or by design, helped America and its citizens to define themselves. Others can decide whether Franklin is overrated, whether he is a philosopher and whether he is a living inspiration to American know-how or a museum piece whose worth is purely historic. In the throes of assessments and reassessments this much is clear: Whatever one thinks of Franklin and his influence, he is an authentic original. He is that invention—conceived and nurtured in America—whose specifications, whether we admire or denigrate them, are those against which succeeding generations of Americans are still compared.

NOTES

1. The literature on Franklin is, vast. For a very full and recent account of Franklin's remarkable life, see H. W. Brands, *The First American: the Life and Times of Benjamin Franklin*. Carl Van Doren's *Benjamin Franklin* (New York, 1938) has worn very well and remains an important, eminently readable source. See also Edmund S. Morgan, *Benjamin Franklin* (New Haven, 2002.)
2. Quoted by I. B. Cohen in *Science and the Founding Fathers: Science in the Political Thought of Thomas Jefferson, Benjamin Franklin, John Adams and James Madison* (New York, 1995), 180. Cohen's *Benjamin Franklin's Science* (Cambridge, Mass., 1990) is indispensable for anyone who wishes to know almost all one needs to know about Franklin's contributions to the sciences.
3. *The Autobiography of Benjamin Franklin*, ed. Leonard W. Labaree, Ralph L. Ketcham, Helen Boatfield and Helen H. Fineman (New Haven, 1964), 3; hereafter abbreviated as *Autobiography*.
4. Ibid. 3, 4.
5. D. H. Lawrence, *Studies in Classic American Literature* (London, 1924), 20.
6. J. J. Ellis indicts the *Autobiography* on the grounds that Franklin's "emotional seams, cracks, fissures, and failures are hidden beneath a façade of psychological artifices, which are in turn hidden beneath a variety of effectively playful literary masks." *Passionate Sage: the Character and Legacy of John Adams* (New York, 2001), 61.
7. *Autobiography*, 51.
8. Ibid. 53.
9. Ibid. 55.
10. Ibid. 60–61.
11. Ibid. 65. Franklin thus adopted the view that philosophers call "fallibilism."
12. Ibid. 80, 89, 128.
13. Ibid. 97, 297–8.
14. Ibid. 116–17.
15. Ibid. 303–5.
16. Ibid. 24.

17. Ibid.
18. Ibid. 157.
19. Ibid. 1.
20. Daniel W. Howe, *Making the American Self: Jonathan Edwards to Abraham Lincoln* (Cambridge, Mass., 1997), 23.
21. Mitchell Robert Breitwieser, *Cotton Mather and Benjamin Franklin: The Price of Representative Personality* (Cambridge, 1984), 286.
22. *Autobiography*, 149.
23. Ibid. 114; emphasis added.
24. Ibid. 114–15.
25. Ibid. 158.
26. *American Philosophy: A Historical Anthology*, ed. B. MacKinnon (Albany, 1985), 44–45.
27. *Making the American Self*, 25. See also *Autobiography*, 157.
28. *The Writings of Benjamin Franklin*, ed. A. H. Smyth (10 vols., New York, 1905–7), X, 84.
29. *Autobiography*, 53, 261–6.
30. *Studies in Classic American Literature*, 16.
31. *An Essay Concerning Human Understanding*, Bk. II, ch. xxvii, sections 17–29.
32. *A Treatise of Human Nature*, ed. L. A. Selby-Bigge, rev. P. H. Nidditch (Oxford, 1978.) 636.
33. *Cotton Mather and Benjamin Franklin*, 185.
34. *Autobiography*, 192.
35. *Cotton Mather and Benjamin Franklin*, 241.
36. *Inheriting the Revolution: The First Generation of Americans* (Cambridge, Mass., 2000), 1–9.
37. *The Works of Benjamin Franklin*, ed. J. Sparks (10 vols., London, 1882), II, 469. See also Breitwieser's analysis of this quotation in *Cotton Mather and Benjamin Franklin*, 177, 224. This text is not yet included in *Papers of Benjamin Franklin*.
38. For Franklin's full account of the construction, range, and sound of this unusual instrument, all of which he provides in a letter to the Italian scientist Giambattista Beccaria, July 13, 1762, see *Papers of Benjamin Franklin*, X, 116–30.
39. *The Writings of Benjamin Franklin*, VIII, 606; emphasis added. This passage from the pamphlet "Information to Those who would move to America" (1782) is quoted at the beginning of Breitwieser's discussion of Franklin. *Cotton Mather and Benjamin Franklin*, 171. Brands briefly interprets the pamphlet and quotation in *The First American*, 633–4.
40. *Autobiography*, 156.
41. *Cotton Mather and Benjamin Franklin*, 254.
42. *Science and the Founding Fathers*, 150; emphasis added.
43. Cohen summarizes Franklin's contributions to electrical theory and describes his adventure with a "common kite" as "one of the most spectacular experiments ever to be performed." Ibid. 149–50.
44. *Democracy in America*, intro. S. Kessler, trans. S. D. Grant (Indianapolis, 2000), 281.
45. *Papers of Benjamin Franklin*, I, 100.
46. *Making the American Self*, 28.
47. *Papers of Benjamin Franklin*, III, 308.
48. Ibid., VII, 340–50, and Max Weber, *The Protestant Ethic and the Spirit of Capitalism*, trans. Talcott Parsons (New York, 1958), 180.
49. *Papers of Benjamin Franklin*, I, 262.
50. See Epicurus's "Letter to Menoeceus," *The Epicurus Reader*, trans. and ed. B. Inwood and L. P. Gerson (Indianapolis, 1994), 30.
51. See, respectively, Aristotle's *Politics*, Bk. VII, ch. 1, and *Nicomachean Ethics*, Bk. IX, ch. 9, in *The Complete Works of Aristotle*, ed. J. Barnes (2 vols., Princeton, 1984), II, 2100–01, 1848.
52. Ibid. 1863.
53. *American Philosophy: A Historical Anthology*, 45; emphasis added.
54. *Papers of Benjamin Franklin*, IV, 227–34.
55. *Papers of Benjamin Franklin*, V, 68–79.
56. Ibid. VIII, 10.
57. Ibid. 451–2.

58. *Autobiography*, 148–60.
59. In 1778 Jean-Antoine Houdon (1741–1828), the most famous sculptor in France, produced the bust of Franklin that is now in the New York Metropolitan Museum of Art.
60. *Letters from an American Farmer* (1782), intro. Warren Barton Blake (New York, 1957), 40.
61. Labaree quotes Parker in his introduction to *Autobiography*, 13.
62. From an "Epitaph Intended for Sir Isaac Newton," quoted in Marjorie Hope Nicolson, *Newton Demands the Muse: Newton's Opticks and the Eighteenth Century Poets* (Princeton, 1946), 37.
63. To be fair, one must admit that women, African Americans, and Native Americans were not among those to whom Franklin generally applied his promises of a free, unlimited, and indeterminate future. That he too was a product of his times, even as he often saw beyond them, is indisputable. See, in this context, *Autobiography*, 197–9.
64. Ibid. 19.

Essay 3
Philosophies of Revolution and Resolution

This essay on the history of philosophy in America is perhaps the most difficult to write. The period under consideration extends roughly from July 4, 1776, to September 17, 1787, from the day that King George III penned in his diary "Nothing much happened" to that late summer afternoon that thirty-nine weary delegates to the Constitutional Convention signed the United States Constitution. In the interval between announcing a formal Declaration of Independence and drafting a document to stabilize an infant nation, there were skirmishes and battles, victories and losses, acts of heroism and treachery. These ceased only when General Charles Cornwallis surrendered to George Washington at Yorktown, October 19, 1781. The story is remarkable and has no antecedent in world history, but what does it have to do with philosophy?

The men who stood at the center of this storm and who drafted the documents and expressed the ideas that decreed and shaped this nation were jurists, lawyers, pamphleteers, planters, scientists, inventors, staymakers, and tax collectors. But were they philosophers? They were certainly not in the business of building philosophical systems. Few capable historians of philosophy would include any of the Founding Fathers, from Franklin to Madison, on even a charitable list of Western philosophers.

So the challenge here is obvious and daunting: Express the philosophical underpinnings of documents at the heart of the struggle for independence and its immediate aftermath, but do so without making the men at its center more philosophical than they were. Obviously, therefore, a good deal of what they wrote has to be omitted on the grounds that it is philosophically anemic or irrelevant. In some sense thinking about and revising a famous pre-Revolutionary rallying cry has helped in preparing this essay: "Taxation without representation is tyranny," and taxing the reader's patience without justification is indefensible.

Thomas Paine, *Common Sense*, January 1776: A Call to Revolutionary Action

Often, stories actually begin before they begin. The same is true when it comes to announcing a date when the American Revolution began in earnest. We know that July 4, 1776, is traditional, but we also know that the press of events had made the Declaration of Independence inevitable long before we celebrate its birthday.

Then there is always the infamous Tea Act of 1773 and the Tea Party in Boston harbor in December of that year. The battle at Lexington and Concord, April 19, 1775, lasted only minutes but makes an excellent candidate for the start of the Revolution thanks to "the shot heard round the world" of Emerson's poem. The distinguished American historian Pauline Maier favors beginning our genuinely national story with the Second Continental Congress that met for the first time in Philadelphia on May 10, 1775.[1]

If there is no absolute agreement on a single date or event to which one can look and insist that the struggle for independence was as a result irrevocable, perhaps Thomas Paine's publication of *Common Sense*, January 9, 1776, is as good a candidate as any other. Noting that this pamphlet struck at the heart of the English monarchy and at anyone who believed that the English constitution served the rights and liberties of America, David Hawke writes: "Paine had forced the hand of Congress. The day *Common Sense* appeared, James Wilson, a moderate, moved that 'Congress may expressly declare to their constituents and the world their present interests respecting an independency, observing the king's speech directly charged us with that design.'"[2] At a minimum, *Common Sense* inflamed further the passions of radicals and helped move moderates and fence sitters to favor independence over compromise.

Nothing in Paine's early years makes him an obvious candidate for instigating a political revolution. Born in England in 1737, he did not immigrate to America until he was almost forty. He had worked in England as a staymaker, sailor, and teacher, and in America he held short-terms jobs as a journalist and clerk of the Pennsylvania Assembly. After the Revolution and after having made his name as author of *Common Sense* and *The Crisis* papers (1776–1783), he returned to England; fled to France, where he was imprisoned for objecting to the execution of Louis XVI; was freed in November 1794 at the request of James Monroe; and returned to America in 1802. He died June 8, 1809, and is buried in New Rochelle, New York.[3]

Coming at just the proper time in the period of growing tensions between England and America, *Common Sense* articulates what colonists and delegates to the Second Continental Congress could not ignore: two clear and compelling arguments. Taken together or treated separately, these arguments are compatible with Paine's abiding confidence in *reason* and *nature*. For example, in his *The Age of Reason, Part I* (1794), an indictment of organized (especially Christian) religion. The central claims are (i) "It is only in the *Creation* that our ideas and conceptions of a *word of God* can unite," and (ii) "It is only by the exercise of reason that man can discover God."[4] For Paine it is (i), which bears on the order and fecundity of nature, that argues for (ii). That is, through the judicious, rational study of nature—not taking on faith the unreliable, sometimes shocking books of the Bible—one is led, scientifically and rationally, to the conclusion that a wise and benevolent God exists.[5] Fine, but what do (i) and (ii), as well as *The Age of Reason* generally, have to do with Paine's earlier arguments for American independence?

The answer is uncomplicated. As Paine sees it—and here we find an unintentional echo of Jonathan Edwards's brief for ordinary understanding in *Freedom of the Will*—common sense tells anyone who will heed it that nature's order is disrupted as long as America is not independent of England. First, "there is something very absurd in supposing a *continent* to be perpetually governed by an *island*. In no instance has *nature* made the satellite larger than the primary planet; and as England and America, with respect to each other, *reverse the common order of nature*, it is evident they belong to different systems—England to Europe, America to itself."[6] Even in an inflammatory pamphlet, such a statement must be taken seriously. Apart from specific abuses, acts of economic suffocation, and a host of restrictions the English have imposed on the Americans, they have perverted the settled balance of nature. When Paine writes, "Nature has deserted the connection, and art cannot supply her place," he is not merely indulging rhetoric that was familiar to eighteenth-century eyes and ears. He obviously wishes to be taken seriously. What improves upon nature is one thing; what violates it is another.[7] The problem is that the English, far from finding in nature an inspiration for generosity, have chosen parsimony and cruelty. They abuse the population of their vast North American satellite and fail to see that it should not be treated as a satellite in the first place.

There is, however, an evil even more unnatural than the disproportion that exists when an island rules a continent, and that is the institution of monarchy. Why for Paine are monarchy and nature incompatible? Here too the answer is a straightforward matter of common sense. In a passage that mimes a good deal of political philosophy from the Renaissance forward, Paine writes, "Society is produced by our wants, and government by our wickedness; the former promotes our happiness *positively* by uniting our affections, the latter *negatively* by restraining our vices."[8] The origins of government, as opposed to society, derive from human tendencies to relax their natural duties to others. This relaxation, which leads to vice, defines legitimate government and its function: "to supply the defect of moral virtue."[9] By restraining the acquisitive behavior of human beings, good government provides the liberty and security for which it was intended.[10]

What is truly unforgivable, according to Paine, is that the English king and parliament have far exceeded the limited powers and business of government and have, acting under the guise of a constitutional monarchy, stifled the economic freedom of Americans and ignored their rights as English citizens. But a closer look at *Common Sense* shows that Paine's argument is even narrower than this. *Common Sense* bears directly on abuses that Americans have suffered and will continue to suffer until and unless they successfully secure their independence—hence Paine's objections to specific acts and impositions imposed upon them and enumerated throughout the work. Still, the basic foundation for his assorted complaints is that the institution of monarchy is unnatural and illegitimate: "How impious is the title of sacred majesty to a worm, who in the midst of his splendor is crumbling into dust."[11] That George III is the specific object of Paine's derision is less important than the grounds for his objections.

Once more, nature itself is the strongest argument against kingship. If a king is treated as the father of a nation, then all his subjects, including adults, are regarded as his children. Children, in the natural order of things, do not have independence. Parents who have authority over them strictly limit their rights. That this should be the model for legitimate government is absurd, unjust and, once again, contrary to nature.[12] Obviously, anyone who illicitly exercises power over another has perverted the equality into which we are naturally born and has also abandoned reason as well. So too Americans or any other human beings who passively allow themselves effectively to become children when they are adults have acted against the canons of their own rationality. This is the *real* argument of *Common Sense* and perhaps also the reason for its title. Just as children, if they are to be adults in fact, have to become independent of their parents, Americans must affirm their independence from the tyranny that masquerades as a constitutional monarchy.

That the monarch at the center of *Common Sense* is English and thereby an enemy of American interests is philosophically, although not politically or economically, beside the point. As Paine states and argues the case, kingship in itself is an aberration; hence its authority must be denied if men are to be free and to enjoy their natural equality. Recognizing this plain fact, which somehow so many people missed or ignored throughout history, is the woof and warp of common sense. The entire argument is neat and tidy. Adults, if they follow the dictates of reason, desire and must retain or, when necessary, reclaim their independence. Failing to do so is to play the part of dependent children, a part that has neither dignity nor advantages except those that accrue to voracious monarchs and their deputies. To grow up is to declare and demand independence, to cut the ties between specious childhood and an illicit father. When demands alone are not enough, revolution is the inevitable step.

In about fifty pages—some of which are inflammatory filler—Paine made the case for an American revolution. The Revolution itself cannot be traced directly and unequivocally to *Common Sense*, any more than it can be treated solely as the effect of the Stamp Act, the Tea Act, or the Intolerable Acts of 1774. But taken together, they were enough to advance the case for freedom from England and to steer a course that the Second Continental Congress seems in retrospect to have been destined to follow. *Common Sense* laid out the grounds for independence. The power of this pamphlet exponentially exceeded its brevity. All that was needed to cast the die was a formal declaration, a declaration that became the most momentous affirmation of independence in world history.[13]

Thomas Jefferson, the Declaration of Independence, a Bill for Establishing Religious Freedom and Founding the University of Virginia: Justification, Toleration, and Education

Among the Founding Fathers, Thomas Jefferson (1743–1826) receives the most attention, and not all of it is flattering. Historians are troubled about Jefferson's secret, but now confirmed, affair with his slave Sally Hemings, by whom he fathered at least one of her children.[14] We are disturbed that Jefferson held slaves and that, unlike George Washington, he refused to call for their emancipation in his will.[15] And we have begun to find out more about his unthinkable policies with respect to Native Americans and their culture.[16] In general, much of the most recent scholarship on this enigmatic man has been more damning than flattering.[17]

On the other side there is Jefferson the American icon. His profile is on the obverse side of the nickel. His massive image is sculpted on Mount Rushmore, and his graceful monument on the Tidal Basin in Washington, D.C., is not far from those of Washington and Lincoln, two other icons with whom he stands toe-to-toe.[18] Obviously, then, there are reasons, notwithstanding his blemishes, that Jefferson's apologists have raised him to the skies. He was the principal author of the Declaration of Independence (1776) and of an unprecedented bill allowing freedom of religion (1786); he served as President of the United States (1801–1809) who successfully urged Congress to approve the Louisiana Purchase from France, doubling the size of his young nation (1803); and he was the founder and architect of the University of Virginia (1825). Add to all this Jefferson's service as Virginia's second governor (1779–1780), Washington's Secretary of State (1789–1793), and John Adams's Vice President (1797–1801).

Where does one begin when the issue is not so much Jefferson's niche in history but rather his contributions to American philosophy? Here the Sage of Monticello is himself helpful. His epitaph, which he wrote and which is engraved on his tombstone in the cemetery of Monticello, reads: "Here was buried Thomas Jefferson Author of the Declaration of American Independance of the Statute of Virginia for religious freedom & Father of the University of Virginia."[19] This is as good a guide as any to what counts as Jefferson's philosophy. For him, for the nation he helped to found, and for those willing to learn something about his philosophy, the Declaration of Independence takes pride of place.

The Declaration of Independence. Chosen by the Second Virginia Convention at Richmond (1775) as a delegate to the Second Continental Congress, after having served six years as a legislator in the Virginia House of Burgesses, the young Jefferson arrived in Philadelphia in June 1775.[20] On June 11, 1776, Adams, Jefferson, Franklin, Robert Livingston, and Roger Sherman were appointed to draft a declaration that captured the Virginian Richard Henry Lee's resolution, "that these United Colonies are, and of right ought to be, free and independent States."[21] Why was Jefferson, who with Adams was chosen by the three others to write the document, the eventual author of the Declaration of Independence? Joseph Ellis's answer is intriguing: ". . . no one at the time regarded drafting the Declaration as a major responsibility or honor. Adams, like Lee, would be needed to lead the debate on the floor. That was the crucial arena. Jefferson was asked to draft the Declaration of Independence . . . because the other eligible authors had more important things to do."[22] And what philosophy did Jefferson express that delegates to the Continental Congress voted to adopt on July 2 and to proclaim on July 4, 1776?

We can begin to answer this question by granting with Ellis that the opening of the second paragraph of the Declaration of Independence, "which has become the most quoted statement of human rights in recorded history as well as the most eloquent justification on behalf of them" is comprised of, "in all probability, the best-known fifty-eight words in American history."[23] These words are also the marrow of the philosophy Jefferson was articulating and defending: "We hold these truths to be self-evident: that all men are created equal; that they are endowed by their creator with certain inherent and inalienable rights; that among these are life, liberty, & the pursuit of happiness: that to secure these rights, governments are instituted among men, deriving their just powers from the consent of the governed."[24]

The extent to which Jefferson was influenced by Locke's *Second Treatise of Government* (1690), by the eighteenth-century Scottish philosopher Francis Hutcheson, and by his own older contemporary George Mason, principal author of the Virginia Declaration of Rights (1776), is a matter of scholarly discussion and debate. Yet there is no question that Jefferson was familiar with these thinkers and sources, among others, and there is as little reason to doubt that he called upon them, especially upon Locke, in writing this portion of the Declaration.[25]

When Jefferson writes about self-evidence and universal equality, what does he have in mind? Ultimately, the answer that anyone gives is conjectural because Jefferson does not say in the Declaration or elsewhere. But in general, philosophers describe a "self-evident" truth as a proposition that is transparently and necessarily true. Anyone who understands the language in which such a proposition is expressed immediately sees its truth and necessity.[26]

Unfortunately, self-evidence is ambiguous. In a letter to James Madison, September 6, 1789, in which the topic is obligations that one generation might or might not bear subsequent generations, Jefferson writes, "I set out in this ground which I suppose to be self-evident, '*that the earth belongs in usufruct to the living*'; that the dead have neither powers nor rights over it."[27] Richard Matthews says that Jefferson means, "Whenever a member of society dies, the control over the portion of land that he had a right to use while living reverts to society. He also says that in this short passage there are for Jefferson *two* self-evident truths."[28] But one can ask reasonable questions about this account of Jefferson's remarks: (i) Does Jefferson's self-evident truth really mean that when a member of society dies, the portion of the land he used returns to society? This sounds more like an interpretation of Jefferson's remark than another way of stating the proposition itself. If, after all, one can intelligently ask, "Does the proposition 'The earth belongs in usufruct to the living' mean the same thing as the proposition 'When a member of society dies, his right to the use of a piece of land reverts to society'," then there is a question whether either proposition is self-evident. Self-evidence is supposed to carry with it the absolute conviction of direct intuition. Does Jefferson's remark to Madison meet this criterion for entry-level self-evidence?

Is it also the case that (ii) Jefferson makes two distinct self-evident claims, as Matthews says he does? One could just as well maintain that this is at best intended by Jefferson to be a single self-evident proposition and that "The Dead have neither power nor right over it [the earth]," he is simply offering an alternative statement of the same proposition. If questions (i) and (ii) are legitimate, it is clear that the appeal to self-evidence is suspect.

None of this is to say that Jefferson is wrong to assert universal equality and "inalienable rights to life, liberty and the pursuit of happiness." Whether, however, these rights are self-evident and exactly what Jefferson understands by "self-evident" remain open questions. In light of these observations and questions, Morton White may be correct to claim that Jefferson should have stayed with "sacred and undeniable," as against "self-evident," truths.[29] This was the phase that appeared in the Rough Draft but that the drafting committee changed in the version that it submitted to the full Congress, although a commentator who maintains that "undeniable" suffers as many ambiguities would be on firm ground.

Then there is the persistent question: To whom is it "self-evident" that "all men are created equal"? If self-evident truths are those that are transparently true to people who know the language in which they are expressed, then presumably they are self-evident to *everyone* who at least speaks and understands the language involved. But neat as this is, it invites further ambiguities. How *well* does someone have to understand English to see immediately that all men are created equal? Does the "We" who "hold these truths to be self-evident" designate those white men who drafted and approved the Declaration of Independence, or does it also designate other Americans who, although not among the intellectually elect, would be asked or commanded to take up arms against the British?

The fact is that there is no way to pronounce with confidence, far less with certainty, who the "We" are. About all one can say with a measure of security is that it must include the drafters and signers of the Declaration. There is simply no way to determine from the document or its context how far beyond the authors and delegates "we" extends. Referring to Jefferson's "A Bill for the More General Diffusion of Knowledge" (1778) and the *Notes on the State of Virginia* (1787), his only book, White asserts and speculates: "Jefferson believed that those he called men of science were intellectually superior to others and that those who were really equipped to see the Lockean self-evidence of his truths in the Declaration may have made up a comparatively small number in spite of the rhetorical suggestion that the signers were speaking for *all* Americans in 1776."[30] The difficulty with White's speculation is that it depends upon inferring from documents written after the Declaration, which do not bear on issues of self-evidence, what Jefferson meant in the Declaration.

The entire issue is complicated further by Jefferson's belief in a "moral sense" that "is given to all human beings in a stronger or weaker degree." This sense can somehow be guided and even improved by reason, but it is distinct from reason: "State a moral case to a ploughman & a professor. The former will decide it as well, & often better than the latter, *because he has not been led astray by artificial rules*."[31] He writes something similar in his famous, passionate love letter to Maria Cosway (October 12, 1786), the married English-Italian woman he befriended in Paris. In this letter the sentimental *Heart* declares to the dispassionate *Head*: "Morals were too essential to the happiness of man to be risked on the incertain combinations of the head. She laid their foundations therefore in sentiment, not in science."[32] One might read these passages as Jefferson's brief for a kind of unerring common sense (not so different from the faith in common sense that we have seen in Edwards and Paine) and construct an argument that self-evident apprehension of the truth is not solely the province of reason.[33] As a consequence, everyone with this sense is able to grasp immediately the truths that "We hold . . . to be self-evident."[34] On this reading "We" is virtually all-inclusive, although in the Declaration itself there is no way to determine whether women and African Americans (whose equality to white men was denied in practice) were also among those to whom universal equality—as well as the rights to life, liberty, and the opportunity to achieve happiness—was self-evident in principle.[35]

The trouble with this reading is that the language of the Declaration belies it. The moral sense may well have been an ascendant principle in the decades after Jefferson composed the Declaration, but to argue for its importance before 1785, when he wrote to Peter Carr about this sense, is to make an inference without any evidence to support it. The language is that of a Lockean rationalist, not of a moral sentimentalist. Although anyone is free to speculate about Jefferson's understanding of self-evidence, the best evidence points to the influence of Locke's *Second Treatise of Government* and *An Essay Concerning Human Understanding*. In each of these classics, self-evident apprehension of a truth is an act of intuitive, rational cognition and not the perception of a moral sense.[36]

Philosophers and historians also wonder what being "created equal" means and implies. If Jefferson was philosophically indebted to Locke, then there is good reason to assume that his understanding of equality was not very different from that of Locke in the *Second Treatise of Government*. We should therefore see without any inferences or abstract demonstrations that, "Because all men have been created equal in the sense of having been given the same nature and the same advantages, they should also be treated as equal in the sense that no one of them should depend on the will of any other man (unless God has by a manifest declaration given one man dominion over others)."[37] What does this mean?

If all men *are* essentially equal, then it is not a matter of inference but of intuition (self-evident understanding) that they *ought* to be treated equally. Some might wonder, as many philosophers have, how the prescriptive "ought" can be extracted intuitively or demonstratively from the descriptive "are," but there is no evidence that this concerned Jefferson. To him, insofar as the Declaration of Independence is an affirmation of what naturally free and equal human beings ought to do when their freedom and equality are usurped and denied, it is self-evident that equals ought to be treated as equals.[38]

There is no great difficulty in the claim that free and equal human beings have, and that we see self-evidently that they have, the indefeasible right to life and to the means to preserve it. Even Thomas Hobbes, in defending the rational transfer of virtually all one's rights in the interest or hope of peace, insists that no man can surrender his natural right to life. To do so would be to yield what is "*good to himself*," which no rational being can do.[39] For Hobbes, however, what is good for oneself amounts to little more than relative security and the likelihood that one will live his full allotment of years in peace. In a real sense, therefore, the pursuit of happiness for Hobbes is success at preserving one's life.[40]

Jefferson is not a Hobbesian. Life and freedom are clearly necessary conditions for the effective pursuit of happiness, but they are not sufficient. What Jefferson means by happiness, which all men must be free to pursue, is not spelled out in the Declaration. Andrew Burstein, in his portrait of Jefferson as a man of deep and sometimes conflicting sentiments, writes, "To Thomas Jefferson 'pursuit of happiness' implied the erection of a sturdy framework . . . ; its primary meaning was the potential to be independent and creative."[41] Looked at within the context of the Declaration, Burstein's formulation is a bit too general. He is not, however, to blame since Jefferson leaves wide open what he understands by "happiness." More than that, he does not include a natural, inalienable right to *property*, which we would expect to see in a doctrinaire Lockean. The inescapable conclusion, then, is that Jefferson is neither a Lockean clone nor a man who dances to exactly the same music as George Mason, who wrote in the preamble to the Virginia Bill of

Rights in May 1776: "All men are created equally free and independent and have certain inherent and natural rights . . . , among which are the enjoyment of life and liberty, with the means of acquiring and possessing property, and pursuing and obtaining happiness and safety."[42]

That the Declaration does not include acquiring and holding property as one of the "inalienable rights" tells us that Jefferson regarded the right to property as acquired, as an artifact made possible by political societies and protected by their man-made laws.[43] That the "pursuit of happiness" is on that short list of "inalienable rights" does not tell us what happiness is, but it does tell us that all men are entitled to seek it. In this respect Jefferson, as well as George Mason, are in the company of Socrates, Plato, and Aristotle. All of them regard it as axiomatic that human beings desire happiness and desire it as an end.[44] And if it is true that human beings desire happiness as an inherently valuable goal, then for Jefferson it is self-evident that they ought to be allowed to pursue the object of their desire so long as they do not inhibit or threaten others who pursue the objects of their own legitimate desires. Jefferson's position seems to be that what "is" the case (All human beings desire happiness) "ought," in the permissive sense of "ought," to be the case (All men ought to, i.e., have the right to, pursue their own happiness). One of the limited but legitimate functions of government is to protect this right in addition to citizens' rights to life and freedom. This is the reason "governments are instituted among men" and that when they are so instituted they derive "their just powers from the consent of the governed." A government that threatens this right is self-evidently illegitimate and ought to be replaced: ". . . whenever any form of government becomes destructive of these ends, it is the right of the people to alter or abolish it, & to institute new government, laying it's [*sic*] foundation of such principles, & organizing it's [*sic*] powers in such form, as to them shall seem most likely to effect their safety & happiness."[45]

Happiness is almost certainly many different things to many different people; hence what makes Jefferson or a philosopher happy may miss the mark for the sturdy farmers whose virtue he praises in *Notes on the State of Virginia*, "Query XIX."[46] What is self-evident, therefore, is not that happiness consists of *x*, *y*, or *z* but that every man and woman knows when he or she is happy. It is no less self-evident to those who are unhappy that they are unhappy. In the Declaration of Independence, which was tantamount to a declaration of war, there was no more need to spell out minutely the nature of happiness than to give a philosophical account of freedom or security.

People do not replace and reconstitute a new government for "light and transient causes," but after "a long train of abuses and usurpations" becomes insupportable and cannot be resolved peacefully, revolution is the only course that remains; thus Jefferson, looking with the authority of Locke "to heaven," writes as he concludes the Declaration and the list of abuses that necessitated it,[47] "We therefore the representatives of the United States of America in General Congress assembled, appealing to the supreme judge of the world for the rectitude of our intentions, do in the name, & by the authority of the good people of these colonies, solemnly publish & declare that these united colonies are & of right ought to be free & independent states."[48]

In the final analysis, then, Jefferson's philosophy of revolution, which became the American philosophy of revolution, is spare and intuitive. There are ambiguities in the Declaration of Independence but not many subtleties. Once the case is clear that the English are oppressors of the people, not their benign representatives and ministers, the course of action is clear. And if ever philosophy calls for action, as well as theory, the philosophy of the Declaration most certainly does. That it took Jefferson no more than two weeks to draft this extraordinary document is surprising if we ponder its impact and its standing as one of America's sacred documents. On the other hand, when we know that he had and understood his sources, principally Locke, the achievement is less surprising. What is truly remarkable in this case is that a call for independence and the philosophy that underpins it are indebted to philosophers and philosophies thoroughly at home in England, the nation of America's oppressors.

Jefferson on Religion. To write briefly about Jefferson's philosophy of religion, it is unnecessary to speculate about whether he saw himself as religious or, more specifically, as a Christian. Ellis, who knows as much as one can know of this enigmatic man, says that if Jefferson had candidly summarized his religious sentiments, "he would have described himself as a deist who admired the ethical teachings of Jesus as a man rather than as the son of God . . ."[49]

We know this much about Jefferson's religious beliefs from some of his letters and writings. Like Edwards and Paine, he thought that empirical evidence pointed to the existence of an intelligent and powerful creator. Like Paine, he was impatient with the Christian mythology that obscures the simple message of the Christian faith.[50] Unlike Edwards, he did not believe that the creator in the least resembled the God portrayed by Calvin.[51]

Like Paine and other deists of the eighteenth century, Jefferson not only believed that reason validates a belief in God's existence, but that revelation actually threatens well-founded religious convictions: "Indeed I think that every Christian sect gives a great handle to Atheism by their general dogma that, *without a revelation*, there would not be sufficient proof of the being of a god. Now one sixth of mankind only are supposed to be Christians: the other five sixths then, who do not believe in the Jewish and Christian revelation, are without a knolege [*sic*] of the existence of a God!"[52]

As a deist and apologist for rational religion, Jefferson is far from being a traditional Christian. In a letter to Joseph Priestly, himself a freethinker, Jefferson praises the moral precepts of Jesus just as Paine had in *The Age of Reason, Part I*, and in a letter to the physician Benjamin Rush he is explicit in what sense he regards himself as a Christian: "To the corruptions of Christianity I am indeed opposed; but not to the genuine precepts of Jesus himself. I am a Christian, in the only sense he wished any one to be; sincerely attached to his doctrines, in preference to all others; ascribing to himself every *human* excellence; & believing he never claimed any other."[53]

Jefferson also worried about the dark side of religion, especially about Christian priests, who like corrupt politicians, foster dangerous zeal and schisms: "It is contest of opinions in politics as well as religion which makes us take great interest in them, and bestow our money liberally on those who furnish aliment to our appetite."[54] Beyond this, religious practitioners "who live by mystery & *charlatanerie*" first oppose and then threaten the development of independent thought and intellectual growth.[55] And those who wish to impose their religious beliefs on others, thereby cutting off free expression and inquiry, must deal with Jefferson's indignation: "I have sworn upon the altar of god, eternal hostility against every form of tyranny over the mind of man."[56] Here Jefferson is close to a version of Immanuel Kant's imperative "*Sapere aude!* 'Have courage to use your own reason!'—that is the motto of Enlightenment."[57] Anything, including the imposition of religious dogma and doctrine, that interferes with or compromises the power and right to think for oneself is anathema to Jefferson as it was to Kant, Paine, Voltaire, and others who spoke for the values of the secular Enlightenment.[58] This brings us, of course, to the second item on Jefferson's list of his truly important achievements, an act granting freedom of religion and much more.

A Bill for Establishing Religious Freedom in Virginia. The opening clauses of the Bill for Establishing Religious Freedom in Virginia tell us immediately what we need to know about the provisions that follow.[59] Referring to representatives to the Virginia House of Burgesses, Jefferson writes that we are

> *well aware that the opinions and belief of men depend not on their own will, but follow involuntarily the evidence proposed to their minds; that Almighty God hath created the mind free, and manifested his supreme will that free it shall remain by making it altogether insusceptible of restraint*; that all attempts to influence it by temporal punishments, or burthens, or by civil incapacitations, tend only to beget habits of hypocrisy and meanness.[60]

Here it all stands. Free minds, hallmarks of what we require to be human, cannot be swayed by threats and by penalties. Evidence, not state authority, induces genuine belief. Our unfettered minds, left to their own devices, enable us to suspend, affirm, and revise our judgments. Intellectual freedom is the core of Jefferson's own religion: ". . . error of opinion may be tolerated where reason is left free to combat it,"[61] and "free inquiry must be indulged . . . , how can we wish others to indulge it while we refuse it ourselves?"[62] A state which requires religious beliefs from its citizens, and which exacts penalties from those who refuse to conform, violates "civil rights."[63]

This Bill, like the Declaration of Independence, declares a philosophy and then demands that elected representatives of the people act on it. Where ratifying the Declaration was almost immediate, a few years would pass before Virginia's legislators followed Jefferson's lead. While other deists in Europe and America inveighed against state religion, the corruption of the clergy, and compelling any citizen "to furnish contributions of money for the propagation of opinions which he disbelieves and abhors," Jefferson did more. While he was serving as America's minister to France, his friend Madison guided the bill through the Virginia Assembly where it became a law in 1786 and the model for similar laws in other states, as well as for the First Amendment to the United States Constitution.

The central provision of this momentous Bill is in section II: "We the General Assembly of Virginia do enact that no man shall be compelled to frequent or support any religious worship, place, or ministry whatsoever, nor shall be enforced, restrained, molested or burthened in his body or goods, nor shall otherwise suffer, on account of his religious opinions of belief." As a consequence "all men shall be free to profess, and by argument to maintain, their opinions in matters of religion," with no effect on their other rights and liberties.[64] This is, of course, consistent with Jefferson's attitudes toward government in general: Where government has no business it must restrict and mind its own business. "A wise and frugal Government, which shall restrain men from injuring one another, shall leave them otherwise free to regulate their own pursuits of industry and improvement, and shall not take from the mouth of labor the bread it has earned. This is the sum of good government . . ."[65]

If good government is necessarily restricted, in matters of conscience and personal belief (which neither harm nor threaten anyone else) it should never intersect with religion. Citizens ought, as an indisputable consequence, to be free to worship *as* they please and *if* they please. By statute, citizens of Virginia have more than freedom *of* religion. They have freedom *from* religion.[66] In spite of what the ancient preacher says in Ecclesiastes, with the bill there is something new under the sun, a revolutionary law for which Jefferson in his role as philosopher-statesman is responsible.

Jefferson's Philosophy of Education and the University of Virginia. We come now to the third and final element of Jefferson's epitaph, the project that occupied him in the last years of his long life, "Father of the University of Virginia." His views on education are not limited to what is required to establish and to attend a university that was meant to be competitive with, even better than, Harvard and Yale. In *Notes on the State of Virginia*, "Query XIV," he outlines a complex system of elementary schools that would provide a brief and basic education (literally reading, writing, and arithmetic) for the young male children of citizens. (Jefferson was not opposed to education for girls and young women but admitted that he had never given it serious attention, except where his own daughters' education was the issue.[67]) The best students would go on to a secondary school where they could learn something about the sciences, history, and classical languages. Most of the cost for educating young Virginians would come from state taxes.

What is the rationale for providing education at public expense? Jefferson's answer is unambiguous. Literate and well-informed citizens are necessary to the public and private good. In a letter to George Wythe from Paris, August 13, 1786, Jefferson is emphatic: "I think by far the most important bill in our whole code is that for the diffusion of knowledge among the people. No other sure foundation can be devised, for the preservation of freedom and happiness. . . . Preach my dear Sir, a crusade against ignorance; establish and improve the law for educating the common people."[68]

A Bill for the More General Diffusion of Knowledge, the bill to which Jefferson refers and of which he is the author, treats as axiomatic—as "self-evident"—that the surest fence against the degeneracy of democracy into tyranny is "to illuminate, as far as practicable, the minds of the people at large."[69] If the connection between knowledge and freedom is not axiomatic, then Jefferson's inference is easy enough to follow. Informed citizens are better equipped to detect the manner in which, and the means by which, their representatives cease to look to the public interest. Knowledge, which leads to intellectual independence, is the bedfellow of political liberty and responsible leadership;[70] therefore the distribution of knowledge must not be limited to the wealthy or to the aristocratic "fit and few." That is why the cost of improving the minds of its citizens is to be borne by the state, "the indigence of the greater number disabling them from so educating, at their own expense, those of their children whom nature hath fitly formed and disposed to become useful instruments for the public, it is better that such should be sought for and educated at the common expense of all, than that the happiness of all should be confided to the weak or wicked."[71]

The culmination of Jefferson's educational system is the implementation of his plan for the University of Virginia, the source for "statesmen, legislators and judges, on whom public prosperity and individual happiness are so much to depend."[72] The ideal of a higher education and of Jefferson's philosophy of education is thus as practical as it is theoretical. Well-educated young men must know the principles of agriculture, commerce, and manufacturing, as well as pure mathematics, the physical sciences, languages, and arts. This is the training ground for leaders of the state, and the quality of their leadership stands in proportion to the knowledge they have accumulated. This Jeffersonian vision is a philosophical echo of the cultivation of philosopher-kings in Plato's utopian *Republic*.

Even the splendid architecture of the University, making it visually the most remarkable university in America, ministers to Jefferson's educational philosophy as well as to his aesthetic preferences.

> At the head of the composition he placed not a chapel or an administration building, as might have been the case in Europe, but a library, the source of learning essential to a fledgling nation. Reaching out from the library in two symmetrical arms he added pavilions to serve as classrooms and housing—but also as social and recreational gathering places—for both faculty and students. The arrangement had the added virtue of forcing all members of the community into regular contact . . . Down the middle was the Lawn, a great grass common to be shared by all. It originally opened out to an endless westward view—literally and symbolically toward the future of a country yet to be explored.[73]

This architectural plan, requiring intimacy and exchanges among professors, students, and visitors, gives physical shape to Jefferson's conception of an "academical village." Instruction is diffused and absorbed by all the citizens of this intellectual township.

In many ways the University is a manifestation of so much that is Jeffersonian outside the sphere of education. Jefferson wanted the University government to be as close to a democracy as he could make it, consistent with the recognition that young men were not yet ready to take on the higher roles of leadership, and left it to the Board of Visitors (akin to a board of regents in twenty-first century American universities) "to devise and perfect a proper system of government, which . . . will be more likely to nourish in the minds of our youth the combined spirit of order and self-respect, so congenial with our political institutions, and so important to be woven into the American character."[74] In short a superior educational system, like a democratic political system, needs order and direction, but it must not be an autocracy. Where the voices of the students can be heard, they should be heard. Where their desires are congruent with the mission of higher education, their desires are to be given serious consideration.

Conspicuous by its absence and consistent with Jefferson's minimalism, the University of Virginia was to have no president. The Board of Visitors had a president, and that was all the administrative authority this new university required. More remarkable for any early nineteenth-century university but almost predictable given Jefferson's attitude toward religion, his university would have neither a professor of divinity nor a commanding chapel.[75] The great Rotunda (library) at the eastern end of the Lawn, not a house of worship, would be the center of the University of Virginia, an institution where free and open inquiry takes precedence over the doctrines and dogmas of sectarian faith.[76] Here, in brick and mortar, as well as in thoughts and on paper, Jefferson found an outlet late in life for his celebration of reason and intellectual autonomy.

But only those young men who distinguished themselves in secondary schools would be allowed advancement to Jefferson's University. By this constant system of elimination and selection, the intellectually elect and morally fit get a chance to prepare themselves for lives of high responsibility. These, not "an artificial aristocracy founded on wealth and birth," are authentic Jeffersonian aristocrats: "The natural aristocracy I consider as the most precious gift of nature for the instruction, the trusts, and government of society. And indeed it would have been inconsistent in creation to have formed man for the social state, and not to have provided virtue and wisdom enough to manage the concerns of the society."[77] Therefore, while Jefferson praises the morally intuitive ploughman and the upright farmer, the class of scholars and statesmen is populated by "the best geniusses" [*sic*] who have been "raked from the rubbish annually."[78] Jefferson is, then, an elitist as well as populist, but for him the elite are those who have earned their privileges by the power and labor of their minds, not by the size of their inheritance or the antiquity of their family names. In this respect, as with his attitudes toward liberty and religion, he is at home among other famous apologists for the values of the European and American Enlightenment.

John Adams, *A Defense of the Constitution of Governments of the United States of America* (1786–1787) and *Discourses on Davila* (1791): A Balancing Act

John Adams (1735–1826) lacked the dramatic instincts and timing of Paine. Short, portly, and abrasive, he did not possess the elegant reserve of Jefferson. Adams correctly anticipated, as three of his best biographers tell us, that he would not be remembered with the awe that adheres to Washington, Franklin, and Jefferson.[79]

Still, he was a Harvard-educated lawyer, a delegate from Massachusetts to the First and Second Continental Congress, Commissioner from the United States to France in 1778, a negotiator and signer of the Treaty of Paris that officially ended the Revolutionary War (1783), first ambassador from the United States to Great Britain (1785–1788), a two-term Vice President under Washington (1789–1797), and a one-term President (1797–1801).

Like many of the other Founding Fathers, Adams also had time to put his political thoughts on paper. The *Discourses on Davila*, principally a translation of Enrico Davila's *History of the Civil Wars of France*, includes Adams's views of human behavior and its connection to the political philosophy in his earlier *Defense of the Constitutions of Government of the United States of America*.[80] What stands out is Adams's picture of human behavior when laws and the political institutions do not restrain it. Indeed, he is in many ways a secular voice of the New England Calvinists from whom he descended. Perhaps this is what Paul Conkin has in mind when he writes, "Adams found no fault with the Puritan past. . . . Even in his one area of overwhelming interest—politics—he had no serious quarrel with his Calvinist predecessors."[81] In finding little or nothing to criticize among his Puritan antecedents, Adams is especially pessimistic about human nature. Generally discounting moralists who speak of human benevolence and altruism, Adams's darker view is that most of what we do is motivated by a desire for esteem, power, and personal enrichment.[82]

Insofar as we are human, we are emotional as well as rational: "The affectation of being exempted from passions is inhuman."[83] And because we are driven by our passions, not always ruled by reason, we need government: "Consider that government is intended to set bounds to passion which nature has not limited; and to assist reason, conscience, justice and truth in controlling interest without which it would be as unjust and uncontrollable."[84] Adams sees himself as a realist, and as a realist he refuses to entertain utopian visions of human perfectibility. We can, if we wish, call some people "good" to set them apart from those we call "bad," but finally, at least for Adams, basic passions—that can lead to self-destruction and the destruction of others—are what animate every man and woman. From his point of view, this fact of human motivation is indisputable; hence political theorists who ignore it will produce schemes that have no bearing on the world and behavior they should address.[85]

Given the acquisitive, self-serving nature of human beings, the issue to which Adams turns his attention in the *Defense of the Constitutions* is the kind of government that best addresses the competing needs of American citizens and at the same time keeps their passions in check. Adams addresses a critic of assorted state constitutions—including the constitution he drafted for his own state of Massachusetts—and is writing in the wake of a successful, unprecedented Revolution.[86] The emphasis has therefore shifted from *revolution* to *resolution*. What kind of government resolves the issues that led to revolution, struggle, and independence? If post-Revolutionary Americans could not respond, they would have won the Revolution at too great a cost. Victory in the field is inconsequential without a plan and the resolve to produce a quieter, lasting triumph at the Constitutional Convention of 1787. Delegates convening in Philadelphia during that long summer had permanently to eliminate the wrongs and to secure the rights for which battles were fought. Adams, serving his country in England, knew the stakes and confronted matters with his pen. If his writings are not so well known as those enshrined in our National Archives, they are, philosophically and practically, not less important.

Paine's *Common Sense* made revolution inevitable, and Jefferson's *Declaration* made its justification immortal. Adams's draft for the Massachusetts constitution and his sometimes turgid *Defense* helped to make all of it—the victories, setbacks, suffering, and expense of the Revolution—worth the effort.[87]

What did Adams contribute? The answer can be summed up by two words: "skepticism" and "equilibrium." Of what was Adams skeptical? (i) Republics and (ii) claims that all human beings are equal.[88] Despite being among the fifty-six delegates who signed the Declaration of Independence and affirmed that "all men are created equal," by or before the mid-1780s Adams had reservations about universal equality. "Was there, or will there ever be, a nation whose individuals were all equal in *natural* and acquired qualities, in virtues, talents, and riches? The answer of all mankind must be in the negative."[89] If we have to make the case that Jefferson was in some respects an elitist, no such effort is required of Adams. He spells out the conditions that set men apart. They include differences produced by *wealth*, *birth*, and the *order of nature* itself.[90]

What about wealth? "There is an inequality of wealth; some individuals, whether by descent from ancestors or from greater skill, industry, and success in business, have estates both in lands and goods of great value; others have no property at all."[91] Between these two extremes, we find most other human beings. And what of birth? "The children of illustrious families have generally greater advantages of education and earlier opportunities to be acquainted with public characters and informed of public affaires than those of meaner ones, or even than those in middle life."[92] This inequality provides them openings and advantages in the professions, and in life generally, that others do not enjoy.[93]

Not every inequality is the product of a good family name or a personal fortune. Some human beings are *naturally* wiser, more talented, stronger, and more virtuous than others. Instead of denying or minimizing this kind of inequality, Adams acknowledges it and insists that in forming a government, special attention must be given to this natural aristocracy. "These sources of inequality, which are common to every people and can never be altered by any because they are founded in the constitution of nature—this *natural aristocracy* among mankind has been dilated upon because it is a fact essential to be considered in the institution of a government."[94] Furthermore, this inequality of virtue, talent and intelligence can be either "the brightest ornament and glory of the nation" or that which guarantees "the destruction of the commonwealth."

This brings us to the core of Adams's political philosophy, *viz.*, to his insistence that a stable, just republic is impossible in the absence of an equilibrium of the powers that constitute it. Adams was divided. On the one hand, he wanted to see the United States take shape as a democratic republic. Why revolt if only to replace British autocracy with homegrown tyranny? On the other hand, his knowledge of history told him that republics are fragile and likely to erode into oppressive oligarchies or into anarchical opposition between the aristocracy and ordinary people who seek some of the privileges of the propertied class.[95] How, then, do well-meaning men, such as those assembled at the Constitutional Convention, construct a republic that addresses the rights of all its citizens and that protects the property of those who have legitimate titles to it?

Adams's answer is that a lasting and true republic must be fashioned as skilled machinists fashion scales, namely with a balance of opposing forces or with what political scientists call "checks and balances." This brings us to the matter of "equilibrium." Briefly, as Samuel Eliot Morison summarizes it, Adams's position is this: "Any 'pure' governmental form degenerated into something else—pure democracy into class tyranny or anarchy, pure aristocracy into selfish oligarchy, pure monarchy into absolutism. Hence, to secure the happiness of the people, a government must be a mixture of the three: a strong chief executive to represent the principle of authority, a senate to represent property, and a lower house to represent the multitude."[96]

Ideally, each branch would be a check on the actions of the other branches. The lower house (House of Representatives) would press the advantages of ordinary men and women, but the Senate, representing the propertied class, would counterbalance any legislative excesses passed by the House. Conversely, the House should vigilantly guard the rights of the people against senatorial attempts to turn representative democracy into government for the privileged few. A strong chief executive has the power to guard the interests of the nation as a whole but, like the English king under a parliamentary system, must also answer to the legislative branches. At the center of this mixed government looms Adams's fundamental distrust of any single assembly or executive to protect interests greater than its own. The interests of all the citizens are no more likely to be served by common people than they are by a much smaller class of natural aristocrats or by even the best available chief magistrate. Here Adams speaks for himself:

> As to usurping others' rights, they are all three equally guilty when unlimited in power. No wise man will trust either with an opportunity; and every judicious legislator will set all three to watch and control each other. We may appeal to every page of history . . . , for proofs irrefragable, that the people, when they have been unchecked, have been as unjust, tyrannical, brutal, barbarous, and cruel as any king of senate possessed of uncontrollable power.[97]

Far too many political philosophers, who "have echoed and reechoed each other's visionary language," believe that human beings will always consult their reason and appeal to their moral sense. They would certainly reject Adams's views as needlessly pessimistic, but as he sees it they are mistaken. They are ignorant of history and of human nature: "The passions and appetites are parts of human nature as well as reason and the moral sense. In the institution of government it must be remembered that, although reason ought always to govern individuals, it certainly never did since the Fall, and never will till the Millennium."[98]

Ellis thinks that Adams reaches his position with regard to governmental checks and balances by generalizing from what he finds when he turns his attention to himself: ". . . there were powerful passions deep in the individual soul and in the people-at-large that required restraint. What struck some of his colleagues as irritability was actually a by-product of the internal struggle with his own vanity and ambition, the nervous energy generated by the incessant operation of his own internal checks and balances."[99]

Fragile republics, disparities and inequality among human beings, and a balance of powers that produces an equilibrium—these are the woof and warp of Adams's political philosophy and are reflected in the ratified Constitution. His idea of a Senate, composed of natural aristocrats, stood from 1787 until 1913, when the seventeenth amendment replaced the appointment of senators with direct elections by all eligible voters. Ellis, who is one of Adams's most vigorous and articulate apologists, sees Adams's view of the Senate as "a combined haven and detention center for America's elite," and Ellis could not be less sympathetic to it as a serious component in thoughtful political science: "His view of the Senate, well, that was sheer lunacy."[100]

Adams was willing to acknowledge that the constitutional separation of powers exhibited a profound debt to America's former overlord, but he did not see why this should be grounds for dismissing the idea. Once the emphasis had shifted from winning the Revolution to producing a just and effective government, there was no reason to reject the fruits of English ingenuity simply because they were English. With a few adjustments, including the rejection of royalty and all titles of nobility, Adams believed that the English system could be adapted to America. "In this instance, argued Adams, there was virtue in imitation; the English constitution was 'the result of the most mature deliberation on universal history and philosophy'."[101] That England lost the war was not to say that England had lost its influence.

James Madison, *The Federalist Papers*: A Brief for Constitutional Government

We come finally to James Madison (1751–1836), Jefferson's Virginia confidant and Secretary of State, member of the Continental Congress and Constitutional Convention, fourth President of the United States (1809–1817) and, as a consequence of his generally successful maneuvering and campaign for a strong federal government, "Father of the Constitution."[102] Part of that campaign was a series of eighty-five papers, published in the New York press (October 27, 1787–May 28, 1788) under the pseudonym "Publius." Written by Madison, Alexander Hamilton, and John Jay, for the purpose of persuading the state convention of New York to ratify the Constitution, *The Federalist* was probably less important to determining the vote for ratification than for classically expounding and defending a constitutional federation of states.

The emphasis goes to Madison, rather than to Hamilton or Jay, because he was significantly the first among equals. His contributions to *The Federalist*, including even Hamilton's sustained argument for the expanded powers of the federal courts and for judicial review (No. 78), are truly the most revolutionary. Hamilton, another unabashed elitist, made no secret that he had doubts about democracy and spent a good deal of his most creative energy arguing that the proposed Constitution include safeguards against the excesses of common men and those who represent them (Nos. 9, 68, 73). Jay wrote only five of the papers (Nos. 2–5, 64) and, rather than provide careful analyses, reminded readers of what most of them already knew: Citizens surrender some of their personal rights to secure the protection of any government, and a strong federal government is best equipped to protect citizens against foreign aggression.[103]

This brings us back to Madison, whose achievements seem out of proportion to such a small, shy man. Ellis writes of Madison, "He did not look the part. At five feet six and less than 140 pounds 'little Jemmy Madison' had the frail and discernibly fragile appearance of a career librarian or schoolmaster, forever lingering on the edge of some fatal ailment, overmatched by the daily demands of ordinary life."[104] If, however, someone wished to press the timeless philosophical distinction between appearance and reality, Madison would serve the purpose. What is *real*? This personally inconspicuous man, who merely *appears* to be "the epitome of insignificance," is, more than anyone else, responsible for the Constitution and for the Convention that shaped it, for the decision of the Virginia ratifying convention to approve the Constitution, for the Bill of Rights and its passage by the First Congress (1791).[105] Madison's résumé casts him as one of the most remarkable Americans of any generation, and what makes him philosophically arresting is the kind of arguments he advances in *The Federalist*, especially in his famous treatment of factions in No. 10.

More ink has been spilled on *The Federalist*, No. 10, than on any of the other eighty-four papers. It has been interpreted by so many scholars and in so many ways that Madison emerges from it, depending on whom one reads, as an economic determinist and thus as a proto-Marxist, as a social scientist and psychologist, as an imitator of Hume and as an innovator whose central thesis is his own.[106] Under the circumstances and given the aims of this study, the chance to say something new about Madison asymptotically approaches zero. Still, no space is wasted in pointing out the importance of Madison's observations and arguments.

The problem is simple enough to understand, but to opponents of the Constitution its solution did not seem to lie in a strong federal government. In any democratic or representative (republican) government, one must always worry about what Adams called the "tyranny of the majority."[107] Where the vote of the majority becomes law, the voice and sometimes the rights of the minority go unheeded. Add to this the problem of factions, about which Madison says: "By a faction I understand a number of citizens, whether amounting to a majority or minority of the whole, who are united and actuated by some common impulse of passion, or of interest, adverse to the rights of other citizens, or to the permanent and aggregates of the community."[108] The potential for mischief is obvious. Again, if one faction constitutes a majority of the citizens in a polity, all other citizens—whether united by common passions and interests or not—are rendered politically impotent. Their rights and privileges are only nominal. If there are multiple factions and none of them constitutes a majority of the citizens, there is the potential for fragmentation, endless bickering and the effective loss of constructive governmental action.

The remedies for factionalism itself are either too harsh or impossibly out of the question. The harsh remedy is to deny citizens their freedom to constitute factions. This remedy "is worse than the disease. Liberty is to faction, what air is to fire, an aliment without which it instantly expires. But it could not be less folly to abolish liberty, which is essential to political life, because it nourishes faction, than it would be to wish the annihilation of air, which is essential to animal life, because it imparts to fire its destructive agency."[109] The impossible remedy is to supply "to every citizen the same opinions, the same passions, and the same interests." That this is both wishful and baleful thinking is clear. Men differ widely in reason and in their capacity to control their passions through the application of fallible reason. And there is more:

> The diversity in the faculties of men, from which the rights of property originate, is not less an insuperable obstacle to a uniformity of interests. From the protection of different and unequal faculties of acquiring property, the possession of different degrees and kinds of property immediately results: and from the influence of these on the sentiments and views of the respective proprietors, ensues a division of the society into different interests and parties.[110]

Important as property and rights to property are in generating factions, we cannot look to property alone to account for them. Human beings, subject to the conditions of political societies, develop "zeal for different opinions concerning religion, concerning Government and many other points"—an observation Madison also makes in his celebrated letter to Jefferson of October 24, 1787. In fact our inclination to develop antagonisms enables comparative trifles to ignite our passions, which express themselves not only in factions but in open conflicts that threaten the individual welfare of other human beings and that of society as a whole.[111]

Factions, their causes, and effects are expressions of a recalcitrant fact about human nature and character. In what is probably the most famous passage from *The Federalist*, Madison muses on human frailty and on government as an institution devised to deal with it: "But what is government itself but the greatest of all reflections on human nature? If men were angels, no government would be necessary. If angels were to govern men, neither external nor internal controuls [*sic*] on government would be necessary" (No. 51).[112] And although Madison, like Jefferson, sees property as an artifact of political societies, he has no reservations in describing it as, more than the other causes of factions, the most serious source of political divisions and factionalism: "The most common and durable source of factions, has been the various and unequal distribution of property. Those who hold, and those who are without property, have ever formed distinct interests in society."[113] That in any political and economic society there will be tensions, hence factions, between debtors and creditors, landed aristocrats and merchants, manufacturers and laborers is never in dispute. The remedy lies in adopting a republican government, "by which I mean a government in which the scheme of representation takes place . . . , and promises the cure for which we are seeking."[114]

A republic differs from a pure democracy in two ways. In a republic (i) a small number of citizens is elected by all the citizens, who can vote to represent them in governmental matters. In a democracy, the citizens themselves vote directly, not through elected representatives, on all matters of state and public policy. And (ii) a republic has a "greater number of citizens, and greater sphere of country" than a democracy.[115] There is nothing remarkable about (i), but (ii), which Madison must have known from reading Hume, was almost a shock to eighteenth-century readers. Why?

Hume, near the end of his "Idea of a Perfect Commonwealth," had written, "Though it is more difficult to form a republican government in an extensive country than in a city, there is more facility when once it is formed, or preserving it steady and uniform, *without tumult and faction.*"[116] Hume had turned conventional wisdom upside down, and Madison had followed his lead. The traditional presumption had been that republics have a chance of succeeding and lasting only in relatively small cities like Venice or Geneva, but a republican government spread over an entire nation was supposed to be doomed from the outset by too many people and too much geography.[117]

Madison says so much the worse for conventional thinking. Because in a republican government, many citizens elect relatively few to represent them in government, the geographical expanse and the population can be greater than that of a direct, participatory democracy.[118] There will never be thousands, much less hundreds of thousands, of citizens assembling in one place to try, albeit unsuccessfully, to conduct the nation's business. The United States, instead of being too big and too populous for the proposed constitution, is a perfect candidate for the republican form of government endorsed by the Constitutional Convention.

Making the proposed constitution the law of the land, that is, the law of a federation of states, can diminish legitimate concerns about factions. Size and population do not allow factions to breed and multiply as they do within the narrow, teeming perimeters of a crowded city-state. Madison sees the issue almost as a case in applied mathematics. Smaller populations necessarily spawn fewer "distinct parties and interests"; hence, since the number of people is insufficient to allow numerous factions, it is easier to come by a majority within a single faction. The rest follows inevitably: "the smaller the number of individuals composing a majority, and the smaller the compass within which they are placed, the more easily will they concert and execute their plans of oppression." On the other hand, enlarging the territory and multiplying the population increases the number of different factions and diverse interests. This greatly diminishes the likelihood that any majority will be generated whose numbers are great enough to divest other citizens of their rights, a point that Madison makes in his October 27, 1787, letter to Jefferson: "In a large Society, the people are broken into so many interests and parties, that a common sentiment is less likely to be felt, and the requisite concert less likely to be formed, by a majority of the whole. The same security seems requisite for the civil as for the religious rights of individuals."[119]

Stripped to the bone, Madison's argument and the philosophy that underpins it are pessimistic.[120] Because men are not angels and because nothing in human nature is likely to change for the better, we must deal with the world as we find it. Given self-interest, the fallibility of reason, and the strength of human passions, men and women frequently err regarding their own interests and threaten the interests of others. Factions, which are facts of social, political, and economic life, are too often the aggregate manifestations of individual flaws. The most enlightened and decent legislators, justices, and magistrates lack the alchemical skills to turn men into angels and factions into agencies for the common good. The best alternative to blunt the force of self-interest, passions, parties, and factions is to abandon alchemy for chemistry, in other words, to spread the poison of factionalism so far and wide that it is too dilute to do serious harm. Heal the patient (a foundering, anemic union under the Articles of Confederation) with a remedy (the Constitution of 1787) proportionate to its illness: "In the extent and proper structure of the union, therefore, we behold a republican remedy for the diseases most incident to republican government."[121]

Madison was far less a strict federalist than a pragmatist, and as a pragmatist he knew that bold initiatives were essential for the United States to remain a nation. There is, however, a dark side to his pragmatism. To induce the southern states, especially South Carolina and Georgia, to ratify the Constitution, he and the other federalists would say little publicly about slavery, and for the purpose of ratification he would tacitly treat slaves as property. As Morton White puts it, "Justice, *the* end of government in *Number 51*, was justice to citizens, not to slaves. In *The Federalist*, by carefully choosing 'Citizens', Madison managed to avoid attacking what he had once called the most oppressive dominion ever exercised by man over man."[122] We know now what only delegates to the Constitutional Convention knew on June 6, 1787, when Madison spoke to them about the evils of slavery and the slave trade. The Convention met in secrecy, and delegates agreed not to say or print anything about their deliberations for fifty years.[123]

Madison must have believed that to make the United States a great nation, one that responds to the promises declared by Paine and Jefferson, the Constitution had to be ratified and given its chance to make good on the promises that animated the Revolution. It is sad and unfortunate that one of those promises was not to abolish slavery.

Madison contributed to *The Federalist* because he understood well and feared deeply the risks of inaction. He stressed only the issues that he had to address if New York and the other states were to be persuaded to adopt a document drafted in just over three months and designed to give the United States a new and lasting government. He accepted the role of a vocal federalist not so much because he wished to but because he thought he had to. As a consequence of his effort and that of other less distinguished men who gathered in the summer of 1787, a new nation—still tainted by institutional slavery and the denial of basic rights to women—survived adolescence and made it to adulthood. The document they drafted, and approved, served then and serves now as the cornerstone for an expansive republic that had no precedent anywhere else in the world. That the republic has lasted more than two centuries, that its Constitution is elastic enough to have eventually eliminated some of the remnants and unthinkable evils of eighteenth- and nineteenth-century injustice,[124] is a monument to a shy, slight Virginian who, when we talk about the Constitution, is transformed into the most imposing Founding Father.

Postscript

The Founding Fathers had succeeded against all odds. Under their leadership, the colonies managed to separate themselves from England, and a loose confederation of states became the United States. Each state had become part of a nation that was politically and economically free of the monarchy, titles of nobility, and suffocating laws of inheritance.

There was, however, unfinished business that was not about political or economic autonomy. The Founding Fathers had borrowed from English scientists, philosophers, and institutions, for example, Jefferson from Locke and Adams from England's parliamentary-monarchical system of checks and balances. The finest American universities modeled their curricula on what Oxford and Cambridge offered their well-born students. Even Jefferson, the consummate Anglophobe, tried to attract English and other European scholars to a life of instruction and research at the University of Virginia, although his hopes were not realized until years after his death.

So too in the arts and sciences, Americans looked first to England for sources and inspiration. Domestic, academic, and urban architecture (Monticello and the University of Virginia excepted) borrowed liberally, before and after the Revolution, from the buildings and architectural pattern books of Georgian and Greek Revival England. American portraiture frequently mimed the styles of Thomas Gainsborough and Joshua Reynolds. Benjamin West (1738–1820) was born and reared in Philadelphia but became one of America's greatest painters by first becoming one of its most famous expatriates, studying in Italy from 1759 to 1763 and moving to London, where he painted for the balance of his life. Gilbert Stuart (1755–1828), one of the most successful American portrait painters of his time, spent seventeen years refining his talents in England and Ireland.[125] The finest American furniture copied English imports or the elegant rococo pieces that Thomas Chippendale described in *The Gentleman and Cabinet Maker's Director* (1754).[126] American literature had not yet found a muse. Newton's *Principia* and *Opticks* were still firmly in command on both sides of the Atlantic. Benjamin Franklin, himself a scientist of the first rank, proposed the American Philosophical Society for advancing practical and theoretical knowledge.[127] Its mission was an adaptation of Robert Hooke's charter for the great Royal Society of London, of which Franklin was himself a member.

None of this is surprising. The political transition from British America to the United States of America had taken time and had been unaccountably difficult. The cost in lives and resources was incalculable. Cultural emancipation was nowhere promised in the Declaration of Independence or the Constitution. Freeing America from intellectual and aesthetic dependence would take time and effort. It would have to wait its turn. The men and women responsible for that effort, especially those who contributed to the American philosophical tradition, are those to whose labors we look in the following essays.

NOTES

1. *American Scripture: Making the Declaration of Independence* (New York, 1997), xx–xxi.
2. David Hawke *The Colonial Experience*, (Indianapolis, 1966), 586–7.
3. Thomas Paine, *Common Sense and Other Political Writings*, ed. N. F. Adkins (Indianapolis, 1953), vii–x. Subsequent citations to *Common Sense* are keyed to this edition.
4. *The Age of Reason, Part I*, ed. and intro. Alburey Castell (Indianapolis, 1957), 25, 26.

5. Ibid. 26, 58–9. In broad outline, Paine's rendering of the design argument for the existence of God is similar to Edwards's working assumptions and conclusions in "The Spider Letter." The difference between them is that for Edwards the phenomena in nature establish the existence of the God worshipped by strict Protestants; whereas for Paine the same sort of data certify that God exists and that the revelations and prophecies of Judaism and Christianity are irrelevant to true religion.
6. Ibid. 26; emphasis added. One can make a case that Paine's objection to the Quebec Act of 1774, one of the "Intolerable Acts," which placed North America territory west of the Ohio River under Quebec's control, was the Parliament's artificial effort to shrink the boundaries of continental North America. So understood, it is from Paine's perspective another example of England's efforts to narrow by law what it could not accomplish by nature (47–8, 148, note 29).
7. Ibid. 33.
8. Ibid. 4.
9. Ibid. 5.
10. Ibid. 6.
11. Ibid. 10.
12. Ibid. 16.
13. Competitors might be the *Magna Carta* of 1215 or the Declaration of the Rights of Man in 1689, but the scope of these documents falls short of what the Declaration of Independence affirms.
14. For the DNA evidence that confirms to a level approaching certainty that Jefferson fathered at least one of Sally Hemings's children and for a discussion of this evidence, see Eugene A. Foster et al., "Jefferson Fathered Slave's Last Child," *Nature*, 396, 27–8, and Eric S. Lander and Joseph J. Ellis, "Founding Father," ibid. 13–14.
15. Here too the literature is vast. Among the best recent discussions of Jefferson's puzzling attitudes toward slavery in theory and slave-owning in fact is that in Joseph J. Ellis, *American Sphinx: The Character of Thomas Jefferson* (New York, 1997), 86–9, 144–52. See also Robert F. and Lee Baldwin Dalzell, *George Washington's Mount Vernon: at Home in Revolutionary America* (New York, 1998), 218–19.
16. Ibid. 200–202. See also Anthony F. C. Wallace, *Jefferson and the Indians: the Tragic Fate of the First Americans* (Cambridge, Mass., 1999).
17. In *Founding Brothers: The Revolutionary Generation* (New York, 2000), Joseph J. Ellis devotes the better part of chapters 5 and 6 to Jefferson and John Adams. Where honesty, humanity, and loyalty are concerned, Adams comes out on top. For additional perspectives by other respected historians, see Garry Wills, "Storm Over Jefferson," *The New York Review of Books*, March 23, 2000, 16–18.
18. *American Sphinx*, 3–5.
19. The spelling and punctuation are Jefferson's. See *Thomas Jefferson, Writings*, ed. Merrill D. Peterson (New York, 1984), 706; hereafter abbreviated as *Writings*.
20. For a brief sketch of Jefferson's life, including his schooling and practicing law in Williamsburg, see *The Political Writings of Thomas Jefferson: Representative Selections*, ed. Edward Dumbauld (Indianapolis, 1955), xi–xvi.
21. *American Scripture*, 43, 98; *American Sphinx*, 48–9.
22. Ibid. 49. Maier says all the other committee members contributed something to Jefferson's Declaration, and she adds, "In the end, the efforts of these five men produced a workable draft that the Congress itself . . . made into a distinguished document by an act of group editing that has to be one of the great marvels of history. *American Scripture*, 98.
23. *American Sphinx*, 53–4.
24. *Writings*, 19.
25. See Carl Becker's classic *The Declaration of Independence: A Study in the History of Political Ideas* (New York, 1922); Morton White, *The Philosophy of the American Revolution* (New York, 1978); Garry Wills, *Inventing America: Jefferson's Declaration of Independence* (Garden City, 1978); and *American Scripture*, 135–40. For a summary of the prevailing and opposing views, see *American Sphinx*, 56–9.

26. For an analysis of the career and shades of meaning of "self-evident," see *The Philosophy of the American Revolution*, 9–96.
27. *Writings*, 959.
28. Richard K. Matthews, *The Radical Politics of Thomas Jefferson: a Revisionist View* (Lawrence, Kansas, 1984), 20.
29. *The Philosophy of the American Revolution*, 76–7, 160–61.
30. Ibid. 138.
31. From a letter to Peter Carr, August 10, 1787, in *Writings*, 901, 902; emphasis added.
32. Ibid. 874; cf. 815.
33. Some interpreters believe common sense and moral sentiment—hence views developed by philosophers of the Scottish Enlightenment such as Hutcheson, David Hume, Thomas Reid, and Dugald Stewart—are inseparable from Jefferson's account of self-evident truths. Garry Wills, in *Inventing America: Jefferson's Declaration of Independence*, is prominent among those who read Jefferson in this light. White, rejecting this position, shows that Jefferson, Locke, and the "Scottish School" agreed that moral judgments, whether self-evident or inferential, are "properly rational." See *The Philosophy of the American Revolution*, 113–27, and Daniel W. Howe, *Making the American Self* (Cambridge, Mass., 1997), 48–77.
34. See *American Sphinx*, 57–8, and *The Philosophy of the American Revolution*, 97–127.
35. There are some remarks about the status of women immediately following the Revolution in Joyce Appleby's *Inheriting the Revolution: the First Generation of Americans* (Cambridge, Mass., 2000), 8, 150–54, 169.
36. In addition to White's arguments for this interpretation, see Douglass Adair's remarks in "The Jefferson Scandals," *Fame and the Founding Fathers*, ed. T. Colbourn (Indianapolis, 1974), 259.
37. *The Philosophy of the American Revolution*, 74. White develops his analysis in great and convincing detail on pages 62–72. Richard Henry Lee's belief and own words were that the Declaration was "copied from Locke's treatise on government" (ibid. 64), and in a letter to the painter John Trumbull, February 15, 1789, Jefferson says that "Bacon, Locke and Newton" are "the three greatest men that have ever lived, without any exception." *Writings*, 939.
38. Ellis says that for Jefferson "what makes human beings fully human, and in that sense equal, was the moral sense." *American Sphinx*, 58. White, without denying the importance to Jefferson of the moral sense, disagrees: "The common feelings of human nature, being expressed by the subordinate faculty of the moral sense, did not *need* to be referred to in the Declaration once the voice of the superior faculty of reason had spoken." *The Philosophy of the American Revolution*, 115.
39. *Leviathan* (1651), ed. Edwin Curley (Indianapolis, 1994), I, xiv, 8.
40. Ibid. I, xi, 1–2.
41. Andrew Burstein, *The Inner Jefferson: Portrait of a Grieving Optimist* (Charlottesville, 1995), 9.
42. Quoted in *American Sphinx*, 55.
43. See *The Philosophy of the American Revolution*, 213–21.
44. See R. E. Allen's commentary to his translation of *The Dialogues of Plato, Volume II: The Symposium* (New Haven, 1991), 64–5.
45. *Writings*, 19.
46. Ibid. 290–91. See also 300–301 and Jefferson's letter to Jean Baptiste Say, February 1, 1804 (1143–4).
47. For Locke's defense of revolution and an appeal to God for the right to revolt, see the *Second Treatise of Government*, chapter XIX, sections 241–3. Jefferson took the phrase "a long train of abuses" from this chapter, section 225.
48. *Writings*, 23–4.
49. *American Sphinx*, 259.
50. See Jefferson's letter to John Adams, April 11, 1823. *Writings*, 1469.
51. Ibid. 1466–7; emphasis added.
52. Ibid., emphasis added.

53. Ibid. 1122; April 21, 1803. See also Jefferson's letter to his friend Charles Thompson, January 9, 1816, in which he describes his "wee-little book" that he assembled from Jesus's precepts in the Gospels. He adds that this shows he is a "*real Christian*," that is, a follower of Jesus's moral philosophy (1373).
54. Jefferson to Robert S. Livingston, September 9, 1801. *Writings*, 1091.
55. Jefferson to Joseph Priestly, March 21, 1801. Ibid. 1085–6.
56. Jefferson to Benjamin Rush, September 23, 1800. Ibid. 1082.
57. From "What Is Enlightenment?" (1784) in Kant, *Foundations of the Metaphysics of Morals* (Indianapolis, 1959), 85.
58. For a comprehensive study of the Enlightenment, see Peter Gay, *The Enlightenment: an Interpretation* (2 vols., New York, 1966).
59. *Writings*, 346–8.
60. Ibid. 346; emphasis added.
61. *Writings*, 493.
62. Ibid. 286.
63. Ibid. 347.
64. Ibid.
65. Ibid. 494.
66. Compare the Constitution of the Commonwealth of Massachusetts, Chapter I, Article ii, which grants freedom of religion but declares a "duty of all men in society, publicly, and at stated seasons, to worship the SUPREME BEING."
67. Jefferson to Nathaniel Burwell, March 14, 1818. Ibid. 1411–13.
68. Ibid. 859.
69. Ibid. 365.
70. Ibid.
71. Ibid.
72. Ibid. 459.
73. Carter Wiseman, *Shaping a Nation: Twentieth Century American Architecture and Its Makers* (New York, 1998), 22.
74. *Writings*, 469.
75. Ibid. 467.
76. Desmond Guinness and Julius T. Sadler, *Mr. Jefferson, Architect* (New York, 1973), 125.
77. Jefferson to John Adams, October 28, 1813; *Writings*, 1306.
78. Ibid. 272. See also Jefferson's letter to Edward Carrington, January 16, 1787, for remarks that at once celebrate and patronize unsophisticated Americans (880–81).
79. The best recent studies of Adams are Ellis's *Passionate Sage: The Character of John Adams* (New York, 1993) and David McCullough's *John Adams* (New York, 2001).
80. The civil wars about which Davila wrote were those in France near the close of the sixteenth century, not the French Revolution, although Adams was not sympathetic with the character and outcome of that Revolution.
81. Paul Conkin, *Puritans and Pragmatists: Eight Eminent Thinkers* (New York, 1968), 112.
82. *The Political Writings of John Adams*, ed. G. A. Peek (Indianapolis, 1954), 176–84, 189–90; hereafter abbreviated as *Political Writings of Adams*.
83. Ibid. 190.
84. Ibid. 191.
85. Ibid. 192.
86. The proximate cause for Adams's work were the criticisms of American state constitutions in a letter that Anne-Robert-Jacques Turgot, a French economist and friend of Franklin, wrote to the English political philosopher Richard Price. Ibid. 105–7.
87. *Puritans and Pragmatists*, 111. For similar, although somewhat more tempered, assessments of Adams's political thought see I. Bernard Cohen, *Science and the Founding Fathers*, 228; and Ellis in *The Passionate Sage*, 172–3.
88. Adams's worries about Shay's Rebellion (1786–7) in his own state of Massachusetts may have exacerbated his doubts about republican governments and presumptions that all men are equal. See Samuel Eliot Morison, *The Oxford History of the American People* (3 vols., New York, 1972), I, 390–94.

89. *Political Writings of Adams*, 133; emphasis added.
90. For Ellis's compelling summary of Adams's belief in a natural aristocracy, see *Passionate Sage*, 156–65.
91. Ibid.
92. Ibid. 134.
93. Ibid. 137.
94. Ibid. 139; emphasis added. The difference between Adams and Jefferson is not whether there is a natural aristocracy but whether it should have a special place (Senate) in a democratic republic. See Jefferson's letter to Adams, October 28, 1813; *Writings*, 1304–10.
95. Maier briefly discusses Adams's concerns about republican governments. *American Scripture*, 34–6.
96. *The Oxford History of the American People*, I, 360.
97. *Political Writings of Adams*, 155.
98. Ibid. 159.
99. *Passionate Sage*, 46; cf. 165–6.
100. Ibid. 153; cf. 155. Ellis notes that Adams first articulates his views on the makeup of a senate, as well as his reasons for having one, in the earlier *Dissertation on the Canon and Feudal Law* (1765).
101. T. Colbourn, *The Lamp of Experience: Whig History and the Intellectual Origins of the American Revolution* (Chapel Hill, 1965), 104.
102. For an arresting account of the reasons that Madison's presidency was less distinguished than the career that led up to it, see Gary Willis, *James Madison* (New York, 2002).
103. For a discussion of Jay's political philosophy and his contribution to *The Federalist*, see Morton White, *Philosophy, The Federalist and the Constitution* (New York, 1987), 149, 150–55, 160.
104. *Founding Brothers*, 53.
105. Ibid. 52–3.
106. See, respectively, Charles A. Beard, *An Economic Interpretation of the Constitution of the United States* (New York, 1913); White, *Philosophy, The Federalist and the Constitution*, 51–81; and Douglass Adair, "'That Politics May Be Reduced to a Science'," in *Fame and the Founding Fathers*, 132–51.
107. *Political Writings of Adams*, 154.
108. Alexander Hamilton, John Jay, and James Madison, *The Federalist*, intro. Edward M. Earle (New York, 1938), 54.
109. Ibid. 55.
110. Ibid.
111. Ibid. 55–6.
112. Ibid. 337.
113. Ibid. 56. This famous assertion led Beard to conclude that Madison was both an economic determinist and advocate of an economic theory of history. White goes to great lengths to show that Beard is mistaken on both counts, that Madison's remarks on the importance of economic causes of factions is not grounds for claiming that economic considerations are the only causes of factions. *Philosophy, The Federalist, and the Constitution*, 56–81.
114. *The Federalist*, 59.
115. Ibid.
116. *Essays: Moral, Political and Literary* ed. E. F. Miller (Indianapolis, 1985), 527; emphasis added.
117. Again, see Adair's commentary in *Fame and the Founding Fathers*, 139–50.
118. *The Federalist*, 59–60.
119. For the entire letter, see *The Origins of the American Constitution: a Documentary History*, ed. Michael Kammen (New York, 1986), 65–76. See also White's discussion of this letter and the influence in it of Hume's "Of Parties in General." *Philosophy, The Federalist, and the Constitution*, 75–76.
120. For some comments on Madison's pessimism, see Gordon S. Wood, *The Creation of the American Republic, 1776–1787* (Chapel Hill, 1969), 472, 577.

121. Ibid. 62.
122. Ibid. 222. White explores and criticizes the legerdemain by which Madison manages to avoid the issue of slavery in the papers he contributed to *The Federalist* (168–71, 221–3). For some more sympathetic observations, see Kammen's introduction to *The Origins of the American Constitution*, xvii–xviii.
123. Ibid. xviii, 56.
124. Amendments 13, 14, 15, 17, and 19 address the racism, elitism, and sexism that neither the federalists nor many of their most outspoken adversaries were prepared to address in 1787–1788.
125. See E. P. Richardson, *A Short History of Painting in America, the Story of 450 Years* (New York, 1963), 1–6, 80–81.
126. Germain Bazin, *Baroque and Rococo Art*, trans. J. Griffith, reprint (London, 1985), 269–70.
127. See H. W. Brands, *The First American: the Life and Times of Benjamin Franklin* (New York, 2000), 169–71.

Essay 4
New England Transcendentalism: Emerson, Thoreau, and the Case for Completing the American Revolution

In his introduction to *The American Transcendentalists*, Perry Miller says that "almost as much has been written about the New England Transcendentalists as they ever wrote by themselves."[1] Miller is right; hence, the problem for those of us who dare to write about the history of philosophy in America is obvious. On whom and what, among the Transcendentalists and their writings, does one concentrate in order to describe the movement and to say something worth reading about its place in the development of philosophy in nineteenth-century America? This task is made more difficult since it is common for some interpreters to treat Emerson and Thoreau, the obvious candidates for our attention, as talented essayists but as only marginal philosophers.[2]

If, however, we are prepared in this essay, as in previous essays, to suspend our search for a precise definition of "philosophy" or "philosopher" and can agree that philosophers are at least determined to criticize conventional thinking and to provoke reflection, then we can say that the New England Transcendentalists are more than philosophical enough for the purposes of this study. They were less interested in arguing than, for example, the critical Socrates and less dramatic than Nietzsche. But like Socrates and Nietzsche, the Transcendentalists were determined to attack the foundations of conventionalism and to urge the men and women of their generation, that of America in the 1830s and 1840s, to think and act for themselves.

As a point of departure, we can adopt as a working hypothesis Perry Miller's characterization of what unifies the different voices and threads of New England Transcendentalism: ". . . we may . . . see in the Transcendentalists not so much a collection of exotic ideologues as the first outcry of the heart against the materialistic pressures of a business civilization. Protestant to the core, they turn their protest against what is customarily called the "Protestant ethic": they refuse to labor in a proper calling, conscientiously cultivate the arts of leisure, and strive to avoid making money."[3] This account may need to be modified as the discussion develops, but it is never very far from what Emerson, Thoreau, and their like-minded friends say when they encourage changes in America and its citizens.

Emerson and "Our National Intellectual Declaration of Independence": A Call for the Emancipation of American Genius[4]

Ralph Waldo Emerson (1803–1882), one of the most familiar figures in American letters, was born in Boston exactly one hundred years after Jonathan Edwards. At age eight, following the death of his father William, it fell to Emerson and his four brothers to care for their mother and aunt. Emerson attended Harvard College and Divinity School (1817–1825). In 1829 he became pastor of the Second Unitarian Church in the north end of Boston, a church whose roots extended back to 1650 and to the leadership of Increase and Cotton Mather.[5] In the same year he married Ellen Tucker, who died in 1831.[6] Profoundly saddened by this loss and perhaps by a related loss of conventional faith, he resigned his position in 1832 claiming that he could no longer accept the sacrament of the Lord's Supper. Between 1832 and 1833 Emerson traveled extensively through England and Continental Europe, meeting, among others, the romantic poets Coleridge and Wordsworth and the essayist Thomas Carlyle. Returning to the United States, he became a successful public lecturer by 1833 and married Lydia Jackson in 1835. Together, though perhaps not always in perfect harmony, they lived in Concord and reared four children, although their first son Waldo died before his sixth birthday (1842).

For two years (1842–1844) Emerson was editor of *The Dial*, the publication of the Transcendental Club, but neither the Club nor *The Dial* lasted. Emerson and his Transcendentalist associates (Margaret Fuller, first editor of *The Dial*, and George Ripley, founder of the experimental Brook Farm community) were not destined to travel the same roads. Emerson found unity in common philosophical points of view, not in gatherings and institutional commitments. To a certain extent, what was true for Emerson was true for Transcendentalism as well:

> Whatever transcendentalism was, it was not suited to institutionalizing. It gave birth to no academy; it flourished in no college or seminary. It had two collective expressions during its heyday (the club and the magazine called *The Dial*) but could only manage one at a time. The last meeting of the club was in 1840, the year *The Dial* was founded.[7]

Emerson spent the balance of his life composing essays, lecturing, writing poetry, concerning himself with political and social reform—especially the increasingly divisive issue of slavery—and traveling. The last ten years of his life amounted to a prolonged period of mental decline. He died of pneumonia at his home in Concord, April 27, 1882.[8]

Obviously, it is much easier to provide an epitome of Emerson's life than of the philosophy that he made it his occupation (literally an *occupation* on the modestly lucrative lecture circuit) to promulgate. The sources for Transcendentalism, whether they determine the content of Emerson's essays and lectures or those of his philosophical confederates, are disparate: Platonism, Neoplatonism, eighteenth- and early nineteenth-century German philosophy, Renaissance mysticism and, of course, English romantic literature. With some of these sources in mind, Miller suggests that one can refine the definition of "Transcendentalists" and see them "as children of the Puritan past who, having been emancipated by Unitarianism from New England's original Calvinism, found a new religious expression in forms derived from romantic literature and from the philosophical idealism of Germany."[9] This clearly applies to Emerson for whom Immanuel Kant's *The Critique of Pure Reason* (1781), one of the greatest books in Western philosophy, is the principal philosophical source in his essay "The Transcendentalist" (1841), which articulates some of the dominant features of Emersonian Transcendentalism. Miller's definition also applies to Emerson insofar as Wordsworth's romantic indictment of materialism in "The World is too much with Us" (1802–1804) could serve as an interpretive gloss on so many of Emerson's objections to a generation of Americans for whom "getting and spending" had become a corrupt religion.

Two facets of American life, together with his own romantic temperament, motivated Emerson: the explosive manufacturing and commercial development that increasingly shaped America's character, and preoccupation with literary, artistic, and other cultural influences forged across the Atlantic. What for Emerson is wrong with each of these manifestations of middle nineteenth-century American life?

Men and women who are busy acquiring and spending might suppress or never confront their authentic natures. This is the message of the opening paragraphs of "The American Scholar." Laboring men, seeing themselves as what they do rather than as what they are, remain detached from their essential *selves*: "The tradesman scarcely ever gives an ideal worth to his work, but is ridden by the routine of his craft, and the soul is subject to dollars. The priest becomes a form; the attorney, a statute-book; the mechanic, a machine; the sailor, a rope of a ship."[10] In short, with the burgeoning commercialism and industrialism of the Northeast during the 1820s–1840s (i.e., canals and railroads to facilitate trade, the expansion of business in everything from whale oil to clocks, the beginnings of corporate America and of banking enterprises, the textile mills in Massachusetts and labor unrest),[11] Emerson's romantic vision of pastoral America was showing signs of a dark and sooty underbelly. Emerson's observations and fears in "The American Scholar" reflect what so distressed him about the Victorian English:

> Man in England submits to be a product of political economy. On a bleak moor, a mill is built, a banking-house is opened, and men come in, as water in a sluiceway, and towns and cities rise. Man is made as a Birmingham button. The rapid doubling of the population dates from Watt's steam engine. A landlord who owns a province says, "the tenantry are unprofitable; let me have sheep."[12]

There is no reason to be surprised that Emerson laments the disillusioned Englishmen whose copies are spreading throughout the American East: ". . . the machine unmans the user. What he gains in making cloth, he loses in general power. There should be temperance in making cloth as well as in eating . . . The robust rural

Saxon degenerates in the mills to the Leicester stockinger, to the imbecile Manchester spinner,—far on the way to be spiders and needles."[13] This unpleasant image is also interchangeable with that of industrial life in Charles Dickens's Coketown.[14] In "The American Scholar," as in other essays, one can justly note that Emerson's passion for originality is occasionally compromised by his liberal appeal to themes that he would like to have been original with him.

What about America's attraction to the culture born and nurtured across the great ocean? The first paragraph of *Nature* announces a sentiment that recurs in several essays and lectures. It describes one of the central concerns of Emerson's critical philosophy:

> Our age is retrospective. It builds sepulchres of the fathers. It writes biographies, histories, and criticism. The foregoing generations beheld God and nature face to face; we, through their eyes. Why should not we also enjoy an original relation to the universe? *Why should we not have a poetry and philosophy of insight and not of tradition, and a religion by revelation to us, and not the history of theirs?* . . . The sun shines to-day also. . . . *Let us demand our own works and laws and worship.*[15]

This famous passage declares that Americans remain trapped, by tradition and by the tired formulas of ancestral religions, European culture and, most generally, the past. Until we recognize our dependence and break free of it, the Revolution of 1776 remains incomplete.[16]

We must, however, note that even more famous than what Emerson says at the beginning of *Nature* is his claim in "Self-Reliance" that "A foolish consistency is the hobgoblin of little minds, adored by little statesmen and philosophers and divines. *With consistency a great soul has simply nothing to do.*"[17] The best evidence that this is not merely rhetoric is Emerson's own inconsistency. While, for example, he extols the virtue of originality and urges his American sisters and brothers to follow their own creative instincts, he puts together a philosophy that is not radically new. He frankly acknowledges that part of his philosophy, hence of his Transcendentalism, is an American variation on selected European philosophical and literary themes. One might justifiably claim that absent the influence of Kant and Coleridge, Emerson's philosophy would have been very different from what it is.[18] But for these two great lights of European thought and literature, we might know Emerson only as a poet and social critic. The admonition, "Do as I say, not as I do" seems particularly apt where Emerson's version of New England Transcendentalism is concerned. Emerson's message, even when applied to him, was ahead of its time.

The same inconsistency plagues Emerson's romantic objections to commerce and to worldliness. He is, as we will see, a philosophical romantic, and romantics tend to be suspicious of business and industry. We have already discovered as much in Emerson's trenchant criticism of the English middle-class temperament. Romantics are fearful and disdainful of factories and, in William Blake's nearly immortal phrase, of the "dark satanic mills" that corrupt the land, air, and water, destroy overworked laborers, and sully the idyllic image of unspoiled nature.[19]

In spite of all this, in his lecture "The Young American," delivered to members of the Mercantile Library Association of Boston, February 7, 1844, we discover Emerson as a vigorous apologist for "the expansion of 'trade', which was his word for the vigorous infant . . . better known as industrial capitalism."[20] One might say that given his young audience, with a keen interest in manufacturing and trade, we should be neither surprised nor too critical of Emerson's unabashed brief for the development of America's railroads and for the expansion of American business. One could also point out that the opening paragraph of this lecture, like that of *Nature*, restates Emerson's persistent concern that America finds its cultural identity across the Atlantic: "It is remarkable, that poor people have their intellectual culture from one country, and their duties from another. Our books are European. . . . A gulf yawns for the young American between his education and his work."[21]

The work that "The Young American" celebrates is not the life of creative genius; rather, it is the muscle and brawn of capitalist energy. When Emerson adds that "America is beginning to assert itself, and Europe is receding in the same degree," he is not talking about the invention and growth of culture, literature, and the arts. Immediately he explains himself: "There is no American who has not been stimulated to reflection by the facilities now in progress of construction for travel and the transportation of goods in the United States. The alleged effect to augment disproportionately the size of cities, is in a rapid course of fulfillment in this metropolis of New England."[22]

Here the prose sounds more like that which Vanderbilt, Carnegie, and Rockefeller would have savored. "Not only is distance annihilated, but when, as now, the locomotive and the steamboat, like enormous shuttles, shoot every day across the thousand various threads of national descent and employment, and bind them fast in one web, and hourly assimilation goes forward, and there is no danger that local peculiarities and hostilities should be preserved."[23]

Emerson's naiveté is palpable. Railroads and steamboats facilitated the movement of goods and people, but they did little to subdue sectionalism or to secure America's national unity. After all, the rails and rivers moved north and south, as well as east and west, and the Civil War—the bloody realization of sectionalism as secessionism—was only seventeen years away. And as Emerson strives in this lecture to blend capitalist modes of transportation with his romantic prepossessions about untrammeled nature, the resulting picture is out of focus: "In an uneven country the railroad is a fine object in the making. It has introduced a multitude of picturesque traits into our pastoral scenery. The tunneling of mountains, the bridging of streams, the bold mole carried out into a broad silent meadow . . . , keep the senses and imagination active; and the varied aspects of the enterprise make it the topic of all companies, in cars and boats, and by firesides."[24]

Even if one buys what Leo Marx describes as Emerson's perplexing "ability to join enthusiasm for technological progress with a 'romantic' love of nature and contempt for cities," what about those who labored impossible, endless hours to build the railroads or to maintain the "waterwheels at Lowell" that power the factories?[25] How is the creativity and imagination of Irish immigrant laborers liberated by the demands that successful capitalists make upon them? How is their life any different from the English working class in Birmingham and Manchester? Emerson's answer belies the insuperable problems that so many immigrants suffered in the squalid slums of New York, Boston, and Philadelphia in the early middle of the nineteenth century.[26]

> And yet their plight is not so grievous as it seems. They escape from the squalid despair of their condition at home, into the unlimited opportunities of their existence here, must be reckoned a gain. The Irish father and mother are very ill paid, and are victims of fraud and private oppression; but their children are instantly received into the schools of the country; they grow up in perfect communication and equality with the native children . . .[27]

This is a remarkable claim from a man who knows the facts and whose basic philosophy, at which we will look in the following section, exploits the venerable distinction between appearance and reality. The facts were that the Irish children and grandchildren confronted prejudice and suffered from scurrilous stereotypes in Protestant America. And Emerson surely knew that day laborers in America may have fared somewhat better than those in London, Liverpool, and Dublin, but the optimistic sketch in "The Young American" is unsupported by the facts.

Although Robert D. Richardson seems unclear what a biographer should say about Emerson and the argument of "The Young American," he tries to put the best face on its message: "Though Emerson was alive to the abuses of commerce . . . , he praised the commercial spirit in 'The Young American' because it also represented a new, more democratic form of social organization than feudalism. Emerson is virtually alone among American writers in his endorsement of the principle of commerce. Most American writers have been antibusiness, many—including Thoreau—vehemently so."[28] If Richardson is correct, the inconsistency between Emerson's complaints in *English Traits* and his celebration in "The Young American" of commercial ingenuity may not be so paradoxical as it appears. The opposition between industry and the best in nature, as Emerson describes it throughout *Nature*, need not be threatening.[29] As Marx puts it, "If technology is the creation of man, who is the product of nature, then how can the machine in the landscape be thought to represent an unresolvable conflict?"[30] This is easier to ask than to answer. There is very little in what we might call the *essential* Emerson, that is, Emerson as he recites the first principles of Transcendentalism, that fits with the commercial and industrial side of human behavior. To see whether there is a central inconsistency between Emerson in "The Young American" and Emerson in the essays and lectures in which he describes Transcendentalists, we must turn to some of his principal writings.

Ralph Waldo to Edward Bliss Emerson, May 31, 1834, and "The Transcendentalist": A Revival of Metaphysical Impulses

What is the marrow of Emerson's Transcendentalism? One can probably come closest to finding the answer in Emerson's letter to his brother Edward (1805–1834) and in "The Transcendentalist," a lecture Emerson gave at Boston's Masonic

Temple in December 1841. His letter antedates "The Young American" by nine years and "The Transcendentalist" by three. There is nothing in the longer or shorter interval to suggest that Emerson had jettisoned his commitments to Transcendentalism or that he had substantially modified them. So it is difficult to see any point of convergence or congruence between the intuitionism of these earlier writings and the capitalist apologetics of "The Young American." What, then, is Transcendentalism as Emerson characterizes it?

Referring in his letter to what Transcendentalists believe, Emerson writes to Edward:

> Philosophy [Transcendentalism] affirms that the outward world is only phenomenal & the whole concern of dinners of tailors of gigs of balls whereof men make such account is a quite relative & temporary one—an intricate dream—the exhalation of the present state of the Soul—wherein the *Understanding* works incessantly as if it were real but the eternal *Reason* when now & then she is allowed to speak declares it is an accident of smoke nowise related to his permanent attributes. Now that I have used the words, let me ask you do you draw the distinction of Milton Coleridge & the Germans between *Reason* & *Understanding*. *I think it is a philosophy itself.*[31]

When Emerson praises *Reason*, but merely describes the *Understanding*, he is prolonging a difference between two modes of knowing, that is, a difference that in some form reaches at least as far back as Plato. But Emerson's immediate sources are neither Plato nor Neoplatonists; they are primarily Coleridge and Kant. Coleridge and Emerson read Kant, but Emerson (and possibly Coleridge) misread or misappropriated him in a way that traditional Kantians could never have approved. For religious and philosophical reasons that need not detain us, Coleridge drew a firm distinction that Emerson made his own. In *Aids to Reflection* (1828), Coleridge wrote of a difference in *kind* between *Reason* and *Understanding*:

> 1. Understanding is discursive. . . . Reason is fixed. 2. The understanding in all its judgments refers to some other faculty as its ultimate authority. . . . The reason in all its decisions appeals to itself as the ground and *substance* of their truth. 3. Understanding is the faculty of reflection. . . . Reason of contemplation. Reason is indeed much nearer to Sense than to Understanding: for Reason . . . is a direct aspect of truth, an inward beholding, having a similar relation to the intelligible or spiritual, as sense has to the material or phenomenal.[32]

Coleridge says what Emerson writes in his letter to Edward. Human *Understanding*, like animal understanding, is restricted to the level of ordinary experience, that which we glean from using and reflecting on the contents of one or more of the five conventional senses. For an empiricist, all knowing begins with what the five senses and the understanding supply us. As a consequence, nothing is in the intellect that is not first in the senses.[33] To tell an empiricist that there is a more fundamental way to know and that there are "objects" that we know only through this more fundamental conduit to knowledge is, for the empiricist, to try to transform senseless talk into profound insights.

Neither Coleridge nor Emerson was, however, an empiricist. Each believed emphatically that *Reason* is a faculty or capacity that all human beings possess. It is a faculty that enables them to reach beyond the world of the senses, to *transcend* that world, and to encounter immediately and unerringly all that is real, true, and valuable. This is how Emerson makes the point as he explains his philosophy to Edward:

> The Understanding toils all the time, compares, contrives, adds, argues . . . , dwelling in the present the expedient the customary. Beasts have some understanding but no Reason. Reason is potentially perfect in every man—Understanding in very different degrees of strength. The thoughts of youth, & 'first thoughts,' are the revelations of Reason.[34] . . . But understanding that wrinkled calculator the steward of our house to whom is committed the support of our animal life contradicts evermore the affirmations of Reason & points at Custom & Interest & persuades one man that the declarations of Reason are false & another that they are at least impractical.[35]

The prose is Emerson's. Its most proximate source is Coleridge; hence we look in vain for the originality that Emerson demands from others.[36] More important is what Emerson, moving in a lockstep with Coleridge, has in mind.

Emerson means that every human being is equipped to move beyond or beneath the world of sensation and to discern that which does not appear among the sensuous phenomena of daily experience and *Understanding*. *Reason* apprehends directly the aesthetic, moral, and spiritual qualities or absolutes that are at most approximated in the world of empirical facts and relations on which the practical understanding bears. The *Understanding* helps us to get about in the world of conventional experience. It tells us the best way to secure some nonmoral, nonaesthetic, nonspiritual end and is, therefore, merely useful. But what about someone who seeks more than utility, someone who wants values, beauty, and truth or answers to perennial questions like "What is ultimate reality?" and "What makes life worth living?" For Emerson such a person must appeal to *Reason*, which alone reveals what he seeks or answers his urgent philosophical questions.

Elizabeth Flower and Murray Murphey believe one can state some of this more directly. They write in their discussion of Emerson, "Transcendentalism was an attempt to rescue man from nature and reestablish his spiritual character. This is why Emerson's great manifesto was entitled *Nature*."[37] Emerson and less well-known Transcendentalists, such as his cousin George Ripley, affirm for all people what Edwards restricted to those fortunate Calvinists whom God sanctified.[38] With the broad and far more democratic reach of Transcendentalism, Emerson asserts that everyone possesses the capacity to employ *Reason* and that everyone is spiritual or, what for him is the same thing, supernatural.

Anyone may, of course, adopt a philosophy for assorted reasons. We will see in the next section that there are some straightforward reasons Emerson and his associates, disheartened by the uninspired message of Unitarianism, sought an alternative religious philosophy. Nor is it surprising that secure in their spiritually rich philosophy, they should look with jaundice on the smug materialists and empiricists for whom nothing is real if it is not, in fact or in principle, sensuous: "The materialist . . . mocks at fine-spun theories, at star-gazers and dreamers, and believes that his life is solid, that he at least takes nothing for granted, but knows where he stands, and what he does." The following observation from "The Transcendentalist" is a warning that this sense of security is wafer-thin: "Yet how easy it is to show him, that he is also a phantom walking and working amid phantoms, and that he need only ask a question or two beyond his daily questions, to find his solid universe growing dim and impalpable before his sense."[39]

Is anything surprising in Emerson's view of a materialist? The answer comes from Emerson's statement of every Transcendentalist's debt to Kant. Once more we see the tension in Emerson between his demand for originality and an admission that his debts may be more profound than his originality:[40]

> [T]he Idealism of the present day acquired the name Transcendental, from the use of the term by Immanuel Kant, of Konigsberg, who replied to the skeptical philosophy of Locke, which insisted that there was nothing in the intellect which was not previously in the experience of the senses, by showing that there was a very important class of ideas . . . , which did not come by experience, but through which experience was acquired; that these were the intuitions of the mind itself; and he denominated them *Transcendental* forms.[41]

The surprise in this passage is that Emerson either does not realize or does not quite acknowledge the difference between New England Transcendentalism and what Kant advances. The point goes beyond terminology. Kant did believe he was differentiating correct philosophy from limited empiricism. He insisted, contrary to Locke and Hume, that we do not merely take in the data of experience but that we ourselves bring something to our experience of the world of sense. The Kantian position is complex, but this much is clear: Kant was not an intuitionist or patron of *Reason* in Emerson's sense.

Kant was convinced that we play an essential role in shaping the content and conditions under which we perceive things, such as in time and space. He was also convinced that our perception can never transcend the world of phenomena, the world that Emerson says is the derivative, unreal order in which the merely practical understanding operates. The world that Emersonian *Reason* penetrates and lays bare, which might correspond roughly to what Kant calls the *noumenal* order, is for Kant inaccessible. It is a world that Kant posits but that no one can know.[42]

Even without trying to penetrate Kant's philosophy, we can detect two levels of inconsistency in Emerson's attempts to explain New England Transcendentalism. First, he borrows liberally from European thought in order to build an American philosophy that serves the struggle for intellectual emancipation from the Old World. Second, he calls liberally on Kant in order to provide authority for a philosophy of transcendence, a metaphysics anchored in *Reason*, yet Kant denied the possibility of transcendent insights and intuitions. Far from being in any consistent way a Kantian, Emerson seems to flout Kant's insistence that metaphysical claims have no place even in the richest sources of human knowledge.[43]

"The American Scholar" and "The Divinity School Address": Transcendentalism as Admonition

"The American Scholar," delivered to Harvard's Phi Beta Kappa chapter on August 31, 1837, is one of Emerson's most famous lectures and, with "The Divinity School Address," one of his most insistent calls to a certain kind of action. As an address to young and older scholars about the character of true scholarship, as against the products of bookworms, it also presents a glimpse of Emerson at his most provocative. That the address and its imperatives might not have been clear enough even for his talented audience is suggested by a listener who conceded "It was well spoken" but wondered "how many were in my own predicament of making little of it."[44]

Emerson senses that Americans are making some progress—are heeding that first paragraph of *Nature*—such that "Our day of dependence, our long apprenticeship to the learning of other lands, draws to a close."[45] This progress is good but not good enough. Less dependence does not amount to independence. The specific deficiencies and dependencies in America's college-educated scholars are manifest when we consider their use, misuse, or indifference to the tools and sources of genuine inspiration. What are these sources and tools?

First, there is nature itself. This is the grand source of inspiration to the true scholar, but the language in which Emerson expresses this fact is opaque. The problem is that Emerson tries, using the speech and metaphors of the *Understanding*, to describe nature insofar as it is the object and inspiration of *Reason*. His words look back to *Nature* and ahead to his essays "The Over-Soul" and "Circles," both of which were published in 1841:

> The first in time and the first in importance of the influences upon the mind is that of nature. . . . The scholar must needs stand wistful and admiring before this great spectacle. . . . What is nature to him? There is never a beginning, there is never an end to the *inexplicable continuity of this web of God*, but always circular power returning into itself. Therein it resembles his own spirit, whose beginning, whose ending he never can find—so entire, so boundless.[46]

Emerson's interpreters see this as a debt to Emanuel Swedenborg (1688–1772), the Swedish scientist and metaphysician who was driven by "the avowed search for the soul and the idea that everything that exists on the physical plane—our world of space and time—has a counterpart in the immaterial world of mind. This is Swedenborg's famous doctrine of correspondences."[47] Second, they read these Emersonian remarks as his brief for a kind of panentheism which holds, according to Morton White, "that each man's Reason is Universal Reason and that our souls are parts of a huge Over-soul much as harbors are parts of the ocean."[48]

Even if the abbreviated metaphysical sampler in "The American Scholar" is not so clear as we might wish, we can induce from it some important themes that characterize this address and other essays as well. If we are part of the spiritual Over-Soul, then we ourselves are spiritual beings, and if laws of our nature correspond to those of the Over-Soul, no great leap is needed to see that we are far more remarkable than we appear to the narrow *Understanding*. As beings whose nature and laws are spiritual, not material, we are all remarkable. This is what *Reason* knows and assures us if we will but heed its message.

If each of us is an extraordinary being but realizes this only by turning from empirical *Understanding*, which can reveal nothing of our spiritual being and divinity, then Emerson's mission in "The American Scholar" is to wake us to our capacity for original insights and creative activity. But there are serious impediments to Emerson's conception of authentic scholarly self-reliance. One of these is the suffocating influence of the past, "in whatever form, whether of literature, of art, of institutions. . . . Books are the best type of the influence of the Past, and perhaps we shall get at the truth . . . by considering their value alone."[49]

Great books can be valuable to the authentic scholar, but they can also be insidious and stultifying. Which they are has far more to do with the way the scholar employs them than with what they actually say. "Man Thinking," Emerson's phrase for the truly creative knight of *Reason*, reads and consults books as a source for inspiration. The bookworm, the dry scholar who reads and analyzes the great books handed down to us, sees himself—consciously or otherwise—as a chronicler, not as a creator. Heedless of *Reason* and working only with the uninspired tools of *Understanding*, he is the unfortunate product of American scholarship: "Hence, instead of Man Thinking, we have the bookworm."[50] Bookishness and academic institutions that sustain it (including Emerson's Harvard) "look backward and not forward. But genius always looks forward. *The eyes of man are set in his forehead, not in his hindhead*. Man hopes. Genius creates."[51]

Like nature and books, when they are used as they should be, action too can educate the American scholar and thereby make him a self-reliant pioneer of American culture. Here too obstacles must be overcome: "There goes in the world a notion that the scholar should be a recluse, a valetudinarian,—as unfit for any handiwork or public labor, as a penknife for an axe. The so-called 'practical men' sneer at speculative men, as if because they speculate or *see*, they could do nothing."[52] Sounding very much like Walt Whitman, whose poetry verges on what Transcendentalists espouse, Emerson is persuaded that although "Action is with the scholar subordinate . . . , it is essential." It is important as a resource on which true scholars can draw. Addressing his scholarly audience, Emerson says, "Life is our dictionary. Years are well spent in country labors; in town—in the insight into trades and manufactures; in frank intercourse with many men and women. . . . This is the way to learn grammar. Colleges and books only copy the language which the field and the work-yard made."[53] If Emerson is not quite an anti-intellectual he is at least a highbrow populist.

Action in its numerous forms is virtually inexhaustible. Action for the serious scholar is not fundamentally intended to alter the world but to wake his or her sleeping muse. Cornel West, claiming "the enshrinement of activity and energy was commonplace in the various forms of North Atlantic romanticisms," says it best. "For Emerson, the goal of activity is not simply domination, but also provocation; the telos of movement and flux is not solely mastery but also *stimulation*."[54]

The message is clear even when Emerson's prose is not: The American scholar must not follow the paths of European counterparts. "We have listened too long to the courtly muses of Europe." He must emulate in scholarship the energy and determination of Americans pursuing activities that, *prima facie*, could hardly be more different from scholarship: manual labor, commerce, agriculture, and industry. West characterizes as "parochial" Emerson's "preoccupation with America" and, as a direct result, his demand that Americans root themselves in America and find their creative expression in the native soil.[55] West may be correct, but if he does not miss Emerson's endless demands for homegrown culture and inspiration, he at least understates it.

Emerson knew the value of European arts and literature. So too did Harvard's intellectually elect who had come to hear him speak. But Emerson was determined that American scholars, poets, novelists and philosophers somehow recognize that the value of European culture does not argue the need for an American inferiority complex. A time for artistic experimentalism, the time for creative men and women to listen to their own *Reason*, was at hand. The proper model was not the centuries of accumulated European culture. For Emerson it was the political and economic institutions of a growing and solvent republic—the hallmarks of a self-reliant nation in its sixty-second year—that should wake and emancipate the drowsy genius of every American scholar.

"The Divinity School Address" is a first cousin to "The American Scholar." Delivered to Harvard's tiny graduating class of divinity students and to their guests, Emerson's concern was to indict the bankrupt Unitarianism, which had become so prominent in New England, and to speak for Transcendentalist alternatives.[56] Just as "The American Scholar" is a frontal attack on the poverty of traditional, derivative scholarship, "The Divinity School Address" is a broadside against historical Christianity, even in its liberal Unitarian expression. Flower and Murphey go as far as to say that the most potent cause for the emergence of Transcendentalism "lay in the profound failure of Unitarianism to provide a basis for *spiritual religion*."[57] This is too narrow. The causes of Transcendentalism, like any other movement or school of thought, are numerous and various. Still, there is no doubt that Emerson and his circle looked with jaundice on the excessive rationalism and historical orientation of the Christianity in which they were reared.

"The Divinity School Address," like "The American Scholar," is bifocal. There is first a two-pronged criticism of Christianity as Emerson finds it preached and generally practiced in New England, and this is followed by an admonition to approach faith in a new and radical manner. The core of "The Divinity School Address" asserts itself after some preliminary restatement of intensely romantic Transcendentalist terrain.[58] After an opening litany to natural beauty, in stark contrast to the barrenness of conventional preaching, Emerson makes his key points.

> In . . . contemplating Jesus, we become very sensible of the first defect of historical Christianity. Historical Christianity has fallen into the error that corrupts all attempts to communicate religion. As it appears to us, and as it has appeared for ages, it is not the doctrine of the soul, but an exaggeration of the personal, the positive, the ritual. It has dwelt, it dwells, with noxious exaggeration about the *person* of Jesus. . . . The manner in which his name is surrounded with expressions, which were once sallies of admiration and love, but are now petrified into official titles, kills all generous sympathy and liking.[59]

In direct terms, Emerson's first complaint is that Christianity, rooted in history and tradition, makes Jesus more than human and thereby diminishes the divinity that the rest of us share as spiritual elements of the one great Soul. For Emerson this is the error of tradition. Seeing Christ as human, and in that regard like the rest of us, is for Emerson to see him as a spiritual being: "That which shows God in me, fortifies me. That which shows God out of me, makes me a wart and a wen. There is no longer a necessary reason for my being."[60] The first great failure of historical Christianity is, therefore, that it denies our potential to make of ourselves as much as we are prepared to invest in ourselves. Historical Christianity's approach strikes at the heart of Transcendentalist belief in individual incentive, autonomy, and the creative power of *Reason*.

The second failure of Christianity-as-usual is "Men have come to speak of the revelation as somewhat long ago given and done, as if God were dead. The injury to faith throttles the preacher; and the goodliest of institutions becomes an uncertain and inarticulate voice."[61] Here Emerson means that official doctrine stifles the creative voice of *Reason*. Transcendentalists believe that men and women are equipped to declare the spiritual, poetic, artistic, and literary declarations of their *Reason*, but orthodoxy, including that of the Unitarians, denies them the authority. Thus in religion, as in scholarship, human beings, living a banal life of the *Understanding*, are discouraged from transcending institutionally imposed impediments to an inspired life of *Reason*.

An account of the failures of Christianity is not sufficient for Emerson; he must also identify remedies. At the foundation of Emerson's plea for change is a call to preachers: ". . . the priest's Sabbath has lost the splendor of nature; it is unlovely; we are glad when it is done."[62] The conventional preacher, like the bookworm, fails almost grotesquely to stimulate those who endure his sermons. Once again, the familiar call to a complete declaration of American independence must reach beyond politics, economics, literature, and the arts. It must include those who preach the faith, some of whom Emerson tries to reach in "The Divinity School Address."[63]

Emerson urges this class of Harvard Divinity School graduates "to go alone." They must turn away from what is routine and toward their own spiritual reservoirs. They must do this with confidence so that those to whom they preach can find meaning and vitality in their remarks and sermons: "Yourself a newborn bard of the Holy Ghost,—cast behind you all conformity, and acquaint men at first hand with Deity."[64] This is a thinly veiled indictment of the organized religions that Emerson rejected.

Emerson's religious message in this address is intimately tied to the central theme of his other hortative lectures. The function of the true preacher is to induce others to take seriously their own divinity, their own attachment to "the all-knowing Spirit." Until and unless men of faith are serious about this duty, religious practice in America will fail to touch our spiritual natures. The value of each individual soul, as well as the obligations and expectations of good men and women, will linger in the shade. Religions will remain little more than theatrical ritual. Our essential natures will remain trapped and none of us will be able to discover and revel in the life that manifests our self-worth and induces us to acknowledge the value of everyone else in the human community.

"Self-Reliance" (1841): Autonomy as a Virtue, Conformity as a Vice

"Self-Reliance," perhaps Emerson's best-known essay, is a clarion call urging all men and women to become self-sufficient and independent. In this sense it recalls familiar themes and admonitions from his earlier lectures and writings. It is also another demand that all of us recognize our inner genius and act on what we discover by heeding the directive of *Reason*: "A man should learn to detect and watch that gleam of light which flashes across his mind from within, more than the lustre of the firmament of bards and sages."[65] Emerson also admonishes each of us to "Trust thyself." The presumption, once more, is that insofar as everyone is part of God or the Over-Soul, each of us has the dignity and value that enables us to act under our own guidance. We are, however, properly guided only if we acknowledge *Reason*. By now the point is familiar: The courage for self-reliant, self-initiated action arises from the intuitions that *Reason* supplies. The *Understanding* offers nothing to confirm our own limitless capacity for contemplation and action.

Why for Emerson are self-reliance, solitude, and nonconformity so intimately connected? Here too the answer is transparent: "Society everywhere is in conspiracy against the manhood of every one of its members."[66] The cacophony and demands of social life drown out what *Reason* offers. To the extent that we embrace the customs of society, to roughly the same degree do we look away from our true selves that only *Reason* can express. As a consequence Emerson is emphatic, "Whoso would be a man must be a nonconformist."[67]

Because being a true man or woman requires as a necessary but not sufficient condition that one be indifferent to social demands and esteem bestowed by others, it follows for Emerson that "What I must do, is all that concerns me; not what the people think. This rule . . . may serve for the whole distinction between greatness and meanness . . . ; *the great man is he who in the midst of the crowd keeps with perfect sweetness the independence of solitude.*"[68] Emerson is idealistic, not foolish. He knows that nonconformity and inattention to social convention can be as difficult to practice as it is to resist the persistent censure of those who expect everyone to join them and to conform. Still, confronting the challenges that make us great human beings is, whatever the discomfort, necessary.

The benefits that one reaps from acting on Emerson's advice are metaphysical *and* practical. Turning to *Reason* enables one who does so to recognize a spiritual self that is eclipsed by the inconsequential reach of the empirical *Understanding*. Discovering one's divine and spiritual being leads to the confidence to act on one's own (self-reliance).[69] Self-reliance presumes a self-worth and the well-founded belief that one can transcend the shallow expectations that society anticipates from each of its members. Transcendence and recognition of one's own genius can yield great achievements—whether in literature, the visual arts, the sciences, or religion—that benefit the society from which self-reliant men and women retreat.

Something like a litmus test for determining whether we are self-reliant is our attitude toward consistency: "A foolish consistency is the hobgoblin of little minds, adored by little statesmen and philosophers and divines. With consistency a great soul has simply nothing to do. . . . To be great is to be misunderstood."[70] Emerson means that self-reliant people have the right to change their minds as they find a need or opportunity. We should not be so wedded to what we have said and done that words and deeds inhibit us from making different claims and adopting different courses of action. A willingness to escape the fetters of what we said and did yesterday, last month, or last year exhibits our confidence that intuitions and the soul that underpins them can and do change. Only the timorous conformist will lack confidence to consult and to follow the lead of *Reason* when it rejects yesterday's plans in favor of today's alternatives.

In "Self-Reliance" Emerson again looks with jaundice on that version of conformity that invokes the past, other countries, familiar religions, and Old World culture. So much of this indicates that self-reliance has not taken hold either at the national level or at the individual level. Lacking confidence in a native culture and in ourselves, we look beyond our frontiers to attainments of great men of the remote past. "It is for want of self-culture that the superstition of Travelling . . . retains its fascination for all educated Americans. They who made England, Italy, or Greece venerable in the imagination, did so by sticking fast where they were, like an axis of the earth."[71] So long as our architecture is determined by the buildings of Doric Greece or Europe's northern Gothic, America and its artists are ignorant of self-reliance: "As our religion, our Education, our Art look abroad, so does our spirit of society."[72] Looking abroad, seeking external praise and worshipping as our ancestors worshipped are declarations of *dependence*, and dependence will never do. The nucleus of Emerson's message throughout "Self-Reliance," his demand for a self-willed isolation from the herd, inspires the closing sentiment of the essay: "Nothing can bring you peace but yourself."[73]

Emersonian Shortcomings

From the perspective of a critic, there are some flaws in Emerson's Transcendentalism. An obvious complaint is that Emerson charts a direct and dangerous path toward intellectual anarchy. If, after all, the true preacher, scholar, scientist, poet, and artist looks only to *Reason* and to his own spark of divine genius, what is the use of instruction, of the relation between a master and an apprentice, of standards for excellence in the arts and sciences? Further, Emerson endlessly inveighs against tradition, but many people find tradition indispensable. What, for example, would attorneys and judges do without the established traditions that underlie the common law which, in turn, protects just human beings from those who are unjust? And why should anyone take seriously Emerson's directive to follow the lead of inner "Spontaneity or Instinct"?[74] One-hundred-fifty years before Emerson penned these thoughts, Locke argued against religious enthusiasts who believed themselves inwardly inspired.[75]

This is a fair criticism for anyone who maintains some sort of public, objective epistemology. If one accepts a hypothesis, knowledge-claim, or standard only if it passes through hoops of the *Understanding*, then appeals to *Reason* and to metaphysical "truths" and "standards" are nonsense. For Emerson, however, those who side with the *Understanding* against *Reason* are critics because they believe that truth and determinations of excellence are detected only by the *Understanding*. He will not be at all impressed by criticisms that make their point of departure the demands of empirical intelligence. Put more directly, we can say that for Emerson those who live by the rules and limitations of the *Understanding* are correct that within the realm of the *Understanding* we do not find *Reason's* truths and realities, but this is just to concede that they are unwilling to take *Reason* seriously.

A second criticism is that Transcendentalism is the bedfellow of subjectivism. If each of us is in principle able to discern through *Reason* ultimate truths and realities, how can we ever distinguish true from false claims when two or more men or women claim (1) to intuit some truth but (2) reach supposed "truths" that contradict each other? Here it is not sufficient to turn one's back on consistency. These are two or more intuitionists who have already accepted Emerson's admonition to push beyond the limits of the *Understanding* and to use *Reason* to get at ultimate reality and truth. Emerson grasps the complaint: "The populace think that your rejection of popular standards is a rejection of all standard, and mere antinomianism; and the bold sensualist will use the name of philosophy to gild his crimes. *But the law of consciousness abides*."[76]

Here too an Emersonian reply is available; it is the reply one can expect from other metaphysicians as well. When two or more Transcendentalists reach opposed "truths" or widely differing descriptions of reality, it is not really the case that each one is employing *Reason*. *Reason*, as far as Emerson is concerned, reaches immutable facts, laws, and truths. Further, everyone who turns earnestly to *Reason* will reach the same facts, laws, and truths.[77] When, therefore, men and women appealing to their *Reason* reach different facts or laws and opposing "truths," at least one of them is not actually appealing to *Reason*. Uniformity of beliefs and certainties about reality are guaranteed where the conviction that one is using *Reason* is itself a fact. Where the declarations of *Reason* are mutually exclusive, one of these declarations is an imposter and must really be a product of the *Understanding*.

Critics will never get to Emerson. He is untouched by their complaints because his philosophy is insulated from criticism in general. There is no way to push objections that Emerson and his circle would take seriously. How can critics tellingly refute any of Emerson's metaphysical claims? If they attack them from the inside, so to speak, they fail because nothing he says either expresses or entails a contradiction. If they attack them from the outside they fail because no objective facts, which are the property of the *Understanding*, can be mustered to invalidate metaphysical claims. The facts and truths of *Reason* occupy a realm of insight and discourse that have no commerce with the ephemeral facts and relative truths that belong to the order of *Understanding*. So it is that in a letter to his friend Margaret Fuller (March 14, 1841), first editor of the *Dial* (1840–1842) and apologist for Transcendentalism, Emerson celebrates his philosophy and berates a specific "sinful empiric," that is, a pseudo-scientific hypnotist who is fettered by his *Understanding*.[78] Critics of Emerson's thought and plans are, as he sees it, like this small-minded "empiric." They will not discard their empirical blinders in order to give *Reason* a chance to show that what they criticize is exactly what they are missing, namely the ripe and nourishing fruits of Emersonian intuition.

Thoreau, *Walden* (1854): A Transcendentalist at Work

Henry David Thoreau (1817–1862) lived most of his life in Concord, Massachusetts. He attended Harvard and worked for a time with his father in manufacturing pencils. Insofar as gainful employment was never an end for Thoreau, as an adult he worked only briefly, first as Emerson's hired man and later for Emerson's brother William as a tutor to his children. Attracted to Transcendentalism in his senior year at Harvard (1837), he participated in the Transcendental Club and contributed occasional essays to *The Dial*. He had hoped to marry Ellen Sewall, but she showed no interest in the prospect. Thoreau's principal concerns, apart from Ellen, were his love for nature and his distress at America's social and political inequities, especially institutional slavery and the "unfair" imposition of taxes.[79]

To satisfy the aims of this essay, it is unnecessary to spend as much time on Thoreau as on Emerson. Emerson, unlike Thoreau, takes the trouble to propound a generally unified philosophy that is admittedly opaque and occasionally at odds with itself. One can nonetheless distill the essence of New England Transcendentalism from Emerson's best-known lectures and essays. Furthermore, philosophical doctrine and nuances transported Thoreau less than actually living the philosophy he embraced, so there is not much gained in a line-by-line exegesis of *Walden*.

Because *Walden* is a classic in American literature, it attracts a variety of interpreters. For some of these interpreters, *Walden* is a chronicle of Thoreau's reverence for "the simplicity and divine unity of nature, . . . his faith in man, . . . his own sturdy individualism, . . . his deep-rooted love for one place as the epitome of the universe."[80] For James Russell Lowell, writing in 1865, *Walden* is a literary masterpiece, but one whose message is a familiar expression of romanticism and unreflective nature-worship. Referring to Thoreau and to his influences, Lowell writes:

> I look upon a great deal of the modern sentimentalism about Nature as a mark of disease. . . . To a man of wholesome constitution the wilderness is well enough for a mood or a vacation, but not for a habit of life. Those who have most loudly announced their passion for seclusion and their intimacy with nature . . . , have been mostly sentimentalists, unreal men, misanthropes on the spindle side, solacing an uneasy suspicion of themselves by professing contempt for their kind.[81]

For F. O. Mathiessen, one should recognize in *Walden* that the apparently accidental arrangement of its chapters is actually an expression of well-conceived and purposeful order. As a consequence, according to Mathiessen, what makes Thoreau's book a true work of American literary art is its organic unity, especially as it mirrors the part of Thoreau's life that he lived on the forested fringes of Walden Pond.[82] But for Mathiessen too, *Walden* is better literature than philosophy.

Leo Marx, whose interpretation of the romantic tradition in American literature is consistently illuminating, believes that readers of *Walden* should not see Thoreau's life in the woods as some literal effort to find Arcadia in Massachusetts: "For Thoreau the realization of the golden age is, finally, a matter of private and, in fact, literary experience. Since it has nothing to do with the environment, with social institutions, or material reality . . . , then the writer's *physical location is of no great moment*."[83]

In the opening paragraph of *Walden*, which introduces the long section "Economy," Thoreau writes that he spent "two years and two months" in a house that he built "on the shore of Walden Pond" (1845–1847). He also announces his reasons for retreating briefly to Walden. There is nothing philosophical, far less transcendental, about his declared motives. It seemed to him a good place for doing some business: "My purpose in going to Walden Pond was not to live cheaply nor to live dearly there, but to transact some private business with the fewest obstacles."[84] If we take Thoreau at his word, this famous account of a retreat to a pastoral setting is his choice because commerce can flourish without municipal codes and fees or the insidious hand of still larger government, which binds the invisible hand of free trade. Moreover, in the forest he can make do with shelter that is enough for his needs, not for the factitious needs of polite society and its frivolous tastes. There too he can find natural beauty, the beauty that all of us can afford: "now, a taste for the beautiful is most cultivated out of doors, where there is no house and no housekeeper."[85]

So understood, then, Thoreau's desire to escape "civilized" society, to build himself a house that is simple enough to fall within his means and adequate enough to answer his needs, is not so much a primitive urge as it is an answer to a simple question: Where can I go to earn what I require and to live on what I earn? The answer is Walden because its woods insulate Thoreau from tawdry ornaments masquerading as life's necessities and from impositions that tax all that he makes, grows, owns, or sells. Here too the Emersonian brief for self-reliance finds its realization in Thoreau. If, after all, Thoreau can build his shelter with little or no assistance, the case for self-reliance and self-satisfaction makes its way from lecture halls into the forest. Thoreau is convinced that a self-reliant man should build for himself just as he should think for himself.[86]

Throughout his account of the expenses involved in building and planting, Thoreau prepares systematic lists of his costs and meager agricultural revenues. In these lists, we cannot miss the way that he, far more than Emerson, is sometimes willing to follow the lead of the *Understanding*.[87] "Assuming that natural facts properly perceived and accurately transcribed yield the truth, Thoreau adopts the tone of a hard-headed empiricist."[88] The point is clear, and we have reviewed it several times: Emerson's *Reason* is suited to penetrate to the depths of reality. *Understanding*, as we have also seen, functions practically, and this is fine for Thoreau since he, not Emerson, faces a binary task.

A pastoral retreat to the Walden woods and pond is both a *practical* and *philosophical* undertaking. Building, harvesting, buying, and selling require useful calculations and accurate records of expenses and revenues. If there is to be a deeper meaning to this retreat, that which *Reason* lays bare, it occurs when Thoreau is situated and secure in an environment that is most hospitable to the work of *Reason*. In the comparatively quiet isolation of the woods, Thoreau can escape the demands and cacophony of the "madding crowd." But securing and maintaining that setting require resources known to and calculated by the *Understanding*. One discovers through the *Understanding* that self-reliance is more economical than dependence, that simplicity is just as efficient as excess and much less expensive, and that the ability to live life on one's own terms is better suited to self-discovery and to the discovery of the metaphysical ties between oneself and the larger world.[89]

Further, "the man who goes alone" is better equipped to absorb the charm and beauty of a pastoral life, a life that even at the level of the conventional senses and *Understanding* draws one toward the mysteries that lurk beneath the surfaces. He need not explain or modify his rituals to suit another's whims and expectations: "Every morning was a cheerful invitation to make my life of equal simplicity, and I may say innocence, with Nature herself. . . . I got up early and bathed in the pond; this was a religious exercise, and one of the best things I did."[90] This and other private rituals that liberate Thoreau from seeing himself as what he *does*, rather than as what he *is*, made Walden his choice: "I went to the woods because I wished to live deliberately, to front only the essential facts of life, and see if I could learn what it had to teach, and not, when I came to die, discover that I had not lived." Among the many things he learned was a series of ineffable facts about the universe and a place in it that is almost what Emerson tried to convey in "The Over-Soul."

Thoreau's vision of nature is affected, like Emerson's "The Young American," by the railroad, the commanding emblem of industrial and commercial progress: "The Fitchburg Railroad touches the pond about a hundred rods south of where I dwell. I usually go to the village [Concord] along its causeway, and am, as it were, related to society by this link." As the train tracks link Thoreau to Concord, so too does it link Concord and its surrounding countryside to the great cities of the East: "With such huge and lumbering civility, the country hands a chair to the city. All the Indian huckleberry hills are stripped, all the cranberry meadows are raked into the city. Up comes the cotton, down goes the woven cloth . . ."[91] What is the image that Thoreau conveys in his account of the railroad's permanent intrusion into the New England wilderness? Marx believes it is obvious: "[Thoreau] says that the pastoral way of life—pastoralism in the literal, agrarian sense—is being whirled past and away. It is doomed. . . . The first thing to do, then, the only sensible thing to do, is get off the track."[92]

Thoreau realizes that he can retreat to Walden Pond and build a house on its shores. That, after all, is what he has done. As easily as he can take to the woods, the railroad can pass through them, alter their contours, and displace their inhabitants. One does not have to like industrial progress, but disliking it and arresting it are far different from each other. Thoreau intimates as much early in the brief section "Solitude." Ruminating on the value of being alone and of being left alone, he writes: "I have my horizon bounded by woods all to myself; a distant view of the railroad where it touches the pond on the one hand, and of the fence which skirts the woodland road on the other. But for the most part it is as solitary where

I live as on the prairies."[93] "For the most part" is not, of course, the same as "for now and the indeterminate future." Even adjacent to Walden Pond, which is itself a modest distance from the village of Concord, Thoreau cannot consistently enjoy the solitude he prefers. Visitors come calling and sometimes remain several days in his guest room. The railroad, carriage roads, and foot paths serve to remind him that even when he seems to be alone he is not truly alone.

So too the bean field Thoreau cultivates, perhaps as an attempt to give life to the agrarian ideal, is not quite a failure, but neither is it a success. When he subtracts his costs from his sales, excluding the hard work of planting, harvesting, and selling his crop, the profit is $8.71.[94] Anticipated profits, which are often disappointing and sometimes far closer to losses, do not produce the noble farmer whose virtue is enhanced by contact with the soil, water, and sun. The facts are otherwise: ". . . the farmer leads the meanest of lives. He knows Nature but as a robber." And if Thoreau's efforts with beans are typical, the average farmer is not even very good at being a robber. The farmer of mythology is not the one Thoreau finds or emulates in and near Walden: "The true husbandman will cease from anxiety, as the squirrels manifest no concern whether the woods will bear chestnuts this year or not, and finish his labor with every day. Relinquishing all claim to the produce of his fields . . ."[95]

More than halfway through *Walden*, the section "The Ponds" evokes romantic and idyllic images of untouched nature that readers associate with Thoreau's love of the wilderness. After he presents a list of the fish, frogs, and tortoises that live in the pond, he describes the trees that surround it: "There Nature has woven a natural selvage, and the eye rises by just gradation from the low shrubs of the shore to the highest trees. There are few traces of man's hand to be seen. The water laves the shore as it did a thousand years ago. A lake is the landscape's most beautiful and expressive feature. *It is earth's eye; looking into which the beholder, measures the depth of his own nature.*"[96]

Readers must, however, be careful. Thoreau is Emerson's disciple and this quotation could have come from Emerson's *Nature*, but neither of these facts suggests that the wilderness is permanent or that nature will always be a resource for those eager to practice self-reliance and to pursue enlightenment. The intrusive side of trade and industry always lurks: "But since I left these shores the woodchoppers have still further laid them waste, and now for many a year there will be no more rambling through the aisles of the wood, with occasional vistas through which you see the water. My Muse must be excused if she is silent henceforth. How can you expect the birds to sing when their groves are cut down?" So too there is always the problem of the "devilish Iron Horse, whose ear-rendering neigh is heard throughout the town . . . and he it is that has browsed off all the woods on Walden shore."[97]

As *Walden* advances toward its conclusion, Thoreau describes the wild mice, partridges, woodcocks and, with the fine eye of a careful naturalist, famously narrates the battle between legions of red and black ants. Here, as in his sections "Winter Animals" and "The Pond in Winter," we can safely infer that Thoreau's quest for metaphysical knowledge, despite its importance, never overawes his talents as a careful empiricist who wishes to discover all he can about nature's "clockwork." An especially rich example of Thoreau's capacity to fuse spiritual awe with a scientist's observational skills is his account of the pond and its shore as they come alive in early spring. Here he sees himself situated "as if in a peculiar sense I stood in the laboratory of the Artist who made the world and me . . ." Here too he produces one of his celebrated paeans to nature: "We can never have enough of Nature. We must be refreshed by the sight of inexhaustible vigor, vast and Titanic features . . . , the wilderness with its living and decaying trees, the thunder cloud. . . . We need to witness our own limits transgressed, and some life pasturing freely where we never wander."[98]

Thoreau's celebration of nature is in the end also a celebration of self-realization. His two years adjacent to Walden Pond had helped him to see past the dross that in most human beings stunts their spiritual growth and awareness: "I left the woods for as good a reason as I went there. Perhaps it seemed to me that I had several more lives to live, and could not spare any more time for that one."[99] Having acquired the capacity to live simply and frugally, he had learned a good deal that would take him through life beyond the woods: "In proportion as he simplifies his life, the laws of the universe will appear less complex, solitude will not be solitude, nor poverty poverty, nor weakness weakness."[100] Following Emerson, Thoreau too disparages those who find nothing of value in American culture: "Some are dinning in our ears that we Americans . . . , are intellectual dwarfs compared with the ancients, or even the Elizabethan men. But what is that to the purpose? A living dog is better than a dead lion. Shall a man go and hang himself because he belongs to the race of pygmies, and not be the biggest pygmy that he can? Let every one mind his own business, and endeavor to be what he was made."

Minding one's own business is what underpins the most famous lines in *Walden* and the most famous lines in Thoreau: "If a man does not keep pace with his companions, perhaps it is because he hears a different drummer. Let him step to the music which he hears, however measured or far away."[101] This is the echo of what Thoreau found and admired in "Self-Reliance."

In the last pages of *Walden*, Thoreau admonishes us to love our lives, to prize truth far more than wealth, and to prefer our own company to that of others who require constant companionship and approval. This is the comparatively simple and, for Thoreau, obvious formula for securing satisfaction and enrichment. Everything else is like a thick fog that obscures and frustrates every inclination to reach what is valuable.

Conclusion

Even those who read *Walden* with approval must be careful in interpreting its message. Thoreau is Emerson's follower, not his clone. Where Emerson is confident that those who turn from *Understanding* to *Reason* will be amply rewarded, Thoreau is more cautious. Amidst the celebration of dwelling close to nature and simplifying one's life, he is clear that the *path* to a meaningful life is not the same as a meaningful life. We have seen that even though Thoreau describes the most authentic life and answers affirmatively the familiar philosophical question "Is life worth living?" he makes no promises that living as he did in Walden will yield the enlightenment and freedom that elude most of us. He always knew what he was up against and what the Transcendentalists had to overcome. In his lecture "Walking" (June 1862), published barely a month after his death, he said "I wish to speak a word for Nature, for absolute freedom and wildness, as contrasted with a freedom and culture merely civil—to regard man as an inhabitant . . . of Nature, rather than as a member of society. . . ."[102]

Thoreau saw the need to promote, at the end of his life, the message of the Transcendentalists which was scarcely audible against the background of countless praises for polite civilization, material progress, and the security of traditional religious institutions.[103] It is, after all, one thing to talk about human spirituality and kinship with nature, but it is another to persuade skeptics to take such talk seriously. When Thoreau says, "in the Wilderness is the preservation of the World," he knows that preserving the wilderness is difficult. Captains of industry and transportation wish to exploit what is wild if it is also rich. Trying to save the wilderness for one's own generation and for generations to follow may be hopeless. What makes this serious for Thoreau is that the wilderness (unrefined nature) is the laboratory where self-reliant pioneers and travelers manage to find the rarest of all natural resources, namely, themselves.[104]

Thoreau worries deeply about the fetters that inhibit self-realization and the flowering of genius. Not only is intimacy with nature encumbered by railroads, commerce, ice cutters, and others who prefer monetary profit to a piece of wilderness, but government is itself complicit in limiting the freedom it is supposed to protect. In his brief *Resistance to Civil Government* (1849), we find Thoreau inveighing against governmental intrusion into the lives of Americans: "'That government is best which governs not at all'. . . . The government itself which is only the mode which the people have chosen to execute their will, is equally liable to be abused and perverted before the people can act through it. Witness the present Mexican war, the work of comparatively a few individuals using the standing government as their tool."[105]

Thoreau's solution to government interference, military aggression, and failure to press the case for abolition was refusing to pay the Massachusetts poll tax. As a result, he was jailed a single night for tax evasion. Thoreau's contempt for government is well-known. So too is his belief in passive resistance and his description of the rare state or government that deserves the allegiance of its citizens: "There will never be a really free and enlightened State, until the State comes to recognize the individual as *a higher and independent power*, from which all its own power and authority are derived, and treats him accordingly."[106]

If all of this is familiar, why mention it? The answer is that government, as Thoreau sees it, inhibits the flowering of personal autonomy in much the same way that commercial intruders affect the hardy men and women who prefer life in the woods to life in a town or city. Thoreau believes that government, just like railroads and merchants, circumscribes freedom more than it advances it. Governmental prerogatives threaten the opportunities that Thoreau and Emerson value as crucial pathways to individual emancipation.

Government and capitalist exploitation of the wilderness are indistinguishable in their threat to the dignity of human beings. To be human is at a minimum to be free. To be free is to be able to act without restrictions and, thereby, to express one's genius and goodness. And what does government have to do with any of this? At the federal level it taxes its citizens so that it can prosecute the Mexican war. It does not ask whether they wish to support such a war and thus denies them a choice to accept expansionist policies that in 1846–1848 were part of America's "manifest destiny." The states cannot make war, but they can copy the taxing power of the federal government and thereby restrict, even impoverish, their citizens.

Captains of industry, bankers, and railroad magnates have no authority to tax, but given their economic power and political influence they can, using their machinery, tracks, and revenue bonds, subdue the wilderness that in the 1840s stretched two thousand miles from the eastern frontier to the mountain West. For Thoreau, the shrinking West was the place to be as free as circumstances permitted. He writes in the essay "Walking":

> Eastward I go only by force; but westward I go free. . . . It is hard for me to believe that I shall find fair landscapes or sufficient wilderness and freedom behind the eastern horizon. I am not excited by the prospect of a walk thither; but I believe that the forest which I see in the western horizon stretched uninterruptedly toward the setting sun, and there are no towns nor cities in it of enough consequence to disturb me.[107]

The trouble with Thoreau's vision of the western myth is that it is an ideal at odds with the facts. This may be the general problem with Transcendentalism.

Thoreau and Emerson value nature for reasons that are opposed to the more basic drives of a muscular young nation, an adolescent nation that must, like any other adolescent, grow. Throughout *Walden, Resistance to Civil Government* and essays like "Walking," Thoreau indicts the forces of change because the changes they make are inhospitable to the Transcendentalist picture of free, divine human beings. Thoreau sees a nation on the move, but the movement, which serves the developing middle class and the much smaller class of wealthy capitalists, is the enemy. Men and women at mid-century wish to be part of the economic action. After all, its fruits are tangible, and economic emancipation is far easier for most people to grasp and to appreciate than ethereal or spiritual freedom attained through rejoining nature.

In the end, Thoreau's problem is that his philosophical platform, which surely borders on anarchism in *Resistance to Civil Government*, had very few takers. Even among the sympathetic cluster of Transcendentalists, Thoreau was notable for practicing the philosophy he preached. Emerson's and Thoreau's picture of human beings as more than human is uplifting, but it is hard to sell to practical, tough-minded people. If there was a right time to try to urge Americans to slow down, to preserve the wilderness, and to disregard the powers of government, the last years of Thoreau's life were not that time. The United States was about to enter the Gilded Age, an age of unprecedented expansion and economic activity.

Transcendentalism could not take hold as a pervasive philosophy of life. By 1850, possibly a bit earlier, it had run its short course and would yield to pragmatism. Pragmatists demand engagement over retreat. They would characterize problems as what we solve rather than evade. If a virile nation could somehow select a philosophy that mirrored its character, pragmatism was a more obvious choice than Transcendentalism. Transcendentalism might have thrived in another setting, but if philosophy were to have a chance to move beyond the academy and to touch the people (always part of Emerson's hopes), practicality and a willingness to deal with the available world would have to be its creed. Pragmatists, as we will see, knew and appreciated this fact. Transcendentalists denied it. Transcendentalism is a museum piece. Pragmatism, the subject of essays to follow, is with us even now.

NOTES

1. *The American Transcendentalists: Their Prose and Poetry* (New York, 1957), x.
2. This is the drift of Tony Tanner's introduction to his edition of Emerson's *Essays and Poems* (London, 1995), xxi–xxix.
3. *The American Transcendentalists*, ix–x.
4. This is the title Oliver Wendell Holmes gave to "The American Scholar." *Robert D. Richardson Emerson: the Mind on Fire*, (Berkeley, 1995), 263.
5. Ibid. 89.
6. Richardson begins his study with an account of Emerson's macabre visit to his late wife's coffin (March 29, 1832), fourteen months after her untimely death. Ibid. 3–5.
7. Ibid. 250.
8. Ibid. 572–3.
9. *The American Transcendentalists*, ix.
10. *The Collected Works of Ralph Waldo Emerson:* Nature, *Addresses, and Lectures*, ed. R. E. Spiller and A. R. Ferguson (5 Vols., Cambridge, Mass., 1971–), I, 53; hereafter abbreviated as Nature, *Addresses, and Lectures*.
11. See John Steel Gordon, *The Great Game: the Emergence of Wall Street as a World Power, 1653–2000* (New York, 1999), 53–69.
12. *The Collected Works of Ralph Waldo Emerson: English Traits*, ed. P. Nicoloff, R. E. Burkholder, and D. E. Wilson, (Cambridge, Mass., 1994), V, 54.
13. Ibid. V, 94.
14. Charles Dickens, *Hard Times* (1854).
15. Nature, *Addresses, and Lectures*, 7; emphasis added.
16. Emerson, *Essays and Poems*, xxi.
17. *The Collected Works of Ralph Waldo Emerson: Essays, First Series*, ed. J. Slater, A. R. Ferguson and J. F. Carr (Cambridge, Mass., 1979), II, 33; emphasis added.
18. Morton White, *Pragmatism and the American Mind* (New York, 1973), 16.
19. For an abbreviated discussion of Emerson as a romantic, see White's comparison between him and Jefferson. *Pragmatism and the American Mind*, 17–19.
20. This is quoted from the editors' introduction to the lecture in Nature, *Addresses, and Lectures*, 217.
21. Ibid. 222.
22. Ibid. 222, 223.
23. Ibid. 223–4.
24. Ibid. 224.
25. Leo Marx, *The Machine in the Garden: Technology and the Pastoral Ideal in America* (New York, 1964), 232.
26. See Edwin G. Burrows and Mike Wallace, *Gotham: A History of New York City to 1898* (New York, 1999), 542–6, 555–6.
27. Nature, *Addresses, and Lectures*, 225.
28. *Emerson: the Mind on Fire*, 394.
29. Nature, *Addresses, and Lectures*, chs. iii, vi–vii.

30. *The Machine in the Garden*, 242.
31. Quoted without revisions in punctuation from *The Selected Letters of Ralph Waldo Emerson*, ed. Joel Myerson (New York, 1997), 133; emphasis added.
32. *The Collected Works of Samuel Taylor Coleridge: Aids to Reflection*, ed. K Coburn, B. Winer and J. Beer (16 vols., Princeton, 1993), IX, 223.
33. For Locke's classic statement of empiricist epistemology, see *An Essay Concerning Human Understanding*, II, i, 2.
34. This reference to youth may be a vestige that Emerson found in William Blake, Wordsworth, and others who believed that children are closer to the truth, to the spiritual and real, than those who are conditioned by practical demands of routine living to rely on their senses and understanding.
35. *The Selected Letters of Ralph Waldo Emerson*, 133.
36. *Documents in the History of American Philosophy*, ed. Morton White (New York, 1972), 99–101.
37. Elizabeth Flower and Murray Murphey, *A History of American Philosophy*, (New York, 1977), I, 402.
38. Morton White makes some instructive comments about Ripley's version of Transcendentalism. See *Science and Sentiment in America*, (New York, 1972), 81–4.
39. Nature, *Addresses, and Lectures*, 202.
40. None of this takes into account Emerson's debts to the Scottish Common Sense school of philosophy, to Adam Smith and Thomas Reid. Richardson discusses these debts in *Emerson: the Mind on Fire*, 29–33.
41. Nature, *Addresses, and Lectures*, 206–7.
42. *The Critique of Pure Reason* (1781), trans. N. K. Smith (New York, 1953), 93.
43. See White's comments on Emerson's liberal exploitation of previous philosophies. *Science and Sentiment in America*, 100.
44. These are the words of John Peirce, about whom the editors of Emerson's addresses write, "[He] was known as one who never missed and never understood the meaning of such academic occasions." Nature, *Addresses, and Lectures*, 50.
45. Ibid. 52.
46. Ibid. 54; emphasis added.
47. *Emerson: the Mind on Fire*, 198.
48. *Science and Sentiment in America*, 107. Panentheism, rather than pantheism, seems the appropriate word insofar as Emerson apparently believed that while each of us is a part of the Over-Soul, the Over-Soul is more than nature and its human manifestations.
49. Nature, *Addresses, and Lectures*, 55.
50. Ibid. 56.
51. Ibid. 57; emphasis added.
52. Ibid. 59.
53. Ibid. 60–1. Cornel West believes that Emerson is inconsistent in his evaluation of working men and women. *The American Evasion of Philosophy: A Genealogy of Pragmatism* (Madison, 1989), 23–4, 28–34.
54. Ibid. 25, 26; emphasis added.
55. Ibid. 26.
56. The address itself, given July 15, 1838, reached an audience of six graduates, their families, friends, and professors. *Emerson: the Mind on Fire*, 288.
57. *A History of Philosophy in America* I, 402; emphasis added. Perry Miller seems to share the assessment of Flower and Murphey. *The American Transcendentalists*, ix.
58. The first two pages are reminders in their tone and content of the paean to beautiful, idyllic nature in *Nature*. See *Nature, Addresses, and Lectures*, 76–7.
59. Ibid. 82.
60. Ibid. 82–3.
61. Ibid. 84.
62. Nature, *Addresses, and Lectures*, 85.
63. Ibid. 87–8.
64. Ibid. 90.

65. *Essays: First Series,* 27.
66. Ibid. 29.
67. Ibid.
68. Ibid. 31; emphasis added.
69. *Essays: First Series,* 37–9.
70. Ibid. 33–4.
71. Ibid. 46.
72. Ibid. 47–8.
73. Ibid. 51.
74. Ibid. 37.
75. *An Essay Concerning Human Understanding,* IV, xix, 16.
76. *Essays: First Series,* 42; emphasis added.
77. Nature, *Addresses, and Lectures,* 63.
78. *The Selected Letters of Ralph Waldo Emerson,* 247–8.
79. For a full, searching study of Thoreau's life, see Robert D. Richardson Jr., *Thoreau: A Life of the Mind* (Berkeley, 1986).
80. *The American Tradition in Literature,* ed. Sculley Bradley, et al., 5th edition (New York, 1981), 700.
81. Reprinted in *Walden and Resistance to Civil Government,* ed. W. Rossi, 2d edition (New York, 1992), 338–9, from *The Writings of James Russell Lowell* (12, vols., Boston, 1890).
82. Reprinted from Mathiessen's *American Renaissance* (Oxford, 1941) in *Walden and Resistance to Civil Government,* 343–9.
83. *The Machine in the Garden,* 264; emphasis added.
84. *Walden and Resistance to Civil Government,* 13.
85. Ibid. 26.
86. Ibid. 31.
87. Ibid. 33, 37, 40–1.
88. Ibid. *The Machine in the Garden,* 243.
89. *Walden and Resistance to Civil Government,* 49.
90. Ibid. 60.
91. Ibid. 78.
92. *The Machine in the Garden,* 254.
93. *Walden and Resistance to Civil Government,* 88.
94. Ibid. 108–10.
95. Ibid. 112.
96. Ibid. 1–5.
97. Ibid. 129.
98. Ibid. 212.
99. Ibid. 215.
100. Ibid. 109.
101. Ibid. 217.
102. Reprinted in *The American Transcendentalists,* 143.
103. Ibid. 144–5.
104. See Robert Nash, *Wilderness and the American Mind,* 3rd edition (New Haven, 1982), 85–6.
105. *Walden and Resistance to Civil Government,* 226.
106. Ibid. 245; emphasis added.
107. *The American Transcendentalists: Their Prose and Poetry,* 144.

Essay 5
Chauncey Wright, a Positivist Precursor to American Pragmatism

With Chauncey Wright, we approach the outer boundaries of pragmatism. Characterizing pragmatism is difficult, yet it is undeniably important for anyone whose task is to read or write a history of American philosophy. Morton White describes Charles Sanders Peirce (1839–1914) and William James (1842–1910) as "the first really original American philosophers," and he characterizes Wright (1830–1875), their intellectual precursor, as a thinker who "entered the American philosophical scene like one of those Darwinian variations about which he wrote so knowledgeably."[1] Add John Dewey (1859–1953) to this short list, and the names of the original pragmatists and the American who influenced them are in hand. But naming the classic pragmatists, or their predecessor, is certainly different from knowing what, if anything, unites all of them philosophically.

We know, then, the overriding problems in this essay and the one that follows: What do historians and philosophers mean when they call Peirce, James, and Dewey "pragmatists"? What are the sources from which pragmatism emerges, or does it originate *ex nihilo* in the third quarter of the nineteenth century? To answer these questions, it is first useful to have a brief look at what characterizes the thought of Chauncey Wright to see how his philosophical views anticipate those of the three most celebrated pragmatists. With Wright's thought and influence in mind, one also learns something of the nonphilosophical factors, especially Darwinism, that help to account for the pragmatists' principal aims and themes as they come into focus from the early 1870s to the opening decades of the twentieth century.

Chauncey Wright as Darwin's American Voice and Something More

A few students of pragmatism and its antecedents know that Wright "was the senior member of the discussion group—C. S. Peirce later called it 'The Metaphysical Club'—which met in Cambridge, Massachusetts, in the early 1870's."[2] Members of the club, including Peirce, William James, and Oliver Wendell Holmes, Jr., gathered informally for only about nine months, but some historians of philosophy believe that it was the source from which pragmatism emerged. Unfortunately, what we know of the Club and its deliberations is not substantial;

hence, to trace the roots of pragmatism to its weekly Saturday meetings in 1872 is not very helpful.[3]

Apart from his role in The Metaphysical Club, we know that Wright was a Harvard-educated mathematician who studied biology under Louis Agassiz, the "foremost biologist in America . . . and teacher of Wright, Peirce and James," and that Wright lectured briefly at Harvard first in psychology (1870) and then in mathematical physics (1874).[4] We also know that in 1872 he visited Darwin in England and that he contributed pro-Darwinian articles to the *North American Review* and the *Nation*. He derived a modest income from his employment with the *American Ephemeris and Nautical Almanac*, a federal publication for which he produced navigational tables that provided the positions of celestial bodies.[5] Wright's good friend Charles Eliot Norton published Wright's essays posthumously in 1877 and called the collection *Philosophical Discussions* (1877). James B. Thayer who, like Wright, came from Northampton, Massachusetts, and was his classmate at Harvard, published Wright's *Letters* in 1878.[6]

Wright was a large man who drank too much and who spoke among friends more comfortably than he lectured to his few students. In the end, his appetites and perhaps alcoholism killed him. At forty-five, with Henry James at his side, he died of a stroke.[7]

Wright on Darwinian Evolution and Spencerian Evolutionism: Praises and Objections

Wright was one of Darwin's first American apologists.[8] To Mrs. J. P. Lesley, a family friend, he wrote (February 12, 1860), after having finished Darwin's *The Origin of Species* (1859), that he was a convert to Darwin's newly published theory: "I believe that this development theory is a true account of nature, and no more atheistical than that approved theory of creation . . ."[9]

For Wright there was no doubt that what came to be known as "Darwinism" was destined to take its place on the top shelf of scientific discovery. Darwin's genius was that he assembled evidence for his view of emergent species and reasoned conclusively from the evidence to a hypothesis which came to be regarded for what it is, namely a well-founded biological theory: "In the half century preceding the publication of the *Origin of Species*, inductive evidence on the subject had accumulated greatly outweighing all that was previously known; and the *Origin of Species* is not less remarkable as a compend and discussion of this evidence than for the ingenuity of its explanation."[10]

Because the Darwinian theory is supported by the facts from which it arose, just as it points to novel facts that it can explain, we should not think of Darwin—or for that matter of the great Newton—as some sort of purely intuitive genius who contrived his thesis without any attention to the empirical data that sustain it:

> It may seem strange to many readers to be told that Mr. Darwin, the most consummately speculative genius of our times, is no more a maker of hypotheses than Newton was, who . . . wrote the often quoted but much misunderstood words, *Hypotheses non fingo*. "For," he adds, "whatever is not

> deduced from the phenomena is to be called an hypothesis; and hypotheses, whether metaphysical or physical, whether of occult qualities or mechanical, have no place in experimental philosophy. . . ."[11]

Wright objects to those in any branch of legitimate inquiry who frame hypotheses, but neither provide evidence that they are tied to sensory observations nor account for otherwise puzzling or inexplicable facts. For Wright, as for Newton, the test of any hypothesis is whether there is evidence in its favor. If there is none, then it is useless, and for Wright and his pragmatist successors what is useless has no place in the canons of meaningful inquiry.

Darwin's theory, spelled out fully and carefully in *The Origin of Species*, is not indictable on the grounds that it amounts to an empty hypothesis. As Wright sees it, this theory, with its emphasis on natural selection, accounts for new and mutant species. As a result, Wright was impatient with scientists like the English biologist St. George Mivart (1827–1900) who granted evolution but not natural selection as its engine. For Darwin and Wright, natural selection determines blindly the selection of traits that enable an organism to adapt to its environment and that dooms others that lack these traits. Natural selection is, therefore, at the center of Darwinism. As Menand puts it, "Natural selection . . . explains *how* changes occur in nature—by the relative reproductive success of the marginally better adapted. But natural selection does not dictate *what* those changes shall be. It is a process without a mind."[12] And Wright says, "We may remark by the way that Mr. Mivart's definite thesis, 'that natural selection is not *the* origin of species', is really not *the* question. No more was ever claimed for it than that it is the most influential of the agencies through which species have been modified."

Wright admires and defends Darwin but admits that *The Origin of Species* probably should have made clearer that references to *accidental* changes do not mean *uncaused* changes.[13] Darwin is not arguing for a world in which events occur by chance and in which nature's laws, especially the law of universal causation, take occasional holidays. The universal law of causation is no less firm in Darwin's world than it is in the worlds of his critics. In Darwin's biology, "accident" is a stipulative term that is not to be taken literally: "The accidental causes of science are only 'accidents' relatively to the intelligence of a man. . . . An accident is what cannot be anticipated from what we know, or by any intelligence, perhaps, which is less than omniscient. . . ."[14]

As Wright sees nature and the sciences, there are universal laws that govern biological phenomena just as there are universal laws in physics that govern bodies in motion. Because these laws are often generalized facts of or about nature, the world is in principle amenable to the scientists' desires to know more about it. The scientific assumption that nature is uniform and at base intelligible is directly opposed to the possibility of uncaused events. What follows, therefore, is that anyone who believes accidents are uncaused occurrences misreads *The Origin of Species* and also misses the bedrock presumptions of empirical science. Wright recognizes that the belief in nature's lawlike character can be stretched beyond what serious science and nature can bear. In this context the name Herbert Spencer comes to mind.

Spencer (1820–1903) was an English philosopher of the second rank but a vigorous supporter of Darwin and a familiar philosophical voice in America, as well as in England, during the middle decades of the nineteenth century. Spencer was among the most widely read philosophers in England and America when Wright was in his own philosophical prime. He, not Darwin, coined the phrase "survival of the fittest" as he spread the Darwinian gospel.[15] He also articulated and defended "Social Darwinism" and thus the view that the strongest capitalists will—and should—eliminate their weaker competitors in a free market economy.[16]

Spencer's understanding of Darwin was not so much defective as it was liberal, and in the essay "The Philosophy of Herbert Spencer" (1865), Wright found it necessary to show where and how this idiosyncratic approach to Darwinism miscarried.[17] Spencer believed that the fundamental law of evolution had a generality that reached far beyond its application to the plants and animals that were the subjects of *The Origin of Species*. In "Progress: Its Law and Consequences" (1857), Spencer wrote: "Now, we propose . . . to show that this *law of organic progress is the law of all progress*. Whether it be in the development of the earth, in the development of life upon its surface, in the development of society, of government, of manufactures . . . , this same evolution of the simple into the complex, through successive differentiations, holds throughout. . . ."[18]

Wright has numerous objections to Spencer's rendering of Darwin's theory. First, he objects to the characterization of the law of evolution through natural selection as a "law of organic *progress*." "Progress," despite its importance to Victorian philosophers and social theorists, is a word that Wright uses with caution.[19] We can, of course, talk about scientific progress if we mean that scientific investigation and understanding narrow the gap between what we wish to know and what we come to know. But to characterize what a hard science studies, such as the evolutionary development in plants or animals from those that are simple to those that are complex, is to assume that "progressive" and "complex" are synonyms. This is not what Darwin claims, and this is what Wright rejects.

There is no evidence of beginnings and goals in nature, yet progress presumes some movement toward an end. Until and unless empirical evidence is forthcoming, and Wright doubts that any ever will appear, "it would be better if science itself were purified of this idea [progress]."[20] Menand adds, "Wright did not consider himself an evolutionist. To him the term denoted a belief that the world was getting, on some definition, 'better'. His loyalty was only to the theory of natural selection. . . ."[21]

Just as bad as the misuse or misapplication of "progress" is Spencer's determination to export the laws of Darwinian evolution for service that exceeds their appropriate, verifiable scope. This is the "evolutionism" to which Wright so vigorously objects:

> Mr. Spencer's law is founded on examples, of which only one class, the facts of embryology, are properly scientific. . . . Theories of society and of the character of social progress . . . , and theories on the origins and the causes of cosmical bodies and their arrangements, are all liable to the taint of teleological and cosmological conceptions,—to spring from the order which the mind imposes upon what it imperfectly observes . . .[22]

We see in this passage that Wright is as dismissive of Spencer's zeal to find or to impose evolutionary change where no evidence confirms its existence as he is of theists and metaphysicians who deny the theory of evolution even where it unquestionably applies.

Wright looks with further jaundice on Spencerian talk about "Equilibration," a word petrified in Spencer's dictionary of empty neologisms. This word denotes the end of any evolutionary sequence. At this stage, according to Spencer, all tendencies to "a definite, coherent heterogeneity, through continuous differentiations and integrations" are finished. "Life is balanced. The worlds are completed."[23]

Here, Spencer has exceeded exponentially the rigors and rules of empirical science and induction. He has failed entirely "to distinguish . . . between what is demonstrative or scientifically probable, and what is imaginary or poetically probable. . . . To do this adequately is the work of time, patience, and science, *following the methods of experimental philosophy rather than those of Mr. Spencer*."[24] He has flouted the procedures of the strict sciences by transmuting Darwin's restricted theory of evolution into a universal evolutionism. There is no scientific warrant for doing so, and Wright has nothing but contempt for Spencer's procedures.[25] Indeed, Spencer has, even while trying hard to be forward-looking, taken a step backward in the direction of ancient science.

What separates ancient science, with its few successes, from the spectacular discoveries and theories of the sciences from the late Renaissance to Darwin? Wright has an answer: ". . . the ancients followed 'the subjective method', or appealed for the verification of their theories to natural beliefs, while the moderns follow 'the objective method', or appeal to new and independent experimental evidence."[26] What does Wright mean, and what does it have to do with his criticisms of Spencer?

Wright means just what he says. The difference in the results of ancient and modern science has little to do with the origins of hypotheses or with the common view that ancient science was a deductive enterprise from a priori first principles and that modern science is principally inductive. Even if there is some truth in this view, it is insufficient to answer the question at hand. The fundamental answer lies again in the distinction between methods. The objective method, that of modern scientists, "is verification by sensuous tests, tests of sensible experience,—a deduction from theory of consequences, of which we may have sensible experiences if they be true."[27] The approach of those who employ the subjective method is different. This is a method that "appeals to the tests of internal evidence, tests of reason, and the data of self-consciousness."[28] Anyone who thinks that Wright's methodological distinctions belong to an era that is long past might do well to read Jacob Bronowski, the eminent mathematician and biologist, who reviewed James Watson's *The Double Helix* (1968): "[*The Double Helix*] will bring home to the nonscientist how the scientific method really works: that we *invent* a model and then *test* its consequences, and that it is this conjunction of imagination and realism that constitutes the inductive method."[29]

Bronowski's remarks are close to Wright's insistence that "whatever the origin, real or ideal, the *value* of these theories can only be tested . . . by an appeal to sensible experience, by deductions from them of consequences which we can confirm by the undoubted testimony of the senses."[30] At some point in the process of scientific discovery and explanation, every hypothesis worth taking seriously "must still show credentials from the senses."[31] The problem with Spencer's evolutionism and his Law of Evolution is that they neither draw from the phenomena we have already experienced nor do they cite future observations that would confirm their speculative foundations. Spencer explains nothing further. He simply uses Darwin's theory and intellectual equipment to try to account for more than Darwin intended in *The Origin of Species* and for far more than the theory of evolution is equipped to explain.[32]

In a sense, Spencer is prolonging and anticipating similar excesses in the promiscuous employment of revolutionary scientific laws and theories. In the eighteenth century, Newtonians were in bloom all over Europe and America. But there was no justification for Jonathan Edwards to try to arrogate Newtonian *gravitas* to account for sinners' unavoidable tendency to slide into the abyss.[33] One can make the same complaint against poets who had little understanding of Newton's *Opticks*, but who were sure that this great work opened doors to aesthetics, morality, and philosophy.[34]

Even in the twentieth and twenty-first centuries, no one needs to be told that Einstein's theory of relativity (in which the speed of light is a constant) has become the common property of those who believe that everything, from ethics and social customs to artistic and literary tastes, is *relative*. The misappropriation of theories, like Spencer's determination to overwork Darwin's insights, leads to pseudoscientific nonsense that is, epistemologically indefensible.

Wright, not Spencer, was an early positivist when the issue was the status of hypotheses, laws, and theories. Menand says, "What Wright meant by positivism was . . . an absolute distinction between facts and values. Fact was the province of science and value was the province of . . . metaphysics. Wright thought that metaphysical speculation—ideas about the origin, end, and meaning of life—came naturally to human beings. He didn't condemn such ideas out of hand. He just thought they should never be confused with science."[35] The way to avoid the confusion that concerned Wright is to see whether the idea (proposition) in question can be verified empirically or experimentally. This is the marrow of Wright's positivism. The demand for verification, which can in principle be satisfied by anyone else who is curious about an idea or proposition, was also the core of Auguste Comte's (1798–1857) and John Stuart Mill's (1806–1873) philosophies of science. Wright favored Mill over other earlier positivists because he was brilliant and because his brilliance was packaged in the body of an Englishman. Wright's own "English" ancestral pride shines through when he praises Mill and adds, "though eight generations removed from English soil, I am still an Englishman. . . ."[36] Obviously, Emerson's zeal for homegrown genius did not touch Wright. What counts for Wright is the fruitfulness of the idea that is advanced, not its national pedigree.

Insofar as public verification is the test for the scientific character of a putative scientific claim, the incapacity in principle to verify or disconfirm the claim empirically establishes that it was never scientific in the first place. It may be a normative, religious, or metaphysical claim, but this family of assertions has nothing to do with the sciences. Yet Wright is more generous than some other positivists. He does not believe that every proposition must be discarded as meaningless insofar as it lacks scientific or empirical credentials: "I am not so much a positivist as to deny that mystical and poetical philosophies are valuable products of human genius; but then they must be works of real genius,—of a Plato, a Hegel, or an Emerson."[37] So, to take a prominent and recurrent case, there is the troublesome conflict between religious doctrine and scientific theory. Must science and religion be at odds?

Wright's answer to this question is no, insofar as the province of the sciences (empirical facts and verifiable occurrences) is separate and distinct from the province of religion, with its trans-phenomenal assertions about the nature of God and origin of the universe:[38] "[I]t is denied by the physical philosopher that causes and effects in natural phenomena can be interpreted into the terms of natural theology by any key which science itself affords. . . . The belief on other grounds that there *are* final causes, that the universe exists for some purpose, is one thing; but the belief that science discloses, or that science can disclose, what this purpose is, is quite a different thing."[39] Sounding more like a fideist (one who believes religious doctrine as a matter of faith, not of rational evidence) than a scientific critic of religion, Wright insists that "there is nothing in science or philosophy which can legitimately rebuke his [a theist's] enthusiasm—nothing, unless it be the dogmatism which would presumptuously interpret as science what is only manifest to faith, or would require of faith that it shall justify itself by proofs."[40]

For Wright every supposed conflict between scientific and religious utterances is spurious because scientific claims and conclusions are cognitive, while those of religion are noncognitive products of *feeling*.[41] In a letter to the Unitarian preacher Francis E. Abbot, July 9, 1867, Wright defends positivism against its religious critics: "This philosophy denies nothing of orthodoxy except its confidence; but it discriminates between the desirableness of a belief and the evidence thereof. Faith is in this philosophy what it is with St. Paul, a *sentiment*, not a faculty of knowledge."[42] Whether Wright understands St. Paul need not trouble us. What counts for understanding Wright is that in denying faith its epistemic credentials and insisting on only its emotive character, he also denies the possibility of meaningful tension and disagreements between theists and scientists. Hinting, as twentieth-century positivists would do seventy-five years later, that the declarations of religion and speculative metaphysics are closer to feelings of poets than to descriptions and predictions of scientists, there is no common ground from which *significant* debates can arise.[43]

Since arguments between those who speak for the sciences and those who speak for religion are meaningless, time spent on sterile debates is misspent. "That there is a fundamental distinction between the natures of scientific and religious ideas ought never be doubted; *but that contradiction can arise*, except between religious and superstitious ideas, *ought not for a moment be admitted*."[44] So too, treating the sciences as natural theologians do is as shortsighted as insisting upon an antagonism between them.[45] No science is a handmaid to faith. Scientists, as long as they are engaged in their scientific activities, have no business involving themselves in any theological and metaphysical issues. Theologians, whether awed by the mysteries of the universe or dealing with the daily, earth-bound needs of their congregations, have as little business asking the sciences, as natural theologians routinely do, to do their work or to follow their spiritual lead.

The Source for Self-Consciousness: Wright's Too Facile Hypothesis?

Before leaving Wright and advancing to the pragmatists he inspired with his brief for evolution and the productive application of the scientific method, it might be helpful to say something about his "Evolution of Self-Consciousness."[46] The chief purpose of this essay is to establish against critics of Darwinism that self-consciousness and the use of reflective language evolve from antecedent causes and are not supernatural characteristics of human beings. Wright believes that those who accept the theory of evolution know that a power like self-consciousness emerges gradually in its full expression but is present latently or potentially in causes and powers that came before human beings.[47]

The difference between animal intelligence and human intelligence—a difference in degree, not in kind[48]—is that human beings can think abstractly or form concepts. Animals can at best associate inner signs (impressions) with outward signs (objects or events). Human beings can move from outward signs to inner signs (impressions) and reflect on these inner signs themselves, thus producing what we might describe as ideas of ideas (concepts). In self-conscious beings, then, one finds a capacity to think about thoughts themselves, not merely on exterior objects or events. This, stripped to the core, is Wright's account of the reflective capacity that to belongs uniquely to man:[49] "[R]eflection is a distinct faculty, and though, perhaps, not peculiar to man, is in him so prominent and marked in its effects on the individual mind, that it may be regarded as his most essential and elementary distinction in kind. *For differences of degrees in causes make differences of kinds in effects.*"[50]

Wright sees his hypothesis as emancipating a biological phenomenon from the grasp of dreamy metaphysicians: "Reflection would thus be, not what most metaphysicians appear to regard it, a fundamentally new faculty in man . . . ; but it would be determined in its contrasts with other mental faculties by the nature of its objects."[51] Skeptics can applaud Wright's naturalistic account of the origins and objects of reflection, but they should wonder what to say about Wright's alternative to a kind of preternatural higher consciousness in human beings.

Wright criticizes Spencer and, in objecting to the "subjective method," also the Transcendentalists for their unanchored speculations and for their inattention to sensory modes of verification. One could object on the same grounds to Wright and his speculative account of the origins of self-consciousness, that is, origins that must for him be consistent with evolutionary theory. If, however, we read all sixty-eight pages of "Evolution of Self-Consciousness," we find the kind of speculation that Wright rejects, namely speculation and theorizing that do not produce conclusions or consequences which can be confirmed or disconfirmed. Wright offers a hypothesis that he describes as superior to that of metaphysical spiritualists because it does not posit self-consciousness as a mysterious capacity somehow infused in men alone.[52]

His hypothesis stands as an alternative to what metaphysicians suggest, but Wright himself insists that a hypothesis is only as good as the evidence that supports it, yet he produces no solid evidence to support his version of the emergence of self-conscious reflection.[53] If there is good reason to indict metaphysicians for their extravagance, there is equally good reason to complain that Wright is in this case indifferent to the "objective method" that he describes as the working center of modern, fruitful science. Even into the present, there is uncertainty and disagreement among prominent Darwinians how to account for thought that is specifically or uniquely human and for the language we use to express the content of our thoughts.[54]

Wright's Place in American Philosophy: A Closing Observation

Historians of American philosophy should be careful neither to minimize nor to exaggerate the significance of Chauncey Wright. He was among the first American thinkers, whether working in or outside the sciences, to grasp the importance of Darwin's theory of evolution. He was also one of the first to see its misdirected use to misguided natural theologians and to those, like Spencer, who argued that evolutionary change exhibits nature's progress toward some ideal.

On the other hand, although Wright was a highly trained mathematician and talented thinker, he was neither a great mathematician nor a philosopher for the ages. His own contributions to mathematics and philosophy do not shape either discipline in any indispensable manner. We read Wright today, following a long period in which his name was dormant, largely because of other philosophers he knew and influenced, that is, those who were part of the Metaphysical Club of 1872. His ideas on change, evolution, and positivism touched each of them and to some degree shaped the philosophy identified as "pragmatism." He insisted on the primacy of *change* but not as the metaphysical reality that underpins the phenomena. Wright's account of change was everywhere evident at the level of observation and experience: "Nothing is exempt from change. Worlds are formed and dissipated. Races of organic beings grow up like their constituent individual members, and disappear like these. Nothing shows a trace of an original, immutable nature, except the unchangeable laws of change."[55]

Wright's attitude toward change affected his pragmatist successors. As a consequence, part of their rendering of philosophy's mission was to help us confront and deal with a world in flux. They too recognized that change is a fact of life and that otherworldly philosophers like Plato, who venerate eternity and disparage mutation, are mistaken.[56] Their philosophies, insofar as they advocate fleeing from the problems, as well as the opportunities, in the order of sense and experience, are pusillanimous. Change is inescapable, and Darwin's theory of evolution exemplifies more cogently than other advances in the sciences that this is so. In an America that was profoundly shaken by civil war and unprecedented industrial growth, no one could escape the pervasiveness of mutation. Wright went a step further and was a step ahead of most other bright and thoughtful Americans. He saw in the life sciences that Darwin was correct: Mutation and evolution were inseparable from the persistence of life itself.

Wright explained to those intellectuals—the great circle of philosophers who wrote and taught during the Gilded Age—that Darwin's theory and the facts that sustained it were indisputable. The evolution of living organisms is nature's purposeless way of announcing that change, not stasis, is ubiquitous and is necessary for the transformations that geological time and fossil records validate. In a period of intellectual and political upheaval in America, a philosopher's choices were disarmingly simple.[57] He could choose recalcitrance over acceptance and deny the Darwinian rendering of evolutionary change, described and defended in *The Origin of Species*, or he could subscribe to the procedures and rigors of the scientific method, and yield to the evidence that the organic world was conspicuous for its alterations, not for its imaginary fixity.

Wright was philosopher and scientist enough to make a case for the greatest of all biological theories. He was also independent-minded enough to break with aging Transcendentalists, assorted spiritualists, and mystics for whom man was a supernatural capstone to life's chain of being. He was confident enough to insist upon the "objective method," the scientific method as we still understand it, that would display the uselessness of the "subjective method," which looked to an inner voice (Reason or Intuition), not outer evidence, to "confirm" its dubious insights.

Wright's legacy was himself, understood as a dramatic intrusion into the evolution of American thought. Striving to emancipate philosophy from the remnants of New England Transcendentalism and from the remains of metaphysics as usual, he was able to persuade members of his small circle to take a hard, fresh look at the job of philosophy.

What emerged from this circle was an open-minded willingness to take up a philosophy that was adapted to an era in American history and that was crafted to address, not to sidestep, life's problems. Counterfactual claims are tricky and contemporary philosophers continue to debate how to confirm them, but perhaps it is not too risky to suggest that *if* there had been no Wright, American pragmatism would have developed ideas different from those that are inseparable from it. One might even suggest, without extravagance, that but for this mild-mannered import from Northampton to Cambridge, American pragmatism might itself never have emerged.

But enough. We know that when Wright was not writing about the development of self-consciousness, he had no patience with insupportable hypotheses. This is not the place for idle hypotheses about what, except for Wright's efforts, might have happened to the development and character of philosophy in America. Instead, it is appropriate to turn our attention to the philosophers whom Wright influenced, which takes us to the next essay and to the great triumvirs of pragmatism.

NOTES

1. *Science and Sentiment in America*, (New York, 1972) 296, 298.
2. *The Philosophical Writings of Chauncey Wright*, ed. Edward H. Madden (New York, 1958), vii; hereafter abbreviated as *Writings of Chauncey Wright*.
3. The most substantial recent study is Louis Menand's *The Metaphysical Club: A Story of Ideas in America* (New York, 2001), 201–32; hereafter abbreviated as *The Metaphysical*

Club. For a still useful account of the Club and of Wright's contributions to its philosophical interests, see Philip P. Wiener, *Evolution and the Founders of Pragmatism*, reprint (Philadelphia, 1972), 18–69.

4. *Evolution and the Founders of Pragmatism*, 32.
5. *The Metaphysical Club*, 206.
6. *Writings of Chauncey Wright*, viii.
7. *The Metaphysical Club*, 231.
8. *Evolution and the Founders of Pragmatism*, 31.
9. *Letters of Chauncey Wright*, ed. James Bradley Thayer (Cambridge, Mass., 1878), 43.
10. From "Evolution and Its Explanation," *North American Review* (1871), 63–6, in *Writings of Chauncey Wright*, 31.
11. From "The Logic of Biology," *North American Review* (1871), 72–5; (1872), 22–4, in *Writings of Chauncey Wright*, 32. Wright treats Newton and Darwin as comparable or, better, incomparable geniuses working in two different sciences. This makes even more shortsighted Kant's confidence that the biological sciences will never produce "another Newton . . . who shall make comprehensible by us the production of a blade of grass according to natural laws which no design has ordered." *Critique of Judgment* (1790), trans. J. H. Bernard (New York, 1951), 248.
12. *The Metaphysical Club*, 123.
13. From "The Meaning of 'Accident'," *North American Review* (1871), 67–9, 78, 80–1, in *Writings of Chauncey Wright*, 36.
14. Ibid. 37, 38.
15. Daniel C. Dennett, *Darwin's Dangerous Idea: Evolution and the Meanings of Life* (New York, 1995), 393.
16. Ibid. 461–3; and Alan Trachtenberg, *The Incorporation of America: Culture and Society in the Gilded Age* (New York, 1982), 81.
17. "The Philosophy of Herbert Spencer," *North American Review* (1865), in Wright's *Philosophical Discussions* ed. Charles Eliot Norton (New York, 1877), 43–96.
18. Quoted from *Romanticism and Evolution: the Nineteenth Century*, ed. B. Wilshire (New York, 1968), 236; emphasis added. For the complete selection, see pages 234–44.
19. Wiener points out that although many evolutionary philosophers in the second half of the nineteenth century confounded "historical and logical problems in an over-optimistic faith in the inevitability of progress, none of our pragmatic thinkers failed to criticize prevailing belief in automatic progress guaranteed by infallible dogmas or inflexible traditions." *Evolution and the Founders of Pragmatism*, 29.
20. *Writings of Chauncey Wright*, 21.
21. *The Metaphysical Club*, 209.
22. "The Philosophy of Herbert Spencer," *Philosophical Discussions*, 73. See also pages 74–7.
23. Ibid. 80.
24. Ibid. 81; emphasis added.
25. Ibid. 77.
26. Ibid. 48–9.
27. Ibid. 46.
28. Ibid.
29. Jacob Bronowski, "Honest Jim and the Tinker Toy Model," reprinted in James D. Watson, *The Double Helix: A Personal Account of the Structure of DNA*, ed. G. S. Stent (New York, 1980), 201.
30. "The Philosophy of Herbert Spencer," *Philosophical Discussions*, 47.
31. Ibid.
32. Ibid. 72–3.
33. See *A Jonathan Edwards Reader*, ed. John E. Smith, Harry S. Stout, and Kenneth P. Minkema (New Haven, 1995), 89–90.
34. See Marjorie Hope Nicolson's analysis in *Newton Demands the Muse: Newton's Opticks and Eighteenth Century Poets* (Princeton, 1946).
35. *The Metaphysical Club*, 207.
36. From a letter to Mrs. J. P. Lesley, May 7, 1871, in *Letters of Chauncey Wright*, 219.

37. From Wright to Norton, July 24, 1866, in *Letters of Chauncey Wright*, 87.
38. "Natural Theology as a Positive Science," *North American Review* (1865), in *Philosophical Discussions*, 40.
39. Ibid. 36.
40. Ibid. 41.
41. "The Philosophy of Herbert Spencer," in *Philosophical Discussions*, 92.
42. *Letters of Chauncey Wright*, 103; emphasis added. For a similar statement of Wright on faith, see page 381.
43. A. J. Ayer, certainly the best known positivist writing in English, is less charitable than Wright. He is emphatic that the metaphysician does not even rise to the level of a poet. *Language, Truth, and Logic*, 2d edition (New York, 1946), 44–5.
44. *Philosophical Discussions*, 36; emphasis added.
45. Ibid. 52–3.
46. From the *North American Review* (1873), in *Philosophical Discussions*, 199–266.
47. Ibid. 200–201.
48. Ibid. 217. Darwin, in *The Descent of Man* (1871), writes, "Spiritual powers cannot be compared or classed by the naturalist: but he may endeavour to shew, as I have done, that *the mental faculties of man and the lower animals do not differ in kind, although immensely in degree*"; emphasis added. See ed. Philip Appleman, 3rd ed., (New York, 2001), *Darwin*, 223.
49. Ibid. 211–19.
50. Ibid. 217; emphasis added.
51. Ibid. See also page 203.
52. Wiener makes an instructive observation about the ties between Wright's approach to self-consciousness and Kant's by "attempting to show the continuity of instinctive sensory reactions and the more guided apprehensions of reflective thinking." *Evolution and the Founders of Pragmatism*, 88.
53. "The Philosophy of Herbert Spencer," *Philosophical Discussions*, 48–9.
54. See, for example, Dennett's discussion of the views of Noam Chomsky, the philosopher and linguist, and Stephen J. Gould, the geologist and biologist. What unifies these thinkers is their endorsement of Darwinism. What separates them is how to account for the origins of a language that expresses concepts, generalities and reflective thoughts. *Darwin's Dangerous Idea*, 135, 138, 341–2, 384, 395.
55. "The Philosophy of Herbert Spencer," *Philosophical Discussions*, 74.
56. See Plato, *Cratylus*, 439d–440b.
57. For some background on this period and some brief discussion of the thought that characterized the Gilded Age, see *The Incorporation of America: Culture and Society in the Gilded Age*, chs. 2–6.

Essay 6
Charles Sanders Peirce, William James, and John Dewey: Founders of Pragmatism, a Philosophy Made in America

A. O. Lovejoy (1873–1962), the American philosopher and historian of ideas, wrote "The Thirteen Pragmatisms, II" in order "to discriminate all the more important doctrines going under the name of pragmatism which can be shown to be not only distinct, but also logically independent. . . ."[1] There is nothing subtle about Lovejoy's position. Pragmatism came in so many varieties that it makes very little sense to talk about the word "pragmatism" as if it denotes a single philosophy: "Each pragmatism of the thirteen should manifestly be given a name of its own, if confusion in future discussions is to be avoided."[2]

Lovejoy may be exaggerating the case. Those who study pragmatism, or pragmatisms, and who have read "The Thirteen Pragmatisms" can decide for themselves the merits of Lovejoy's complaint. What philosophers rarely debate is that Charles Sanders Peirce was a pioneering pragmatist, whether they have in view a single philosophy or a baker's dozen that go by the same name. To know anything at all about pragmatism or about thirteen different pragmatic philosophies is to know something about Peirce's mature philosophy.

Charles Sanders Peirce (1839–1914)

A few words about the man Charles Sanders Peirce are necessary. He was born in 1839 and reared in Cambridge, Massachusetts. Peirce's father Benjamin was Harvard's most distinguished mathematician.[3] He saw that Charles, the second of five children, had enormous intellectual potential and did all he could to encourage Charles to employ his talents. Far from denying his father's authority, the younger Peirce describes himself as having "inhabited a laboratory from the age of six until long past maturity."[4] Unfortunately, Charles had personal failings and problems of health to match his mental gifts:

> Charles suffered from facial neuralgia . . . , and used opium (then a commonly prescribed painkiller) for relief, apparently developing an addiction. Later in life he relied on ether, morphine, and cocaine as well. He was also an assiduous womanizer as well. . . . His neuralgia, and the drugs he used to alleviate it, made him susceptible to violent fits of temper.[5]

Despite these problems, Peirce found some peace with his wife Harriet Melusina Fay, whom he married in 1862. She too had flaws, including a contempt for all immigrants. That she could help Peirce to lead a calmer life, despite her own simmering intolerance, tells us a bit more about the level of his own volatility.[6]

With his father's help and influence Peirce found employment in 1861 as a mathematician with the United States Coast Survey. He stayed with this agency until his retirement in 1887. Peirce never managed to secure a permanent position as a professor, but he did lecture part-time in philosophy and logic at the newly founded Johns Hopkins University (1879–1884). According to Justus Buchler, who wrote in the middle decades of the twentieth century about Peirce's philosophy, there are very few thinkers like Peirce—great intellectuals who manage to affect so limited an audience during their lifetimes:

> [Peirce's] inability to secure a regular teaching position . . . and to have his work published in book form partly account for this fact, and so does his unwillingness to "water down" ideas for whatever audience he reached. But his effect on other thinkers has been great: the philosophies of Royce, James, and Dewey would lack some of their most distinctive emphases if his influence were subtracted.[7]

"The Fixation of Belief" (1877) and "How to Make Our Ideas Clear" (1878): A Philosophy of Science Takes Shape

In "Concerning the Author," a condensed autobiographical essay, Peirce writes a little about the circumstances through which he came to intellectual maturity. In addition to his association with Chauncey Wright, his study of Kant, Hegel, and the fourteenth-century philosopher Duns Scotus, Peirce spent many of his formative years experimenting in a chemistry laboratory. He was equally at home in the sciences and in philosophy, and it is important to know that the physical sciences and their method helped shape many of his philosophical beliefs and choices.[8]

Among Peirce's most celebrated essays, as well as one that shows how seriously he took his scientific background and its suitability for nonscientific modes of inquiry, "The Fixation of Belief" stands out. Here he writes, "The object of reasoning is to find out, from the consideration of what we already know, something else which we do not know. Consequently, reasoning is good if it be such as to give a true conclusion from true premisses [*sic*], and not otherwise. Thus the question of validity is purely one of fact and not of thinking."[9] Peirce means, among other things, that the soundness and validity of inferences is strictly a function of the facts and the relation between facts that the premises and conclusion of the inference express. Facts and discovering them are what count to a scientist who refuses to allow his prepossessions to interfere with his approach to a problem that concerns him.[10]

This prologue brings Peirce to the center of his treatment of inquiry, which in its turns presents him the opportunity to discuss how we manage to "fix," that is, to reach secure beliefs: "We generally know when we wish to ask a question and when we wish to pronounce a judgment, for there is a dissimilarity between the sensation of doubting and that of believing. But that is not all which distinguishes doubt from belief. *There is a practical difference.*"[11] The latter difference is that with belief come dispositions or habits of *action*; whereas doubt leads to *inaction*. And there is another difference as well: "Doubt is an uneasy and dissatisfied state from which we struggle to free ourselves and pass into the state of belief; while the latter is a calm and satisfactory state which we do not wish to avoid, or to change to a belief in anything else."[12]

This account of doubt is almost biological. "The irritation of doubt causes a struggle to attain a state of belief. I shall term the struggle *Inquiry*, though it must be admitted that this is sometimes not a very apt designation." Moreover, this "*irritation of doubt* is the only immediate motive for the struggle to attain belief."[13] Irritation is visceral. It makes the doubter as uneasy in his way as the discomfort that stimulates an oyster to produce cells that encase an irritating grain of sand in a protective pearl. Once the irritation is relieved, the oyster's simple comfort is restored; so too through productive inquiry the irritation of doubt is eliminated and replaced by satisfying belief: "With doubt, therefore, the struggle begins, and with the cessation of doubt it ends."[14] As if to stress further the organic, urgent character of authentic doubt, Peirce articulates a thinly veiled criticism of Descartes: ". . . the mere putting of a proposition into the interrogative form does not stimulate the mind to any *struggle* after belief."[15]

But how do we go about securing the beliefs that give us at least temporary calm and mitigate our distress? Peirce describes four methods but insists that only one works. One way to come by beliefs, a way that almost announces its failure, is through the method of *tenacity*. Here one simply chooses or retains a belief and expects that it will be secure and satisfying. But Peirce insists that social practice is against this effort to maintain a belief. Why? "The man who adopts it will find that other men think differently from him, and it will be apt to occur to him, in some saner moment, that their opinions are quite as good as his own. . . . Unless we make ourselves hermits, we shall necessarily influence each other's opinions; so that the problem becomes how to fix belief, not in the individual merely, but in the community."[16]

An approach to securing belief within a community is through *authority*, but this method is noxious and ineffective. This is the method that stoops to cruelty; it is the method employed by tyrants and despots. Over men and women who are weak, this method is effective. But there are always in any society people who do think and who have seen or read about different societies with beliefs and doctrines at variance with their own. More than that, they are also open-minded and are drawn to consider "there is no reason to rate their own views at a higher value than those of other nations and other centuries; thus giving rise to *doubts* in their minds."[17] This will never do since a method for "fixing" belief is meant to overcome doubts.

A third method, the a priori method, may answer doubts with imposing metaphysical systems and elaborate philosophical architecture like that which we find in Plato, but the problem is its scanty equipment for displacing our doubts. Peirce has in mind demonstrative metaphysical systems that begin with first principles that have no factual basis, and then purport to deduce subaltern certainties from their primary truths. Philosophers might try to believe the axioms, postulates, and theorems of their elaborate systems, yet in the end they cannot make their effort subdue doubt.[18]

With the a priori method we encounter the recurrent problem of unanchored hypotheses, masquerading as first principles. If one has no evidence that the first principles of an elaborate metaphysics are ultimate truths about reality, then all that follows from these principles shares in their insecurity. This is presumably why Peirce discounts this method with the observation that "its failure has been the most manifest."[19]

The only method left and the only one Peirce endorses, as eliminating doubts in favor of beliefs, is the *method of science*. This is the approach to inquiry "by which our beliefs may be determined by nothing human, but by some external permanency—by something upon which our thinking has no effect."[20] Among all the methods surveyed, this is the one that provides objectivity; it is also the one that can yield durable, comfort-producing beliefs even as it purges nagging, irritating doubts. The fundamental hypothesis of this method is: "There are Real things, whose characters are entirely independent of our opinions about them; those Reals affect our senses according to regular laws, and, though our sensations are as different as are our relations to the objects, yet, by taking advantage of the laws of perception, we can ascertain by reasoning how things *really and truly are*."[21]

We notice here that Peirce is not troubled by persistent philosophical questions of whether in perception we can ever get beyond appearances to see whether there is some basic reality about which a certain class of propositions, those confirmed by the scientific method, is true. Rather, he presumes that the scientific method takes us to, and even defines, reality insofar as using this method never leads to doubts about its practice; hence reality and what is true of it amount to what the scientific method discloses. "Experience of the method has not led us to doubt it, but, on the contrary, scientific investigation has had the most wonderful triumphs in the way of settling opinion."[22]

Even people who through habit are disinclined to abandon what they tenaciously believe, or believe through imposition of authority—if they use the method that requires observation, scrupulous reasoning, testing, and public confirmation of its results—are won over. As converts to the scientific method, the displacement of doubt produces for Peirce the truth that makes them free and beliefs that make them comfortable.

There are some points to keep in mind as Peirce describes and celebrates the scientific method and both its epistemological and therapeutic consequences. First, his conviction that this method takes us to truth and reality is a presumption. There is no way to confirm, using the scientific method, that it reaches what is ultimately the case. Peirce admits as much when he writes, "If [scientific] investigation cannot be regarded as proving that there are Real things, it at least does not lead to a contrary conclusion. . . ."[23] But given that there is no better method than the scientific method, where "fixing" beliefs and diminishing doubts are ends in view, there is no other method available to confirm that a scientific investigator has arrived at reality and what is true of it.

Second, despite Peirce's seemingly unrestrained praises for the method of the sciences, Cornell West points out what we will turn to a little later in this essay: "Peirce carefully and cautiously *restricts* the application of the scientific method . . . to the scientific community involved in rational inquiry. The authority of the scientific method does not hold sway in ethics and religion. In this sense science is neither a guide to conduct nor an instrument for a practical end."[24]

Finally, we notice from Peirce's account of four different methods for "fixing" belief how fragile beliefs seem to be. In three of the four methods, coming to believe some proposition is far less difficult than maintaining the belief. A great deal of interference, often competing views within a diverse society, threatens what might have begun life as a firmly held belief. That the case is different with regard to beliefs confirmed by the scientific method is at once a testament to the solvency of that method and a recognition that the set of possible beliefs is on surprisingly unsteady ground. Only scientifically based beliefs in what is true and real stand a chance of lasting.

"How to Make our Ideas Clear" stands to Peirce's statement of the pragmatic maxim as "The Fixation of Belief" does to his conception and defense of the scientific method. These two essays are canonical and indispensable for those who are curious about the scientific side of Peirce that draws philosophers to him. We will see in the next section that understanding Peirce solely as a philosopher of science is to miss or omit another facet of his larger philosophy. For now, however, it is important to determine the salient elements of "How to Make Our Ideas Clear."

The opening third of this essay amounts to a prolonged knife-in-the-back of Descartes and the Cartesians. When the issue is clarifying our ideas, Descartes gives us nothing but a suspect method that moves from the Scholastic method of authority (especially that of Aristotle) to his own rendering of what Peirce sees as subjectivism. Rejecting Descartes's insistence that the inability to doubt proposition P guarantees the certainty of P, Peirce adds: "But since, evidently, not all ideas are true, he was led to note, as the first condition of infallibility, that they must be clear. The distinction between an idea *seeming* clear and really being so, never occurred to him."[25]

As Vincent Calopietro points out, Peirce has no objections to doubt in itself, but the value of doubt must not be overstated. Descartes's error was an enthusiasm for overstatement:

> The value of doubt, of calling into question what has not been questioned thus far, is itself beyond doubt; but it is a double illusion to suppose that (1) we can simultaneously call everything into question and (2) having done so, can establish some truth once and for all. As doubters, we can profitably go into the retail business, but are destined to bankrupt ourselves by trying to erect a wholesale outlet.[26]

If, as Peirce believes, Cartesianism is and ought to be an extinct philosophy, it falls to him to try to explain "how to make our ideas clear." To make our ideas clear or, what is the same thing, to determine and sometimes to settle their meaning, "we have, therefore, simply to determine what habits it produces, for what a thing means is simply what habits it involves."[27] Here we have the connection between Peirce on the nature of belief and on the search for meaning. "The essence of belief is the establishment of a habit: and different beliefs are distinguished by the different modes of action to which they give rise."[28]

Peirce is now prepared to declare his famous pragmatic maxim, namely the admonition to settle disputes or determine the meaning of a proposition as it designates some property or thing: "It appears, then, that the rule for attaining the *third grade* of clearness of apprehension is as follows: *Consider what effects, that might conceivably have practical bearings, we conceive the object of our conception to have. Then, our conception of these effects is the whole of our conception of the object.*"[29] Two points are important at the outset. When Peirce talks about "effects," he means "sensible effects." He says, immediately before announcing the maxim, "Our idea of anything *is* our idea of its sensible effects; and if we fancy that we have any other we deceive ourselves." What Peirce has in mind emerges from examples of the application of the maxim.

With this much in hand, Peirce turns to the application of the maxim in order to exhibit its content. What, for example, do we mean when we call something "*hard*"? We mean, Peirce says, that there are few other things that can scratch it, but to determine what we mean by saying "X is hard," we must appeal to an operational test. We might appeal to a traditional geological scratch test and say "X is hard" means "Any attempt to scratch X with a mineral softer than a diamond fails." This test also provides a translation of "soft" into operational language that says if certain sensible effects (scratches) appear on X, following specified operations, then X is not soft. Absent that test, or one similar to it, we have no idea what the words "hard" and "soft" mean. "There is absolutely no difference between a hard and a soft thing so long as they are not brought to the test."[30]

We find the same approach to "a clear idea of Weight." Here, as in the case above, to say "X is heavy" is to say, "Absent a counter-force X will fall." This is our complete and clear idea of weight. In this translation of one proposition into one that clarifies it, we do not know anything more about the presence of gravity in our universe, "but what we mean by the force itself is completely involved in its effects."[31] In this case, as in that of *hardness*, we notice that Peirce's use of the pragmatic maxim is intentionally narrowed by an appeal to "sensible effects."

To determine whether an idea of something is meaningful and amenable to clarification is to be able to provide a public, verifiable criterion that depends upon the manifestation of appropriate facts in experience; hence we cannot clarify or verify any metaphysical claims. Metaphysical claims are, after all, those that are meant to assert something about states of being or about trans-experiential objects that do not reveal themselves to any of our sensuous experiences. Given Peirce's criterion for clarifying our ideas, we can know that an idea of P, where P is said to have no sensible properties or effects, is inherently unclear, and insofar as it is unclear, our idea of P carries with it none of the advantages of a scientist's or scientifically minded philosopher's search for knowledge and intelligible concepts.

Peirce concludes "How to Make Our Ideas Clear" with a return to the issue he confronted in "The Fixation of Belief": can we have a clear idea of the *real*? This is a question that has occupied philosophers from Plato and Aristotle forward. Using the pragmatic maxim to try to determine whether and, if so, what sensible effects *real things* produce, Peirce finds that the only sensible effect real things cause is our belief in them. "The question therefore is, how is true belief (or belief in the real) distinguished from false belief (or belief in fiction)?"[32] His answer has to do with the independence of the real and once more with the state of mind it produces in people, by far the great majority, who are persuaded that there are some such realities. Here, as in many of Peirce's other essays, scientific investigation is the model to which he appeals: "The opinion which is fated to be ultimately agreed to by all who investigate, is what we mean by the truth, and the object represented in this opinion is the real. That is the way I would explain reality."[33]

Reality impinges on us everywhere and thereby induces belief that there is something we are entitled to call "reality." It also raises our expectation that through meaningful inquiry we will come closer to knowing it.[34] This expectation, which is coordinate with our *belief* that there are real things and independent occurrences, is the most imposing example of Peirce's glowing account of "scientific men."

Because Peirce is eager to show how to make our ideas clear, he is particularly eager to clarify the ideas of *science* and scientific practitioners. What might be surprising is how far this clear idea is from what we intuitively think of as pragmatism:

> If a proposition is to be applied to action, it has to be embraced, or believed without reservation. There is no room for doubt, which can only paralyze action. But the scientific spirit requires a man to be at all times ready to dump his whole cartload of beliefs, the moment experience is against them. . . . Thus the real character of science is destroyed as soon as it is made an adjunct to conduct.[35]

Since, as Peirce sees it, worthwhile science bears on "useless things," the only consequences that count for scientists are those that come nearer what is characteristic of reality. To demand that good scientists concern themselves with practical results or productive applications of their investigations and theories is to misunderstand scientific goals. Asking a scientist what good his work is or does, with the expectation that he will point to some beneficial consequence, displays indefensible ignorance of the scientific enterprise. "To employ these rare minds on such work ["the study of useless things"] is like running a steam engine by burning diamonds."[36]

Peirce knows that those who seek a philosophy are not concerned exclusively, or dominantly, with the sciences. But for him the scientific method and attitudes of scientists, are paradigms for meaningful inquiry in any area. This is principally why he writes in "The Essentials of Pragmatism" that it is advisable to change the name of his philosophy from "pragmatism" to "pragmaticism." Peirce had hopes that he could recapture the essence of pragmatism from those who adopted it and understood it more loosely than Peirce intended: ". . . the writer . . . , feels that it is time to kiss his child good-by and relinquish it to its higher destiny; while to serve the precise purpose of expressing the original definition, he begs to announce the birth of the word 'pragmaticism', which is ugly enough to be safe from kidnappers."[37]

In the end, whether we choose to call it "pragmatism" or "pragmaticism," Peirce's philosophy uses its pragmatic maxim to determine the perimeters and character of authentic inquiry. This philosophy is surely akin to Wright's brand of positivism, but there is a difference that no one who wishes to understand Peirce can overlook. Peirce puts the point simply enough, but in this case simplicity and clarity might not be congruent: ". . . instead of merely jeering at metaphysics, like other prope-positivists . . . , the pragmaticist extracts from it a precious essence, which will serve to give precious light to cosmology and physics."[38] He seems to mean that the pragmatic maxim exposes "ontological metaphysics" as either "meaningless gibberish" or as "downright absurd," but leaves room for a species of meaningful propositions that *cannot* be resolved into identifiable sensible effects or habits of action.[39] But this claim may be too facile insofar as Peirce says in the same essay, while surveying the strengths of pragmatism: "*Any hypothesis, therefore, may be admissible . . . provided it be capable of experimental verification, and only in so far as it is capable of such verification. This is approximately the doctrine of pragmatism.*"[40] Somehow Peirce believes he can reconcile his insistence on the ties that bind meaningfulness to verifiability and still open the door to a certain kind of metaphysical claim.

The way Peirce tries to reconcile his pragmatism, a verification theory of meaning, and claims that seem unverifiable bear on misinterpretations of Peirce's thought and motivation. Some scholars and historians have made the leap that a philosophy inspired by the scientific method is a perfect bedfellow for hyperkinetic industrial America in the 1870s and later, but this leap is questionable. We have just seen that for Peirce it does not follow that our most scientifically respectable beliefs are essentially practical or have any bearing on a desire to profit from our accumulated knowledge. Looking for a philosophy (in post–Civil War America) that focuses on the needs of practical, active, acquisitive people has little to do with Peirce's view of scientific inquiry or of scientists themselves.[41] We should not be at all surprised when Peirce writes: "If a man occupies himself with investigating the truth of some question for some ulterior purpose, such as to make money, or to amend his life, or to benefit his fellows, he may be ever so much better than a scientific man . . . *but he is not a scientific man*."[42] What does any of this have to do with Peirce's surprising remarks about at least some metaphysical claims?

Peirce's Scientific Pragmatism and His Metaphysics: A Period of Adjustment or Persistently Troubled Marriage?

Readers who go beyond Peirce's most familiar essays, like "The Fixation of Belief" and "How to Make Our Ideas Clear," discover what can fairly be described as a metaphysical facet of the man and his thought. After all, in "How to Make Our Ideas Clear," Peirce insists that ". . . metaphysics is a subject much more curious than useful, the knowledge of which . . . serves chiefly to enable us to keep clear of it. . . ."[43] Contrast this remark with what emerges from papers like "The Architecture of Theories" (1891) or "Evolutionary Love" (1893). In the latter Peirce offers a speculative account of the origins of life, scientific laws, and the universe itself:

> [W]e can readily foresee what sort of metaphysics would be constructed from those conceptions [chance, law and "habit-taking"]. Like some of the most ancient and some of the most recent speculations it would be a Cosmogonic Philosophy. It would suppose that in the beginning—infinitely remote—there was a chaos of unpersonalized feeling, which being without connection of regularity would properly be without existence. This feeling, sporting here and there in pure arbitrariness, would have started the germ of a generalizing tendency.[44]

So too in "Synechism, Fallibilism, and Evolution" (1897) we find:

> In view of the principle of continuity, the supreme guide in framing philosophical hypotheses, we must . . . regard matter as mind whose habits have become fixed, so as to lose the power of forming them and losing them, while mind is to be regarded as a chemical genus of extreme complexity and instability. . . . *All this, according to the writer, constitutes a hypothesis capable of being tested by experiment.*[45]

Peirce does not say how anyone could go about confirming this hypothesis, but to claim—appearances notwithstanding—that it is not metaphysics and to confirm such a claim are very different matters.

Even for those who might think that Peirce's brand of pragmatism leaves no place for God, he has a reposte. He believes in God, and he also believes that "we can catch a fragment of His thought, as it were," insofar as our scientific discoveries allow "us to *predict* what will be the course of nature." If one asks what, besides references to nature's regularity, points to God's existence, Peirce answers with more of an admonition than an explanation: ". . . as to God, open your eyes—and your heart, which is also a perceptive organ—and you will see him."[46] When Peirce describes the heart as "a perceptive organ," visions and reminders of Jonathan Edwards's "sense of the heart" return. Peirce was an Anglican, not a Calvinist, but we can still be surprised by language that sounds more mystical—more Transcendental—than positivistic. He goes even further and says that to deny that "direct experience" furnishes us with the idea of God is to violate the key regulative precept of his description of the scientific method: "*Do not block the way of inquiry.*"[47]

How does a laboratory man and a positivist make room in his philosophy for both evolutionism and speculative metaphysics? The question is difficult to answer, especially when Peirce articulates a metaphysical hypothesis and then claims that in principle, if not in fact, it can be tested experimentally.[48] David Gruender, in "Pragmatism, Science, and Metaphysics," thinks that Peirce can make good the marriage between his metaphysics and pragmatic positivism. Referring specifically to Peirce's "sometimes speculative thinking in metaphysics," he adds:

> He has theories about basic categories in nature and in human life, theories about relationships between them, from the role of evolutionary theory to inductive methods. . . . But all of these theories arise out of the stimulus of experience and the selection and deliberation that follow, and all have

> consequences for human action. Likewise, all are fallible . . . , and Peirce offered them in the spirit of an inquirer who hopes others will carry on the investigations he has begun. . . .[49]

This sounds good, but will it do? Even if metaphysical theories and speculation originate in experience, this alone does not make them consistent with Peirce's pragmatic maxim. Wright argued, as we have seen, that the viability of a scientific theory has almost nothing to do with its origins and almost everything to do with its being verifiable. But to say that we might conduct ourselves in one way or another as a consequence of adopting a certain metaphysical hypothesis does not make the hypothesis verifiable.

An idealist like Bishop Berkeley was confident that everything—including all physical objects—is a collection of ideas in a perceiving mind, but how do the idealist's actions and expectations confirm his belief? The only way that they could do so is through his acting a certain way and expecting a set of consequences to follow *if* the universe is entirely mental, and Berkeley insists that we will and should behave in exactly the same ways whether we think the universe is mental or material. Acting on the idealist's hypothesis is far from verifying an idealist's hypothesis, but it is also the case that acting on Peirce's metaphysical speculations falls far short of what Peirce requires from the pragmatic maxim.[50]

There is also the problem of Peirce's doctrine of *fallibilism*. As a fallibilist he claims, "we cannot in any way reach perfect certitude nor exactitude. We never can be absolutely sure of anything, nor can we with any probability ascertain the exact value of any measure or general ratio."[51] This position is far from novel. "Many of the greatest minds of all time have held it for true." The doctrine applies to the issue of "absolute certainty concerning questions of fact." We are inclined to think first of empirical facts, but presumably Peirce regards metaphysical hypotheses as statements that are supposed to introduce a special kind of facts, in other words, facts that do not confront our senses directly nor appear to us through any inference that we can confirm with our senses. The implication is that all metaphysical pronouncements, like all ordinary empirical statements, are uncertain; hence it seems the claims of metaphysicians, including those of Peirce in his metaphysical essays, labor under two difficulties. First, they cannot be verified and, second, because they cannot be verified, their status is that of fallible conjectures that are suspect precisely because nothing from actual or possible experience can be enlisted to count in their favor.

Peirce against the Stereotypes: A Closing Observation

Peirce's willingness to make room for a certain kind of metaphysics, namely the kind that he approves, is not what we expect from reading only his most famous essays. We can say the same thing about his attitudes toward nineteenth-century American capitalism. These are just as surprising if we embrace standard accounts of pragmatism as the philosophical complement to a growing, commercial America. Instead of shaping the contours of his pragmatism around America as he found it, Peirce was more inclined to worry about America and about the industrial Western world in general: ". . . the conviction of the nineteenth century is that progress takes place by virtue of every individual's striving for himself with all his might and trampling his neighbour under foot whenever he gets a chance to do so. This may actually be called the *Gospel of Greed*.[52]

The pursuit of profit and the assumption that such a pursuit is the vital "business" of life leave Peirce cold and disappointed, but this is his assessment of the nineteenth century or what he also calls the "Economical Century." He fears that "Americanism" amounts to "the worship of business, the life in which the fertilizing stream of genial sentiment dries up or shrinks to a rill of comic tit-bits."[53]

Cornell West writes that Peirce's antipathy toward capitalism and commercialism have a good deal to do with his respect for the sciences: ". . . just as Emerson deploys the rhetoric of a market society against this society in defense of human personality [individuality], so Peirce uses the rhetoric of the natural sciences against the rugged individualism of his day for the sake of individuality in community."[54] Peirce understands the sciences as social disciplines or enterprises in which fine minds work collectively (but not by denying individual attainments) toward the truth as a shared goal. There is, however, probably something more at, or near, the bottom of Peirce's indictment of economic materialism and "an exaggeration of the beneficial effects of greed. . . ."[55]

We might keep in mind Peirce's remarks about the best scientists who pursue their studies apart from questions of application and practicality.[56] Their passion for truth and understanding is not guided by a need to link their discoveries to developing better machines for fabricating products or to perfecting processes for maximizing industrial production. The issue for Peirce is the too narrow notion that scientific discovery and knowledge are worthwhile just because of their potential utility. This is to forget the inherent value of thoughtful inquiry and to treat the individual sciences as instruments of personal and corporate aggrandizement. It is to impinge upon the spirit of uninhibited investigation that is essential to successful scientific activity.[57]

There is also the issue of *imagination* that is of first importance to Peirce's conception of pure scientific activity: "It is not too much to say that next after the passion to learn there is no quality so indispensable to the successful prosecution of science as imagination. . . . The scientific imagination dreams of explanations and laws."[58] Scientific activity at its highest and most inspired registers requires scientists whose imaginations are as prodigious as their skills. Any limitation on the imagination inhibits pure scientific progress, and for Peirce research and experimentation for the sake of a better product or new commodity manifests reigning in the powers of scientific imagination. Science as the servant of manufacturing, distribution, and trade lacks the purity and integrity that Peirce demands.[59]

Given Peirce's view of the sciences and of their proper "business," a view that may have been too severe or rarefied for the sensibilities of America's Gilded Age (c. 1870–1910), there should be no need to ask, "What good is dispassionate inquiry?" For him its good is transparent. No, science never gives us "absolute certainty, absolute exactitude, absolute universality." To expect any of these from the sciences is to expect more than they can deliver.[60] If, however, Aristotle was correct and some human beings pursue "science in order to know, and not for any utilitarian end," then Peirce too is correct.[61] Scientific knowledge is the reward for directed, scrupulous scientific activity. Sincere and capable scientists revel in their increased intellectual grip on the universe. For them, as for Peirce, that is more than a sufficient compensation for their time, effort, and occasional disappointment. Whether or how scientific knowledge leads to wealth and to a more comfortable life is the concern of industrialists, developers, and bankers, not of Peirce.

A discussion of Peirce should conclude with a few reminders. Peirce is a pragmatist who is sometimes indifferent to consequences. He is a positivist who tolerates metaphysics and speculates about the ultimate "stuff" and origins of an evolving universe. He philosophizes throughout the Gilded Age but remains deeply suspicious of the commercial and monopolistic character that nearly defines the age. He values reason deeply but also writes positively about the role of habits in conduct and feeling in religion. Perhaps Peirce is Lovejoy's best argument for his claim that describing any philosopher as a "pragmatist" invites a measure of ambiguity.

William James (1842–1910)

William James is in some sense the star of the pragmatists' show. The most widely read of the grand American triumvirate, he is also a stylist of the highest water and, like Peirce, as much at home in the sciences—experimental psychology and medicine—as in philosophy.[62] He and Henry, truly a world-class novelist, are probably the most distinguished brothers in American history. Their father Henry James, Sr., was an eccentric dilettante whose interests ranged from religious philosophy and the pseudosciences to the mystical writings of Emanuel Swedenborg.

The Jameses were not old-line American aristocrats. Unlike Wright and Peirce, both of whom could trace their American roots into the late seventeenth century, they were New York descendents of Irish immigrants who had to win their social success with a mix of charm, talent, and intellectual attainment.[63] William's attainments were prodigious. He entered Harvard in 1861 and was graduated with a medical degree in 1869. It was, however, disciplines in which he had no formal training that interested him more than medicine. After a period as a lecturer at Harvard in anatomy and physiology, he began teaching philosophy and psychology. In 1880 he was named an assistant professor of philosophy. Two years earlier he had married Alice Howe Gibbons and eventually became the father of five children.[64]

Despite being the effective leader of the Harvard Department of Philosophy in its golden age, William was never fully satisfied with himself as a philosopher or an educator. There are some periods in James's life in which it is not an exaggeration to say that he was almost pathologically dissatisfied with himself.[65] "He always felt himself at a disadvantage in arguments with people with a real training in logic. . . . And when he retired from teaching, he complained to Henry that 'as a *professor* I always felt myself a sham, with its chief duties of being a walking encyclopedia of erudition'."[66]

What matters for understanding the history of philosophy in America is how others assess James, not how he assesses himself. The prevailing view of his colleagues, successors, and readers, including many who did not or do not endorse his pragmatism, is that he stands at or near the summit of what is worth celebrating in American philosophy. According to Morton White,

> After the reader escapes earlier imitators of British and continental philosophy, he discovers in the case of James a new intellectual globe, a luminary about whom the American philosophical world rotated for a generation beginning in 1890, when James' great *Principles of Psychology* appeared. James . . . was unquestionably the central figure in the pragmatic movement at the turn of the century, the major spokesman for *America's distinctive philosophy*.[67]

If White is correct, with James, Emerson's wish for a cultural declaration of independence finds its first philosophical realization. What are some of the essential features of James's pragmatism?

The Pragmatic Method for Settling Disputes and the Pragmatic Theory of Truth: James on the Meaning of Pragmatism

Pragmatism (1907), dedicated "to the memory of John Stuart Mill from whom I first learned the pragmatic openness of mind," is James's summary of philosophical themes and theses that he had promoted earlier in his career. In "What Pragmatism Means," the second chapter of this book, James undertakes briefly to describe the two elements that, more than any others, entitled him to call his philosophy "pragmatism."

The first of these elements is "*the pragmatic method*," which James characterizes as "primarily a method of settling metaphysical disputes that might otherwise be interminable." Given, for example, competing philosophical "notions," such as whether we are free or determined, whether the world is one or many, whether the universe is material or spiritual, Jamesian pragmatists summon their method "to try to interpret each notion by tracing its respective practical consequences. What difference would it practically make to any one if this notion rather than that notion were true?"[68] If it turns out that those who debate some metaphysical alternatives are unable to find a practical (consequential) difference between them, "then the alternatives mean *practically* the same thing, and all dispute is idle."[69]

Although James gives Peirce full credit for having been the first to state the pragmatic principle or maxim, it is clear that he had interpreted and used the maxim far more elastically than Peirce had intended. This was Peirce's complaint and the source of his decision to rename his own philosophy "pragmaticism." In general terms, James goes beyond Peirce in deriving a nest of characteristics from one who looks to practical consequences of choices and hypotheses:

> A pragmatist turns his back resolutely . . . upon a lot of inveterate habits dear to professional philosophers. He turns away from abstraction and insufficiency, from verbal solutions . . . , from fixed principles, closed systems, and

> pretended absolutes and origins. He turns toward concreteness and adequacy, *towards facts, toward action and towards power.* That means the empiricist temper regnant and the rationalist temper sincerely given up.[70]

But this "empiricist temper," with its emphasis on consequences and the power that comes from the application of the philosophical intellect to trying to solve real problems, is not anti-metaphysical. Here we find a fundamental difference between Peirce and James. Peirce maintains some metaphysical beliefs. James, whatever his personal beliefs, offers a philosophy that is careful to separate metaphysical claims from an open-door policy toward metaphysical and religious convictions. This is the point and the difference. Where Peirce says that eons ago everything was primordial, undifferentiated *feeling*, James says that if the belief truly matters to someone that eons past all was feeling and if this belief makes a difference in how she lives or confronts life here and now, then whoever believes this metaphysical thesis is justified solely on the grounds that it makes a difference to her.

For James, therefore, the importance of the pragmatic method is that it opens doors that other philosophies, such as Platonism, Absolute Idealism, and logical positivism, close. The criterion for accepting or for rejecting a metaphysical, moral, or religious hypothesis is, first, what the hypothesis offers a putative believer and, second, what additional roads to enrichment it might offer to anyone else who accepts it. So understood, "what the pragmatic method means" is an *"attitude of looking away from first things, principles, 'categories,' supposed necessities; and of looking towards last things, fruits, consequences, facts."*[71]

James admits that praising the pragmatic method and its emphasis on the "cash-value" of ideas is not the same as explaining it. We address his attempt to explain how the method works in the next section. For the present, however, we should look at another hat that James's pragmatism wears, namely, at pragmatism as it designates a theory of truth that Peirce, among others, rejected as much too subjective.[72]

Peirce and James do agree that the fundamental laws of the established sciences, such as Galileo's law of falling bodies or Kepler's laws of planetary motion, "are only approximations." They are not part of some absolute "transcript of reality"; rather, according to James,

> "[T]ruth" in our ideas and beliefs means the same thing that it means in the sciences. It means . . . nothing but this, *that ideas (which themselves are but parts of our experience) become true just in so far as they help us to get into satisfactory relation with other parts of our experience. . . .* Any idea upon which we can ride, so to speak; any idea that will carry us prosperously from any one part of our experience to any other part, linking things satisfactorily, working securely, simplifying, saving labor; is true for just so much, true in so far forth, true *instrumentally.*[73]

One might complain that the problem with this view of truth is not so much that it is too subjective but that it is circular. It says that "true ideas" are ideas that are "true *instrumentally*." If, however, we are not yet clear what it means for an idea or statement to be true, we are no nearer the mark in being told that this category of ideas or statements is instrumentally true.

Putting the problem of circularity aside, we come back to a scientific example from James's view of truth. In the sciences it is always possible, as history so frequently shows, that a theory can be threatened by data that do not square with it. We need only think of the phases of Venus and the retrograde movement of the planets as inexplicable within the ancient Ptolemaic picture of a heliocentric solar system. Copernicus, zealous for a comprehensive, less complicated picture of the solar system, found that shifting the position of the earth and sun in the Ptolemaic system provides what he sought. The move to a heliocentric system and away from one that is geocentric allowed Copernicus and his successors to retain a good deal that Ptolemy had worked out in geometrical detail.

For James the Copernican theory is *true* because it does a better job of harmonizing established and formerly inexplicable data. Moreover, it does its job without requiring that astronomers jettison established beliefs that hold both for the Ptolemaic and Copernican systems: "This new idea is then adopted as the true one. It preserves the older stock of truths with a minimum of modification, stretching them just enough to make them admit the novelty, but conceiving that in ways as familiar as the case leaves possible."[74]

Against critics of the pragmatic theory of truth, James maintains that this view of truth is neither so subjective nor so elastic as we might at first think. He insists that our older stock of truths controls and restricts us from too easily conferring the epithet "true" on this or that novel proposition. He believes that most of us are essentially conservative where our long-held beliefs and theories are concerned. We will relinquish these beliefs and theories if and only if new and commanding evidence of otherwise unexplained experiences leaves us no choice.

On the other hand, James certainly says enough about truth that one wonders how seriously to take his remarks with respect to the durability of established truths. After all, he writes: "A new opinion counts as 'true' just in proportion as it gratifies the individual's desire to assimilate the novel in his experience to his beliefs in stock. . . . *When old truth grows, then, by new truth's addition, it is for subjective reasons. . . .*"[75] This surely looks like the kind of subjectivism about which Peirce and critics of pragmatism worry. If, however, we look a little closer, James's subjective approach to truth may be more benign than it first appears. He notes, for example, that pragmatists approach truth as they approach other questions that cannot be resolved by appeals to empirical criteria: "'Grant an idea or belief to be true', it says, 'what concrete difference will its being true make in anyone's actual life . . . what, in short, is the truth's cash-value in experiential terms?'"[76]

Once pragmatism asks these questions, the answers emerge: "*True ideas are those that we can assimilate . . . and verify. False ideas are those that we cannot*. That is the practical difference it makes to us to have true ideas; that, therefore, is the meaning of truth. . . ."[77] James says that this is the thesis he is concerned to defend. On this view truth is not a "stagnant property" that belongs to some ideas but not to others; rather, truth is part of a dynamic process. An idea "*becomes* true, is *made* true by events. Its verity *is* in fact an event, a process: the process namely of its verifying itself, its veri-*fication*."[78]

The displeasure that critics experience at reading remarks like those James makes about truth stand in more or less direct proportion to their own prepossessions about truth. If a critic maintains some version of the correspondence theory of truth, the theory that a proposition like "Snow is white" is true if and only if snow is white, then James's talk about truth as a process, truth as about what happens to an idea, truth as performing a marriage function within our experience, sounds odd. But if James's critics look at the way that he actually describes true ideas or statements and if one is willing to appeal to the scientific model that James has in mind, his conception of truths is less idiosyncratic.

A working scientist develops or considers a hypothesis and asks, among other things, whether it is congruent with those facts that he wishes to explain. To make this determination, he tests the hypothesis against both established beliefs about which he has no doubts and against novel beliefs that he wishes to justify and to explain. The test of whether hypothesis *a* can successfully connect established beliefs to new and still tentative beliefs is to see whether experience and observation verify, corroborate, and assimilate *a*. This amounts to asking whether beliefs about which we are comfortable, hence have no grounds to doubt, and novel beliefs about which we would like to be comfortable confirm *a* and find their explanations through *a*.[79]

If we couple this model of scientific verification to James's bewilderment about what anyone could mean, given the correspondence theory of truth, by claiming that true ideas "copy" or "agree with" the objects of which they are true, then the pragmatic theory of truth loses a great deal of its shock value.[80] James's position comes to this: We are entitled to call "true" those beliefs or statements that conform to our experience and that do not jar or unsettle already established truths. Far from being radically at odds with a standard correspondence theory, the difference between the pragmatic and traditional theories of truth is that pragmatists emphasize the emergence of truths as part of a process and correspondence theorists claim, according to James, that they discern a one-for-one fixed relation between some state of affairs and some statement purporting to report that state of affairs. Pragmatists like James emphasize activity and engagement; correspondence theorists settle for passive apprehension of a static relation between things or events and ideas of these things or events. According to Bruce Wilshire, in a searching essay on James, the point to keep in mind is this:

> Truth must be an actual co-creation of our inquiring selves and the rest of the world. So, about any *determinable* matter, James wants to say that *once a question is asked* (his emphasis) there is the possibility of only one true answer. . . . Lacking evidence, we do not know which answer this is. All we can responsibly mean by truth is the answer that would come to our question were we to get the evidence.[81]

Throughout this talk about truth and true beliefs, the fundamental issue for James is the process involved in coming to what we call "true," not the subjectivity of truth. In most cases, pragmatists like James call "true" or "false" exactly what everyone else calls "true" or "false." When James comes close to the position "A proposition is true when believing it maximizes desire-satisfaction," his readers and interpreters need to look carefully at the context.[82] In cases in which our persistent, unsettling doubts cannot be eliminated by the empirical or logical verification of comforting beliefs, in other words, cases that involve metaphysical and religious questions, we are entitled to believe what produces comfort, fruitful activity, and helpful consequences.

So understood, then, verifiable and unverifiable beliefs, which are not even verifiable in principle, serve the same function: They harmonize our experiences and integrate them in such a way that we are better equipped to get about in the world. The difference between these distinct sets of beliefs—and it is undeniably a major difference—is that one of them, the set which is religious and metaphysical, does its job even though its beliefs cannot be confirmed.

For James doing the job is what finally matters most. If for some people a belief in God, the existence of an immaterial soul, and free will satisfies previously unfulfilled desires and gives life meaning that it otherwise lacks, then so much the better for this set of beliefs. Calling beliefs "true" does not mean they correspond to anything. We have already seen that James cannot make sense of this view of truth.[83] Calling them "true" insofar as they enable believers to act and to profit from the consequences of their actions is another matter. In this context "*p* is true" means the same thing as "*p* leads to actions, attitudes, commitments and habits that are life-enriching." If, therefore, a true belief is one that makes a difference and that promotes some good, then the pragmatic conception of truth is entirely at home within the framework of James's pragmatism.

Denying Agnosticism and Acquiring Commitment: "The Will to Believe" and "Is Life Worth Living?"

"The Will to Believe" (1896), an address to the philosophy clubs of Yale and Brown, has emerged as James's most famous philosophical essay. More clearly than in any of his other essays, we see here his rendering of pragmatism at work. James's concern is the "defense of our right to adopt a believing attitude in religious matters" even when "our merely logical intellect may not have been coerced."[84]

In order to defend the "right" at issue, James employs some terminology: (a) *hypothesis* designates anything that someone might consider believing, where *deadness* marks a hypothesis that neither appeals to the person in question nor induces any inclination to act. *Liveness*, on the other hand, marks a hypothesis that appeals to someone and induces in him or her an inclination to act. Finally, (b) *option* amounts to a decision between two hypotheses. Such an option can be *living* or *dead*, *forced* or *avoidable*, and *momentous* or *trivial*.[85]

Whether an option between hypotheses is living or dead, forced or avoidable, momentous or trivial depends upon the person who confronts it and has nothing to do with a set of intrinsic properties. Referring to the remarkable French philosopher, mathematician, and physicist Blaise Pascal (1623–1662) as his antecedent, James says that the option whether to believe in the God of orthodox Catholics makes no impression on a confirmed atheist, Muslim or Protestant. "It is evident that unless there be some pre-existing tendency to believe in masses and holy water, the option offered to the will by Pascal is not a living option."[86]

James's position against agnostics who refuse to affirm or to deny a proposition, unless they are compelled by logical arguments or by firm empirical evidence, is that we often believe things for which no logically compelling arguments and no hard evidence exist: "Here in this room, we all of us believe in molecules and the conservation of energy, in democracy and necessary progress . . . , *all for no reasons worthy of the name*."[87] This is the claim that brings James to his basic thesis: "*Our passional nature not only lawfully may, but must, decide an option between propositions, whenever it is a genuine option that cannot by its nature be decided on intellectual grounds; for to say, under such circumstances, 'Do not decide, but leave the option open,' is itself a passional decision—just like deciding yes or no, and it is attended with the same risk of losing the truth*."[88]

To those who reject an appeal to anyone's "passional nature" on the grounds that such an appeal is romantic, irrational nonsense, James replies with one of those lines that are as quotable as they are informative: "Objective evidence and certitude are doubtless very fine ideals to play with, but where on this moonlit and dream-visited planet are they found?"[89]

Agnostics, to whom the essay is directed, insist that in all matters, "*We must know the truth; and we must avoid error*." Although James agrees that on balance it would be better to be right than wrong, he also knows that in spite of our caution we err frequently.[90] In certain cases, therefore, our "passional nature" is entitled to choose when the decision in favor of option *a* over option *b* cannot be guided by the intellect. In other cases, when a choice between competing hypotheses can in principle be settled rationally or empirically, we are obligated to suspend judgment and to wait on the evidence or the demonstration.[91]

James's concern in "The Will to Believe" is that class of questions, hypotheses, and options that *cannot* be answered or selected on the basis of what works in the sciences, mathematics, and logic. Science can tell us what is the case, not what *ought* to be the case or what is of greater *worth* than something else. Here we must find our answers in "what Pascal calls our heart" and James calls our "passional nature"; for they cannot come from anything else. Furthermore, James's position in this context is one he also defends in "Is Life Worth Living?" (1895), in which faith and passional commitment are described as creating facts that otherwise never would have existed: "There are . . . cases where a fact cannot come at all unless a preliminary faith exists in its coming. *And where faith in a fact can create the fact*, that would be an insane logic which would say that faith running ahead of scientific evidence is the 'lowest kind of immorality' into which a thinking being can fall."[92]

With all of this in mind and with a firm conviction that empirical data and demonstrative arguments will never be in a position to settle religious and moral questions, James writes that religion says (1) "*The best things are the more eternal things*," and (2) "*We are better off even now if we believe her first affirmation to be true*."[93] Those who cannot even confront the possibility that (1) and (2) might be true are outside the audience to whom James speaks throughout "The Will to Believe." He is addressing the thoughtful, open-minded agnostic, not the doctrinaire atheist. He is speaking to those who agree with him that nothing in the sciences or the canons of logic can answer religious questions but who cannot bring themselves to believe or act on what falls outside the data of sense and the deductions of reason. James is making clear one of the many ways in which his pragmatism reveals and revels in its "*anti-intellectualist* tendencies."[94]

For those open-minded members of his audience and for those who later read "The Will to Believe," James is insisting that religion is a momentous option. Why? In choosing to adopt the religious hypothesis, we are supposed to gain "even now . . . a certain vital good." He is also persuaded that "religion is a *forced* option so far as that good goes." If we insist upon the agnostic suspension of judgment, we deny ourselves all possibilities for the good as obviously as if we chose to disbelieve. For James, then, a skeptic's withholding assent is an option of its own: "*Better risk loss of truth than chance or error*—that is your faith vetoer's exact position."[95] This expression of skeptical or agnostic rationality, withholding judgment until clinching evidence settles the issue, is far from rational. Waiting on evidence before making a life-changing commitment, when the demand for agnostic-erasing evidence is never satisfied, is for James foolish and self-denying: "I . . . cannot see my way to accepting the agnostic rules for truth-seeking, or willfully to agree to keep my willing nature out of the game . . . *a rule of thinking which would absolutely prevent me from acknowledging certain kinds of truth if those kinds of truth were really there, would be an irrational rule.*"[96]

We have already seen that James, as an empiricist and fallibilist, has the strongest possible doubts that we will ever come by absolute truth, what he describes as truth with a capital "T." Anyone can wait for absolute truth, "but if we do so, we do so at our peril as much as if we believed. In either case we *act*, taking our life in our hands." In the final analysis James shares and endorses Pascal's insistence that belief can be secured in a way that has nothing to do with the principles of established rationality. Both agree: "*Le coeur a ses raisons que la raison ne connait pas.*"[97]

"Is Life Worth Living?" (1895), a lecture to the Harvard YMCA, is in some respects a codicil to "The Will to Believe." Can one argue convincingly to the extreme skeptic, such as the suicidal man or woman, that life is valuable enough to continue living? This is the task that James sets for himself. The skeptic he wishes to convince is one who believes in an indifferent universe that may be governed by "an awful power that neither hates nor loves, but rolls all things together meaninglessly to a common doom. This is an uncanny, a sinister, a nightmare view of life. . . ."[98] But even this skeptic, freed from the burdens imposed upon him by a religious conscience and poised to aid others with no supermundane expectations, can find worth, meaning, and purposes in living: "Thus, then, we see that mere instinctive curiosity, pugnacity, and honor may make life on a purely naturalistic basis seem worth living from day to day to men who have cast away all metaphysics . . . , but who are resolved to owe nothing as yet to religion and its more positive gifts."[99] And in "What Makes a Life Significant" (1892), James argues that a significant life can be crafted by those of us who take up ideals and combine them "with pluck and will," as well as "dogged endurance and insensibility to danger." The union of these is what matters. "There must be some sort of fusion, some chemical combination among these principles, for a life objectively and thoroughly significant to result."[100]

We know from "The Will to Believe" that the life that is truly worth living, and worth living in overdrive, is a religious life, which is lived on the belief "that there stretches beyond this visible world an unseen world of which we know nothing positive, but in its relation to which the true significance of our present mundane life consists."[101] More than this, James is persuaded "that we have a right to believe" that the order within our gaze and grasp is partial. We are entitled to believe that there is a spiritual order that, on faith and trust, argues the case that life is worth living.

In remarks that prefigure what we have already seen in "The Will to Believe," James insists that the sciences cannot answer all our questions about the universe, and they can answer none of our questions about the meaning and purpose of life. For those disposed to believe that life is truly meaningful only if there is an invisible spiritual universe beyond our visible world, science has nothing to say: "And if needs of ours outrun the visible universe, why *may* not that be a sign that an invisible universe is there? What, in short, has authority to debar us from trusting our religious demands?"[102] If scientists say that their discoveries trump our religious faith and hopes, James replies that the sciences at their best have only a fragmentary glimpse of the nature of things. Authentic faith and belief, the position of positivist scientists notwithstanding, sometimes generate facts rather than discover them. "Suppose . . . that you are climbing a mountain, and have worked yourself into a position from which the only escape is by a terrible leap. Have faith that you can . . . make it, and your feet are nerved to the accomplishment."[103]

This same kind of faith can also make it true that life is worth living. If a person finds joy, in spite of persistent evil and misfortunes, "in trusting ever the larger whole," has he not himself made life worth living? This is James's rhetorical question, and this is his answer: "This life is worth living, we can say, *since it is what we make it, from the moral point of view*; and we are determined to make it from that point of view . . . a success."[104] From this perspective, the objections of scientists who are constantly searching for palpable evidence do not matter to the faithful. James ends "Is Life Worth Living?" with an admonition: "Be not afraid of life. Believe that life *is* worth living, and your belief will create the fact."[105]

Criticisms of James's position in "The Will to Believe" and "Is Life Worth Living?" persist. Agnostics will still insist that genuine beliefs must be generated and sustained by the kind of evidence that scientists demand. Philosophical empiricists and positivists will insist that James abandons his own empiricist commitments when it suits him to do so. Still others, even if they wish to be sympathetic to James's justification of faith and the value of life, will argue that a willingness to believe and belief itself are two different matters. Even as Peirce insists that doubts are not generated merely by putting a question mark after a statement, so James's critics can remind him that the will to believe is not enough to produce the belief at issue. Nonetheless, what critics reject does not alter what James affirms. Morton White is, therefore, justified to describe James as "a grandchild, if not a child, of the romantic movement" and to add that James "sympathetically quoted Pascal's statement about the *heart's* reasons, and vigorously contended for the view that metaphysical and religious truth may be established by *sentiment* rather than by reason."[106]

"A World of Pure Experience" (1904): James's Generous Empiricism

At the conclusion of a discussion of James's philosophy, it is appropriate to say a few words about an element of his mature philosophy that is perhaps logically independent of his pragmatism, namely what he calls "Radical Empiricism" in the essay "A World of Pure Experience." James writes that radical empiricism as distinct from the empiricism of Berkeley, Hume, and Mill "must neither admit into its constructions any element that is not directly experienced," nor fail to do "full justice to conjunctive relations."[107] What makes this empiricism radical?

From at least as far back as Plato's *Theaetetus*, Berkeley's *Principles of Human Knowledge* (1710), and Hume's *A Treatise of Human Nature* (1739–1740), empiricists, or those who speak for or against the principles of empiricism, have granted there are problems knowing just what to say about *relations*.[108] That they are "objects" of immediate or direct experience is Hume's position, but his attempt to deal with them as such objects is strained in his treatment of spatial and temporal relations.[109] Berkeley, despite his claim in the first section of the *Principles* that all "*objects* of human knowledge" are *ideas*, admits in the second edition of the *Principles* "that *ideas, spirits* and *relations* are all in their respective kinds the objects of human knowledge . . . , and that the term 'idea' would be improperly extended to signify everything we know or have any notion of."[110]

James's solution, which he thinks makes a semi-chaotic world more coherent and which conforms to the character of direct experience, is to treat relations, especially *conjunctive* relations, as no different from any other data of immediate experience. Referring to the status that radical empiricism accords to relations—spatial and temporal relations, causal relations, relations between the ideas and experiences that constitute individual self-conscious minds—James writes: "Radical empiricism . . . is fair to both the unity and the disconnection. It finds no reason for treating either as illusory. It allots to each its definite sphere of description, and agrees that there appear to be actual forces at work which tend, as time goes on, to make the unity greater."[111]

Once James admits conjunctive relations as ingredients of experience whose credentials are as impeccable as any of the other data in an empiricist's picture of the world, artificial problems of philosophy should disappear. We need not, for example, try to account for personal identity or for individual selves through fictions like a substantial and metaphysical *mind, soul, spirit*, or *ego*. These baseless "entities" fail to explain the unity of consciousness and they fall outside the range of all possible knowledge.[112] On the other hand, when Hume denies all such metaphysical accounts of self-identity or self-consciousness, he also concedes that he is at a loss to explain the source for the unmistakable reality of self-consciousness.[113]

Radical empiricism cuts through this Gordian knot. It agrees with Hume that we are not justified to affirm the reality of mental substances when we can never encounter them in experience. It disagrees with Hume that we find no conjunctive relations when we turn our attention toward ourselves and seek principles to account for the unity of ourselves. We find, according to James, just those conjunctive and intimate relations that unify the impressions, ideas, perceptions, and memories that each of us are entitled to call absolutely his or her own.

Beyond what James says about relations and about the experiential limits of knowledge, he also borrows a theme from his theory of truth and incorporates it into his epistemology. Just as he could not make sense of the way that truth, beliefs, or propositions are held to represent or copy the facts about which they are supposed to be true, so too in his epistemology he discards representation or correspondence in favor of process and success. When we claim to know something, some object or state of affairs, what we mean on analysis is that given a certain process and end in view, the process is successful and the end in view is reached.[114]

In more concrete terms, to say that *S* knows *p*, where *S* is the knowing subject and *p* is the object of knowledge, is for James to say (1) *S* believes that *p*; (2) various steps or occurrences in *S*'s experience verify *p*; and (3) these steps or occurrences justify *S*'s belief that *p*.[115] As James sees it, this picture of knowledge and of how we come to know does not violate what common sense understands or would understand by knowledge if unphilosophical men and women thought about their claims to know something. Furthermore, this theory of knowledge does away with the traditional problem of representative perception, in other words, a problem that leads to difficulties accounting for our knowledge of the world when we cannot bridge the gap between the phenomena we know and the trans-phenomenal world to which we have no sensuous access.[116]

Whether one considers James's account of the pragmatic method, the pragmatic theory of truth, or the foundations of radical empiricism, a constant theme is always present. That theme—when it is contrasted with positivism or with metaphysics that affirms its version of idealism, materialism, or the Absolute—is an endorsement of plasticity and generosity. James makes no secret of his pluralist, nominalist, empiricist prepossessions, nor is he deaf to alternative philosophical voices. And his open-ended theory of truth, like Peirce's most general first principle, does not block the road to inquiry. A position that squares with "any element that is directly experienced" is welcome to takes its place within the open arms of Jamesian pragmatism.

And, as we have just seen, no theory of knowledge is tested by its failure to answer this unanswerable question: Do the data of our immediate experience represent, copy, or correspond to realities that are beyond all possible experience? Instead, pragmatists like James ask whether we can know facts by tracing a chain of experiences to the point that they validate what we believe or certify what we hope is the case.[117] This he insists is the theory of knowledge that is bound to the argument in *Essays in Radical Empiricism*. By omitting the self-defeating search for what is inherently unknowable and by admitting that conjunctive relations are as much a part of experience as are the disjunctive relations defended by traditional empiricists like Hume and Mill, we can reasonably satisfy our desire to know.

One would have to force the issue to characterize James's pragmatism as emblematic of the American spirit, even if there were no ambiguity about what the

American spirit is. To be sure, he speaks for progress and objects to capitalism only when middle-class men and women, who are often capitalists themselves, lose their zest for life and trade adventure for the unthreatening comfort of their neighborhoods and clubhouses.[118] But if there is something about James's philosophical thought that is shaped by America, it is probably the openness and willingness to embrace change and to venture beyond what is familiar. James is not the philosophical equivalent of a pioneer heading into the western sun, hoping to find a better life and to make his fortune as well. Still, like restless pioneers who sought more than what they could find at home and who were prepared to take chances to find it, James announces and promotes a kind of philosophical restlessness.

The agnostic should willingly and willfully act, thus risk being mistaken on the chance that he might find something more fulfilling than his doubts. The too cautious positivist-empiricist should entertain the possibility that there are metaphysical realities if, in so doing, his deepest longings are satisfied and thereby make a positive difference in the way he lives. The seeker after truth should understand that the absolute, immutable truth he desires is the kind of truth that he will never find. But this should not deter him from searching for tentative truths that might displace what he has comfortably believed for some time.

The ideas at the foundations of James's pragmatism belonged to James, but the backdrop against which they develop is probably the general direction of American life and culture just after (and even before) the Civil War. Citizens of the United States—except those descended from slaves who remained enslaved by institutional segregation—were unfettered by class distinctions, a state church, or the intrusions of a suffocating government. There was room to grow, and there were abundant opportunities to explore. It is simplistic to claim that James's philosophical thought was the effect of the national atmosphere; it is far less simplistic to claim that Jamesian optimism and his endorsement of risks for the sake of rewarding consequences reflected this atmosphere.

Seventy-five years before James reached his philosophical stride, the Duc de La Rochefoucauld-Liancourt spent three years in the northeastern United States. His primary observation was that America ". . . is a country in flux"; hence "that which is true today as regards its population, its establishments . . . , its commerce will not be true six months from now."[119] This is an observation that James almost certainly would have approved. Inertia, security at the expense of novelty, the veneration of specious eternal truth, and comfort with the *status quo* are for James threats to lives worth living: "It is, indeed, a remarkable fact that sufferings and hardships do not, as a rule, abate the love of life; they seem, on the contrary, usually to give it keener zest. The sovereign source of melancholy is repletion. Need and struggle are what excite and inspire us; our hour of triumph is what brings the void."[120] For better or for worse, the United States in the last decades of the nineteenth century and in the first decade of the twentieth century—the United States that James knew in his philosophical maturity—was bursting with vitality. Some of this national *brio*, expressed in expansionist policies and in echoes of Manifest Destiny, is difficult to celebrate. Our concern here is not to judge America's past but to recognize it as a hospitable backdrop to James's philosophy. If pragmatism was likely to root somewhere, it was in the United States that this philosophy found fertile ground for germination and growth. To extend this botanical metaphor, James took the decisive step: He made pragmatism the first philosophy to bloom in America without a heavy dose of foreign additives.

John Dewey (1859–1952)

John Dewey was born in Burlington, Vermont, in the year that Darwin published *The Origin of Species* and lived until 1952. He received his bachelor's degree from the University of Vermont, after which he spent two years teaching secondary school in Oil City, Pennsylvania. Dewey returned to Vermont where he taught briefly and submitted essays to the *Journal of Speculative Philosophy*. Encouraged by his first formal steps in the world of published philosophy, he entered Johns Hopkins as a graduate student. There he studied logic under Peirce but was more interested in the philosophy of Hegel, which was fashionable for a time in some American universities. After receiving his Ph.D., Dewey became an instructor at the University of Michigan. He remained in Ann Arbor for ten years.

Dewey moved from Michigan in 1894 to accept a professorship and to head the Department of Philosophy and Psychology at the recently founded University of Chicago. He left Chicago in 1904 to join the faculty of Columbia University and remained at Columbia until he retired from teaching in 1930. Retirement from life as a university professor did not result in retirement from the philosophical life. Residing in New York until his death, Dewey continued to write, lecture, and embrace assorted liberal, social, and political causes.

Books that Dewey wrote after his retirement include *Philosophy and Civilization* (1931), *Art as Experience* (1934), *Liberalism and Social Action* (1935), and *Logic: The Theory of Inquiry* (1938). From the time that he died to the present, excluding a relatively short period in the 1950s and 1960s when pragmatism fell out of fashion, Dewey has been widely regarded as the most significant American philosopher of the twentieth century. With the revival of pragmatism that continues into the early years of the present century, coupled with the tendency of positivists to edge closer to the thinking of pragmatists, there is little doubt that Dewey's philosophy, like that of the other great pragmatists, will endure and influence generations of philosophers still unborn.[121]

"The Influence of Darwin on Philosophy" (1909): Dewey in Defense of Darwin

If an author is not quite clear where to begin some observations on Dewey's philosophy, he or she can justifiably start with Dewey's lectures on Darwin, which he gave at Columbia University in 1909. The date, fifty years after the publication of *The Origin of Species*, is auspicious. More important for purposes of this essay than its ceremonial bow to Darwin, Dewey's lecture "The Influence of Darwin on Philosophy" provides unambiguous hints into the nature of his own philosophical leanings just beyond the midpoint of a long and productive life.

What is central in Dewey's praise for Darwin is the value of change. Dewey looks with disdain on the ancient Greek belief, which was carried into the nineteenth century, that species are fixed and immutable. That they are immutable is not only a fact, according to ancient, medieval, and early-modern philosophers; it is good. On this pre-Darwinian picture of knowledge and its objects, change amounts almost to a four-letter word:

> Since . . . the scene of nature which directly confronts us is in change, nature as directly and practically experienced does not satisfy the conditions of knowledge. Human experience is in flux, and hence the instrumentalities of sense-perception and of inference based upon observation are condemned in advance. Science is compelled to aim at realities lying behind and beyond the processes of nature, and to carry on its search for these realities by means of rational forms transcending ordinary modes of perception and inference.[122]

This passage includes themes that are vintage Dewey and that would repeat themselves in his later writings. Here also is Dewey's impatience with philosophers who devalue experiential changes that, in his view, scientists and philosophers should try to know. And here, of course, is his rejection of any philosophy that posits some transcendent world of fixity as the supposed reality toward which all inquiry should aim.

Darwin insisted that species are not fixed realities and that new species come into being throughout time even as some older species disappear forever: "When [Darwin] said of species what Galileo had said of the earth, *e pur se muove*, he emancipated, once for all, genetic questions and experimental ideas as an organon of asking questions and looking for explanations."[123] Although Dewey admits in "The Influence of Darwin on Philosophy" that it is still too early to know precisely how Darwin's theory will affect philosophy, the outlines of its impact are visible. The notion of a purposeful world, aspiring by some occult spiritual forces to realize its goal, loses whatever respectability it has managed to retain.

The argument from design, advancing from the world as a well-crafted artifact to an intelligent and inexpressibly powerful God as its architect, no longer appeals to reflective men and women: "If all organic adaptations are due simply to constant variation and the elimination of those variations which are harmful in the struggles for existence that is brought about by excessive reproduction, there is no call for a prior intelligent causal force to plan and preordain them."[124]

When the preoccupation with the universe as a product of an omnipotent God recedes, philosophy can turn to the business that Dewey always favors and understands as its proper role: "Interest shifts from the wholesale essence back of special changes to the question of how special changes serve and defeat concrete purposes."[125] The problems that vex us even as they demand our attention, as well as the opportunities this world can provide, become the proper interest of philosophers who neither fear nor debase change. Philosophy is forced to become respectable, to deal with problems and rich possibilities that confront us and that refuse to fade into the mists of rarefied metaphysics and idealized religions.

What is at the core of Dewey's praise for Darwinian science and for its effects on philosophy? It is his belief that intellectual progress takes place when apologists for discredited ideas—philosophers who debate whether the universe is the product of design or of chance and who cannot imagine that it is neither—revise their thinking. "Old questions are solved by disappearing, evaporating, while new questions corresponding to the changed attitude of endeavor and preference take their place. . . . Doubtless the greatest dissolvent in contemporary thought of old questions . . . , is the one effected by the scientific revolution that found its climax in the 'Origin of Species'."[126]

Whether Dewey promotes Darwinian biology as the spur to correct thinking, or whether he is antecedently firm about what philosophy should be doing and is glad that Darwin provides support, is not entirely clear. Either way, this much is beyond question: Whatever its source, Dewey saw that the job of philosophy was—as Francis Bacon, Thomas Hobbes, and Karl Marx had seen before him—to know the world in order to alter it to human advantage.

In whatever manner Dewey came by this working assumption, Darwin's emphasis on the effects of change in nature served as a reminder that changing the world is possible through the intervention of directed thought and experimentalism. The key is to engage the world, not to flee from it. Darwinian science served, at least in Dewey's estimation, as an eminently successful reminder that man-made change can be imposed on the world where natural changes are already at home. This is the world of our acquaintance and the world in which we must live. It is a world of which we are naturally a part.

The Denial of the Mind-Body Distinction: A Defense of Naturalism

Dewey's understanding of mind is that of a confirmed naturalist who is impatient with specious dualities. And once he denies the mind-body distinction, he introduces elements into our mental life that point directly to his rendering of pragmatism. So he writes in *Art as Experience* (1934): "Popular psychology and much so-called scientific psychology have been pretty thoroughly infected by the idea of the separateness of mind and body. . . . The separation, when it is once made, certainly confirms the theory that mind, soul, and spirit can exist and go through their operations without any interaction of the organism with its environment."[127]

The denial of this facet of dualism is not new with Dewey. Aristotle rejected Plato's dualism, claiming his own alternative that the soul is the form of the body, not an independent substance that for sixty-five or seventy years takes up residence in a body. Spinoza does the same when he rejects the Cartesian view that "man in Nature . . . [is] a dominion within a dominion," and we have already seen in Essay 5 that Chauncey Wright makes no sense of the position that the human mind is a supernatural intrusion into an organic body.[128]

Dewey goes beyond his predecessors to add that when we use "mind" in its usual acceptation, not as a term of art, we are very close to the proper meaning of the word and what it denotes:

> It seems to me . . . , that the idiomatic use of the word "mind" gives a much more truly scientific, and philosophic, approach to the actual facts of the case

> than does the technical one. For in its non-technical use, "mind" denotes every mode and variety of interest in, and concern for, things: practical, intellectual, and emotional. It never denotes anything self-contained, isolated from the world of persons and things, but is always used with respect to situations, events, objects, persons and groups.[129]

This estrangement of mind from its body and of an intelligent organism from its environment is what Dewey cannot tolerate. Apart from amounting to a counterfeit dualism, which has nothing but the reveries of metaphysicians on which to rest, this estrangement is yet another effort to remove human beings from the natural world to which, like every other organism, they belong.

Dualists, whatever their intent, separate putatively spiritual minds, together with their various cognitive faculties, from the activities and forces that our bodies cannot escape. The inevitable consequence is the factitious notion that minds are insulated from the demands that nature makes on our bodies.[130] A related and no less important consequence is that the proper activity of a mind is to know, while that of bodies is to engage with nature. On this account, therefore, leisure is the condition that enables a mind to discharge its role. The clutter of nature is what those who labor, those whose bodies are also their tools, must daily confront.[131] Human beings at leisure thus find a way to emancipate themselves from the messy and threatening world of change. Commenting on this aspect of Dewey's objections, Joseph Ratner writes that the calm and security we all seek is, according to doctrinaire dualists, unavailable in the world that we encounter at the level of sense and conventional experience. "[T]he royal road that has time and again been sought by all peoples is the road of imagining another world wherein none of the hardships and at least all the delights of this world are to be found and perpetually enjoyed."[132]

Dewey finds nothing except our desire for security that supports mind-body dualism. He believes and insists that once philosophers disabuse themselves of this hollow blend of spiritualism, religion, and insecurity, they can turn their attention to the world to which they belong and which is the appropriate and authentic "object" of inquiry and knowledge.[133] "We may reject the traditional dualism. In my conviction we should reject it. We cannot be scientific save as we seek for the physiological, the physical factor in every emotional, intellectual and volitional experience."[134]

The Quest for Certainty: The Problems of Dualism Enlarged

The interaction of mind and body is what philosophers and historians of philosophy usually have in mind when they discuss the problem of dualism. This was, for example, Descartes's emphasis when he tried in *The Passions of the Soul* (1649) to explain how mind and body, two ontologically independent substances, could possibly interact causally. For Dewey, however, dualism shows itself in the broader landscape of Western philosophy, which includes the writings of Plato, Aristotle, Descartes, Kant, and others whose reputations are less august than those of these giants. We discover a good deal about this dualistic contagion in *The Quest for Certainty*.

Once ancient philosophers took that initial step of seeing human beings as duplexes of rational minds and sensing bodies, a host of consequences in theories and judgments followed. First, as we have already seen in "The Influence of Darwin on Philosophy," one niche developed for serious inquiry (the rational activity of mind) and another, lower realm for conventional action.[135] There was also a cleavage between pure mental activity and mere practical action. Practical activity of any kind occurs in the order of change, not that of authentic being. By dint of this fact alone, practice is inherently inferior to disinterested thought.

Moreover, buying into the view that there are two distinct orders, one that is real and the other that is mutable and less real, leads to a division between knowledge and belief. "[Knowledge] is demonstrative, necessary—that is, sure. Belief on the contrary is only opinion; in its uncertainty and mere probability, it relates to the world of change as knowledge corresponds to the realm of true reality."[136] This leads to the division that Dewey finds most troubling and wishes most to overcome, namely that between what is and what merely becomes:

> The realm of the practical is the region of change, and change is always contingent; it has an element of chance that cannot be eliminated. . . . What *is*, in the full and pregnant sense of the word, is always, eternally. It is self-contradictory for that which *is* to alter. . . . That which *comes* to be, never truly is. . . . The world of generation is the world of decay and destruction. Whenever one thing comes into being something else passes out of being.[137]

Again, anyone who reads "The Influence of Darwin of Philosophy" sees what little tolerance Dewey has for a philosophy or philosophical movement that indicts change and situates all value and reality in an immutable order, an order that has no being outside the minds of those who invent it.

A willingness to take change seriously and the tension between theory and practice are not the only causalities of dualism. If real objects of knowledge are supposed to be unchanging realities, then there is no way, in fact or in principle, to know the world in which most of us admit that we live. What Dewey calls the "spectator theory of knowledge" is the result. On this theory objects of knowledge are subsistent entities that passively await our coming to know them. We apprehend them immediately and as they are. On the other side, sensible objects in the world of conventional experience are always mediated by the condition of the perceiver or knower and by the medium through which our attempts to get at them is distorted or refracted.[138] These facts and consequences of dualism lead Dewey to the principal thesis of *A Quest for Certainty* and to a thesis that is central to his entire philosophy:

> All of these notions about certainty and the fixed, about the nature of the real world, about the nature of the mind and its organs of knowing, are completely bound up with one another, and their consequences ramify into practically all important ideas entertained upon any philosophic question. They

> all flow—such is my basic thesis—from the separation (set up in the interest of the quest for absolute certainty) between theory and practice, knowledge and action.[139]

The trouble with this binary view of the world is that it is spurious.

Flight from the world of our experience, expectations, successes, and frustrations, always underpinned by the background effort to acquire certainty and its comforts, inevitably fails. No matter how hard we try and no matter what theories we contrive, the natural world, the world that drew the scientific attention of Galileo, Newton, Franklin, and Darwin, is irrefragable. It intrudes upon and pulls at us as much as it intrudes upon every other organism. The natural world is here to stay; its pull is too strong to permit the most metaphysically driven philosophers to escape it. What, therefore, can we do to find a measure of comfort, even happiness, within this real world, since from Dewey's perspective we will find it no where else?

Experience, Inquiry, Experimentalism, and Truth: Indispensable Elements in Dewey's Philosophy

Knowing what Dewey criticizes and rejects is obviously different from knowing what he promotes. If, however, students of philosophy in America do not have some idea of Dewey's own thought, not simply his objections to what others have thought, their picture of Dewey is fragmentary. Beyond that, they will be pressed to say why Dewey is routinely described as a pragmatist. We need, therefore, to get some idea about what Dewey defends and about why he defends it.

We begin with a few words about Dewey's conception of experience, but getting at this conception is by no means straightforward. Still, we can infer from titles of books such as *Experience and Nature* and *Art as Experience* that Dewey's interest in the character of experience is not casual. One of the problems of saying, narrowly just what Dewey understands by experience is that sometimes he is content to tell us what it is not: It is not principally "a knowledge-affair" but is "an affair of the intercourse of a living being with its physical and social environment," nor is it chiefly "a psychical thing, infected throughout by 'subjectivity'." Experience is not the record of what is past. "[E]xperience in its vital form is experimental, an effort to change the given." Even the sometimes elusive nature of aesthetic experience is not for Dewey radically divorced from other kinds of experience: "In as far as the development of an experience is *controlled* through reference to these immediately felt relations of order and fulfillment, that experience becomes dominantly esthetic in nature. The urge to action becomes an urge to that kind of action which will result in an object satisfying in direct perception."[140] A few pages later Dewey adds, "In a distinctively esthetic experience, characteristics that are subdued in other experiences are dominant . . . namely, the characteristics in virtue of which the experience is an integrated complete experience on its own account."[141]

Aesthetic experiences produce a satisfaction that one may not find in other experiences, but it is a mistake to think of aesthetic objects, the moving causes for aesthetic experiences, as occupying an inherently distinct class from that of other objects. A Renaissance painter or sculptor produces a lifelike portrait or bust, which generates an aesthetic experience in those who look carefully at it, but the portrait or bust was also produced to help remember someone in a dynasty. So if the likeness does its job, the aesthetic experience also has practical or instrumental consequences. There are other motives at work as well as those that are an artist's aesthetic aims. Haydn composed the lyrical Farewell Symphony no. 45. This is a composition of musical art, but it also was a practical hint in November 1772 to his patron that the orchestra has been overworked and that it was time to let the musicians return to their homes for a rest.[142]

Experience, despite what eighteenth- and nineteenth-century empiricists believe, is not atomistic and disjunctive; rather, it "is pregnant with connections." Traditionalists treat experience and thought as "antithetical terms." These traditionalists, whether they are identified as rationalists or as empiricists, believe:

> Inference . . . goes beyond experience; hence it is either invalid, or else a measure of desperation by which, using experience as a springboard, we jump out to a world of stable things and other selves. But experience, taken free of the restrictions imposed by the older concept, is full of inference. There is, apparently, no conscious experience without inference; reflection is native and constant.[143]

To this quotation and the previous remarks about what experience is and is not, we can add Richard Bernstein's observation that Dewey's treatment of experience develops and changes as Dewey himself moves philosophically from a brief interest in Hegelian idealism to the settled pragmatic naturalism of his later years.[144] What does Dewey finally understand by experience?

Never far from the influence of Darwin and the biological revolution that Darwin's evolutionary theory introduced, Dewey says that to understand the meaning of "experience" is to keep in mind the actual relations between an organism and its environment. Above all else, this requires us to exorcise the notion that experience is little more than a living organism's passive reception of sensory data that act upon it from without.

> Experience becomes an affair primarily of doing. The organism does not stand about . . . waiting for something to turn up. It does not wait passive and inert for something to impress itself upon it from without. The organism acts in accordance with its own structure, simple or complex upon its surroundings. . . . The living creature undergoes, suffers, the consequences of its own behavior. *This close connection between doing and suffering or undergoing forms what we call experience.*[145]

And in *Experience and Nature*, at the beginning of Dewey's discussion of the proper philosophical method, we read ". . . experience is *of* as well as *in* nature. It is not experience which is experienced, but nature—stones, plants, animals, diseases, health, temperature, electricity, and so on. Things interacting in certain ways *are* experience; they are what is experienced."[146]

Is this conception of experience, "as constituting the entire field of man's relation to the universe so broad as to be useless?" This is George Geiger's question and Geiger, one of Dewey's many interpreters, certainly knew what questions had to be asked and answered. Does Dewey tell us enough about experience as he calls upon and employs it in his philosophy?[147] The answer is yes. Dewey's use of experience is not so general that it ceases to be useful. We must simply understand its importance in designating transactions, that is, connections, between organisms and their environment. So understood, experience names everything "that passes between the organism and its surroundings." Geiger concludes "that 'experience' stands for all commerce between man and nature—the gross, the physical, and the automatic as well as the refined and self-conscious."[148]

Granting that Geiger correctly describes what Dewey has to say about the nature of experience, how does his view of experience as "all commerce between man and nature," whether that commerce is reactive and noncognitive or purposeful and cognitive, help us to understand the larger fabric of Dewey's philosophy? To answer this question is to know what Dewey says about inquiry, that is, about the species of transaction that generally involves putting questions to nature and our environment. It is also an answer that shows an important side of Dewey's debt to Peirce.

In *Logic: The Theory of Inquiry*, Dewey offers his definition of "inquiry": "*Inquiry is the controlled or directed transformation of an indeterminate situation into one that is so determinate in its constituent distinctions and relations as to convert the elements of the original situation into a unified whole.*"[149] Like other aspects of Dewey's writings, this definition of "inquiry" does not tell us immediately all that we wish to know about the subject, but we can make a start by linking it to what he says about experience.

If experience involves all kinds of transactions between human beings and their environment, inquiry is a far more specific transaction between our world and us. How does Deweyan inquiry arise? As natural organisms, we are sometimes disturbed, puzzled, confused, or unsettled by interruptions in the continuity of our experience.[150] In some cases we feel, in other cases we recognize intellectually, a perturbation in our environment that we wish to eliminate or, at a minimum, mitigate. Anything that provokes or unsettles us can be a call to knowledge, a call to deploy our intelligence and thereby, in revising or developing new practices, to overcome what troubles us.[151] Thus, our need to know something is contextual. It arises from some real need and does not emerge *ex nihilo*.

We can express the same point in more specific terms by following Dewey's lead in *The Quest for Certainty*: "Uncertainty is primarily a practical matter. It signifies uncertainty of the *issue* of present experiences; these are fraught with peril as well as inherently objectionable. Action to get rid of the objectionable has no warrant of success and is itself perilous. . . . The natural tendency of man is to do something at once; there is impatience with suspense, and lust for immediate action."[152]

What Dewey describes in this text is the "problematic situation." This is the irritation that something in our environment causes, but reacting or blindly acting leaves the problematic situation and its attendant irritation unresolved. If anything at all turns this state of affairs into a problem to be addressed and solved it is thinking or what Dewey describes as "deferred action." With the judicious application of thought as a substitute for undirected responses to the irritation or uncertainty that leads to irritation, the problematic situation is transformed into a problem: "The first and most obvious effect of this change in the quality of action is that the dubious or problematic situation becomes *a* problem. The risky character that pervades a situation as a whole is translated into an object of inquiry that locates what the trouble is, and hence facilitates projection of methods and means of dealing with it."[153]

The problematic situation becomes a problem for those organisms that, possessing and employing mental capabilities, can respond "to the doubtful as such." The possession of mental capacities, in addition to qualities that are solely emotional and volitional, is what marks the distinctive and often fruitful response to what is doubtful and uncertain. Dewey is here issuing his defense for deferred, as opposed to purely emotional, reactions to whatever is problematic: "The intellectual phase of mental action is identical with an *indirect* mode of response, one whose purpose is to locate the nature of the trouble and form an idea of how it may be dealt with—so that operations may be directed in view of an intended solution."[154]

All in all, then, a problematic situation is so generic as to be indistinct. An organism feels the irritation of that situation but is not prepared to deal with what it finds irritating. The use of intelligence applied to the uncertain, doubtful, or irritating situation makes it, more narrowly, a problem. Intelligence enables those who have it to discover and to focus their attention on precisely what leads to uncertainty and discomfort. So too the further application of intelligence, as it seeks greater understanding of what is doubtful and what can be done to replace doubts with comparatively stable beliefs, often (but not always) ends in a problem solved. This solution, made possible by the deferred action that is effected through intelligence, amounts to knowledge: "Anything that may be called knowledge, or a known object, marks a question answered, a difficulty disposed of, a confusion cleared up, an inconsistency reduced to coherence, a perplexity mastered."[155]

At the same time, Dewey is able to express and, as he sees it, to solve that persistent problem to which we have already referred in a previous section. What is mind, and how do we account for its capacity to intercede in nature if it is not already part of nature? Dewey's answer is to treat mind *instrumentally*, not to reify it. "There is no separate 'mind' gifted in and of itself with a faculty of thought. . . . Thinking is objectively discoverable as that mode of serial responsive behavior to a problematic situation in which transition to the relatively settled and clear is effected."[156] Mind is present wherever human beings respond productively to problematic situations. Thought is what enables agents to treat problematic situations as problems that they can solve. Once "mind" and "thought" are described in terms of what some human beings do in cases that require action to secure beneficial consequences, traditional worries about how minds and bodies interact, or how thinking differs metaphysically from sensing, lose their sting.[157]

Dewey also notes the sense in which action, guided by the cognitive arsenal for directed inquiry, is indispensable to productive consequences or problem solving. "Experimental operations change existing conditions. Reasoning, as such, can provide means for effecting the change of conditions but by itself it cannot change it. Only execution of existential operations directed by an idea in which ratiocination terminates can bring about the reordering of environing conditions required to produce a settled and unified situation."[158]

This anatomy of experience, inquiry, and the instrumental character of thinking permits Dewey to address additional issues to which he refers throughout the development of his philosophy. First, if thinking well is not alone sufficient to bring about changes in one's environment and, as a result, in one's comfort and security, then we see again that the persistent separation between people who think and people who labor is wafer thin. Beneficial consequences, the kind that Dewey and other pragmatists praise, depend on instrumental thinking. Guided, thoughtful action is still action; hence, the notion is defective that the truly happy man or woman is the purely intellectual man or woman.[159]

Happiness for Dewey requires the solution of problems and the comfort consequent on overcoming that class of problems that unsettle the relation between human beings and their environment. Acting rationally and deliberately, thereby trying through intelligent and deferred action to change the problematic features of our surroundings, is necessary for helping anyone to secure the happiness he or she wants. If this looks more like an unexceptional truism than a serious philosophical claim, then one should see why Dewey recurrently invites his readers to review the history of philosophy, with special attention to that artificial division between thinking and doing: "The effective condition of the integration of all divided purposes and conflicts of belief is the realization that intelligent action is the sole ultimate resource of mankind in every field whatsoever."[160] Whether this is or is not a truism is secondary to the dominant historical facts of Western philosophy, facts that for Dewey are detrimental to the reputation and value of all philosophy. As long as contemplation is regarded as superior to practice and to knowing the world of change, and as long as speculative hypotheses occupy a higher order than experimentalism, change and knowledge are inimical.[161] It is no exaggeration to say Dewey is incredulous that so many philosophers turn away from the world that confronts them on the grounds that, when judged against the criteria for authentic knowledge, it is unknowable and unworthy of being known.

A second point is also worth making. Although Dewey, following Peirce, characterizes doubt and uncertainty as uncomfortable because he believes that for most of us that is what they are, he too is an apologist for the attitude, as well as the method, of scientists who ask their own questions of an environment that extends from microbes to stars. This is where we see most clearly the difference between "ordinary thinking and thinking that is scrupulous." What is the difference?

> A disciplined mind takes delight in the problematic, and cherishes it until a way out is found that approves itself upon examination. The questionable becomes an active questioning, a search; desire for the emotion of certitude gives place to quest for objects by which the obscure and unsettled may be developed into the stable and clear. *The scientific attitude may almost be defined as that which is capable of enjoying the doubtful.*[162]

The model for scrupulous thinking is that which we find in the sciences. Scientists, as Dewey understands them, do more than try to understand nature or to unlock its secrets, although this is unquestionably part of their vocation.

Inventive scientists, far from merely wishing to know nature as it confronts them, are eager, as experimentalists rather than unimaginative empiricists, to alter the data and to put questions to nature whose answers pose additional questions. The process is unending, but its immediate consequences are a more subdued natural world, one that answers human needs and questions.[163]

> As long, for example, as water is taken to be just the thing which we directly experience it to be, we can put it to a few direct uses. . . . When, however, water is treated not as the glistening, rippling object with the variety of qualities that delight the eye, ear, and palate, but as something symbolized by H_2O, something from which these qualities are completely absent, it becomes amenable to all sorts of other modes of control and adapted to other uses.[164]

Whether or not it is intentional, Dewey hints at Francis Bacon's metaphorical sketch of the emphasis in a proper scientific method. Bacon writes in the first book of his *New Organon* (1620): "Those who have handled sciences have been either men of experiment or men of dogmas. The men of experiment are like the ant; they only collect and use. The reasoners resemble spiders who make cobwebs out of their own substance. But the bee takes a middle course. It gathers its material from the flowers of the garden and of the field, but transforms and digests it by a power of its own."[165]

Bacon's ants, although he calls them "men of experiment," are pure inductivists who collect data but have no idea what to do with the data they amass. Their catalogs of nature's contents are neither instructive nor groundbreaking. Spiders, like metaphysical dogmatists, fashion elegant webs out of their own constitutions, but these webs, like the hypotheses of speculative philosophers, have no bearing on experience and, as fabulous hypotheses, never touch ground. Only bees, traditional symbols for fruitful industry, take from nature what they can use and then convert it into something that would never have existed without their effort. Despite the different terminology, Bacon's bees are very close to Deweyan experimentalists.[166]

Given Dewey's commitments to experimentalism as the most satisfactory expression of inquiry, we can ask how he understands the connection between inquiry and truth. Dewey raises this question in the *Reconstruction in Philosophy* and in other writings.[167] In one of his clearest accounts of truth, which is reminiscent of what James said earlier about the same subject, Dewey writes:

> Now an idea or conception is a claim or injunction or plan to act in a certain way as to arrive at the clearing up of a specific situation. When the claim or pretension or plan is acted upon it *guides us truly or falsely*; it leads to our end or away from it. Its active, dynamic function is the all-important thing about it, and in the quality of activity induced by it lies all its truth and falsity. The hypothesis that works is the *true* one; and *truth* is an abstract noun applied to a collection of cases, actual, foreseen and desired, that receive confirmation in their works and consequences.[168]

A few lines later Dewey adds that treating what is true in terms of intended and fruitful consequences does not entail, as critics of the pragmatic theory of truth maintain, that "true" and "false" are subjective epithets. Dewey has in mind a far more public and objective treatment of what we call "true," one that matches the public and objective character of the experimental method. He tells us that we do not describe a public road as useful because it enables brigands to ambush innocent travelers. Its usefulness "is measured by whether it actually functions as a road, as a means of easy and effective *public* transportation and communication. And so with the serviceableness of an idea or hypothesis as a measure of its truth."[169]

None of this silences every persistent philosophical critic. Bertrand Russell (1872–1970), to take a notable case, admired the pragmatists' commitment to empiricism but rejected the pragmatic theory of truth, whether it is that of James or Dewey:

> [W]e cannot agree that when we say a belief is true we mean that it is a hypothesis which 'works,' especially if we mean by this to take account of its excellent effects, and not merely of the truth of its consequences. . . . And if the pragmatist states that utility is to be merely a *criterion* of truth, we shall reply first, that it is not a useful criterion, because it is usually harder to discover whether a belief is useful than whether it is true. . . . Finally, therefore, the pragmatist theory of truth is to be condemned on the ground that it does not 'work.'[170]

No doubt, Dewey and James were often criticized for their view of truth because of the language they used to express it. To say that "ideas . . . become true" or that ideas "will be true . . . in the sense of being good for so much" seems obviously wrong to those who are accustomed to think that "true" and "false" are qualities of propositions that either do or do not correspond to the facts. Even when they point out to their critics that there is no significant way to give content to mirroring, copying, or corresponding to facts, nonpragmatists remain unconvinced.[171]

Again Russell casts his lot with unimpressed critics: "Scepticism is of the very essence of the pragmatic philosophy: nothing is certain, everything is liable to revision, and the attainment of any truth in which we can rest securely is impossible."[172] Russell probably rejects pragmatism less for its "scepticism" than because *he* sees pragmatists as a species of sophists who praise their own assumptions and theories more than truth itself.[173]

Dewey and the Marrow of Democracy, Communication, and the "Great Community"

Before concluding this discussion of Dewey, it is necessary to say a few words about his political and social attitudes. Their influence persisted and spread throughout the United States from the late 1920s forward, and remain alive into the present.[174]

Dewey was no stranger to America's social and political problems. He knew of the class divisions of the late nineteenth century, and he outlived by decades the hopes of the Progressive era, whose brief life and appeal ended with the conclusion of World War I. In a series of books, among which *The Public and Its Problems* (1927) is the most significant, Dewey attempts to address the problems of American political, social, cultural, and economic life.[175] One of these problems, to which Dewey gives his full attention, is the shift in America from an agricultural to an industrial nation. For Dewey, the political institutions that helped to secure and to protect the "pre-industrial age" were not suited to perform a cognate task in an age of technology and grand industrial capitalism. One can safely make the observation that for Dewey the "same forces that have brought about the forms of democratic government," such as extension of the right to vote and the democratic election of executives and legislators, had not produced either a government or society that seriously addresses the needs of the whole public: "'The new age of human relationships' has no political agencies worthy of it. The democratic public is still largely inchoate and unorganized."[176]

What is particularly serious from Dewey's perspective is the "eclipse of the public." Political theorists of the liberal and capitalist stripe never weary of chanting a litany to individualism. Dewey finds nothing wrong with extolling individualism, except insofar as individualism itself exists at the expense of a cohesive public. "What has happened to the public in the century and a half since the theory of political democracy was urged with such assurance and hope?"[177] Dewey's answer is that the machine age, whatever its benefits, has produced fragmentation. There are so many different groups, unions, managers, wholesalers, retailers, and consumers that the ideal of a homogenous public, with a cluster of shared values, has lost out to innumerable separate publics. "There are too many publics and too much of public concern for our existing resources to cope with."[178]

But the problems that inhibit the generation of the public, which Dewey admires were daunting. Whether it is the economic consequences of World War I that were taking shape on the eve of the Great Depression, or the failure of the federal government to answer the needs of America's citizens, the results were antagonistic to the birth of the "Great Community." Helplessness overawed any spirit of optimism: "Men feel that they are caught in the sweep of forces too vast to understand or master. *Thought is brought to a standstill and action paralyzed.*"[179]

Dewey also notices that Americans, no less than citizens of other countries, find considerable competition for their social and political concerns. Until hints of permanent prosperity were shattered on October 29, 1929, the machine age provided amusement and inappropriate diversion from public matters. Dewey's view is that men and women of his generation were endlessly willing to discuss what amuses them, what actors they prefer and what music they listen to on their radios. On the other hand, it is far more difficult "to sustain conversation on a political theme; and once initiated, it is quickly dismissed with a yawn."[180] We can add to this the degree of mobility that was unprecedented in Dewey's America. Products of industry and technology generated opportunities for mobility on a grand scale, and Americans found these opportunities too difficult to resist. "How can a public be organized, we may ask, when literally it does not stay in place?"[181]

In spite of all one might say about social ills and fragmentation, Dewey is far from blaming technology and capitalism alone for the nation's shortcomings and needs. He is no Neo-Marxist eager to destroy old institutions and to distribute capital and its sources to the workers of the world or, more narrowly, to the workers of America.[182] Dewey believes the disunity that so troubles him has largely to do with the paucity of ideas that enable us to understand the new mode of living which comes with "steam, electricity and machinery." We cannot live intellectually or sentimentally in the past when we are confronted by a nation rife with change and novel opportunities. We stand apart from each other even when we have the tools that permit us to come together and to communicate more easily than at any other time in history. Unless there is such communication, "the public will remain shadowy and formless, seeking spasmodically for itself, but seizing and holding its shadow rather than its substance."[183] Dewey's confidence in the unifying power of communication is a piece with his endorsement of scientific activity and knowledge, but what about communication outside the sciences? "Till the Great Society is converted into a Great Community, the Public will remain in eclipse. Communication can alone create a great community."[184]

For Dewey, the problem in *The Public and Its Problems* is to locate and declare the conditions that can enable the transformation of a Great Society into a Great Community. This in turn is to explain how the mere germ of a community can grow into a unified *democratic* community, where democracy "is the idea of community life itself." When we find some association of activity "whose consequences are appreciated as good by all singular persons who take part in it" and where what is good is shared and promoted by all who produce it, there we have what Dewey calls a "community."[185] As far as Dewey is concerned, the association of men and women that is necessary to a community does not require explaining. He says of "associated activity," very succinctly, "things are made that way." But on its own this fact does not give us a community. A true community has an essential moral dimension. That dimension acquires content and character through sharing common purposes. Articulating and working toward common ends and goals requires "*communication* as a prerequisite."[186]

Only through communication, through signs and symbols adopted to facilitate the flow and interchange of ideas can men and women discover those "interdependent activities" that promote directed action—action governed by a common wish to implement the fruits of our collective desires. This capacity to communicate, like knowledge itself, arises out of social contexts. These contexts are no more alien to human beings than the habits that help them to live.

We are not moved solely out of understanding what serves our individual interests. We are far more commonly animated by habits of action that reflect "social customs." But as important as habits and the behavior they produce are to survival, they are not what we look to if our interest is to know and shape the Great Community. Here Dewey turns again to scientific method and the knowledge that arises out of its judicious application to a problematic situation.

Dewey is emphatic about the importance of knowledge and its dissemination in the search for the Great Community: "There can be no public without full publicity in respect to all consequences which concern it. Whatever obstructs and restricts publicity, limits and distorts public opinion and checks and distorts thinking on social affairs. Without freedom of expression, not even methods of social inquiry can be developed."[187] Dewey is not simply talking about being allowed to speak one's mind. As in the sciences, so too in the quest for community: "positive freedom is not a state but an act which involves methods and instrumentalities for control of conditions."[188]

And there is more. Even when the sciences help us to understand human nature, and when psychology earns the respect its practitioners desire, they are truly successful only when their results are "published, shared, socially accessible." Here too Dewey and others who seek the Great Community must take a lesson from the sciences. Communicating results in the social sciences—that is, through the data of anthropology, sociology, economics, political science, and psychology—shapes public opinion: "Opinions and beliefs concerning the public presuppose effective and organized inquiry." Informed opinion, itself the consequence of directed inquiry and of knowledge freed from habit, must be public in fact and not simply in name.

What we see, according to Dewey, is that the transformation of society into community (the transformation from people whose private interests are weakly bound up with the interests of others to a "people" vigorously seeking a common good) demands "continuous inquiry," which is connected and constant. This kind of inquiry alone "can provide the material of enduring opinion about public matters."[189] We must not confuse serious, productive inquiry with what is nothing more than the latest news. Telephones, telegraphs, radios, and newspapers make it possible for society to acquire and transmit the news. But news, even if it sometimes informs society, is not always instructive. It can be distorted in the interests of business and government. For Dewey, the growth and transmission of instructive public knowledge are inseparable from the community he seeks.[190]

Nonetheless, for Dewey a "democratic community" is nothing more than a phrase; it requires content to generate value and to secure what is best in men and women. This content is supplied by something more than a nominally representative republic. The people must themselves be involved. They must care deeply to preserve the values that democracies are supposed to protect: freedom, equality, the vote, uninhibited communication, and the unfettered search for knowledge. Out of this symphony of opportunities and potential for productive change a Great Community can develop—"a society in which the ever-expanding and intricately ramifying consequences of associated activities shall be known in the full sense of the word, so that an organized, articulate Public comes into being."[191]

If there are underlying themes in Dewey's remarks, apart from the significance of community and joint activity that looks to an instantiated common good, they are the importance of communication itself and the scientific model for effective communication. Dewey finds nothing vague in his message. To implement and enjoy the values that citizens of a democratic community cherish is at a minimum to know these values and to articulate them to one's friends, neighbors, coworkers, and legislators. To know that these values are worth securing, that they are not empty names for what no one desires, is to use something like the method of the sciences to investigate their social utility. Here the pragmatic Dewey shows his hand: "'Laws of social life . . . are like laws of engineering. If you want certain results, certain means must be found and employed."[192] This amounts to applied science in the service of enriching the lives of men and women as social animals. As the value of scientific discoveries and theories depends in part upon their distribution, so too the benefits of living in a community cannot be tested and certified unless they are freely communicated.[193]

Perhaps it is odd, or perhaps it is fitting, that Dewey closes *The Public and Its Problems* with an approving nod to Emerson, the great apologist for self-reliant individuality. The unity that Emerson found through Reason and a metaphysical participation in the life of the Over-Soul, is a rough anticipation of Dewey's version of a need and source for unity understood as a community: "We lie, as Emerson said, in the lap of an immense intelligence. But that intelligence is dormant and its communications are broken, inarticulate and faint until it possesses the local community as its medium."[194] In very simple terms, Dewey, no less than Emerson, insists that the tension between a democratic society and its individual citizens is sometimes serious but too often overstated. When a democracy functions as it should, society turns itself into a community of needs and common expectations. This is the context, the Great Community, through which and from which the full flowering of self-reliant citizens is possible.[195]

NOTES

1. Reprinted from *Journal of Philosophy* (January 16, 1908), 29–39, in *The Development of American Philosophy*, ed. and intro. by W. G. Muelder, L. Sears, and A. V. Schlabach, 2d edition (New York, 1960), 431.
2. Ibid. 437.
3. Lewis Menand, *The Metaphysical Club*, (New York, 2001), 153.
4. "What Pragmatism Is" (1905), in *The Collected Papers of Charles Sanders Peirce*, ed. Charles Hartshorne, Paul Weiss, and Arthur W. Banks (8 vols., Cambridge, Mass., 1931–58), V, 411. Hereafter abbreviated as CP, followed by the volume and pages cited.
5. *The Metaphysical Club*, 159.
6. Ibid. 162.
7. *Philosophical Writings of Peirce*, ed. Justus Buchler (New York, 1955), ix–x.
8. CP, I, 3–4.
9. Ibid. V, 366.
10. Ibid. 366–7.
11. Ibid. 371; emphasis added.
12. Ibid. 372; cf. 417.
13. Ibid. 375; emphasis added.
14. Ibid. 376.
15. Ibid.; emphasis added.
16. Ibid. 378.
17. Ibid. 382; emphasis added.
18. Ibid. 383.
19. Ibid.
20. Ibid. 384.
21. Ibid.; emphasis added.
22. Ibid.
23. Ibid.
24. Cornell West, *The American Evasion of Philosophy* (Madison, 1989), 46.
25. CP, V, 391.
26. Vincent Calopietro, "Charles Sanders Peirce," in *Pragmatism and Classical American Philosophy: Essential Readings and Interpretive Essays*, ed. John J. Stuhr, 2d edition (Oxford, 2000), 45.
27. CP, V, 400.

28. Ibid. 398.
29. Ibid. 402; emphasis added.
30. Ibid. 403.
31. Ibid.
32. Ibid. 406.
33. Ibid. 407.
34. Ibid. 409.
35. "The Scientific Attitude and Fallibilism" (1896–99), CP, I, 55.
36. Ibid. 76.
37. Ibid. V, 414.
38. Ibid. 423.
39. Ibid.
40. Ibid. 197; emphasis added.
41. For a still instructive account of the American traditions that are never far from the central themes of classical pragmatism, or pragmatisms, see George Herbert Mead (1863–1931), "The Philosophies of Royce, James, and Dewey in their American Setting" (1929), reprinted in *The Development of American Philosophy*, 351–60.
42. CP, I, 45; emphasis added. See also 55 and 78.
43. Ibid. V, 410.
44. Ibid. VI, 33.
45. Ibid. 101; emphasis added.
46. "The Conception of God" (1898), CP, VI, 493.
47. Ibid. I, 135; emphasis added.
48. See Philip P. Wiener's comments in *Evolution and the Founders of Pragmatism* (Cambridge, 1949), 84–6.
49. *The Relevance of Charles Peirce*, ed. Eugene Freeman (La Salle, 1983), 283–4.
50. CP, V, 422.
51. Ibid. I, 147.
52. Ibid. VI, 294.
53. Ibid. I, 673. See also *The American Evasion of Philosophy*, 46–9.
54. Ibid. 45.
55. CP, V, 376.
56. Ibid. I, 76.
57. Ibid. 47.
58. Ibid. 43–4.
59. Ibid. 44.
60. Ibid. 141.
61. See Aristotle, *Metaphysics*, I, ii, 982b, 20–21.
62. For an economical account of James's place and influence in the development of American philosophy and psychology, see Giles Gunn's introduction to James's Pragmatism *and Other Writings* (New York, 2000), vii–xxxi. Hereafter abbreviated as *Pragmatism*.
63. *The Metaphysical Club*, 77.
64. *Pragmatism*, i–ii.
65. See the abbreviated version of Ralph Barton Perry's *The Thought and Character of William James* (Cambridge, Mass., 1948), 359–69.
66. *The Metaphysical Club*, 94.
67. Morton White, *Pragmatism and the American Mind: Essays and Reviews in Philosophy and Intellectual History* (New York, 1973), 31; emphasis added.
68. *Pragmatism*, 25.
69. Ibid.; emphasis added.
70. Ibid. 27; emphasis added.
71. Ibid. 29.
72. Roy Wood Sellars, *Reflections on American Philosophy from Within* (Nôtre Dame, 1969), 33–4.
73. *Pragmatism*, 30.
74. Ibid. 31.

75. Ibid. 32.
76. Ibid. 88.
77. Ibid.
78. Ibid.
79. Replacing irritating doubt with comfortable belief is as important to James as it was to Peirce. Ibid. 31.
80. Ibid. 88.
81. Bruce Wilshire, "The Breathtaking Intimacy of the Material World: William James's Last Thoughts," in *The Cambridge Companion to William James*, ed. Ruth Anna Putnam (Cambridge, 1997), 116.
82. Richard M. Gale, *The Divided Self of William James* (Cambridge, 1999), 118.
83. For a more elaborate rejection of truth as correspondence, see James's essay "Humanism and Truth" (1904), in *Pragmatism*, 146–67. James might also object to the correspondence theory of truth on the grounds that there is no way that we can transcend our actual or possible experience. Since this is so, we are never in a position to determine whether what we experience corresponds to some trans-experiential *reality*. See, for example, James's criticism of representational knowledge in "The Tigers in India" (1895), in *Pragmatism*, 142–5.
84. Ibid. 198.
85. Ibid. 199.
86. Ibid. 201. James refers to Pascal's celebrated "wager." For the terms of the wager and for its foreshadowing of the argument in "The Will to Believe," one can look at any edition of Pascal's posthumously published *Pensées*, paragraph 233.
87. *Pragmatism*, 203; emphasis added.
88. Ibid. 205.
89. Ibid. 207.
90. Ibid. 209–10.
91. Ibid. 211–12.
92. Ibid. 214.
93. Ibid. 214, 215.
94. Ibid. 28. For a chapter on anti-intellectualism in American philosophy, see White's *Pragmatism and the American Mind*, 78–92.
95. *Pragmatism*, 215.
96. Ibid. 216.
97. Ibid. 212. Pascal declares here, "The heart has its reasons about which reason knows nothing at all."
98. Ibid. 226. This is similar to the dark, pessimistic "picture of the last state of the universe" that the English statesman Arthur James Balfour describes and that James quotes in *Pragmatism*, 49.
99. Ibid. 232–3.
100. Ibid. 301. This essay is also a criticism of late nineteenth-century Americans who find meaning in the capitalist comfort (tedium) of the Gilded Age.
101. Ibid. 233.
102. Ibid. 236.
103. Ibid. 238. Compare "facts" in "The Will to Believe." Ibid. 213–14.
104. Ibid. 239.
105. Ibid. 240.
106. *Pragmatism and the American Mind*, 89–90; emphasis added.
107. *Pragmatism*, 315, 316.
108. See *The Collected Dialogues of Plato*, ed. Edith Hamilton and Huntington Cairns (New York, 1961), 889–91; Berkeley's *Principles, Dialogues, and Philosophical Correspondence*, ed. and intro. by Colin Murray Turbayne (Indianapolis, 1965), 65–6; and *A Treatise of Human Nature*, ed. L. A. Selby-Bigge, rev. P. H. Nidditch (Oxford, 1978), 73.
109. *Treatise of Human Nature*, 26–65.
110. *Principles, Dialogues, and Philosophical Correspondence*, 66.
111. *Pragmatism*, 317; compare 324.

112. Descartes admits as much to Hobbes. See Descartes's Third Replies to Hobbes's criticism of the *Meditations*, in *The Philosophical Writings of Descartes*, trans. J. Cottingham, R. Stoothoff, and D. Murdoch (2 vols., Cambridge, 1984), II, 124.
113. *A Treatise of Human Nature*, 636.
114. *Pragmatism*, 323.
115. Compare what is sometimes called the "tripartite conception of knowledge" as Chisholm presents it, in Roderick Chisholm, *Theory of Knowledge*, (Englewood Cliffs, 1977) 2nd ed., 102–18.
116. See *Pragmatism*, 337–9.
117. Ibid. 90–91.
118. "What Makes a Life Significant," *Pragmatism*, 286–9.
119. Quoted by Joyce Appleby in *Inheriting the Revolution*, (Cambridge, MA, 2000), 6.
120. *Pragmatism*, 230.
121. See Morton White, *Science and Sentiment in America*, (New York, 1972), 266–8.
122. John Dewey, *"The Influence of Darwin on Philosophy" and Other Essays in Contemporary Thought* (New York, 1910), 6.
123. Ibid. 9. "*e pur se muove*" in English is "and yet it moves."
124. Ibid. 11–12.
125. Ibid. 15.
126. Ibid. 19.
127. John Dewey, *Art as Experience* (New York, 1934), 262.
128. See Aristotle's *De Anima*, Bk. II, 412a, 1–424b, 19, as well as the enigmatic remarks in Bk. III, 430a, 17–25, and *A Spinoza Reader: The Ethics and Other Works*, ed. and trans. Edwin Curley (Princeton, 1994), 152. This also needs somehow to be reconciled with what Spinoza says in the *Ethics*, Pt. V, prop. 23.
129. *Art as Experience*, 262.
130. John Dewey, *The Quest for Certainty* (New York, 1929), 212–14. See also *Experience and Nature*, 2nd edition (Chicago, 1929), 308.
131. *Art as Experience*, 262.
132. *Intelligence and the Modern World: John Dewey's Philosophy*, ed. and intro. by Joseph Ratner (New York, 1939), 20.
133. That Dewey has not invented a straw-man argument to attack in his objections to dualism is clear from a Platonic dialogue like the *Cratylus*, 429d–440d.
134. From an address Dewey gave to the College of Physicians in St. Louis, 1937, and that is included in *Intelligence and the Modern World*, 827. See also *The Quest for Certainty*, 230–31.
135. *The Quest for Certainty*, 17; emphasis added.
136. Ibid. 18. Dewey's point is nicely illustrated by Plato's distinction between the philosopher (lover of knowledge) and the philodox (lover of opinion), in the *Republic*, 474b–480a.
137. *The Quest for Certainty*, 19.
138. Ibid. 23.
139. Ibid. 23–4.
140. *Art as Experience*, 50.
141. Ibid. 55.
142. Ibid. 50. See also Charles Rosen, *The Classical Style: Haydn, Mozart, Beethoven* (New York, 1972), 146, 147.
143. John Dewey, *On Experience, Nature, and Freedom: Representative Selections*, ed. and intro. by Richard J. Bernstein (Indianapolis, 1960), 19, 20–23.
144. Richard J. Bernstein, "John Dewey," *The Encyclopedia of Philosophy*, ed. Paul Edwards (8 vols. New York, 1967), II, 381.
145. John Dewey, *Reconstruction in Philosophy* (1920), expanded edition (Boston, 1948), 83. Emphasis added.
146. *Experience and Nature*, 4a.
147. *John Dewey in Perspective: A Reassessment* (Oxford, 1958), 14–15.
148. Ibid. 17–18.
149. John Dewey, *Logic: The Theory of Inquiry* (New York, 1938), 66–67.

150. Ibid. 67.
151. *Reconstruction in Philosophy*, 85.
152. *The Quest for Certainty*, 223.
153. Ibid. 223–24.
154. Ibid. 226.
155. Ibid. 226–27. See also what Dewey says in *On Experience, Nature, and Freedom*, 120–27.
156. *The Quest for Certainty*, 227. Compare *Experience and Nature*, 261, 272.
157. *The Quest for Certainty*, 226, 228–31.
158. *On Experience, Nature, and Freedom*, 131.
159. See in this context what Aristotle says about the activity of the happiest possible human beings. *Nicomachean Ethics*, 1178b, 20–24.
160. *The Quest for Certainty*, 252.
161. *Reconstruction in Philosophy*, 98.
162. *The Quest for Certainty*, 228; emphasis added.
163. Ibid. 100–103.
164. Ibid. 105.
165. Francis Bacon, *Selected Philosophical Works*, ed. and intro. by Rose-Mary Sargent (Indianapolis, 1999), 128.
166. For a recent discussion of the problems with Bacon's treatment of inductivism, see Perez Zagorin, *Francis Bacon* (Princeton, 1998), 87–93, 98–103.
167. See, for example, *Experience and Nature*, 288, 310, 321, 410–11.
168. *Reconstruction in Philosophy*, 128–29.
169. Ibid. 129; emphasis added.
170. Bertrand Russell, *Philosophical Essays*, revised edition (London, 1966), 129–30. See also 88–104.
171. Dewey is so fatigued by complaints that pragmatists have no conception of reality, which true statements are supposed to mirror, that he willingly concedes pragmatism "finds that 'reality' is a *denotative* term, a word used to designate indifferently everything that happens." "The Need for a Recovery of Philosophy" (1917), in *Of Experience, Nature, and Freedom*, 59.
172. *Philosophical Essays*, 105.
173. Ibid.
174. Bruce Kuklick, *A History of Philosophy in America*, (Oxford, 2001), 189.
175. Ibid.
176. John Dewey, *The Public and Its Problems* (New York, 1927), 109.
177. Ibid. 125–6.
178. Ibid. 126.
179. Ibid. 135; emphasis added. See also 137.
180. Ibid. 139.
181. Ibid. 140.
182. George Geiger, *John Dewey in Perspective* (New York, 1964), 179–84.
183. *The Public and Its Problems*, 142.
184. Ibid. See also pages 98 and 126–7.
185. Ibid. 149.
186. Ibid. 152.
187. Ibid. 167.
188. Ibid. 168.
189. Ibid. 178.
190. Ibid. 184.
191. Ibid.
192. Ibid. 197.
193. Ibid. 216–18.
194. Ibid. 219. For more on Dewey's social thought and elements that foreshadow the argument of *The Public and Its Problems*, see *Reconstruction in Philosophy*, 148–64.
195. *Reconstruction in Philosophy*, 152–3.

Essay 7
Josiah Royce, Idealist and Absolute Pragmatist: Unity, the Absolute, and Loyalty

With Josiah Royce (1855–1916) and his brand of idealism, we come to a brief interlude between the naturalist empiricism of the pragmatists and the naturalist realism of George Santayana (1863–1952), the subject of Essay 8. Royce, whose philosophy took shape from about 1885 through 1913, stands apart from every other philosopher we have encountered up to this point. He alone began life as a northern Californian who early in life sought his intellectual moorings in the East. At exactly the period in American history when hardy men and women were seeking their fortunes by migrating to the West, Royce was initiating a journey that would enable him to discover and add to the philosophical riches of the East.

Royce was born in the small town of Grass Valley where his father operated a general store to serve gold miners. Even as a very young man, Royce was turned aside by the excesses and lawlessness of the California Sierras whose gold fields and boom towns were havens for "social collapse, lynch law, drunkenness, gambling, murder, and mistreatment of foreigners."[1]

In 1866 the Royces moved to San Francisco. As a student of mining engineering, Josiah was graduated from the University of California in 1875 and was able to spend the following year in Germany, studying in Leipzig and Göttingen. His interest was no longer engineering but rather German philosophy.

On his return from Europe, Royce took up graduate studies in philosophy at Johns Hopkins University and earned a Ph.D. in the spring of 1878. After an unproductive year in Baltimore, Royce returned to Berkeley, where he taught English composition. He was uninspired by his stay in California and lamented his departure from the culturally rich cities in which he had lived during his studies in Germany and the eastern United States.

Royce did not lament long. William James, whom he had met in Boston (1875), took a year's leave from Harvard and arranged to have Royce replace him. But, as R. Jackson Wilson writes, James "gave Royce a striking clue to the situation of the intellectual even in Cambridge. You are not so very much isolated in California. We are all isolated—'columns left alone of a temple once complete.'" It was a warning that Royce must have taken to heart, for even after he had gained academic security at Harvard he never felt quite at home, and his memory often returned to California.[2]

Despite his growing nostalgia for California, toward which he felt "native," Royce remained at Harvard, where he saw himself as merely a New England "resident."[3] Still, his residency in Cambridge was long and fruitful. His writings made him partly responsible, along with those of James and Santayana, for the great Golden Age of the Harvard Department of Philosophy, and when his philosophy went out of fashion, "it was as if the temple of American philosophy itself had collapsed."[4]

An Absolute Experience: Royce and the Convergence of Epistemology, Metaphysics, and Theism

Although there are a few similarities between some aspects of Royce's philosophy and pragmatism, there is a fundamental difference that could allow his friend William James to characterize Royce as one of the many "tender-minded" metaphysicians.[5] The difference is Royce's conviction, for which he argues, that there is an Absolute whom he also characterizes as the Absolute Experience.[6] What does Royce have in mind, and why call him an "idealist" for maintaining the reality of an Absolute Experience?

To answer these questions is first to remind ourselves that for James and for many philosophers before him, there was a recalcitrant problem that philosophers themselves recognized and that their critics raised against them. This problem is explaining how anyone can get beyond private experiences of the world to show that his experience corresponds to the real world, that is to reality itself. This is how James describes a critic's argument as he begins to defend his "radical empiricism": "If a series of experiences be supposed, no one of which is endowed immediately with the self-transcendent function of reference to reality beyond itself, no motive will occur within the series for supposing anything beyond to exist. It will remain subjective . . ."[7]

James's critic notes what countless skeptics, among them Montaigne (1533–1592) and Hume, pointed out before him. An unavoidable fact is that we cannot step outside our own experience to determine whether it represents things as they are in themselves or whether there are any trans-experiential things in themselves whose reality is independent of anyone's experience. James's effort to blunt this familiar criticism is to fall back on his pragmatism and to admit that we are in a lockstep with our experience. He insists, however, that the continuity and uniformity of experience that enable us to navigate and predict *within* experience is enough to address and sometimes to attain "real goals . . . admitted as things given *in* experience."[8] In other words, the pragmatic James evades, as rationally and empirically insoluble, the traditional problem of our knowledge of an external world.

Like James, Royce also has trouble with the representationalist or "intellectualist view of reference that has a mental image mysteriously jump out of its own skin and hit some transcendent target."[9] Royce asks how our own perceptions can tell us anything about an outside world that they are supposed to copy. He grants that they cannot do the job:

> The physical fact never gets directly represented in our mental state; for between the physical fact and our experience of its presence lie the complex conditions that give our sensations their whole specific character. And what is true of our sensations is true of the rest of our experience. As it comes to us, this experience is our specific and mental way of responding to the stimulations which reality gives us. . . .
>
> Thus, then, our experience changes with the current state of our own organizations, rather than reveals the reality beyond; *and this reality beyond, as it is in itself, remains unknowable.*[10]

But Royce believes that this familiar argument is unimpressive. If we answered that the problem of knowledge, that is, the problem of knowing reality just as it is in itself, is intractable, we would be left with nothing more than a skeptic's residue. We would agree with classical skeptics that knowledge of what really is the case—assuming there is some real, objective state of affairs "out there" that is inherently knowable—always exceeds our grasp.

Royce's desire to deny skeptics their victory, in conjunction with his own philosophical and theological prepossessions, leads to his recurrent argument for God or the Absolute—an Absolute Experience. These terms are interchangeable in Royce's writings, and his argument is the same whether it occurs in *The Religious Aspect of Philosophy* (1885), *The Conception of God,* (1898) or *The Sources of Religious Insight* (1912). The argument begins interrogatively: "Is there, not as a mere possibility, any reality? The question: Is there an absolutely organized experience? Is equivalent to the question: Is there an absolute reality? . . . Our actual issue, then, is: Does a real world ultimately exist at all?"[11]

The question that Royce actually wishes to answer, despite the assorted ways that he asks it, is familiar to philosophers. Is there some omniscient reality (God or the Absolute) who knows all that there is to know—past, present, and future—or, what amounts to the same question, is there a being who knows all actual and possible experiences?

Royce's answer is yes, and he believes that even the skeptic's doubts and purported ignorance support his answer. "For my thesis . . . will be that the very nature of human ignorance is such that you cannot conceive or define it apart from the assertion that there is, in truth, at the heart of the world, an Absolute and Universal Intelligence, for which thought and experience, so divided in us, are in complete and harmonious unity."[12]

In order to support this thesis, Royce announces that which stands at the absolute center of his idealism: "Any finite experience either regards itself as suggesting some sort of truth, or does not so regard itself." The second element of this disjunction is of no interest to Royce and has no bearing on his proof. If, however, someone's finite experience suggests a truth of some sort, this is also to say that that experience is part of some larger, far more fully encompassing truth that would be included in the total experience of some absolute, omniscient knower.

A critic might, however, concede as much but reply that this absolute experience, the experience of an absolute knower, is an ideal and nothing more: "There need be no such experience as a concrete actuality."[13]

Here, according to Royce, a serious problem arises for the skeptic. If one grants with the skeptic that no universal experience, which includes all finite experiences, exists except as an ideal, where does this admission leave us? Royce's response is the marrow of his argument for the Absolute: "This ultimate limitation, this finally imprisoned finitude, this absolute fragmentariness and error of the actual experience that aims at the absolute experience when there is no absolute experience at which to aim,—this absolute finiteness and erroneousness of the real experience, I say, will itself be a fact, a truth, a reality, and, as such, just the absolute truth."[14] But for whom or for whose experience will this "absolute truth" exist?

If, in short, a finite knower, whose experience is finite, affirms that there is no absolute knower of absolute truth, that limited knower is caught in an inconsistency. After all, a finite knower, just because of its finitude, "cannot know that there is no unity beyond its fragmentariness." Further, only such an absolute experience could say with assurance: 'Beyond my world there is no further experience actual'."[15] When, therefore, a finite knower or believer asserts that there is no absolute knower of all possible experiences, that knower effectively becomes the Absolute, the knower of ultimate truth and the experiencer of an all-inclusive experience. In *The Sources of Religious Insight*, Royce makes the same point: "To assert then that there is no largest view, no final insight, no experience that is absolute, is to assert that the largest view observes that there is no largest view, that the final insight sees that there is no such insight, that the ultimate experience is aware that there is no ultimate experience. And such an assertion is indeed a self-contradiction."[16]

Royce insists that the only valid and sound conclusion one can draw from his argument is that if some possible truth is also an actual truth, it must be "somewhere experienced" *as* true. For him, it is simply axiomatic that "truth *is*, so far as it is *known*."[17] So, if one wishes seriously to claim as a fact that there is nothing outside or beyond the world of finite experience, this too is a fact that must be known and, insofar as it is such an all-enveloping fact—a fact that bears on the entire scope and limits of knowledge—it can be known only by a knower proportioned to it. And this is to say that it must be known by the Absolute or by "an absolute experience which knew all there is or that genuinely can be known; and the proposition that a totality of finite experience could exist without there being an absolute experience, thus proves to be simply self-contradictory."[18]

Royce's conclusion is supposed to be inescapable: "There is an Absolute Experience, for which the conception of absolute reality, i.e. the conception of a system of ideal truths, is fulfilled by the very contents that get presented to this Experience."[19] This experience, which is the unified whole of which all fragmentary experiences are parts, includes knowledge of all possible experience. So understood, Royce calls it the "Absolute" but is just as happy to call it "God."

This God, who also answers and actualizes an absolutely comprehensive "system of ideal truths," helps us to understand why Royce's philosophy is categorized as Absolute Idealism. The God, for whose existence as an omniscient knower he argues, experiences as a unity the whole of experience and thus all that is true about it. Omnipotence, omnipresence, and omnibenevolence may also be inseparable from the divine nature, but Royce's proof that a God exists depends upon traveling a route from finite, fragmentary knowledge and experience to knowledge that is complete and to every experience that, as possible, is also actual. An ideal knower has all possible ideas; therefore, "absolute idealism," a phrase that refers to the content of an Absolute Experience, identifies the philosophy Royce defends.

Because God is the center of all experience and of all there is, he is also a source of meaning for all finite rational and moral beings. Everyone who is haunted by finitude and by a life that lacks coherence and direction is at the same time a source for finite experiences that, paradoxically, point beyond finitude: ". . . every finite incompleteness and struggle appears as a part of a whole in whose wholeness the fragments find their true place, the ideas their realisation, the seeking its fulfillment, and our whole life its truth, and so its eternal rest,—that peace which transcends the storms of its agony and its restlessness."[20]

If we recognize that our experienced frustrations and failures are embodied in a unified understanding, we can find a measure of calm and comfort. We can know that our experiences belong and fit into the experience of God—that they are more than punctiform fragments that appear and disappear without importance and without a trace: "These things, wherein we taste the bitterness of our finitude, are what they are because they mean more than they contain, imply what is beyond them, refuse to exist by themselves, and . . . assure us of the reality of that fulfillment which is the life of God."[21] And this reality, God and the unified totality of all experiences, puts the lie to any pragmatist's claim, "'There is no whole world; there is no complete view . . . , and the world is just now incomplete, and therefore there is nothing eternal.'" To say this much is for Royce to concede just what he insists upon throughout his different statements of the proof that God, as the center of all experience, exists. This is the message in his response to pragmatists in *The Sources of Religious Insight*: "Of course, every new deed introduces novelties into the temporal world. But . . . , even to assert this is to assert *that the future, and in fact all the future, in all its individual detail, belongs to reality, and forms part of its wholeness.*"[22]

Royce's argument for the existence of an Absolute Experience or Absolute Reality is flawed. Its most serious shortcoming is a consequence of the polar opposites that are supposed to make it successful. The argument is, after all, successful only if some finite being, whose own experience is commensurately finite, asserts confidently "There is no Absolute Experience." But what does one say about the middle ground that splits the relevant polar opposites? On the one side, we have the atheist, the man or woman who emphatically denies the reality of this Absolute Experience as chimerical. On the other side, there is the committed theist for whom the existence of God, Absolute Reality, or an Absolute Experience is not in question. He or she is convinced that such a being exists and provides the meaningfulness that life otherwise lacks. So far, we are talking about the opposites William James notes in "The Will to Believe." For James, as we have seen, the hypothesis that God exists is for a serious theist settled; hence, the question "Does God exist?" is not for the theist "live," "forced," and "momentous."[23]

Those whom James addresses are also those about whom Royce should be concerned, namely open-minded agnostics who, as nondogmatic skeptics, require evidence before they can bring themselves to believe the proposition "God exists." James is impatient with agnostics who wait for evidence before they decide in favor of the religious hypothesis. His impatience is the consequence of his own conviction that no evidence is, or ever will be, forthcoming to validate the claim that God exists. The case with Royce is different.

Royce, whose confidence in reason as a conduit to truth is much greater than James's, believes that reason leaves no choice for the attentive nonbeliever but to become a believer. The problem with Royce's own reasoning is that its aim is badly skewed. It addresses the atheist or, what amounts to the same thing, the dogmatic skeptic who boldly declares, "There is no God; talk of an Absolute Experience is patently false." Whether an atheist is likely to consider Royce's use of reason and the argument that it is supposed to support is questionable. Atheists are usually not swayed by even the best constructed arguments against their irreligion. Royce ought to have been addressing the far less stubborn agnostics who are at least prepared to consider the possibility that "The Absolute Experience exists or is real." The difficulty is that such an agnostic, whom theists presumably have a better chance of winning over than they have of any doctrinaire atheist, does not announce dogmatically, "'Beyond my world there is no further experience actual'".[24]

Royce's problem and a shortcoming of his proof is that it turns on the immovable assertion of an intransigent atheist. If Royce's proof does its job with anyone at all, it does so only with the rarest of thoroughgoing skeptics who might be willing to investigate whether this proof actually warrants careful consideration. Agnostics, who are open to arguments and who are not blind to well-reasoned conclusions, are not those who say, "There is no Absolute Experience beyond our own finite experiences." The salient characteristic of agnosticism is that it disallows and disavows, in the absence of evidence, that some putative state of affairs must be an actual state of affairs. Royce's argument, which depends upon a finite intellect's unsupported claim that no Absolute Experience exists, does not persuade agnostics because it is contrary to an agnostic's determination to suspend judgment unless evidence supports a judgment. And because sincere agnostics have a judicious regard for the truth, they will not blindly make claims that lead to self-contradictions. If they mistakenly make such claims, they will retract them the moment they understand their self-contradictory character. This, as we have also seen, is one of the reasons that James is so utterly impatient with serious agnostics.[25] Openness to evidence is useless when the evidence they require is never available.

A corollary of Royce's proof that there must be an Absolute Experience or that the Absolute exists also helps to get at the poverty of his argument from an agnostic's perspective. Royce says:

> An opinion of yours may be true or false. But when you form an opinion, what are you trying to do? You are trying to anticipate, in some fashion, what a wider view . . . , a fuller insight into your present ideas, and into what they mean, would show you, if you now had that wider view and larger experience. . . . One can express the matter by saying, that you are trying, through your opinions, to predict what a larger insight, if it were present to you . . . , would experience.[26]

But an agnostic who shuns declarations of absolute truth and avoids precipitous judgments that can lead to error falls outside the perimeters of Royce's remarks. Granting their own fallibility and the difficulty inherent in seeking truth or avoiding error, agnostics avoid the pitfalls that are necessary to generate Royce's religious and epistemological conclusions; hence they have no reasons to accede to the premises or conclusion that Royce thinks are unavoidable. Agnostics refuse to "form an opinion" about the existence of a supermundane being with this "wider view and larger experience."

Serious students of Royce's philosophy will not easily dismiss defects in the argument for his central thesis, namely that a real world exists "as the object of some concretely organized experience . . . carried to its absolute limit of completeness."[27] Those of us who are interested in understanding the elements of his thought can, however, note its deficiencies and move on.

Royce and a Passion for Unity

There is no mistaking that Royce is zealous to see the Absolute, the world, and all individual manifestations of the world as unified. This desire for unity is familiar in the history of Western philosophy and science. Plotinus, Spinoza, Emerson, Isaac Newton, and Einstein are only a few well-known thinkers for whom the unity of all reality, the unity of the laws that govern the manifest behavior of all that is real, or the unified method for interpreting that behavior, are irreducibly basic features of the universe. The reasons so many different philosophers and scientists declare this unity are no doubt various. As a consequence, there is no firm explanation why unity was so important to Royce, but there are hints at an answer. Furthermore, these hints help us understand the degree to which Royce could admit that he was in some restricted sense a pragmatist. He writes in *The Philosophy of Loyalty*:

> *We need unity of life.* In recognizing that need my own pragmatism consists. Now, we never find unity present to our human experience in more than a fragmentary shape. We get hints of higher unity. But only the fragmentary unity is won at any moment of our lives. We therefore form ideas—very fallible ideas—of some unity of experience. . . . Now if our ideas are in any case indeed true, then such an unity is as a fact successfully experienced upon a higher level than ours, and is experienced in some conspectus of life which wins what we need . . . , and which has in its wholeness what we seek.[28]

This "need" for unity is described here in almost visceral terms. Our experience and knowledge are disjunctive and evanescent. This might be tolerable for some people, but Royce believes that most of us value unity and wish to see our lives as part of some unified whole.[29]

Consulting James again, although he is not sympathetic with Royce or with other idealists for whom unity is the *sine qua non* of a satisfying life, is instructive with respect to the search for unity among philosophers: "Philosophy has often been defined as the quest or vision of the world's unity." He adds a paragraph later that "the unity of things has always been considered more *illustrious*, as it were, than their variety."[30] And midway through "The One and the Many," James addresses Royce's view that the many things and events of our finite experience exist in "*the one Knower* . . . ; and *as he knows* them, they have one purpose, form one system, tell one tale for him." Because James is unimpressed with any effort to *prove* that this "All-Knower" exists, he treats it as neither more nor less than a hypothesis for which evidence is unavailable.[31]

At the same time that James is criticizing Royce's philosophy, he gives us an insight into the reason that it initially appeals to those who take it seriously. If, as Royce believes, all experiences are unified in "one Knower" who, as a consequence of this absolute knowledge and experience, sees the single unfolding "system" and "purpose" of the universe, then he also sees its plan or what James calls its "tale." As Royce puts it, "An Omniscient Being would have to present to himself all the conceivable relations amongst facts, so that in his world nothing would be fragmentary, disunited, confused, unrelated. To the question: What is the connexion of this and this in the world? The Omniscient Being would simply always find present the fulfilled answer."[32]

One need only look at Royce's adjectives: "fragmentary," "disunited," "confused," and "fulfilled." For him, these are words, except "fulfilled," we use to describe a chaotic world, a world that is in no meaningful way unified. It is one thing to live and to believe, as Royce does, in a world that appears confused but that in fact is a unity known to an absolute mind that experiences it *in toto*. This mind, unlike any finite mind, sees the measure, order, and balance that are part of the unity of a fully known universe. It is a very different thing to confront the world as it appears and to believe that objects and events as they appear are all there is. Were the world just as it appears, those who write with a romantic desperation about its uncertainties and about their own vulnerabilities in such a place would have some justification.[33] But if the world is unified insofar as for the Absolute it is one grand object of experience and knowledge, lamentations are no longer justified. Royce at once concedes the human condition and announces his now familiar antidote:

> We are beset by questions to which we now get no answers. Those questions could only be answered, those bitter problems that pierce our hearts with the keen edge of doubt and wonder . . . , such questions, such problems . . . could only be answered if the flickering ideas then present in the midst of *our* darkness shone steadily in the world of some superhuman experience, of which ours would then seem to be only the remote hint.[34]

One can liken what Royce means in this passage to what Jonathan Bennett says in his provocative study of Spinoza's *Ethics* (1677): "Spinoza assumed that whatever is the case can be explained—that if P then there is a reason why P. . . . It is the refusal to admit brute facts—ones which just *are* so, for no reason."[35] Both Spinoza and Royce see God as a knower of all there is to know. Both believe that a world known by God is one in which every meaningful question has an answer and in which no fact dangles as an unknown and unknowable.

With respect to these claims, it is not surprising to see why Royce sometimes characterizes himself as a kind of pragmatist. For him the existence of God, the most important and uplifting discovery of reason, satisfies more than a theoretical end in view. A firm belief—Royce calls it a certainty—that such a world is real, not merely ideal, has major consequences or "cash value" for those whose belief it is. Their conviction that such a unified world and an Absolute Experience exist provides the satisfaction that no other view of the world can provide. James, like Royce, concedes the consequences of this conviction, but he believes that the yearning for such a world is at base temperamental rather than intellectual; it is felt, not verified. James also believes this preference "is far less an account of this actual world than a clear addition built upon it, a classic sanctuary in which the rationalist fancy may take refuge from the intolerably confused and gothic character which mere facts present."[36]

Whether James's assessment is correct or not, he has obviously captured Royce's passion for unity and for all that a unified universe implies. And whether Royce actually believes that a demonstrative argument establishes his claims about the world and its Absolute Knower, or recognizes that his demonstration is actually subaltern to a basic desire for comforting unity and order, is conjectural. Beyond all conjecture, however, is that Royce's brief for unity commences with God and the universe but by no means ends with them.

Unity and the Self

In his *In Quest of Community*, which includes a substantial chapter on Royce, R. Jackson Wilson writes that Royce, like all other American philosophers of his era, "denied the existence of any 'Soul-Substance' which was given to rather than gotten from experience. . . ." Wilson adds, quoting a letter from Royce to James, that if one has a purpose in life, the past and future can be unified into a "system of memories and hopes" that account for a unique personality or self. Royce makes the point directly: "By this meaning of my life-plan . . . I am defined and created a self."[37]

Royce means that there is no place in his philosophy for the Platonic or Cartesian position that every individual self is a substantial "thing" that informs or temporarily occupies its body. This conception of selfhood and of the seat of personal identity is more metaphysical than even the metaphysically minded Royce could abide.[38] Royce has no more patience with positing metaphysical entities than does a doctrinaire pragmatist like Dewey. And to believe that underpinning the phenomena of my consciousness (or yours) is an ego, to which I have no access unless I call upon some factitious metaphysical intuition, is to believe that which no evidence can support.

Yes, Royce is a metaphysician, but he is not cut from the same cloth as metaphysicians like Jonathan Edwards or Emerson. They appeal, respectively, to the sense of the heart or to Reason in order to employ an additional sense or faculty that takes a Calvinist saint or a New England Transcendentalist to realities that never show themselves among the conventional phenomena of sensing and reasoning.

Royce's most important metaphysical conclusion, that an Absolute Knower exists, is based on an argument that he believes anyone using his or her reason ought to be able to follow. So where Emerson affirms, but does not argue, Royce argues against suspect entities, such as a substantial self or ego to which neither perception nor reason can take us.[39]

Royce means to defend a view of the self that is congruent with what makes sense to him and requires neither metaphysical flights of fancy nor the multiplication of entities. In concrete terms, this means that Royce understands and defines a "self," the seat of personal identity and activity, in a manner that can never satisfy metaphysical intuitionists:

> *I should say that a person, an individual self, may be defined as a human life lived according to a plan*. If a man could live with no plan at all, purposelessly and quite passively, he would in so far be an organism, and also . . . , he would be a psychological specimen, but he would be no personality. Wherever there is personality, there are purposes worked out in life. . . . You are one self just in so far as the life that goes on in connection with your organism has some one purpose running through it.[40]

Royce adds that the purpose or plan to which he refers is in some rudimentary sense present in almost all human beings. Insofar as we try in our own, often unremarkable way to express our individuality in the world, we are aware that our lives are "unified, after a fashion." This is to say at a minimum that all of us realize we are somehow individual unities; hence my experiences set me apart from others and their experiences. This effort, to which we might pay only passing attention, opens the door just enough to indicate some basic purpose, one that might or might not be uniquely my own.[41] In order to know anything more about the self, understood as what for Royce constitutes one's personal identity, a further look at the nature and content of purposes is necessary. This leads, in turn, to a look at the intimate connection between Royce's view of personal identity and his moral point of view.

Personal Identity, Personal Goals, and Moral Commitment

To understand how Royce attempts to account for self-identity or self-consciousness and, thereby, the unity of the self, it might be helpful to recall questions that people often ask, first, of young children and second, of adults: "What do you plan to be when you grow up?" and "What do you do?" These questions in some contexts may be inappropriate and meddlesome, but they are useful for our purposes. What kind of information is the questioner after, and what sort of reply does she anticipate?

If a child answers, "I plan to be a larger human being when I grow up," the person who asked the question is certain to be surprised or annoyed. The same can be said of a mature man or woman who answers, "This is what I do. I breathe; I ingest; I digest; I sleep, and I wake." Whether it is her business or not, the person who asks such questions is expecting answers that describe vocations. Emersonians and

Marxists disapprove of questions that tie one's identity to one's vocation, but their disapproval does not alter what we generally expect as answers to either of these two questions. What about Royce?

Like anyone else whose assumption is that we are what we do, Royce believes "Who am I?" and "Who are you?" are appropriate questions, but their proper answers are not vocational. His persistent claim that "a self is a life in so far as it is unified by a single purpose" has nothing to do with how a person, a self-identical and self-conscious being, makes a living.[42] It has instead to do with an identifiable, unified purpose understood as a particular cause. And this cause enables Royce to link the problem of personal identity, of finding and affirming a self, to his ethical theory—to his philosophy of loyalty—and to his insistent view that who anyone is has a great deal to do with the community to which one belongs:

> [A] self is a life in as far as it is unified by a single purpose. . . . Where loyalty has not yet come to any sort of definiteness, there is so far present only a kind of inarticulate striving to be an individual self. This very search for one's true self is already a sort of life-purpose, which, as far as it goes, individuates the life of the person in question, and gives him a task. But loyalty brings the individual to full moral self-consciousness. It is devoting the self to a cause that . . . first makes it a rational and unified self, instead of what the life of too many a man remains,—namely, a cauldron of seething and bubbling efforts to be somebody. . . .[43]

A good deal of Royce's thought moves through this text, but we can simplify it in order to reach the core of his guiding ideas.

Royce states his case for purposes and goals rather than for inscrutable thinking substances that metaphysical intuitionists claim they detect through acts of introspection. But not just any goals or purposes will do the job. As far as Royce is concerned, and this is more an affirmation than an argument, the unity of conscious named the "self" is generated and maintained only through a morally felicitous kind of action. Loyalty, Royce's supreme moral category, is what requires a human being to do what is right and, in doing what is right, to develop the unified self that other philosophers inevitably miss: "Loyalty shall mean . . . *The willing and practical and thoroughgoing devotion of a person to a cause.* A man is loyal when, first, he has some *cause* to which he is loyal; when, secondly, he *willingly* and *thoroughly* devotes himself to this cause; and when, thirdly, he expresses his devotion in some *sustained and practical way*, by acting steadily in the service of his cause."[44]

Without worrying too much now about what Royce understands by the supreme principle of his moral theory, "*In choosing and in serving the cause to which you are loyal, be, in any case, loyal to loyalty,*" we can trace the threads that tie his general brief for unity to the action that produces individual unity understood as a self and to the greater social unity for which he hopes.[45] Sound moral deliberation and action that are appropriate to attaining moral goals are essential to constituting one's self-identity. The moral self, the only true self for Royce, thinks first of moral goals and then acts to promote them.

Talk of self-identity or self-consciousness is idle in the absence of plans and goals. But—and this is perhaps the irony—to serve oneself by serving a goal, one must act on others' behalf. Such goals-as-service might include helping others to satisfy their legitimate needs, to chart and act on their aspirations, to identify themselves through their own aims. In a very real sense, therefore, one becomes an authentic self in direct proportion to one's willingness to surrender himself or herself to some higher good, one that reaches well beyond the individual human being who acts, works, and strives to improve the lots of other people: "Whenever a cause . . . greater than you are,—a cause social in its nature and capable of linking into one the wills of various individuals, a cause thus at once personal and . . . superpersonal,—whenever, I say, such a cause so arouses your interest that it appears to you worthy to be served with all your might, with all your soul, with all your strength, then this cause awakens in you the spirit of loyalty."[46]

In a direct manner, given Royce's account of identity, personal independence depends, just as self-identity does, on acting for what lies outside oneself. The genuinely independent person is the person who attains and exhibits independence by working in favor of purposes that must take other people into account. On Royce's terms, there is no independence outside a commitment to self-sacrifice, and self-sacrifice requires giving something of oneself to individual human beings, to a society or community in need. This in its turn entails that there is no independent conduct that does not *depend* essentially upon someone or something that is different from the truly independent agent.

There is almost no way to overstate how self-discovery and self-invention distinguish Royce from fellow Americans such as Emerson and Thoreau or from nineteenth-century Europeans such as Kierkegaard (1813–1855) and Nietzsche (1844–1900). Many things separate these four philosophers, but they agree that an authentic person, one who truly knows and shapes himself, learns what is true of himself, at least in part, by escaping the crowd. When these New England Transcendentalists make their case for creation of a unique self, self-awareness or self-identity, and independence, they write about nonconformity and detachment from the conventional values, professions, and activities of society. Kierkegaard insists that the "knight of faith," probably the most authentic and self-knowing character to appear anywhere in his philosophy, is profoundly alone. All that he recognizes either as moral or as lying beyond the boundaries of traditional morality is expressed in his essential isolation from all other beings except God and in the enigmatic notion of "a teleological suspension of the ethical."[47] And Nietzsche's famous "superman," like so many fictional romantics in literature, finds or makes himself without the aid of society, communities, or the moral imperatives of the "herd."[48] For Nietzsche, each of these is far too banal for the needs and realization of the superman.

Royce is not describing supermen, knights of faith, or human beings as expressions of the Over-Soul. He recognizes and finds no reason to lament our social nature: "By virtue of my nature and my social training, I belong to a family, to a community, to a calling, to a state, to humanity. . . . In the meantime, however, I must also choose special causes to serve; and if these causes are to interest me . . . , they must involve me in numerous and often conflicting social tasks."[49] If this text is general, the following sums up specifically a position that Royce maintained at every stage of his writings in philosophical psychology: "I am dependent on my fellow, not only physically, but to the very core of my conscious self-hood, not only for what, physically speaking I am, but for what I take myself to be."[50] Here in straightforward prose, Royce makes clear that absent one's engagement with others, no sense can be made of selfhood. So, once more, self-identity derives from social and community engagement, but not from just any sort of engagement. It depends upon the kind of engagement that demands an active and moral commitment to the welfare of a cause, a nest of causes, or a society from which I—as an "I" or a real self—cannot be separated.

Given Royce's insistence on the ties between goals or life-plans, moral activity, and the service one renders to others in being loyal to loyalty, the issue of worthwhile ends in view is salient in his thought. After all, being loyal to loyalty includes a determination to surrender one's will and energy to promote the welfare or security of some cause larger than oneself, for example, as a mother cares for her family, a volunteer works for a charity, a soldier serves his country, or a statesman strives for world peace and justice. This determination and zeal to work toward the realization of a purpose, when it is a moral determination, has nothing to do with maximizing the self-interest of the agent. Here too we detect a relation between those who are loyal to the causes that draw them in and the unintended, but beneficial, consequences for those who act out of loyalty: "This purpose may in such cases come to consciousness merely as a willing hunger to serve the cause, a proud obedience to the ideal call. *But in any case, wherever loyalty is, there is selfhood, personality, individual purpose embodied in life.*"[51]

Royce anticipates criticisms of his moral theory. Some might complain that the imperative "Be loyal to loyalty" is a blank cartridge that tells us nothing about the value of the cause to which we choose to be loyal. As a consequence, there is always the possibility that one's loyalty can be uninformed or misinformed, and in certain cases my loyalty to a cause may conflict with your loyalty to some other cause. Blind loyalty, which is never what Royce advocates, can lead to unspeakable atrocities like those that were commonplace in Nazi Germany.[52] Royce's good fortune was that he died long before the criminals in command of the Third Reich first perpetrated atrocities and then tried obscenely to justify their crimes by claiming they were behaving out of loyalty to the state.

Although Royce believes that he can reply to various critics of his moral philosophy, one is free to disagree. There is, for example, the serious question whether the supreme principle of loyalty to loyalty can stand on its own as a guide to moral behavior. Without adding an independent principle, namely "In being loyal to loyalty we must respect other agents' loyalty to their causes," the complaint seems reasonable that Royce's ethical theory is incomplete. Can the imperative, "Be loyal to loyalty," tell us unerringly that the causes we serve are just and fair to everyone concerned?

But what concerns Royce far more than predictable criticisms of his philosophy of loyalty is that citizens of the United States are generally indifferent to the value of loyalty and blind to the unifying tendencies inherent in the devotion to a cause. These concerns, which affected Royce deeply, warrant some remarks about the special significance of communities in his mature philosophy.

Royce's treatment of a community is a complicated affair. One of his best accounts of communities and their shortcomings is in *The Problem of Christianity* (1913).[53] There he describes the ideal community as a religious society or something close to it. In this important book, Royce lists the characteristics of an authentic community. The first of these is one that we have already encountered: a community must include individual human beings whose plans possess a moral dimension.[54] The second condition for a true community is that it includes "a number of distinct selves capable of social communication, and, in general, engaged in communication." The third and last condition for a genuine community brings us back to unity: a community "consists in the fact that the ideally extended past and future selves of the members include at least some events which are, for all these selves, *identical*."[55]

When these three conditions are realized, so also is a community. Moral men and women, looking beyond their own interests, act for the communal or collective good. They are sufficiently integrated that they communicate meaningfully with each other and do not exclude others who share in the purposes and goals that, despite individual differences, give the community its character and essential unity. Why, then, are Royce's account of a community and his vision of unity threatened in America during the first years of the twentieth century? His response is more empirical than metaphysical. He thinks that intransigent facts about American life explain why communities of every kind are threatened.

There was first the effect of massive immigration that commenced in the nineteenth century. The initial wave of immigrants, chiefly those from England, Germany, and Ireland, began arriving in the middle 1800s. Between 1850 and 1882, primarily in the West, over three hundred thousand Chinese sought a better life and hoped to find it in the United States. In the 1890s the pattern shifted. This second wave was chiefly Eastern European, Russian, Italian, Greek, Turkish, and Syrian. Fear and bigotry led to actively organized opposition to non-Americans who wished to make America their new home.[56]

Immigration presented a challenge to "established" Americans, what Royce called "the great task that now lies before the American people,—the task of teaching millions of foreign birth and descent to understand and to bear constantly in mind the value of loyalty, the task also of keeping our own loyalty intact in the presence of those enormous complications of social life which the vastness of our country, and the numbers of our foreign immigrants are constantly increasing."[57] But even though this task is necessary, it is not sufficient. Americans must, Royce insists, do all that they can to welcome and train these new and hopeful residents so that developing loyalty and an appropriate moral center is possible, not merely ideal.[58]

Unfortunately, what Royce seeks in the interest of loyalty and its instantiation in morally worthwhile communities was jeopardized by the thing that initially drew foreigners to the United States: "[O]ur national prosperity and our national greatness involve us all in many new temptations to disloyalty. . . . Our young people grow up with a great deal of their attention fixed upon personal success, and also with a great deal of training in sympathetic sentiments; but they get far too little knowledge . . . of what loyalty means."[59] The American family, perhaps the most basic form of community, also founders with the celebration of individualism and denigration of tradition.[60] Royce protests: "No one may rationally say: 'Loyalty can no longer bind me, because from my deepest soul, I feel that I want individual freedom.' For any such outcry comes from an ignorance of what one's deepest soul really wants."[61]

There is also the problem of partisan loyalties, to labor unions, religious cults, and political parties, that are antagonistic to the legitimate ends of communities and to the benign loyalty that Royce values: "Narrow loyalties, side by side with irrational forms of individualism and with a cynical contempt for all loyalty,—these are what we too often see in the life of our country."[62] Furthermore, and here we see Royce's own reflections on the dark shadow of the Gilded Age, the industrial might and wealth of America do nothing to serve the cause of loyalty to loyalty or to maintain a morally valuable community. The "industrial forces, the aggregations of capital" and "enormous physical power" of the nation "excite our loyalty as little as do the trade-winds or the blizzard. They leave our patriotic sentiments cold. The smoke of our civilization hides the very heavens that used to be so near, and the stars to which we were once loyal."[63]

These are the problems, but what are their solutions? Insisting that the loyalty he prizes is neither vague nor unattainable, Royce says, "The spirit of loyalty is practical, is simple, is teachable, and is for all normal men." To instill in other Americans, as well as new arrivals, the need and nature of loyalty to loyalty, and to promote the communities in which loyalty flourishes, it is necessary "*to help them to be less estranged than they are from their own social order.*"[64] Americans need "a new and wiser provincialism." What is this kind of provincialism?

> I mean the sort of provincialism which makes people want to idealize, to adorn, to ennoble, to educate, their own province; to hold sacred its traditions, to honor its worthy dead, to support and to multiply its public possessions. I mean the spirit which shows itself in the multiplying of public libraries, in the laying out of public parks, in the work of local historical associations. . . . I mean also the present form of that spirit which has originated, endowed, and fostered the colleges and universities of our Western towns, cities, and states. . . .[65]

Royce is optimistic that from this wise provincialism, which had thrived in English villages for centuries, a wider loyalty can emerge. He believes that it is possible to train for national loyalty by beginning with provincial loyalties. At the formative stages of training America's youth for a life of loyalty, there must be leaders who can instruct them in the value of loyalty, and there must be causes that can be realized. Royce cites a rather parochial case to illustrate that a wider commitment to loyalty and unity can come to be from unremarkable beginnings: "Even so, the loyalty of the sons of a subjugated nationality, such as the Irish or the Poles, to their country, is kept alive through precisely such an union or the influence of individual leaders with the more impersonal reverence for the idealized, although no longer politically existent nationality."[66]

Preferring to see loyalty arise from provincial beginnings, from organizations, clubs, and philanthropic societies, Royce sounds a cautionary note about the uninhibited growth of "the centralization of national power." This kind of power, which estranges rather than unites citizens to the national good, is "a distinct danger" to the nurturing of loyalty. Royce's apprehension about federalism at the expense of individual freedom is, of course, a familiar theme among libertarians, conservatives, and Jeffersonians.

For Royce, the grand vision of loyalty that stretches from villages to a country, to nations beyond America's own frontiers, and finally to the Absolute is progressive. The moral core of Royce's philosophy begins modestly enough but, properly cultivated and reinforced, reaches to the metaphysical heights of the All-knowing being. At this rarified level no greater unity or loyalty can be expressed, exhibited, or desired.

Ideals, even for an idealist like Royce, are easier to announce than to realize. As long as Americans are estranged from each other and from a society that might provide the unity for which Royce speaks, all litanies to community, devotion to a common good, and loyalty to loyalty are empty. Even a distant approximation to the ideal of unity remains an empty hope. Until and unless training and a passion for loyalty take hold, Hegel will remain prescient in his account of individual "estrangement" from the society in which we live but of which we are not really a part. In America, like Imperial Rome and seventeenth-century France, "as Hegel skillfully points out, the individual comes to regard himself as in relation to social powers, which . . . he cannot understand. The fact that, as in our present civilization, he is formally a free citizen, does not remove his character of self-estrangement from the social world in which he moves."[67] As locked out or alienated from a society to which we could give our unconditional loyalty, we lose, or never discover, goals that supply life's meaning. As a consequence of the indefeasible ties between these goals and who we are, we cannot create selves that answer the questions, "Who am I?" and "What am I doing here?"

Conclusion

What can we say about the "fit" of Royce's idealism into the larger scheme of American philosophy for the few decades that he was a prominent thinker. We can say that the odds were against its staying power almost from the beginning? Writing about the Absolute, loyalty to loyalty and self-sacrifice to some larger good, whatever their inherent value, was far outside the mainstream of what Peirce had done and what James and Dewey were advocating. It is true that Peirce spoke for a community and for the involvement of scientific men in a mutual enterprise that was larger than any one of them. Dewey also insisted upon a philosophy that addressed social problems and imbalances, not merely the needs of Americans acting for their own sakes.[68] And we know from the previous essay that James was a pragmatist who in "The Will to Believe" confidently promoted openness to a belief in God and the value of sincere religious practices.

At base, however, Royce looked backward in a way that the pragmatists did not. His sources were German and English idealism, which had fallen out of fashion in America by the close of the nineteenth century. Idealism would wake again later in the twentieth century and into the first years of the twenty-first century. But the renewed interest in the Neo-Kantians, Neo-Hegelians, and the metaphysician Martin Heidegger (1889–1976) omits Royce, the American philosopher who took up Continental idealism, reshaped it, and made it his own. Perhaps the problem for Royce is straightforward: He promoted a nearly moribund philosophy and did not alter idealism enough to attract readers who already found what they liked in Hegel or F. H. Bradley (1846–1924), the important English idealist. Morton White, addressing the difference between Royce and the pragmatists, puts the matter this way: "... Royce was an intellectual throwback or conservative.... Moreover while an Absolute Idealism like that of Royce was being abandoned by younger philosophers like Dewey, James was hailed by them as a leader who was guiding them out of the idealistic jungle and into the fresh philosophical air of the twentieth century."[69]

If there are some reasons to debate the extent to which the pragmatists produced a philosophy that mirrored its time and thereby won acceptance, there is less reason to question whether Royce's idealism was responsive to urgent American problems. Obviously, his Absolute Experience and his attempt to prove its existence did not emerge from capitalist forces or class divisions that bothered him and that he addresses directly in the *Philosophy of Loyalty*. And it is too simple to reduce Royce's desire for unity to his worries about elitism, alienation, and the disappearance of provincial communities.

Royce is not the first philosopher whose defense of unity helped to shape various elements of his entire philosophy. His vision of every man's and woman's experience as part of the total experience that belongs to the Absolute is not so different from Emerson's belief that all of us are individual elements of one Over-Soul. Both saw this ontological unity as the ultimate ground for correcting virtually every kind of social injustice. If we are all equally expressions of the Over-Soul or elements of the Absolute Experience, there can be no justification for treating one human being or class of human beings less fairly than we treat any other human being or class. To discriminate against someone or some group is for Royce at once immoral and irrational.

But similarities do not mask differences. For Emerson, Reason alone can penetrate the veil of appearances. For Royce no special, trans-experiential faculty is needed. Since, for Royce, one's finite understanding can discover necessary truths about ultimate Reality, this same understanding is more than sufficient to enable us to chart and enact a sturdy moral course. This, at least, is how Royce sees things.

For Royce, whose worries about America were in many ways different from Emerson's, but no less earnest, philosophy can and ought to perform an ameliorative function. That communities were in peril, that the threat of class warfare was deeper in the 1870s and 1880s than at any other period in American history, that entire nationalities (Hungarians, Poles, Irish, Chinese, and Italians) were more often ridiculed than encouraged to pursue their own versions of a good life—these were facts about which Royce was keenly aware. For him one of the truly practical ends of idealism, an end that might help to make sense of the notion that Royce's philosophy is a kind of "Absolute Pragmatism," is to defend a standard of conduct that would elevate our actions. This is a standard to induce thoughtful Americans to generate a spirit of community, tolerance, and unity.[70] This is loyalty to loyalty. Royce, seeing matters in the Republic differently from Emerson or Thoreau in the 1830s and 1840s, grasped what he believed was, as R. Jackson Wilson identifies it, "the most pervasive problem of the period" (1860–1920): "the hopeless insufficiency of the isolated individual."[71]

We find in Royce's philosophy, taken more or less as a whole, two tiers. First, there is the metaphysical tier that argues for the existence of God, provides grounds for religious beliefs, and induces the conviction that the phenomena of all finite experiences are grounded in the essentially limitless experience of the Absolute. There is, again, nothing specifically American about any of this.

Second, there is the tier that is, on the face of it, less metaphysical but that still owes a debt to Royce's metaphysical convictions. As a social critic and moralist, Royce needed no insights or philosophical arguments to identify what was amiss in America as he confronted it. He surely thought that the growth pains of a mammoth, increasingly industrial nation were bound to create some serious problems, and he was no unreflective optimist who believed that in time these problems would solve themselves. The solutions to America's problems required Americans who were prepared to display, in thought and action, loyalty to just and worthwhile purposes, Americans who could dismiss their prejudices, overcome their distrust of foreigners, and diminish any self-absorption that might result from thinking that a "real" human being is an acquisitive and successful merchant, banker, investor, or industrialist.

Standing behind Royce's solution to much of what was wrong in the United States is his certainty that unity, not division, is the natural condition of all that is real and valuable. If the character of the universe is unity, then why should it not be the nature of the nation to be a unity as well? For Royce, this question is rhetorical. Worthy societies, communities, and nations ought in his view to simulate the unity of the universe and, therefore, of the Absolute. As far as he is concerned, there is no problem deriving the prescriptive "ought" from the descriptive "is." Insofar as the foundation of all reality *is* an absolute unity, the deviation from unity (whether it is a deviation that leads to a disjointed and incomplete self, an exclusionary society, or a country that is "United" only in its name) *ought not* to be and *must not* persist.

All of this is the redemptive message of Royce's philosophy. No, Royce did not acquire his taste for metaphysical idealism at Berkeley or Harvard. For that he looked to Europe and made no secret of his debts.[72] But America's shortcomings were, possibly more than any other single factor, what his theory of value, responsibility, and community were meant to correct. If an American philosophy is, among other things, intended to identify and address American problems, there is no denying that Royce's philosophy was American. His message was, after all, supposed to reach beyond the academy and into the cities, villages, streets, mills, and factories of the Republic.

NOTES

1. R. Jackson Wilson, *In Quest of Community: Social Philosophy in the United States, 1860–1920* (New York, 1968), 147–48.
2. Ibid. 150. Most of this information about Royce's early background is from Wilson, pages 144–51.
3. Ibid. 151.
4. Morton White, *Science and Sentiment in America* (New York, 1972), 239.
5. Giles Gunn, *Pragmatism and Other Writings*, (New York, 2000), 10–11. Here after abbreviated as *Pragmatism.*
6. Josiah Royce, Joseph Le Conte, G. H. Howison, and Sidney E. Mezes, *The Conception of God: A Philosophical Discussion Concerning the Nature of the Divine Idea as a Demonstrable Reality* (New York, 1898), 43–4. In this book, Royce lays out the fundamental elements and arguments of his metaphysical idealism. It spares readers a need to turn to *The World and the Individual* (1899), a turgid two-volume work that runs to more than a thousand pages.
7. From James, "Is Radical Empiricism Solipsistic? (1912)" in *Pragmatism*, 337.
8. Ibid. 339.
9. Richard M. Gale, *The Divided Self of William James* (Cambridge, 1999), 167.
10. *The Conception of God*, 17, 18; emphasis added.
11. Ibid. 36–7.
12. Ibid. 15–16.
13. Ibid. 38–39.
14. Ibid. 39–40.
15. Ibid. 40.
16. Josiah Royce, *The Sources of Religious Insight* (New York, 1912), 114.
17. *The Conception of God*, 41.
18. Ibid. See also Royce's recapitulation on page 43. For other analyses of Royce's argument for the Absolute and thus for his version of idealism, see White's remarks in *Science and Sentiment in America*, 221–6, and Gale's *The Divided Self of William James*, 167–8.
19. *The Conception of God*, 43–4.
20. *The Conception of God*, 47.
21. Ibid. 47–8.
22. *The Sources of Religious Insight*, 160, 161.
23. *Pragmatism*, 198–204.
24. *The Conception of God*, 40.
25. *Pragmatism*, 216–17.
26. *The Sources of Religious Insight*, 107.
27. *The Conception of God*, 36.
28. *The Philosophy of Loyalty* (1908), reprint, intro. John J. McDerrmott (Nashville, 1995), 158–59; emphasis added.
29. For Garry Wills's account of the transcendent importance of unity in Lincoln's political thought and as one of the overriding themes of the Gettysburg Address, see *Lincoln at Gettysburg: The Words that Remade America* (New York, 1992), ch. 4.
30. *Pragmatism*, 59.
31. Ibid. 66.
32. *The Conception of God*, 14.
33. This is the character of Hume's preromantic melancholy and lamentations in *A Treatise of Human Nature*, ed. L. A. Selby-Bigge, rev. P. H. Nidditch (Oxford, 1978), I, 263–70.
34. *The Conception of God*, 12; emphasis added.
35. *A Study of Spinoza's Ethics* (Indianapolis, 1984), 29.
36. Ibid. 15.
37. Wilson, *In Quest of Community*, 152.
38. *The Conception of God*, 45–6, and *The World and the Individual* (2 vols., New York, 1899–1901), II, 268.

39. For a point of convergence between Royce and James on the rejection of selves as substances that stand apart from nature, see James "A World of Pure Experience" (1904), reprinted in *Pragmatism*, 315–19.
40. *The Philosophy of Loyalty*, 79; emphasis added. See also *The Conception of God*, 289–96; and Bruce Kuklick, *Josiah Royce: An Intellectual Biography* (Indianapolis, 1972), 156–7.
41. *The Philosophy of Loyalty*, 79.
42. Ibid. 80.
43. Ibid.
44. Ibid. 9.
45. Ibid. 57.
46. Ibid. 72.
47. Soren Kierkegaard, *Fear and Trembling* (1843), trans. Alastair Hannay (London, 1985), 83–95, 104, 106.
48. See *A Nietzsche Reader*, ed. and trans. R. J. Hollingdale (London, 1977), 94–5, 237, 243.
49. *The Philosophy of Loyalty*, 84–5.
50. From "Self Consciousness, Social Consciousness, and Nature" (1895), reprinted in *The Basic Writings of Josiah Royce*, ed. John J. McDermott (2 vols., Chicago, 1969), I, 425–6.
51. *The Philosophy of Loyalty*, 80; emphasis added.
52. Ibid. 48–69. In these pages, Royce surveys objections to his defense of loyalty to loyalty and offers his replies.
53. Josiah Royce, *The Problem of Christianity* (2 vols., New York, 1913), I, 127–59. See also Wilson, *In Quest of Community*, 144–70.
54. *The Problem of Christianity*, II, 60–61, and Kegley, "Josiah Royce," 251.
55. Ibid. 67–8; emphasis added.
56. Steven M. Gillon and Cathy D. Matson, *The American Experiment: A History of the United States* (2 vols., Boston, 2002), II, 731, 754.
57. *The Philosophy of Loyalty*, 99.
58. Ibid. 101.
59. Ibid. 103.
60. Ibid. 104.
61. Ibid. 105.
62. Ibid. 107.
63. Ibid. 113.
64. Ibid. 114.
65. Ibid. 114–15.
66. Ibid. 128.
67. Ibid. 112.
68. John Dewey, *The Public and Its Problems* (New York, 1927), 143–84.
69. *Science and Sentiment in America*, 217–18.
70. For Royce as an advocate of "Absolute Pragmatism," see Kuklick's discussion in *Josiah Royce*, 119–35.
71. *In Quest of Community*, 30.
72. Both his *Lectures on Modern Idealism*, ed. J. Loewenberg (New Haven, 1919) and *The Spirit of Modern Philosophy* (Boston, 1892) make clear that Royce understood and admired the traditions from which he derived his own idealism.

Essay 8
George Santayana, Philosophical Naturalist *Par Excellence* and More

George Santayana was born in Madrid, Spain, in 1863, but at age nine he came with his mother to the United States and was educated, after attending Boston Latin School, at Harvard. In 1889, following graduate study at Harvard under Josiah Royce's direction, he became a member of its Department of Philosophy and eventually rose to the level of a full professor. In 1912 he resigned his position and left the United States for good. That Santayana could willingly leave Harvard surprised many American academics, but it should not have. Throughout his twenty-three years on the faculty, he was generally remote from his colleagues and lived, "so long as he could, a life closer to that of a student."[1]

Santayana was in every sense a man incessantly on the move during nearly the last half of his long life, and by 1952, the year he died in a Roman convent, he had lived in Spain, France, England, and Italy. Nonetheless, Morton White characterizes Santayana as the "sage of American materialism" and as a thinker whose contributions to American philosophy are of the first importance.[2]

"The Genteel Tradition in American Philosophy" (1911)

Our look at Santayana as an American philosopher begins on the eve of his departure from America. He delivered his now classic lecture the "The Genteel Tradition in American Philosophy" at the University of California, Berkeley, on August 25, 1911, and crossed the Atlantic a few weeks later.[3] So it is that he managed to capture the marrow of America's philosophical development, as he saw it, just as he was preparing to go into self-imposed exile. And whether or not one agrees with Santayana's remarks, they constitute the most significant valedictory lecture in the history of philosophy in America.

What is the genteel tradition that he describes and criticizes? This tradition is one that, in its first phase, begins with the Calvinism that English Americans transported across the Atlantic to New England in the 1600s. This, as we know from Essay 1, was the theology that some colonists turned into a philosophy. According to Santayana, whether we have in mind Calvinism on the European or North American side of the Atlantic, we have the same three claims at its center, namely "that sin exists, that sin is punished, and that it is beautiful that sin should be punished."[4] What makes this theology philosophical? "To be a Calvinist philosophically is to feel a fierce pleasure in the existence of misery, especially of one's own, in that this misery seems to manifest the fact that the Absolute is irresponsible or infinite or holy."[5]

This is metaphysics to the bone. For reasons that eternally exceed our finite understanding, we are determined to sin; hence we sin and as a consequence suffer an "agonized conscience" for our transgressions. Our sole hope is that an inaccessible God will save us.

The peculiarities and paradoxes of Calvinism were imported. This too we know from our discussion of Edwards. They did not spring naturally from New England towns and villages. For a time, the peculiarities of Calvinism had a staying power, but as years turned to decades, the virtues of Calvinism, such as hard work and contempt for idleness, justified themselves in securing a better, less taxing existence. Misery became increasingly a matter of religious and philosophical doctrine, but decreasingly a fact of life itself: "people remained honest and helpful out of good sense and good will rather than out of scrupulous adherence to any fixed principles. They retained their instinct for order . . . , but the sanctity of law, to be obeyed for its own sake, began to escape them." The inflexible demands of unyielding Calvinism gradually lost their power, and with them "Calvinism . . . lost its basis in American life."[6]

A reader might insist that Emerson said as much before Santayana. He, no less vigorously than Santayana, complained that America was living in the nineteenth century on a borrowed philosophy. But where Emerson saw his own philosophy as an emancipating, invigorating alternative to Calvinism, Santayana saw it as a second phase of the genteel tradition in philosophy. Emerson and his friends "escaped the mediocrity of the genteel tradition, but they supplied nothing to supplant it in other minds."[7]

Santayana claims that whether the subject is Emerson's rendering of Transcendentalism or that of the German Romantics, a salient feature is "systematic subjectivism." Transcendentalism in all its manifestations "studies the perspectives of knowledge as they radiate from the self." So understood, it is at once an intensely private philosophy that at the same time announces that the private knower grasps truths that are more than subjective presumptions. But in making the individual self the source for knowledge and a criterion for truth, transcendentalists came off as egoists around which the knowable universe centered. Santayana objects not so much to the transcendental theory of knowledge as to the mythology that accompanies it: "Transcendental method . . . produced transcendental myth. A conscientious critique of knowledge was turned into a sham system of nature."[8] The Over-Soul, the spiritual Genius that is an inseparable part of every human being, and the inexpressible flux that Emerson tried to capture in "Circles," are vacant metaphysical abstractions. We have already seen that Reason, the only epistemic conduit to these (suspect) abstractions, takes its stand as an alternative to mere understanding; thus Santayana complains, "[Emerson] was detached, unworldly, contemplative."[9] This "unworldly" detachment is what lies at the seat of the genteel tradition and its shortcomings.

On the face of it, there is no obvious similarity between the harsh verdict of Calvinism that all human beings warrant damnation for their prideful disobedience and the far more sanguine picture of (Emersonian) human beings as divine and as suffused with genius. What would tempt anyone to call "genteel" the incomprehensible wrath of the Calvinist God and the terrifying prospects for sinners? Why does Santayana link these two as elements of a single tradition?

Santayana believes that what unifies Calvinism and Transcendentalism is greater than what separates them. The similarity is that both are gross and disturbing evasions of philosophical responsibility. Both preach an escape from the world that a sturdy American philosopher such as William James rejects. American Calvinists saw the world as a seductive field of play that ceaselessly turns sinners away from the God who alone can save them. For Edwards, as for all others who shared his convictions, sinners must strive against heavy odds to cleanse themselves of every worldly temptation so that perhaps election and heaven, rather than damnation and the abyss, will be their fate. For Emerson and the other New England Transcendentalists, who believed that the world we confront with our senses and understandings is unreal, we must realize that the search for all that is worthwhile depends upon transferring our attention to Reason or metaphysical intuition. For Santayana, then, Calvinists demand turning from the world, and Transcendentalists insist upon discounting it.

If this much captures the genteel tradition to which Santayana objects, what does one say next? An obvious reply is that we have seen this before. Dewey stands out as one of those American thinkers who cannot abide otherworldly philosophers who eschew the world as counterfeit. We know this and are entitled to ask whether Santayana offers anything new. A proper reply is yes and no. Santayana, neither more nor less than Dewey, looks contemptuously on any philosophy whose adherents indulge metaphysical fantasies and wish somehow to take flight from the world of actual experience. In this respect, therefore, Santayana and Dewey are bedfellows. But this masks a difference.

Dewey paints with a wider brush than Santayana. Dewey's objections to Plato and to all other "Platonizing" philosophies is not addressed to excesses and deficiencies that are characteristic of philosophy as it is practiced in the United States. He objects to every philosophy, wherever it is entrenched, that claims to find reality, truth, value, and beauty beyond the world of sensuous experience and experimentalism. Santayana is less catholic, more parochial and most concerned with a tradition that shaped and sullied American philosophy until William James argued that America had had enough of the genteel tradition. In short, Dewey addressed problems in philosophy, and Santayana addressed, in a classic lecture, a central problem in American philosophy. Santayana looked to James and claimed that he, more than any other American thinker, had already justified the attitudes that America needed in order to bury the genteel tradition.

What did James do that so impressed Santayana? First, he understood the genteel tradition. He saw, before Santayana coined the phrase, that the "genteel tradition" had taken hold and in his writings, he did something about it: "His way of thinking and feeling represented the true America, and represented in a measure the whole ultra-modern, radical world."[10] Santayana sees James as no less a romantic than Emerson, but James's romanticism was not quiescent. He did not, as we have already seen, encounter the world as a passive bystander. On the contrary, the world we experience is real and invites us to shape it, not to fly from it. Santayana saw early and clearly that action and risk—indispensable ingredients of James's own pragmatism—would drive the genteel tradition from the temple. James was emphatic about nature's purposes, "which are not to be static harmonies, self-unfolding destinies, the logic of spirit . . . , its purposes are to be concrete endeavours, finite efforts of souls living in an environment which they transform and by which they, too, are affected."[11]

Santayana reminds his audience that James, unlike Calvinists who see the world as unfolding in terms of a plan from which it cannot in the minutest detail waver, treats the universe as "an experiment; it is unfinished." As such, human efforts count for something, and Santayana approves: "This is, so far as I know, a new philosophical vista. . . . It is a vision radically empirical and radically romantic; and as William James himself used to say, the visions and not the arguments of a philosopher are the interesting and influential things about him."[12]

By treating the world as a place in which things can be improved by people who have the will and drive to do so, Santayana believes that James successfully challenged the genteel tradition. "What! The world a gradual improvisation? Creation unpremeditated?"[13] In characterizing this dynamic, melioristic outlook and its consequences for the world in which most of us actually live, Santayana goes beyond a descriptive epitome of James's *Pragmatism*. Santayana praises James for having opened America's intellectual windows, thereby allowing new light to brighten the philosophical future.

In concluding his lecture Santayana says something more, and what he says is also a window through which to glimpse his own naturalism:

> You must feel . . . that you are an offshoot of her (nature's) life: one brave little force among the immense forces. . . . Everything is measurable and conditioned, indefinitely repeated, yet, in repetition, twisted somewhat from its original form. Everywhere is beauty and nowhere permanence, everywhere an incipient harmony, nowhere an intention, nor a responsibility, nor a plan.[14]

What does a philosophy look like insofar as its character corresponds to this view of the universe? This is the question to which we now turn.

Ethics, Rationality, and Naturalism: Santayana Makes His Stand

One way to understand the designation "naturalist" as it applies to Santayana is through his ethical theory. Unfortunately, his treatment of ethics is difficult going and cannot be gleaned from a single book, lecture, or paper. Impediments are not, however, excuses to dismiss an important part of his philosophy.

We begin with Santayana's criticism of the anti-naturalist treatment of ethics or the concept "good" as it plays a role in moral valuation. The classic treatment of this concept from an anti-naturalist standpoint is in G. E. Moore's *Principia Ethica* (1903). Moore (1873–1958), an extraordinarily influential British philosopher and Bertrand Russell, his even more influential colleague, believed that earlier answers to the question "What is good?" were misguided or wrong.[15] Moore makes the central point with his customary economy: "If I am asked 'What is good?' my answer is that good is good, and that is the end of the matter. *Or if I am asked 'How is good to be defined?' my answer is that it cannot be defined, and that is all I have to say about it.*"[16] And Russell says, in Santayana's paraphrase, "The predicate 'good' is indefinable." Santayana adds that according to Russell, "the so-called definitions of 'good'—that is pleasure, the desired, and so forth—are not definitions of the predicate 'good,' but designations of the things to which this predicate is applied by different persons."

Santayana does not object to the position that "good" is indefinable. He agrees. What he cannot understand or accept is Russell's view, like Moore's, that because we cannot define "good" as it functions in ethical evaluation and other modes of moral discourse, it follows that, now quoting Russell directly, "Good and bad . . . are qualities which belong to objects independently of our opinions, just as much as round and square do; and when two people differ as to whether a thing is good, only one of them can be right. . . ."[17] This is what for Santayana characterizes "hypostatic ethics," that is, turning indefinable terms into moral abstractions that are independent of human preferences and beliefs. Santayana, as what Russell calls an "ethical sceptic," is an ethical naturalist, namely one who maintains that evaluative words like "good" and "bad" have no meaning except insofar as they can be translated into the descriptive or naturalistic vocabulary that affirms our aversions, preferences, desires, and fears.

So where Russell and Moore hold that "X is good" means that an indefinable property, designated by the word "good" actually belongs essentially to X, Santayana means that someone, or perhaps some society or culture, desires X. "*To esteem a thing good is to express certain affinities between that thing and the speaker*; and if this is done with self-knowledge and with knowledge of the thing, so that the felt affinity is a real one, the judgment is invulnerable and cannot be asked to rescind itself."[18] Elsewhere, Santayana writes: "*Morality is something natural*. It arises and varies . . . with the nature of the creature whose morality it is. *Morality is something relative*: not that its precepts in any case are optional or arbitrary; for each man they are defined by his innate character and possible forms of happiness and action."[19] In other words, if someone, some group, or society, prefers X to all other alternatives under consideration, then there is nothing more to say or to debate: "X is good" is a true proposition; it is simply not an eternally true proposition.[20]

There are serious issues one can raise against Santayana's normative naturalism.[21] Traditionalists complain that naturalism or relativism amounts to the denial of all values. Santayana admits that as a naturalist he rejects values conceived as reified, unchanging properties of a value-laden universe. For him the universe is value-neutral, and "nature exists for no reason."[22] More important, he finds something therapeutic in the relativism he espouses. Why?

If someone acknowledges that his values are relative to his own desires, even as someone else acknowledges that her values are relative to her own desires, there would be grounds for understanding and acting on something like the following corollary: "Our private sense of justice itself would be acknowledged to have but a relative authority, and while we could not have a higher duty than to follow it, we should seek to meet those whose aims were incompatible with it as we meet things physically inconvenient, without insulting them as if they were morally vile or logically incompatible."[23] Santayana suggests, then, that from naturalism and relativism a hope for greater tolerance makes sense; whereas no absolutist can reasonably entertain this hope.[24]

But another criticism or need for clarification comes to mind when we look again at Santayana's insistence that the desire one has must be mediated by "self-knowledge" and by "knowledge of the thing" that is esteemed. That self-knowledge enters the picture is easy enough to accept. Santayana might mean that the human being who says "I esteem object, action or condition X" might not always know his own mind, that he might not know the difference between reflexively valuing or desiring X and actually desiring it over the long term. We can easily imagine, for example, someone who unreflectively desires to duel for the sake of his honor and the same person who, after reflecting on the possibility of a mortal outcome, no longer desires to duel. Having had the time and discipline to think about the *code duello*, he decides that dueling is bad rather than good.

This interpretation, like Santayana's condition of self-knowledge, hangs by a slender thread. It is odd to maintain that someone who thinks he desires something may not actually desire it. Less odd, but not consistent with what Santayana actually says, is that the person really did desire the thing in question until he learned more about it. Then, under the direction of reason, he ceased to desire it. In this case, however, reflection does not inform a desire; it eliminates it.

No less vexing is what Santayana, the committed relativist, means by "knowledge of the thing." Again, as Santayana reads them, "far from inferring from this diversity of experience that the present good, like the others, corresponds to a particular attitude or interest of ours, Mr. Russell and Mr. Moore infer instead that the presence of the good must be independent of all interests, attitudes, and opinions."[25] If, however, Santayana is correct that normative properties are not really properties of things, then it is difficult to know, first, why Santayana talks about "knowledge of the thing" that is esteemed and, second, what bearing such knowledge has on the value of the "thing" that is known.

Suppose, given this connection between knowing a thing and esteeming it, a reader says that Melville's *Moby-Dick* is good. Let us suppose further that this reader has worked through the novel with great effort and attention, and thus really does *know* it. How, accepting Santayana's view that "good" is an affinity between the reader and *Moby-Dick*, does knowledge of the novel make it good? An absolutist—but probably not Russell or Moore insofar as they insist that "good" is indefinable—might say that in knowing *Moby-Dick* far better than a casual reader, the serious reader has acquired an understanding of the literary qualities and narrative that make this a very good book. At base this is the simple claim that there are properties of the book that make it good and that the attentive reader will likely discover them. Here, therefore, "good" expresses the content that makes something good.

If a relativist such as Santayana means what he says, then carefully reading and re-reading *Moby-Dick* can help our reader learn much more about the book.

He also discovers properties that he never noticed on a preliminary reading. Still, and this is the peculiarity of evaluative relativism in any of its contexts, a reader who shares Santayana's relativistic position is barred from claiming that he discovered how good the book was by coming to know it much better than he had before. If, after all, "good" is indefinable and expresses the desires of a discerning reader, nothing more that one comes to know about *Moby-Dick* makes it good rather than bad. This should be the case if one means, as Santayana does, that "good" or "bad" is not resident in objects or events.

Suppose an apologist for Santayana says that although "good" is not itself inherent in what some of us, or all of us, identify as good, it is still true that certain properties of objects or events cause people who know these properties to say "X is good." The problem with this defense is that it denies exactly what Santayana believes. In declaring himself a relativist, Santayana must deny, if he values consistency, that properties that belong to those objects which we call "good" are responsible for shaping our judgments about the good. Such judgments are noncognitive and have nothing to do with the increase in knowledge: "The ultimate intuitions on which ethics rests are not debatable, for they are not opinions we hazard but *preferences we feel; and it can be neither correct nor incorrect to feel them*."[26] This means, if it means anything at all, that visceral desires, not science, enlightenment, or intellectual progress, are the woof and warp of what is good. Knowing more about an object or action may or may not elicit our praise. Whether it does or does not is accidental, not essential. Someone may call *Moby-Dick* good for no better reason than she calls cherry pie good; someone else may call it bad for no better reason than she calls cherry pie bad. That students of value and literary critics might find Santayana's doctrine bizarre is beside the point. This is the doctrine he tries to justify throughout "Hypostatic Ethics."

Santayana's criticism of Moore and Russell, as well as his insistence upon judgmental relativism, does not exhaust his thoughts on ethical behavior. In *Reason and Science* he returns to the features and problems that we traditionally treat as part of analytic ethics. Late in this volume he distinguishes "Prerational Morality" from "Rational Ethics." Timothy Sprigge writes that for Santayana, "Pre-rational morality is a moral system based on various distinct principles, each presenting a response to some recurrent type of situation, but without forming a well-integrated whole."[27] What does this mean?

We find the hint of an answer when Santayana says early in the chapter titled "Prerational Morality":

> When morality is . . . casual, impulsive . . . , it is what he may call prerational morality. There is indeed reason in it, since every deliberate precept expresses some reflection by which impulses have been compared and modified. But such chance reflection amounts to moral perception, not to moral science. . . . This morality is like knowing chairs from tables and things near from distant things, which is hardly what we mean by natural science.[28]

Later, Santayana calls what he has just described "intuitive ethics," and that is precisely what he has in mind. For whatever "reasons," human beings recognize the need to behave in certain ways that are likely to serve the interest that each of us has in his own welfare, even if we cannot spell out in any coherent manner what counts as welfare.[29] Our intuitions and instincts do for us what reason has not yet been enlisted to do, that is, address the choices that we *sense* or *feel* are most likely to enhance our well-being and that of others with whom we live and whom we daily encounter. Nor are we to think that prerational morality is only a thinly disguised form of egoism. Insofar as one of our feelings and instinct is conscience, moral men and women also feel a need to behave out of benevolence and a desire to see the secure prolongation of society.[30]

The overriding problem with prerational ethics for Santayana is its limitations. This is a morality that articulates "universal laws which are indispensable to any society, and which impose themselves everywhere on men under pain of quick extinction. . . ."[31] There is no system or moral foundation in the purely instinctive grasp of obligations and imperatives. The philosophical moralist must be concerned to settle disputes that inevitably arise as opposed parties fail to agree on the moral worth of a choice, precept, or course of action. So too a reflective moralist seeks, as the history of philosophy confirms, progress in reaching or approximating the truly moral life. She must articulate moral programs and account for their justification. Unfortunately, prerational ethics does none of this: "A moralist who rests in his intuitions may be a good preacher, but hardly deserves the name of philosopher."[32] The patent inadequacies of an instinctive morality lead Santayana to address "Rational Ethics," which is philosophically and practically superior to an unsystematic morality that calls upon feelings and intuitions whenever conduct is justified or enjoined.

Santayana stresses that approaching moral behavior by relying on impulses has no connection to rationally grounded conduct. What repulses or attracts us is of more interest to physicists than to philosophers: "The physical repulsion . . . which everybody feels to habits and interests which he is incapable of sharing is no part of rational estimation. . . . The strongest feelings assigned to the conscience are not moral feelings at all; they express merely physical antipathies."[33] This is not to say that the alternative to acting and reacting out of impulses or feelings, which is acting under the guidance of reason, is acting through the direction of some trans-natural principle of rationality. No naturalist, and certainly not Santayana, would defend that conception of rationality. "Reason is an operation of nature, and has its root there."[34]

Because Santayana indulges no illusions about the force of passions and instincts that are self-serving and that sometimes harm others, he stops short of making extravagant claims in favor of the governing power of reason. He concedes that no "truly rational morality or social regimen" has ever existed and is never likely to exist. Following Plato and Kant, Santayana knows that the raw force of self-destructive and socially destructive inclinations often usurps the authority of reason as an overseer of just and moral conduct. This is not so much pessimism as it is an understanding of human limitations and frailties.[35] Nonetheless, there is no compelling reason to abandon efforts to approximate the ideal of "perfect humanity and perfect justice," a reply that Mill also made to critics who cynically insisted that utilitarians expect more from human beings than anyone would ever *willingly* invest in a moral life.[36] At this point in *Reason in Science*, Santayana begins to talk about rational ethics as what best enables imperfect men and women to move closer to the ideal of a rational morality.

Rational ethics helps us to lay bare the principle that underlies the ideal of rational morality. It tells us what a rational morality requires and ". . . sets forth the method of judgment and estimation which a rational morality would apply universally and express in practice."[37] Looking with admiration at the dialectic method that, according to Plato's dialogues, Socrates used to help others draw nearer to truth or to avoid error, Santayana announces that the method in question enables an agent to find out what he esteems. What he sincerely esteems ought to shape and direct his conduct in any moral context, and it is Socrates's method of questioning, followed by answers which beget new questions, that identifies what he esteems most. "What he really esteems ought to guide his conduct; for to suggest that a rational man ought to do what he feels to be wrong . . . would be to impugn that man's rationality and to discredit one's own."[38] Here Santayana affirms that rational ethics is a species of self-knowledge. Finding out what is right or wrong, good or bad, altruistic or self-serving seems to be an enriched understanding of what one actually desires or values.[39]

As Santayana exhibits the use and value of the method of rational ethics, we find that at base he has in mind what we might characterize as rational autonomy. Someone may be assisted, as several young Athenians were by Socrates, to discover what is right and wrong, just or unjust, virtuous or vicious, but here is the important point at the end of such assistance: "Each man is autonomous and all are respected; and nothing is brought forward except to be submitted to reason and accepted or rejected by the self-questioning heart." Santayana praises Socrates for articulating the necessary and sufficient conditions from which authentic morality arises. Socrates's ethics was not a web of directives sustained by threats against transgressors: "It was a pliant and liberal expression of ideals, inwardly grounded and spontaneously pursued. *It was an exercise in self-knowledge.*"[40] This exercise, if it is sincere, is what identifies the autonomous moral agent.

An autonomous moral agent, unlike those who are acted upon from without, frames goods and values for some purpose: "This functional good is accordingly always relative and good for something. . . . It is identical, as Socrates constantly taught, with the useful, the helpful, the beneficient."[41] And insofar as an autonomous moral agent, to behave autonomously and not simply in harmony with assorted impulses, must act rationally, she must also be *reflective*. "Human instincts are ignorant, multitudinous, and contradictory. To satisfy them as they come is often impossible, and often disastrous. . . . When we apply reason to life we immediately demand that life be consistent, complete and satisfactory when reflected upon and viewed as a whole."[42] Here too Plato comes to mind. A reader conversant with the history of Western philosophy is likely to think of the well-tuned or just soul that Plato describes in the *Republic*, Book IV.

Like Plato, Santayana finds no difficulty making the transition between the just person and the happy person: "If pleasure, because it is commonly a result of satisfied instinct, may by a figure of speech be called the aim of reason, happiness, by a like figure, may be called the aim of reason. *The direct aim of reason is harmony; yet harmony, when made to rule in life, gives reason a noble satisfaction which we call happiness.*" This passage does not mean that happiness is the end at which moral conduct aims. Such a position would lead critics to complain that Santayana is far less concerned with the moral life than with a life of self-love and self-absorption. He makes the more modest claim that happiness is the direct result of the harmonious or well-ordered life, the life of rational direction and discipline: "It is discipline that renders men rational and capable of happiness, by suppressing without hatred what needs to be suppressed to attain a beautiful naturalness."[43]

What do we make of the phrase "a beautiful naturalness"? Is it merely ornamental, something like grace notes in fine music? Is it nothing more than the verbal offspring of Santayana's naturalism? A more likely answer is that this phrase marks the difference between ungoverned naturalism, in which reason plays no special role, and elevated naturalism, that is, morally significant naturalism where the agent's reason (again, one of our natural impulses) exercises its authority. Perhaps this is what Santayana has in view when, concluding the discussion of rational ethics, he adds: "Morality becomes rational precisely by refusing either to accept human nature, as it sprouts, altogether without harmony, or to mutilate it in the haste to make it harmonious."[44] Among other possibilities, he may intend what many other philosophers, from Epicurus (341–271 B.C.E.) to Dewey, understood by the fruits of deferred, reflective action as opposed to choices made in order to secure immediate gratification.[45] The latter choices too often produce results that are far from the good that we intended for others or for ourselves.

The inescapable elements in Santayana's ethics are that he is a relativist; that one of his major concerns is to clarify the common language of moral discourse ("good," "bad," "right," "wrong"), and that, except for an admonition to be reasonable, he does not develop any system of imperatives that morally reflective human beings must follow. Once Santayana announces in "Hypostatic Ethics" that he is a relativist, we know that he will never countenance supposed moral absolutes or necessary and eternal principles of right conduct. His effort to clarify the language of morals and value serves fundamentally to buttress his relativism.

Santayana's committment to relativism tells us in advance of *Reason in Science* not to expect him to produce either a simple or elaborate theory of obligation. An implication of relativism is, after all, that no one moral principle or collection of principles is at base justifiable over some other principle or set of principles.[46] People who, for many different reasons, require a moral universe will be disturbed by the character and consequences of Santayana's relativism. They will probably try to argue against his claim in *The Sense of Beauty* (1896) that ". . . apart from ourselves, and our *human bias*, we can see in such a mechanical world no element of value whatsoever. *In removing consciousness, we have removed the possibility of worth.*"[47] The world to which Santayana refers is our world, the one in which we constantly pass judgments and evaluate conduct. On the other side, those people who deny that the universe is a seat of values will delight in Santayana's message.

We should also see now why Santayana's most comprehensive remarks on ethics are part of *Reason in Science*. Apart from issuing a brief for rationality and its fruits in *The Life of Reason*, Santayana wishes to account for the phenomena of human experience and aspirations. *Reason in Science* is not entirely devoted to philosophy of science. One of its concerns is to see what a science of ethics would look like and whether that kind of science is possible. Unfortunately, as Morton White points out, Santayana does not do the best job making clear what conception of science he employs in confronting these issues. Whether he has in mind the Aristotelian and Euclidean view of science that is an *a priori*, demonstrative enterprise is unclear. But it is no clearer that his model is one of the empirical sciences practiced by classical physicists, chemists, biologists, and geologists.[48]

These ambiguities notwithstanding, Santayana seems to have admired the lead of Spinoza and Hume in their belief that a science of human nature, apart from the ambiguities of "science," might be possible.[49] The burden of the chapters on ethics in *Reason in Science* is to explore what is needed to develop a scientific understanding of moral motivation, as well as the choices that one can anticipate given scientific knowledge of impulses (including reason), feelings, and habits. Santayana is in search of a science of psychology that takes into account the grounds for moral preferences. Psychology, in its turn, is subaltern to physiology and physics insofar as Santayana believes that every occurrence, including any occurrence we call a "choice," is an instance of the mechanical principles of matter in motion.[50]

We are free, of course, to be disappointed that Santayana does not provide and promote an ethical theory, but we have already seen that this is out of the question for a sincere and consistent relativist. His primary interest, when he turns his attention to ethics, is not what we ought to choose in a given context or what we ought to esteem as good without reservation. He wishes, perhaps paradoxically, to ask and to answer this question: "What is required to produce a coherent science of ethics?"

Mind and Epiphenomenalism: Dualism Dismissed

Another route to understanding Santayana's commitment to naturalism is to say something about his philosophy of mind and treatment of consciousness. Like Wright, Peirce, James, Dewey, and Royce, Santayana refuses to treat mind as a thing, and, as a direct consequence, he denies that "mind" or "self" denotes a supernatural principle that intervenes in the natural order and that is not subject to the laws of nature. "To a speculative mind, that had retained an ingenuous sense of nature's inexhaustible resources and of *man's essential continuity with other natural things*, there could be no doubt that similar principles . . . would be seen to preside over all man's action and passion."[51] That mind does not stand outside nature and is not exempt from the pushes and pulls of the mechanical world tells us only what mental activity is not. What it is, however, requires that we turn our attention to that which philosophers call "epiphenomenalism," a view of mind that Spinoza expresses in his *Ethics*, Part II, propositions 11–13. There we find that the mind is the "idea" of the body.[52]

A clearer example of what an epiphenomenalist believes is from Thomas Henry Huxley's defense of Darwin: ". . . [A]ll states of consciousness in us . . . are immediately caused by molecular changes of the brain-substances. . . . [T]here is no proof that any state of consciousness is the cause of change in the motion of matter of the organism. . . ."[53] This is not only a claim that thought is caused by a physical organ, but it is the additional assertion that thought and consciousness stand in an asymmetrical relation to their cause; i.e., the brain produces thought and prospects for self-consciousness, but thoughts are themselves powerless to effect changes in their sources.

With this much as prologue, what about Santayana? His most fruitful discussion of the philosophy of mind is from *Reason in Common Sense*, but in *Reason in Science* we also see why consciousness and thought require Santayana's special treatment. As a thoroughgoing mechanist, he will seek mechanical, material causes for the nature and causes of consciousness. Although explaining the nature and manifestations of mind may pose special difficulties, Santayana will not allow their resolution to become the province of metaphysics. Materialism rules and underlies every promising explanation. This presumption enables Santayana to define "mind" as "the residue of existence, the leavings, so to speak, and parings of experience when the material world has been cut out of the whole cloth."[54] At a minimum, Santayana means here that what we call mind and what we call physical things do not refer to two radically different orders of existence. Because we cannot locate mind somewhere in space or plot its coordinates on a map, we are led to believe that it and the data of consciousness are cut from a "stuff" that is different from tables, chairs, rocks and trees. But this is shoddy thinking. Since mind seems somehow more mysterious than bodies whose locations, movements, and vectors we can discern, many philosophers indulge that mysterious quality and give it a metaphysical status to which it is not entitled: "Whatever stuff has not been absorbed in this construction [of material ingredients], whatever facts of sensation, ideation, or will, do not coalesce with the newest conception of reality, we then call mind."[55]

Santayana also promotes understanding his philosophy of mind in terms borrowed from Aristotle's *De Anima*. There, striving to separate his own treatment of mind from that of Plato, Aristotle denies that mind is a substantial, independent thing; rather, he says that mind is the *form* of the body. Santayana tries to capture a similar idea when he writes, "Now the body is an instrument, the mind its function, the witness and reward of its operation. Mind is the body's entelechy, a value which accrues to the body when it has reached a certain perfection, of which it would be a pity, so to speak, that it should remain unconscious." A paragraph down, Santayana makes the same point using different language: "The soul is the voice of the body's interests; in watching them a man defines the world that sustains him and that conditions all his satisfactions. . . . Simultaneously he discerns his own existence and marks off the inner region of his dreams."[56] This kind of discerning is the marrow of self-consciousness or reflection, and with reflection there also comes a capacity to confront the world in practical terms.

Santayana likens the human brain to a boiling cauldron of ingredients that are endlessly transformed. "When this cerebral reorganization is pertinent to the external situation and renders the man, when he resumes action, more a master of his world, the accompanying thought is said to be practical; for it brings a consciousness of power and an earnest of success."[57] Even if Santayana's metaphors are sometimes strained, what remains unambiguous is his insistence that mind-body dualism is a sophism and that man is not a "conjunction of an automaton with a ghost."[58] Any philosophy that describes mind as a thinking thing is patently misguided. And trying, as so many Cartesians have, to explain causal transactions between three-dimensional bodies and immaterial, dimensionless minds is doomed to fail for the best possible reasons: there are not two different classes of ontologically independent substances and even if there were, no causal transaction between them is intelligible. Underpinning all of this is Santayana's confident mantra: The foundation of all that exists or that can exist is matter and the laws that it obeys. The thoughts that enable us to know something of the world are a fortunate by-product of the material organ that causes them.[59] In themselves, as epiphenomena of matter in motion, they are impotent.

An implication of this philosophy of mind, which Santayana by no means denies, is that thought as the effect of matter occurs with the same necessity that changes in matter occur. What a human being notices in sensing and registers in thinking is no more spontaneous than acceleration of a falling body dropped from a determinate height.[60]

An important element of Santayana's treatment of thought and consciousness is his attitude toward the instrumental value of cognition: "In so far as thought is instrumental it is not worth having, any more than matter, except for its promise; it must terminate in something truly profitable and ultimate which, being good in itself, may lend value to all that led up to it. But this ultimate good is itself consciousness, thought, rational activity."[61] Thought does, of course, provide ways to solve problems, and Santayana has no reason to deny that it does; however, solving problems, especially problems that pose impediments to getting about in the world, cannot exhibit the full and ultimate value of consciousness. In this regard, Santayana is nearer Aristotle's ideal of a human being's highest good and happiness than he is to those who first praise thinking well for its usefulness.[62] "Impulse makes value possible; and the value becomes actual when the impulse issues in processes that give it satisfaction and have a *conscious worth*."[63] In simple and direct terms, Santayana says that successfully to seek meaning and value in life is initially to know where to look. When we look judiciously, we find that no higher good presents itself than the contemplative life, the life of what Aristotle called "*theoria*." Untroubled contemplation provides satisfaction in and by itself. Here, then, Santayana agrees with Socrates, Plato, and Aristotle: A life is more or less rich and more or less worth living to the same degree that it is contemplative.[64]

From this attitude toward life, the perennial philosophical question of whether happiness is attainable is not so difficult to address. If one has the ability and will to indulge consciousness at its higher registers, that is, in contemplation, then happiness is surely attainable insofar as contemplation and happiness are inseparably linked. This is part of what Santayana intends when, near the end of the chapter "How Thought Is Practical," he says, "Thought belongs to the sphere of ultimate results. What, indeed, could be more fitting than that consciousness . . . should be its own excuse for being and should contain its own total value, together with the total value of everything else?"[65]

At one level thought originates mysteriously in the motions of the brain, and in this respect, to borrow once more from Huxley, is something like "the steam-whistle which accompanies the work of a locomotive engine [but] is without influence on its machinery."[66] At another level thought or a collection of thoughts that we call "consciousness" confers value on all that we come to desire.

A host of questions arises about Santayana's epiphenomenal approach to thought and consciousness. How, to take the most prominent problem, does the motion of matter produce ideas?[67] How can one account for this causal relation given a cause that is so radically different from its effect? Thomas Hobbes, a committed mechanist himself, wondered in the seventeenth century about this process since he held that "motion produceth nothing but motion."[68] And if thought, therefore consciousness, is nothing but matter in motion, why has no physicist, psychologist, or neurophysiologist been able to show that this is the case? Moreover, if consciousness can be resolved into the movement of matter, there is no obvious reason that it should, as Santayana claims, lack force. Why should this matter in motion alone be without any of the dynamic properties that all other matter in motion possesses?[69]

Each of these questions is reasonable. None of them is trivial, and all of them have been asked of materialists and epiphenomenalists for perhaps as long as materialism and epiphenomenalism have been promoted.[70] Lacking compelling answers, Santayana is in the position of other philosophical naturalists. He avoids metaphysical "nonsense" and refuses to populate the natural order with supernatural mental substances, but he too is burdened by a philosophy of mind that generates as many problems as the dualism that it is intended to supplant.

Knowledge and Skepticism

Santayana's skepticism is familiar to his followers and critics. Some of them maintain that without understanding both Santayana's skepticism and his solution to it, one does not know the marrow of his philosophy.[71] Others, including Morton White, are less impressed with this aspect of Santayana's thought and do not see it as an impressive contribution to American philosophy.[72] For purposes of this essay, a middle road is judicious. There is a need to know enough about the epistemological side of Santayana to have some grip on his overall philosophy but no need to examine it in great detail because some of what he says in *Scepticism and Animal Faith* (1923) is not unique to Santayana.

The initial chapters of *Scepticism and Animal Faith* extend skepticism about as far as it can reach, and Santayana's mission is to press the case for skepticism in order, he says, "to clear my mind of illusion, even at the price of individual suicide."[73] In this regard Santayana does what others, like Montaigne and Descartes, have done. This amounts to presenting the strongest possible case for skepticism in order to see whether knowledge is possible.

To build a case for extreme skepticism, Santayana begins with what he calls "romantic solipsism," which is roughly a person's incapacity to validate the existence of anything outside himself. So, for example, most of us believe that there was a past and that there will be a future that mirrors the past in its general, lawful behavior. This belief is, however, groundless at base. No one has knowledge of the future, and the claim to know the past does not stand up well against criticism. How can I or anyone else know that what I believe about the past, including my belief that there was a past, is true of anything? The images of my experience that

I identify as elements of the past do not constitute or contribute to knowledge. Referring to these images and to the metaphor of drama, Santayana writes that "... the moment they are out of sight the play is over for them; those outlying regions and those reported events ... are pure fancy."[74]

Doubts about memory and about the past are only one product of skeptical analysis and introspection. Introspection itself is suspect to the extent that a skeptic is asked to believe, as Descartes believed, that a substantial self or mind is the source of ideas, complex thoughts, concepts and the like. At least since Hume, philosophers have produced good arguments against the personal discovery of a "self" or an "ego." We know that Santayana shares these arguments and proclaims that the claim to know such a self has no basis in fact. The most that I find when I turn my attention "inward" is a loosely connected tissue of appearances: "Anything given in intuition is, by definition, an appearance and nothing but an appearance. Of course, if I am a thorough sceptic, I may discredit the existence of anything else, so that this appearance will stand in my philosophy as the only reality. But, then, I must not enlarge nor interpret nor hypostatise it; I must keep it as the mere picture it is, and revert to solipsism of the present moment."[75]

Once I recognize in perception that I confront, or am confronted by, appearances, any remaining claims to knowing anything become increasingly precarious. All my future expectations, insofar as they depend on memory and my trust in the reality of the past, are doubtful. At this point in Santayana's relentless narrative, he confronts skepticism at its highest registers: "Belief in the existence of anything, including myself, is something radically incapable of proof, and resting, like all belief, on some irrational persuasion or prompting of life."[76]

Santayana grants that skepticism when it is "carried to the point of denying change and memory, and the reality of all facts" sounds dogmatic and that if someone seriously entertains skepticism at this level, at least one fact (existence) arises from the ashes of doubt, namely that a strict skeptic is in the act of doubting everything. But a careful skeptic will avoid affirming that this is a fact. He will maintain that the proposition "A skeptic who doubts everything certainly knows that he doubts everything" is itself nothing more than a hypothesis whose truth must be tested. Then he will attempt to show that no indubitably *known* facts can be summoned to verify this hypothesis.[77]

What about someone who says that skeptics overstate their case and that experiencing the "given" at the time one actually experiences it, that is, any immediate datum of consciousness or sensation, exceeds all possible doubt? This sort of critic means simply that in immediately experiencing a color, sound, or odor, or in having an idea of a rainy day, there is no place for the skeptic's doubt. An immediate experience is given in sensation or thought, and there is no basis for denying that it is given. Is this not where Santayana or some other skeptic must grant that at some level, however unimpressive it might be, knowledge is possible?

Santayana is familiar with this argument and has an answer. He replies, "Existences, then, from the point of view of knowledge, are facts or events *affirmed*, not images seen or topics merely entertained."[78] This is to say that the mere having experiences or ideas does not count as knowledge. It tells us nothing about the nature or presumed existence of any external fact or state of affairs.[79] No judgment is involved; no information is purveyed. Having ideas and experiencing sensations lack epistemological credentials. The pivotal point for Santayana is, as it was for Royce in a portion of his argument that an Absolute Experience exists, that experiencing and having ideas do not point beyond themselves to the existence of anything. "... [S]cientific psychology confirms the criticism of knowledge and the experience of life which proclaim that the immediate objects of intuition are mere appearances and that nothing given exists as it is given."[80] In other words, insofar as we are necessarily in touch with the world as we experience it, not with the world as it is in itself, we can never know with certainty whether our experiences actually correspond to or resemble anything outside and independent of us. If, after all, it is the condition of sensitive and intellective subjects that we encounter things (if we actually encounter them at all) only as-sensed, then we can never know or have good reasons to believe that things as-unsensed correspond to or resemble their copies in the "minds" and sensuous fields of conscious subjects.

And what does a potential knower or perceiver experience since it is not the external world of objects as it is in itself? Santayana's answer, which makes his skepticism and its resolution rather difficult to plot, is *essences* or, more simply, *essence*. "My scepticism at last has touched bottom, and my doubt has found honourable rest in the absolutely indubitable. Whatever essence I find and note, that essence and no other is established before me." The skeptic who sincerely seeks knowledge cannot be much satisfied with this indubitable intuition of essences: "To this mirage of the non-existent, or intuition of essence, the pure sceptic is confined. . . . To consider an essence is . . . to enlarge acquaintance with true being; *but it is not even to broach knowledge of fact.*"[81]

In an attempt to get at Santayana's understanding of essences, we can profitably look at a well-known text in Descartes's fifth Meditation. As a prologue to his final proof for the existence of God, Descartes appeals first to a certainty he finds in geometry: "When, for example, I imagine a triangle, even if perhaps no such figure exists, or has ever existed, anywhere outside my thought, there is still a determinate nature, or *essence*, or form of the triangle which is immutable and eternal, and not invented by me or dependent on my mind."[82] Descartes settles on the phrase "true and immutable natures" to include this and other indubitable data that are given in thought. If we go beyond Descartes to include whatever patterns, forms, shapes, and qualities are encountered in cognition and sensation, we have Santayana's essences. Sprigge writes that a skeptic "savours the character of certain forms of being, this colour, this pattern, this idea, and finds it indubitable that they are what they are . . . Santayana calls these forms of being *essences*. . . ."[83] John Lachs adds, "Essences are not physical objects and, if the notion of existence is restricted to items that operate in time and space, they do not exist. This does not mean that they lack reality. On the contrary, they are very real indeed, if only we do not mistakenly suppose that reality must mean the possession of physical or causal power."[84]

These essences *subsist* rather than exist. Because their reality is neither spatial nor temporal, they stand as possibilities that may or may not be realized or instantiated by things and qualities that exist, that is, that come to be in space and time and eventually pass out of being. Sprigge helps us again to see what Santayana is trying to get at in his doctrine of essences. Suppose, to use Sprigge's example, someone says, "Something is orange or nothing is orange." As an instance of what logicians call the Principle of Excluded Middle, the principle that any statement must be either true or false, this proposition is necessarily true. This means in turn "that orange must have ontological status either as exemplified or as unexemplified."[85] But whether the color orange is exemplified or not exemplified in space and time—whether, that is, orange exists or does not exist—that "Something is orange or nothing is orange" is a datum that some mind might apprehend, and the apprehension of its content exceeds even the most extreme skeptical doubt.[86]

Despite the difficulties inherent in Santayana's talk of essences and consequent reservations, one can take essences seriously. They serve Santayana's own skeptical purposes just as he wants them to do: "Nothing is ever present to me except some essence; so that nothing that I possess in intuition, is ever *there*; it can never exist bodily, nor lie in that place or exert that power which belongs to the objects encountered in action." Six lines later, he adds, "The evidence of data is only obviousness; they give no evidence of anything else; they are not witnesses." There is, then, an unbridgeable gap between essences on the one hand and existing objects (if any such objects really exist) on the other.[87] But where does Santayana's distinction, between what we actually intuit immediately and what we merely believe to exist, take us? Even if we choose not to question his doctrine of essences, what does it amount to and where does it lead within his more general theory of knowledge? An answer, or a hint at one, follows: "I have already discovered what this bed-rock of perfect certitude is; somewhat disconcertingly, it turns out to be in the regions of the rarest ether. *I have absolute assurance of nothing save of the character of some given essence; the rest is arbitrary belief or interpretation added by my animal impulse.*"[88]

The account of the limitations of certainty and remarks about "animal impulse," an alternative phrase for "animal faith," help us to answer the question that still remains. If one is talking about knowledge as strict certainty, that is, about the conception of knowledge that we properly identify with Plato, Aristotle, Descartes, Spinoza, Locke (when Locke is being consistent), and many other lesser philosophical lights, then Santayana's position is that of a doctrinaire skeptic: "So long as a knowledge is demanded that shall be intuition, the issue can only be laughter or despair; for if I attain intuition, I have only a phantom object; and if I spurn that and turn to the facts, I have renounced intuition. This assumption alone suffices, therefore, to disprove the possibility of knowledge."[89] With the traditional standard of knowledge as certainty and appropriate objects of knowledge as the "things" about which certainty is possible, Santayana is correct to say that his and similar skeptical arguments disprove the possibility of knowing anything beyond essences.

Consider, for example, Descartes's claim that beyond what we intuit or absolutely demonstrate to be the case—such as any of Euclid's five Axioms ("common notions") or the theorem "The three interior angles of a triangle equal two right angles," respectively—there is no knowledge.[90] Then there is Locke's declaration, "These two, (*viz.*) Intuition and Demonstration, are the degrees of our Knowledge; whatever comes short of one of these, with what assurance soever embraced, is but Faith, or Opinion, but not Knowledge, at least in all general

Truths."[91] These are the conceptions of knowledge Santayana has in mind when he argues for skepticism. The consequences for Santayana and for those who wish to understand the philosophy of *Scepticism and Animal Faith* are clear: If knowledge always amounts to certainty, and if the only certainty we possess lies in the intuition of essences, then we cannot *know* that an external world of bodies exists, that each of us is a unified self or that there are other human beings with whom we frequently come into contact.

Is Santayana a skeptic? Sprigge says that he is not, and this seems to be correct.[92] He is a skeptic if and only if the standard for knowledge and for that which we can know remains what the tradition from Plato into at least the opening decades of the twentieth century endorses. If, however, a philosopher such as Moore or Santayana loosens the criteria for knowing, then regarding Santayana as a skeptic is overdone.[93] And loosening the criteria for knowledge is just what Santayana does: "Plato and many other philosophers . . . have identified science with certitude, and consequently entirely condemned what I call knowledge (which is a form of animal faith) or relegated it to an inferior position, as something merely necessary for life."[94] Santayana, unlike the traditionalists and the restrictions they impose on what counts as knowledge, insists:

> *Knowledge accordingly is belief: belief in a world of events, and especially those parts of it which are near the self, tempting or threatening it. This belief is native to animals. . . . Furthermore, knowledge is true belief. . . .* The object of this tentative knowledge is things in general, whatsoever may be at work (as I am) to disturb me or awake my attention.[95]

Now this revision of what counts as knowledge is also very close to Locke's own addendum when he tries to account for knowledge of an external world and finds that intuition and demonstration fall short of his need. Quite out of the blue, he introduces sensitive knowledge, and adds, "*The notice we have by our Senses, of the existing of Things without* us, though it be not altogether so certain, as our intuitive Knowledge, or the Deductions of our Reason, employ'd about the clear abstract *Ideas* of our own Minds; yet it is an assurance that *deserves the name of Knowledge*."[96]

Santayana's "animal faith" is not much different from Locke's account of sensitive knowledge as an undeniable conviction that there is a world of bodies. "[K]nowledge is true belief grounded in experience, I mean, controlled by outer facts. . . . It arises by a movement of the self sympathetic or responsive to surrounding beings . . . , and at the same time an appropriate correspondence tends to be established between these objects and the beliefs generated under their influence."[97]

If someone were to ask Santayana where, apart from an irrefragable belief, she can look for evidence that supports this nontraditional picture of knowledge, he would be candid and forthright: "In regard to the original articles of the animal creed—that there is a world, that there is a future, that things sought can be found, and things seen can be eaten—no guarantee can possibly be offered. . . . But while life lasts, in one form or another this faith must endure."[98] Here, therefore, the belief that for Santayana amounts to knowledge is far more a matter of the urgency to act and incapacity to doubt than it is the product of empirical verification or rational demonstration. In some sense, one that might reach back to Peirce, animal faith becomes belief (or already amounts to belief) insofar as resolving a problem or answering a question carries this urgency that a troubled or curious agent cannot ignore. This is the kind of urgency that begets and sustains action.[99]

Paul Conkin says it as well as anyone else when he writes about the results of Santayana's epistemological excursions:

> But one can still doubt. . . . Santayana explored to the quick this doubt and drove it relentlessly to its bitter end of complete solipsism. Yet, he conceived such complete skepticism as *practical* foolishness, as a feigned, abstract product of reflection torn asunder from the active life of an animal. . . . Born in the primitive mold of brute experience, reflection reaches the height of practical (not logical) absurdity when it feeds upon itself and denies the existence of matter or, in interpreting its inability to mirror perfectly the whole universe, as license for complete doubt.[100]

This is not skepticism; rather, it is Santayana's rejection of an ideally high standard for knowledge, at least where knowledge of our world and our own minds is the issue. Plato argued in the *Cratylus* (440a–b) that there could be no knowledge of that which changes and that knowledge must, therefore, be of that which is eternal. On this view, it follows that the world of bodies and events in space and time are unknowable. Santayana's move is to deny the Platonic presumption and to allow knowledge far greater latitude.

Santayana continued to believe that the contemplative ideal can well express a human being's highest good: "To cease to live temporally is intellectually to be saved; it is . . . to fade or brighten into the truth, and to become eternal."[101] Contemplation at this level brings with it security, peace, and almost inexpressible happiness. There is, however, an unfortunate or, better, an indisputable fact about being a human animal: life itself is not always secure, peaceful, and serene. It crowds us, threatens us, and calls for remedial action. This is simply a fact about the world and about our abbreviated stay in it. Where this world is concerned, animal faith, not detached contemplation or the intuition of essences, counters forces that might harm us, adjusts to the fortune and misfortune that blindly come our way and, in the end, enables us to fight the good fight.

Conclusion

As with Royce, so also with Santayana: There is more to say, and any stopping point or omission may seem arbitrary. There is, for example, Santayana's view of truth, philosophy of culture, philosophy of religion, and philosophy of art. Each of these areas merits discussion. But since there is not "world enough and time" to review every aspect of his mature philosophy, this much will have to do for the present volume.

But in selecting those elements of Santayana's thought that constitute this essay, one can find a good deal to ponder, accept, or reject. Perhaps some readers will decide that the five-volume *The Life of Reason* or the more compact *Skepticism and Animal Faith* and *Winds of Doctrine* are enough to get at Santayana's beliefs and arguments as he builds a philosophical system. Others, who might wish to learn more about his literary talents, can read *The Last Puritan: A Memoir in the Form of a Novel* (1936), in which "He sympathized with the totally spiritual man, out of place and uneasy in the ordinary tasks of the world."[102] Of Santayana, as of other major philosophers, it is fair to say that no sample of his works—even if it is broadly representative—provides the whole story.

On the other hand, the selections that constitute the core and perimeter of this essay provide more than a taste of what a distinguished thinker and author argued and wrote when he concentrated on issues that are, so to speak, the meat and potatoes of philosophical activity in America and Europe. Whether moral judgments and values are objective and absolute or subjective and variable, whether a person is the totality of his or her experiences or something more, whether the world of appearances and essences is a reliable conduit to the world of existences—each of these issues reaches as far back as the Greek origins of Western philosophy.

What is novel about Santayana is not so much the issues that he chooses to probe but rather the character and results of his curiosity. Only the rarest of philosophers argue incisively for the subjectivity of ethical judgments and at the same time write lyrically about the place of objective reason in morals. Only an unusually clever philosopher first produces compelling arguments for naturalism, —for example, the view that human beings are continuous with nature, that no man or woman is, in John Donne's memorable phrase, "a little world made cunningly"—and next writes in almost spiritual tones about talents and qualities that set us apart (almost qualitatively) from every other animal who shares our planet.[103] Perhaps it is also a rare philosopher who expresses his impatience with metaphysics but is at the same time eager to defend his doctrine of essences, a doctrine that supports an order of infinitely many "things" that do not exist, yet do subsist.[104]

Possibly, although this is mere speculation, Santayana's approach to many philosophical issues and problems mirrors the man. He came to America and left with a deeper understanding of the nature and history of American philosophy than possibly anyone else whom we have discussed. A case for this claim could be made given only the content and analysis of "The Genteel Tradition in Philosophy." Santayana was a master of American culture and society, yet he could not wait to separate himself from both. He saw himself as an exile in the United States throughout the nearly forty years that he lived in Massachusetts and taught at Harvard.

Without pushing any of this too far beyond its tolerances, Santayana's restlessness and estrangement (from his colleagues, from his distinguished university and, for nearly half his life, from the United States) may find an image in his philosophical approach. Ancient skeptics say that they must follow the rules and customs of where they live but that they have no reason to believe that they are following immutable legal or moral verities. Santayana's treatment of skepticism, coupled to his moral relativism, conveys a similar message. Santayana, the philosopher, has no use for vacuous talk about a substantial ego. He says that we will never find any separate self no matter how carefully we search and turn our attention inward. Reading McCormick's fine biography leaves one with a similar opinion of Santayana, the man.[105] He seems more a loosely conjoined bundle of choices, expectations, fears, and disappointments than a thoughtfully crafted, self-made man. His ambivalence about being a full professor at Harvard, but still spending those twenty-three years as a member of the faculty, can suggest someone searching for identity but failing, even in mid-life, to find it. He would not allow himself to be identified with his profession; he would live his long life throughout the United States and Europe but would never find a permanent, satisfying home. Here too, like that which the second-century skeptic Sextus Empiricus describes at the beginning of *Outlines of Pyrrhonism*, he searches but seems never to find whatever it is that he is after.[106]

When we put speculation aside, what remains is a remarkable philosopher whose reach in philosophy is substantial. There are reasons to say of Santayana, without any hyperbole, that he is a good candidate for the epithet "last great *American* philosopher." This is to claim that whether Santayana thought of himself as American, as Spanish, as a citizen of the world, or as a man without a country, he produced a philosophy whose roots run deep into American soil. Yes, he owed philosophical debts to Plato, Aristotle, Spinoza, and others. He was also indebted in some measure to Peirce and James.

What sets Santayana apart from his American successors is the richness of his philosophical understanding and capacity for synthesis. He not only recognized how much American philosophy was determined by its Calvinist and Transcendentalist sources, but he argued persuasively that Jamesian pragmatism broke the stranglehold that had slowed America's philosophical growth. He took on Russell and Moore, both major philosophers by 1910, and so forcefully challenged their ethical theories that Russell changed his view partly in response to Santayana's criticisms.[107] Santayana favored naturalism and enriched it in *The Life of Reason*. He, as much as or more than Dewey, inspired a younger generation of philosophical naturalists. And despite his own distaste for metaphysics, he managed to couple naturalism with realism (i.e., his doctrine of essences) in ways that cut against the grain of anti-metaphysical attitudes that, with a few exceptions—especially the work of Alfred North Whitehead—dominated American philosophy throughout most of the twentieth century.[108]

There is doubtless some irony that Santayana questioned how Dewey could be both a naturalist and a metaphysician in *Experience and Nature*. McCormick wryly comments that Santayana must have known that this is "a question asked many times about his own philosophy."[109] Moreover, the question is fair. Santayana did somehow forge a union, or at least a truce, between sturdy, earthbound naturalism and metaphysical suggestions that the class of essences, of things that do not exist, is as philosophically interesting as existences that endure for a while in space and time. No one in America since Santayana has managed anything close to such a synthesis.

In the end, therefore, one can justly claim that Santayana made unique, important, and lasting contributions to American philosophy, not simply to philosophy developed *in* America. And when he left the United States, he took with him much of what he had thought about as a professor in Harvard's philosophical Golden Age. Santayana's remains are interred in Rome, but his philosophy still lives as a beacon that attracts the attention of those who are eager to know philosophy in America yet have the time to study only its philosophers *par excellence.*

NOTES

1. Timothy L. S. Sprigge, *Santayana: An Examination of His Philosophy* (London, 1974), 27; hereafter abbreviated as *Santayana.*
2. *Science and Sentiment in America,* (New York, 1972), 241. For a brief account of Santayana's life, see *Santayana,* 21–9.
3. The lecture was included in *Winds of Doctrine: Studies in Contemporary Opinion* (1913), in *The Works of George Santayana* (15 vols., New York, 1936), IV, 127–50; hereafter abbreviated as *Works.*
4. Ibid. 129.
5. Ibid. 130.
6. Ibid. 131.
7. Ibid. 132.
8. Ibid.
9. Ibid. 137.
10. Ibid. 355–6. Santayana's enthusiasm for James's approach to philosophy is not matched by his ambivalent attitudes toward James, the man. Louis Menand, *The Metaphysical Club* (New York, 2001), 76–7.
11. *Works,* 143–4.
12. Ibid. 145.
13. Ibid. 146.
14. Ibid. 148–9.
15. Russell states his position in "The Elements of Ethics," in *Philosophical Essays,* revised edition (London, 1966). For summaries of Moore's and Russell's positions, see *Santayana,* 189–90.
16. *Principia Ethica,* reprint (Cambridge, 1962), 6; emphasis added.
17. "Hypostatic Ethics," in *Winds of Doctrine,* 115.
18. George Santayana, *Reason in Science,* from *The Life of Reason,* 2nd edition (5 vols., New York, 1936). *Works,* V, 155; emphasis added.
19. George Santayana, *Persons and Places* (New York, 1943–47), critical edition, ed. Herman J. Saatkamp and intro. Richard C. Lyon (Cambridge, Mass., 1986), 234; emphasis added.
20. For an account and criticism of ethical naturalism, see William K. Frankena, *Ethics,* 2nd edition (Englewood Cliffs, 1973), 96–102.
21. Ibid. 97–101, 109–10.
22. *Works,* VII, 125.
23. Ibid. 124.
24. See Sprigge's comments on Santayana's view of the possibility of beneficial ties between relativism and tolerance. *Santayana,* 195.
25. *Works,* VII, 117–18.
26. Ibid. 118; emphasis added.
27. *Santayana,* 209–10.
28. *Works,* V, 153.
29. For an economical criticism of "intuitive" ethics or what Santayana prefers to call prerational ethics, see John Stuart Mill, *Utilitarianism* (1863), ed. Roger Crisp (Oxford, 1998), 50–51.
30. *Works,* V, 165–66, 167–68.

31. Ibid. 167.
32. Ibid.
33. Ibid. 169.
34. Ibid. 171. See also *Santayana*, 198.
35. *Works*, V, 172.
36. *Utilitarianism*, 64–5.
37. *Works*, V, 173.
38. Ibid. 173–4.
39. See *Santayana*, 191.
40. *Works*, V, 174–5; emphasis added.
41. Ibid. 176. See also Santayana's rejection of tasks that are imposed from the outside and that are also identified as moral, 179.
42. Ibid. 180.
43. Ibid. 182; emphasis added.
44. Ibid. 183.
45. *Santayana*, 199. See also Dewey, *The Quest for Certainty* (New York, 1929), 225–8, and *The Epicurus Reader*, trans. and ed. Brad Inwood and L. P. Gerson (Indianapolis, 1994), 30.
46. For a discussion of this point of view and its implications in Santayana, see ibid. 195–96, and John McCormick, *George Santayana: A Biography* (New York, 1987), 349–50.
47. *Works*, I, 17; emphasis added.
48. *Science and Sentiment in America*, 254–6.
49. See especially, Spinoza's *Ethics*, Preface to Part III, and Hume's *A Treatise of Human Nature*, ed. L. A. Selby-Bigge, rev. P. H. Nidditch (Oxford, 1978), xiii–xix.
50. *Works*, V, 55; emphasis added.
51. Ibid. 54; emphasis added.
52. For a discussion of what Spinoza means by this claim and how it blunts Platonic and Cartesian views of minds or souls as mental substances that are radically different from bodily substances, see Genevieve Lloyd, *Spinoza and the Ethics* (London, 1996), 6–9.
53. Quoted in *The Metaphysical Club*, 259, from "On the Hypothesis that Animals are Automata, and its History," *Fortnightly Review* (1874).
54. *Works*, III, 103; cf. 108.
55. Ibid. 105.
56. Ibid. 161, 162.
57. Ibid. 164.
58. See Gilbert Ryle, *The Concept of Mind* (London, 1949), 15–16. Ryle disparages Cartesian dualism as what he calls "The dogma of the Ghost in the Machine."
59. Ibid. 165–166.
60. Ibid. 167, 169.
61. Ibid. 170–71.
62. Aristotle, *Nicomachean Ethics*, X, viii, 1178b, 20–24. Once again, this is not to claim that Santayana is indifferent to the practical value of intelligence. See his unacknowledged debt to Peirce. *Works*, III, 177.
63. Ibid.; emphasis added.
64. Ibid. 179.
65. Ibid. 181.
66. *The Metaphysical Club*, 259.
67. For a collection of still important papers on this and other problems in philosophy of mind, see *The Philosophy of Mind*, ed. V. C. Chappell (Englewood Cliffs, 1962).
68. *Leviathan* (1651), I, 1, [4].
69. *Works*, III, 172–3.
70. In *An Essay Concerning Human Understanding*, IV, iii, 6, Locke admits the remote possibility that God, as omnipotent, could "superadd to Matter a Faculty of Thinking," but finds nothing to support such a possibility.
71. See John Lachs, "George Santayana," in *Pragmatism and Classical American Philosophy: Essential Readings and Interpretive Essays*, ed. J. Stuhr, 2nd ed. (New York, 2000), 340–48.

72. *Science and Sentiment in America*, 241. White does not even discuss Santayana's epistemology.
73. George Santayana, *Scepticism and Animal Faith* (1923), in *Works*, XIII, 15.
74. *Works*, XIII, 19.
75. Ibid. 26–7.
76. Ibid. 35.
77. Ibid. 40–41.
78. Ibid. 46; emphasis added. Santayana understands by "existence" not what we can say about the data of immediate apprehension (the province of "intuition"), but what bears upon "facts or events believed to occur in nature," 45.
79. For a condensed discussion of the "is" of existence, and thus of the meaning of "existence," see Santayana's "Some Meanings of the Word 'Is'" (1936), in *Works*, XIII, 289–90. Compare some rather different remarks about existence in *Skepticism and Animal Faith*, 121.
80. Ibid. 62.
81. Ibid. 69–70; emphasis added.
82. *The Philosophical Writings of Descartes*, trans. John Cottingham, Robert Stoothoff, and Dugold Murdoch (2 vols., Cambridge, 1985), II, 44–5; emphasis added.
83. *Santayana*, 43.
84. Lachs, "George Santayana," 343. See also on essences McCormick's *George Santayana*, 258–9, 271–2.
85. *Santayana*, 45.
86. For Sprigge's analysis and criticism of Santayana on essences, see *Santayana*, 65–94.
87. *Works*, XIII, 91–2.
88. Ibid. 101; emphasis added.
89. Ibid. 153.
90. *Rules for the Direction of the Mind* (c. 1628), in *The Philosophical Writings of Descartes*, I, 15.
91. *An Essay Concerning Human Understanding*, IV, ii, 14.
92. *Santayana*, 47.
93. See Moore's "Certainty," in *Philosophical Papers* (London, 1959), 223–46.
94. *Works*, XIII, 153.
95. Ibid. 160–62; emphasis added.
96. *An Essay Concerning Human Understanding*, IV, xi, 3.
97. Ibid. 162.
98. Ibid.
99. Ibid. 274–5.
100. Conkin, *Puritans and Pragmatists: Eight Imminent American Thinkers*, 429–30.
101. *Works*, XIII, 115.
102. Paul K. Conkin, *Puritans and Pragmatists* (New York, 1968), 420. Compare also page 472.
103. To take a single case, see what Santayana says about human nature in *Reason in Science*, chapters 5 and 10. *Works*, V, 91–120, 189–216.
104. For striking similarities between Santayana and Alexius von Meinong (1853–1920), the Austrian philosopher who maintained an unusual theory of objects, see Alvin Plantinga, *The Nature of Necessity* (Oxford, 1974), 133, and Bernard Williams, *Descartes: The Project of Pure Enquiry* (Harmondsworth, 1978), 155–6.
105. *George Santayana*. See especially chapters 13, 14, and 15 (178–226).
106. *The Skeptic Way: Sextus Empiricus's Outlines of Pyrrhonism*, trans. and analysis Benson Mates (Oxford, 1996), 89, 224–25.
107. *Santayana*, 189.
108. Whitehead (1861–1948), who collaborated with Russell on the *Principia Mathematica* (1913), left England for a professorship at Harvard (1924) and lived in the United States until his death (1948). *Process and Reality* (1929), his philosophical *magnum opus*, is at certain points impenetrable and is not clearly shaped by anything that is distinctly American.
109. *George Santayana*, 266.

Essay 9
Philosophical Analysts and the Persistence of Pragmatism

This essay, which takes us selectively from the period between the two world wars to the present, features no American philosopher who indisputably stands toe-to-toe with thinkers like Peirce, James, Dewey, or Santayana. The names we encounter from the late 1920s into the first years of the twenty-first century include C. I. Lewis, Brand Blanchard, Wilfred Sellars, Willard Van Orman Quine, Nelson Goodman, Donald Davidson, Hillary Putnam, John Searle, John Rawls, Saul Kripke, Robert Nozick, and Richard Rorty. Each of these men is an important thinker; a few of them are remarkable. But is any of them conspicuously American in the philosophy he defends? Some might argue that a recurrent feature of much middle and later twentieth-century American philosophy is that it could easily have been crafted in Oxford, Cambridge, Berlin, Vienna, or Paris.[1]

With this much as prologue, we will look in this essay at three prominent figures: Lewis, Quine, and Rorty. They span about three quarters of a century in American philosophy, and, together, they help us to understand what—if anything—characterizes the most recent years of academic philosophy in the United States. With an overview of salient themes and problems in their respective philosophies, we can consider in a brief epilogue how philosophy in America reached its present state and where it may be headed in the years to come.

Clarence Irving Lewis: Foundationalism, Epistemology, and Pragmatism Prolonged

In his recent history of American philosophy, Bruce Kuklick characterizes Clarence Irving Lewis (1883–1965) as "the most capable and influential American thinker of the inter-war period." He goes on to describe Lewis's classic *Mind and the World-Order* (1929) as "the paradigmatic twentieth-century epistemological effort in the United States."[2] Lewis studied at Harvard under James and Royce, was on the faculty at Berkeley until 1920, and was invited back to Harvard, where he spent the balance of his academic life.

Lewis was a logician, philosopher of mathematics, and moral theorist, but his enduring significance is his approach to the nature and limits of knowledge. A good place to try to spell out the dominant features of his epistemology is the opening paragraph of "The Pragmatic Element of Knowledge" (1926), in which Lewis writes: "There are three elements in knowledge: the given or immediate data of sense, the concept, and the act which interprets the one by means of the other. In the matrix of thought these are inseparable: they can only be distinguished by *analysis*."[3] What does Lewis mean in this text?

To answer this question, we begin, as Lewis does, with "the given or immediate data of sense." Laurence Bonjour says that in *Mind and the World-Order* and *An Analysis of Knowledge and Valuation* (1946), Lewis presents a classic account of the empirically "given" but adds that Lewis's comments on the "given" are, nonetheless, sketchy.[4] We are, therefore, left to our own resources in an effort to understand both what this central notion means for Lewis and how it functions in his theory of knowledge.

One has a sense why Bonjour criticizes Lewis's remarks on the given from looking at a passage like this one:

> [W]e must distinguish the given from the *object which is* given. The given is presentation of something real, in the normal case at least; *what* is given (given in part) is this real object. But the whatness of this object involves its categorial interpretation; the real object, as known, is a construction put upon this experience of it, and includes much which is not, at the moment, given in the presentation.[5]

If we link this passage with what Lewis says about the "given" and the "concept" as fundamental elements in knowledge, we can make some headway in knowing what constitutes the given.

What is given for Lewis is the ingredient in sensory experience that is basic and indefinable; it is simply experienced. When, for example, I look to my left and experience blue, the content of that experience is the blue that I immediately apprehend. The same can be said for a sound that I experience, an odor that overtakes me, and the textures and tastes of my remaining senses. Each of these is a basic experience with what is given as an ingredient of that raw experience. But there is more.

We cannot say much, indeed we can barely say anything, about what is given in experience because any attempt to give a description goes beyond the given itself. After all, having an experience of **p** and describing **p** are two distinct enterprises. But a failure to describe **p**, where **p** is given in brute experience, is not to maintain that our cognitive capacities are defective or that **p** is so remarkable that it "beggars all description." Here, Lewis may say best what he needs to say: ". . . in a sense the given is ineffable, always. It is that which remains untouched and unaltered, however it is construed by thought. Yet no one but a philosopher could for a moment deny this immediate presence in consciousness of that which no activity of thought can create or alter."[6]

Lewis is also emphatic that recognizing the importance of the given in a theory of knowledge is not to dignify the given and thereby characterize it as an object of knowledge. However surprising this may sound, the claim that the given is necessary to knowledge is not identical to the claim that the given is an object of knowledge. Experiencing a sharp pain or a deep shade of blue is not alone to know anything about pains or colors. We have many good reasons to believe that a three-month-old infant or the family dog has such experiences, but we have no comparable reasons to believe that the infant or dog "knows" the shade of blue or the sharp pain. Lewis is himself willing to endorse the difference between pre-analytic, noncognitive experience and that which interests psychologists and philosophical analysts: "It is indeed the thick experience of the world of things, not the thin given of immediacy, which constitutes the datum for philosophical reflection. We do not see patches of color, but trees and houses; we hear, not indescribable sound, but voices and violins. What we most certainly know are objects and full-bodied facts about them which could be stated in propositions."[7] At first glance, it might appear that Lewis contradicts himself. How, a critic might ask, can he say that we do not see color patches or hear indescribable sounds and at the same time insist that such colors and sounds are given in basic sensory experience?

What Lewis means is that the raw data of experience are not *in themselves* objects of knowledge. What we confront, absent the capacity or equipment for knowing, fits into no categories that we can articulate or to which we can give any content: "We do not have any knowledge merely by being confronted with the given. Without interpretation we should remain forever in the buzzing, blooming confusion of the infant."[8] That we do not know only insofar as we are confronted by the given in sense is, however, not to say that we can know without being so confronted. Lewis is at base a doctrinaire empiricist who says in his own way that there can be nothing in the intellect that is not first in our senses.[9]

Perhaps we can better understand Lewis's treatment of the given if we consider, with Lewis himself, Kant's declarations as he begins to spell out his own theory of knowledge in the *Critique of Pure Reason*. Commenting on the conditions and ingredients that have to be included in a compelling treatment of knowledge, Kant writes: "Without sensibility no object would be given to us, without understanding no object would be thought. *Thoughts without content are empty, intuitions without concepts are blind*. . . . The understanding can intuit nothing, the senses can think nothing."[10] Long before Lewis, Kant insisted that without the raw data of sense—whether we call them "sense-data," the "given," "intuitions," or "sensations"—all talk of knowledge is vacant. The basic data from which knowledge must arise are the contents of sensory experience. For Lewis the basic, inexpressible data of sense are given insofar as they, as ultimate, serve as the foundations for knowledge. As Bonjour puts it, "Thus, for Lewis, basic empirical beliefs are justified by appeal to given experience, which finally constitutes the foundation of empirical knowledge."[11]

Because Lewis conceives the sensuous and experiential foundations for knowledge as he does, he is able to make a further assumption and to advance an additional claim. Insofar as sensory experiences stand at the foundations of experience itself, we need not waste time inquiring about the origins of the given. To make such inquiries is to treat the given as derivative and, as a consequence, to deny the status of the given as ultimate. The search for knowledge begins with what is given or, stated another way, the given is not a point of epistemological departure that is itself preceded by a more basic point of departure. Any such position leads to an infinite regress. We may usefully think of Lewis's "given" as a kind of cognate to Hume's "impressions" of sensation. They present themselves in our experience "originally from unknown causes."

Lewis believes that as long as one restricts oneself to the given—to the immediate content of one's own experience—certain self-referential assertions are immune to doubt. If I say of something in my visual field, "This is white," I am making a claim that may or may not be true. "No matter how fully I may have investigated this objective fact, there will remain some theoretical possibility of mistake. . . ."[12] Whether my assertion is true or false depends upon objective qualities that determine the color of this or that thing.

On the other hand, if I say "This appears white to me," I am reporting on the subjective content of my experience, not on any objective property of an object. And if I am telling the truth and know how to use color-words in the English language, then, according to Lewis, my assertion is indubitable. In such cases, "I restrict myself to what is given; and what I intend by this language is something of which I can have no possible doubt. And the only possible doubt you could have of it—since it concerns an experience of mind—is a doubt whether you grasp correctly what I intend to report, or a doubt whether I am telling the truth or a lie."[13]

The absence of doubt does not, however, entail the presence of knowledge.[14] The certainty of some sensory presentation does not point beyond itself. As far as Lewis is concerned, it conveys no information; hence "the presentation would *mean* nothing to us. . . . It is the interpretation put upon this presentation which constitutes belief in our assertion of some objective fact."[15] And this remark brings us to the role of concepts in Lewis's view of a coherent theory of knowledge.

Concepts are loosely what the mind or understanding imposes upon the given. They are what allow us to use language to talk about objects of knowledge and their properties. When, to take Lewis's own example, I describe something that I confront in sense "as a round, ruddy, tangy-smelling somewhat," my description "means to me 'edible apple'." My interest in what signifies to me an "edible apple" may be the sweet taste that accompanies these other qualities. Nonetheless, the taste I wish to enjoy is not part of what is given in my present experience, so I need what Lewis calls a "conceptual go-cart" to get me from the qualities I confront to the quality I wish to experience and enjoy. And this is where a concept enters the picture:

> Life is full of these undesirable interstices; in fact just so far as it needs to be earnest and active, it is made up of them. It is the function of mind to bridge these by assigning to the present given an interpretation through which it becomes related to, or a sign of, a correlation between certain behavior of my own and the realization of my purpose. . . . I phrase it by saying "That (denoting the given presentation) is a sweet apple (connoting among other things the possible taste)."[16]

Pivotal in this passage is that the concept "apple" is not "given" in my experience. This concept has epistemological and instrumental value, but it is not itself part of my brute experience; rather, it is what makes that brute experience something more than mere presentation. The concept is what makes experience intelligible and, strictly speaking, knowable.

There is a chance that Lewis chose his example from having read the opening section of Berkeley's *Principles of Human Knowledge*, where Berkeley writes, "a certain color, taste, smell, figure and consistence having been observed to go together, are accounted one distinct thing, signified by the name apple." Whether Berkeley was or was not Lewis's source, the two agree: "An object such as an apple is never given; between the real apple in all its complexity and this fragmentary presentation, lies that interval which only interpretation can bridge. The 'objectivity' of this experience means *the verifiability of a further possible experience which is attributed by this interpretation*."[17]

When, therefore, Lewis says, "Knowledge *always* transcends the immediate given," he has in mind a variety of intimately related facts: (1) The given itself enters into knowledge only insofar as it is transformed by a concept into something that we can denote by names such as "apple," "stone," "river," and "chair." (2) The application of concepts to the given enables us to move from the immediate present —the present moment of what is immediately given in sense—to expectations and predictions. If I say, "This is a lime," my experience of selected sensuous qualities unified under the concept "lime" permits me to make claims about what I know and about what is real. I can say, among other things, "This is tart." (3) The test to determine whether I am correct and whether "This is tart" is true lies in its verification or in the possibility of its verification. If it turns out that tasting what I denote a "lime" produces a tart or bitter taste, I can claim to know that this really is a lime (not the content of an hallucination), that "This is tart" is true.

Knowledge of reality and knowledge of the truth depend upon the "interconnectedness of experience and must be verifiable in the pattern of presented experience." Such knowledge reaches beyond the present and informs us that if **a** is also **b** or that **a** has the property **c**, we can verify, in fact or in principle, this conjunction or relation between **a** and **b** or **a** and **c**. In simpler terms, Lewis's position is that in knowing **a**, or that something is **a**, we must know what to expect from **a** or from that which we suspect is **a**. This in basic terms is what Lewis has in mind when he describes the intimate connection between knowledge and verification. And this is also what he has in view when he quotes with approval Peirce's statement of the pragmatic maxim: "'Consider what effects that might conceivably have practical bearings you conceive the objects of your conception to have. Then, your conception of those effects is the whole of your conception of the object.' 'Effects' which are *verifiable* can, in the end, mean nothing more than actual or possible presentations."[18] This passage brings us to another feature of Lewis's epistemology, namely to what he calls "non-terminating judgments."

Non-terminating judgments affirm something about objective reality. When we make these judgments confidently, we do so because nothing in our past experience counts against them. We might say that up to the present, all attempts to verify their truth have been successful. Still, what has been true and continues to be true is not in itself an absolute guarantee that what we judge to be the case will hold into the indefinite future.[19] "Theoretically complete and absolute verification of any objective judgment would be a never-ending task: any actual verification of them is no more than partial; and our assurance of them is always, theoretically, less than certain."[20] The conclusion Lewis draws is not surprising: "The empirical knowledge of particular objects is probable only."[21]

What about the specific function of concepts in empirical knowledge? Lewis's remarks can sometimes make the question seem more obscure than it actually is. He says, ". . . any conceivable experience will be such that it can be subsumed under concepts, and also such that predictive judgments which are genuinely probable will hold of it."[22] What does he mean? When I say, to take one of Lewis's own examples, "This penny is round," I am saying far more than what is immediately given, and I am saying more than "This looks round to me"; hence my subjective experiences are eclipsed by an objective judgment, one that is in principle verifiable and that, failing the test of verification, is erroneous.[23] In this and similar cases—such as "This is hard" or "This is blue"—I am doing more than expressing what is "given" in my private experience. "Round," "hard," and "blue" denote objective properties that are described as belonging to real objects. And what they are, as a consequence of their being identified as objective properties, are elements in predictive "judgments which are subject to verification and liable to error."[24]

The conceptual element in each of these judgments, and in countless others that we make everyday, is what we are prepared to count as "hard," "round," and "blue." The meanings of these words are not part of sensory presentations but once they are established, they determine whether we know, within the limits of empirical knowledge, what we claim to know. If, to borrow an example from Peirce, we define or stipulate that "hard" means "will not be scratched by many other substances," then *knowing* whether "This diamond is hard" depends upon our concept of "hard" and upon a procedure.[25] When I say that the diamond I am holding is hard, which is actually a duplex claim that what I am holding is a diamond and that diamonds resist scratching, I am implicitly making a prediction: "*If* anyone attempts to scratch this stone, *then* he or she will fail." If my operational prediction is verified, then I can claim to know "This stone is a diamond" and "This stone is hard" are true. The stone has passed through the same conceptual hoops through which objects called "diamonds" also pass.[26]

We are entitled to characterize our concepts as a priori just insofar as they determine, antecedent to some experience, whether this or that experience counts or fails as something we know. "The only sense in which categorical interpretation can be a priori is the sense that the *principle* of this interpretation is not subject to recall even if, in the particular case, what is given should fail to conform." Lewis adds a few lines later, "[I]n the case of the categorical principle, if experience does not fit it, then so much the worse for experience."[27] We can take an example that recurs in countless philosophical discussions of definition and the a priori. Suppose as pre–eighteenth-century Europeans we stipulate, "All swans are white" and mean, among other things, that for **x** to be a swan, **x** must be white. If we determine ineluctably that white is inseparable from the definition of "swan," then the English discovery of black swans in Australia turns out not to be a discovery of black swans after all. What we build into our definition or category is determinative.

A critic might object that we ornithologists are being unreasonable and that since the bird at issue has every other swanlike property, we must call it a swan and modify our definition. With this, we can anticipate a heated and prolonged debate between traditionalists and revisionists. But whether traditionalists hold the day or concede the need for an expanded definition, they can always insist that the category that includes swans is not the pawn of our experiences and discoveries. New experiences alone cannot compel us to sacrifice our categories and well-established definitions. These categories are, they might add, what gives experience its content, order, and uniformity. If, on the other hand, a revisionist makes a solid case that with an enriched definition we are in some way able to advance the science of ornithology, perhaps this definition will displace its predecessor.[28]

With his emphasis on the a priori element in knowledge and on categories through which knowledge and richer understanding are possible, Lewis is not very far from Kant's declaration, "But though all our knowledge begins with experience, it does not follow that it all arises out of experience. For it may well be that even our empirical knowledge is made up of what we receive through impressions and of what our own faculty of knowledge . . . supplies from itself."[29] Points of intersection between Kant's philosophy and that of Lewis must not, however, lead anyone to believe that Lewis was a pure Kantian. His view of the a priori establishes that he was not.

We have already seen what Lewis means when he describes concepts as a priori, but there is another species of the a priori that is of first importance to him:

> That truth which is a priori rises from the concept itself. This happens in two ways. In the first place, there is that kind of truth, exemplified most clearly in pure mathematics, which represents the elaboration of concepts in the abstract, *without reference to any particular application of experience*. Second, the concept in its application to the *given* exhibits the predetermined principles of interpretation, the criteria of our distinguishing and relating, of classification, and hence the criteria of reality of any sort.[30]

Up to this point, we have discussed only the second kind of a priori concepts, but what about the first kind, the kind that we most frequently encounter and have in mathematics?

In answering this question, Lewis first advances a definition of the a priori in general: "*The a priori is not a material truth, delimiting or delineating the content of experience as such, but is definitive or analytic in its nature.*"[31] We are to take "definitive" literally in order to understand the character of a priori propositions and knowledge. "Analytic" in this context designates a fact about a priori propositions, namely that we can discover their truth by looking at the intimately related meanings of their terms.[32] The definitions that we employ for a variety of purposes are not pawns or products of experience. They are "necessarily true, true under all possible circumstances, *because definition is legislative*." We define words in specific ways, and they are true just insofar as we, in the most literal sense, make them true. That "triangle" is defined as a plane, closed, three-sided figure was determined—perhaps one should say, "decided"—long before Euclid. Having been determined and accepted, this is *the* definition for "triangle." Even though our experience might have been "other than it is, the definition and its corresponding classification might be inconvenient, useless, or fantastic, but it could not be false. Mind makes classifications and determines meanings. . . ."[33]

The paradigm case for Lewis of a priori knowledge is, therefore, what we find in mathematics. We find that "The truths of mathematics follow merely from definitions which exhibit the meaning of its concepts by purely logical deduction. . . . The content of the subject consists entirely of the rigorous logical analysis of abstract concepts, in entire independence of all data of sense. . . ."[34]

We learn that the a priori is also characteristic of the laws of formal logic. These laws, which Lewis calls "the parliamentary rules of intelligent thought and action," are independent of experience and of all that is given in experience. From the premises "All A is B" and "All B is C," it follows necessarily and a priori that "All A is C." This syllogism is a valid deductive inference, and its validity is independent of the content of any actual or possible experience. Whether there are any real existences or occurrences to substitute for A, B, and C is irrelevant. The syllogism holds whatever the world of our sensory experience is like, and nothing in or beyond our world can change this logical relation between premises and a conclusion.[35]

Lewis says in his own way what Hume had written almost two hundred years earlier, when he distinguished "Relations of Ideas" (a priori propositions) from "Matters of Fact" (propositions whose truth depends upon what exists or happens in the world of our experience). About "Relations of Ideas," Hume wrote, "Propositions of this kind are discoverable by the mere operation of thought, without dependence on what is anywhere existent in the universe."[36]

If we grant with Lewis that a priori concepts and the "given" are two of the three essential elements of knowledge to which we referred near the beginning of this discussion, what about the third element, "the *act* which interprets the one by means of the other"? To answer this question, Lewis turns to pragmatism and offers this sketch of a pragmatist's approach to knowledge: ". . . knowledge is an interpretation, instigated by need or interest and tested by its consequences in action, which individual minds put upon something confronting them or given to them."[37] Apart from the phrase "consequences in action," a reader might continue to wonder why Lewis thinks of himself and his treatment of knowledge as pragmatic. What points to an answer is the remark that "Knowledge arises when we can frame the data of sense in a set of concepts which serve as *guides for action*."[38]

As a concrete example Lewis offers an abbreviated summary of the difference between the Ptolemaic conceptual scheme, which situates an immobile earth at the center of our planetary system, and the Copernican conceptual model in which the sun replaces the earth. Why did the Copernican system eventually displace the Ptolemaic system? Lewis says that the facts in the two cases had very little to do with choosing one over the other. The decision had far more to do with questions of economy and convenience. Copernicus's conception of the solar system is less cumbersome and more efficient than Ptolemy's: "So that the issue between the Ptolemaic and Copernican choice of a frame of motion cannot be decided on the ground that one describes the facts, the other not. Rather the one describes the facts simply and conveniently, the other complexly and most inconveniently. *The only issue is pragmatic*."[39] We favor Copernicus's theory because it makes fewer assumptions and enables astronomers to make their way more easily around their charts, maps, and photographs of the heavens.

Whether we are discussing the advantages of one planetary system over another, or something that is literally more mundane, Lewis's conclusions are the same. The conceptual apparatus that we apply to what is given in experience has as much to do with our needs as it does with what we might too facilely characterize as the truth. Echoing what he finds in James's "Pragmatism's Conception of Truth," Lewis ties truth to verification and to concepts as we use them to bring coherence and organization to experience. We are prepared to call "true" what best coheres with other experience that we already regard as true. This is the truth that is fixed and certain both because we invent it and because it does not depend upon the content of any sensuous experiences.

The truth that Lewis intends when he looks to James as an influence is essentially tied to verification: "Truth here is not fixed, because interpretation is not fixed, but is left for trial and error to determine."[40] We use the epithet "true" to designate a state of affairs that is compatible with other statements we call "true" and that serves our practical purposes better than some alternative, logically possible state of affairs. In the 1940s, the proposition "The quickest way to cook soup is with an electric range or a gas stove" was true. Evidence confirmed it; we could test and verify it over competing claims. For the past forty or fifty years, the proposition "The fastest way to cook soup is with a microwave oven" is true. Our verifiable evidence in experience does not lead to any reasonable grounds for doubting its truth. The result is that what we once called true is no longer true. Newly discovered facts, progress in the sciences, and different modes of interpretation permit us, individually or collectively, to describe some truths (those that are not a priori)—as flexible.[41]

But with respect to Copernicus's *Revolutions of the Celestial Orbs* (1543) and Ptolemy's *Almagest* (c. 150 C.E.), Lewis refuses to say that one is true of our heavens but is now false. Because there are different ways in which to interpret planetary motions, either of these systems, comprehensively worked out in mathematical detail, is true, or can be described as true, of the observational data. "The laws of celestial motion in the two cases would be quite different, and the divergence would extend beyond astronomy to physics. But both would be absolutely and eternally true in their own terms."[42] The choice that astronomers have made is not one between truth and falsity, although it is surely a fact many people believe Copernicus's conceptual system because they believe that it is the (heavenly) truth. A trained astronomer's choice is made on pragmatic grounds.[43] If Copernicus's account of the movement of the planets (including the earth) relative to a stationary sun accounts for the phenomena more fully and with greater efficiency than Ptolemy's, why on pragmatic grounds would he or she defend the truth of the cumbersome Ptolemaic epicycles? There is no compelling reason to do so.

Moreover, Lewis insists that what holds for the attitude of the Copernican astronomer also holds for the more general approach to knowledge and understanding: "Wherever such criteria of comprehensiveness and simplicity, or serviceability for the control of nature, or conformity to human bent and human ways of acting play their part in the determination of . . . conceptual instruments, there is a pragmatic element in knowledge."[44]

Lewis: A Postscript

It is fair to say that Lewis looms more as an important figure in the history of American philosophy than as a persistent influence. He has been the subject of criticism for his approach to the "given," truth and verification.[45] Moreover, criticisms of Lewis's epistemology are not altogether misplaced.

The "given" is the central component of Lewis's philosophy, but even after following what he says about it and what importance he confers upon it, a critic is entitled to ask questions. If, to take a single case, the given in experience is an ultimate category designating ineffable sensory apprehension—"ineffable" at least in *Mind and the World-Order*—what does this really tell us about the foundations of knowledge? That Lewis seeks this foundation and that he finds it in the given is clear enough, but does the given help very much to understand, not simply to name, the foundations of knowledge? To tell us that the given, sense data or *qualia* are the raw materials, without which there can be no knowledge, generates as many questions as it answers. We cannot ask about the causal antecedents of the given since that makes the given derivative rather than foundational. We cannot say much about the given since almost anything we say about it already assumes a superadded conceptual apparatus through which we come to have knowledge. If, therefore, we cannot speak of or know the given as it is in itself, it is hard to say in meaningful terms just how the given functions in knowing.[46] This is not to say that the given fails to play a critical role in knowing. It is to affirm, more modestly, that Lewis does not, despite the centrality of "given" to his philosophy, do enough to explain its role.

There may also be ambiguities about the conceptual component in knowledge. Sometimes Lewis talks about this component as that through which we are able to interpret experience and thereby constitute knowledge. "A mind without past experience would have no knowledge by means of it: for such a mind the apprehension would be exhausted in mere receptivity of presentation, because no interpretation would be suggested or imposed."[47] Fair enough, as far as it goes. We bring to our world expectations, generated by the uniformity of past occurrences, and out of the recollection of these occurrences, we derive probable knowledge.

But other philosophers have different accounts of how we come to this kind or degree of knowledge. Aristotle says this advance to the level of experience, and ultimately to the first principles of demonstrative knowledge (science), arises from our retention or memory of past regularities *in* our perception, not from what we impress upon the sensory manifold.[48] Hume says that the observed regularities in causal sequences produce *habitual* or *customary* expectations that are, on analysis, closer to *feeling* than to cognition.[49] For Lewis, however, this commitment to empiricism leaves a mysterious residue. To claim with Aristotle that knowledge arises from repetition of a certain sort or with Hume that its acquisition is affective is, Lewis believes, to leave the acquisition of knowledge unexplained.

Lewis has no taste for a theory of knowledge that rests on what is mysterious and thus accounts for less than it hides, but what does he say about the system of concepts that we impose upon sense data? He cannot say for certain whether these concepts are cousins to Plato's eternal "ideas" or whether they are our own inventions, although he suspects that they are the latter.[50] To this extent, the conceptual origins of knowledge are certainly something of a mystery. And if we do impose these concepts on the data that we apprehend immediately, and if this is what enables us to claim that we have empirical knowledge of the world, what more can we say about this conceptual or interpretive knowledge? What have other philosophers said?

Locke, to take an important case, treats substance as that which underlies and binds together disparate sensible qualities and so makes them knowable as a single "thing." But he admits that the concept of substance itself answers more to our desire to see the world in a certain way—as constituted by discrete objects to which we can assign names—than it does to anything we can understand. Only because we do not see how the qualities given in sense can exist on their own and unsupported, "we suppose them existing in, and supported by some common subject; *which Support we denote by the name Substance*, though it be certain, we have no clear, or distinct *Idea* of that *thing* we suppose a Support."[51] For Locke, we make disjunctive experience more amenable to our demands for unity and knowledge by employing a concept that does not itself answer to anything we can positively identify.

We find another such case in Hume's famous treatment of causation, specifically his denial that there is any necessary connection between the elements of a causally ordered pair. Our experience never reveals more to us than some event **c** followed in time by another event **e**. Nonetheless, for purposes of unifying and making sense of the world we actually experience—a world in which no event necessarily points to or entails another event—we assume and insist upon a necessary connection between **c** and **e**. But assuming and insisting upon a relation is by no means finding it between two events that are taken to be relata. What helps to unify our world causally and to provide the uniformity we seek is a *fiction*. Finding nothing that necessarily ties **c** and **e** together, we interpret the world as though there were connective tissues, such that some occurrences are more than occurrences; they are causes or effects.[52] Through our imposition of ideas and concepts, we make the world and our experience conjunctive rather than disjunctive.

What do these examples from Locke and Hume have to do with Lewis? All three say that we bring to experience more than experience presents to us. Locke describes his idea of substance as "confused" but still serviceable. Hume tries to account for the origins of our idea of necessary connection in the language of feeling and visceral expectation. Lewis maintains that the concepts we use to interpret experience and thus to make it knowable are a priori. In the end, however, mystery prevails.

Locke freely admits that we cannot know anything positive about the substance that we posit. Hume has nothing but noncognitive answers to questions about the nature and origins of our conviction that some events entail other events. Lewis's interpretive concepts have pragmatic applications but, except for those he describes in branches of mathematics, he does not make clear the origins of these concepts. We provide the structure and knowability for what we encounter immediately in experience. But even after a careful reading of Lewis, something remains unexplained about the categories we use in order to know about their interpretive fusion with the given. The analysis that Lewis provides does not help very much.[53] There is no direct way to determine, even with Lewis's assistance, why the categories of intelligibility—again excepting those of mathematics and geometry—are a priori. From what a priori cast of conceptual characters do we find or derive concepts that give content and structure to what would otherwise remain merely given? Why should we assume with Lewis that knowing the world as discrete objects that are related to each other, so closely related that some predictions could be trusted almost to the level of certainty, arises from the cooperation of sense data and a priori concepts?

Lewis never seems to answer this question. We are left to take it on credit or, more likely, to assume that he was not able fully to separate his own philosophy from the influence of Kant.[54] In the end, Lewis's a priori concepts or categories seem to be a priori almost by default. Unlike the "given," these concepts cannot derive from experience since, after all, their role is to allow us to interpret the given that arise uniquely in experience. Nor can they belong to a special category of what is given in a posteriori experience insofar as what ever emerges directly from experience is the "given" itself. By simple elimination, therefore, the concepts that give cognitive content and intelligibility to the data of experience must be antecedent to and separate from these data.[55]

If the remarks above are correct, it is no exaggeration to think of Lewis as (i) a philosophical analyst, who seeks to separate in thought the elements in knowledge, (ii) a positivist for whom the principle of verification is decisive in the search for truth, (iii) a pragmatist who demands that we ask about the use for knowledge and not only about its nature, and (iv) a Neo-Kantian for whom experience becomes knowable only when we bring concepts of the understanding to bear upon it.

Whether this Neo-Kantian aspect of Lewis's thought makes him an unwilling idealist is unclear and, in any case, reaches beyond the scope of this discussion. But if these remarks are a representative account of the contents of Lewis's philosophy in *Mind and the World-Order* and *An Analysis of Knowledge and Valuation*, we might justly conclude that it is as hard to say just what niche he filled in the history of American philosophy. Perhaps we are best advised to think of Lewis as one who absorbs and offers a selection of trends in American philosophy that we have been following at least since our look at Chauncey Wright. If this is a reasonable claim, one might add that American philosophy in Lewis's hands is not so much a unified theory of knowledge as it is a collection of different philosophies that enjoyed a tentative, transitory union. This union could not, however, last very long. Later analysts would find reasons to doubt that Lewis's synthesis had staying power; hence long before the end of the twentieth century, Lewis's major writings became intellectual curiosities that warrant the admiration of later philosophers but not their allegiance.

Williard Van Orman Quine: Denying Dogmas, Interpreting Reality, and Reconstructing Epistemology

W. V. O. Quine was born in Akron, Ohio (1908), educated at Oberlin and Harvard, served as a lieutenant commander in World War II, and returned to Harvard where he enjoyed a long and distinguished academic career. After retiring from Harvard, he continued writing and defending his philosophy until a very few years before his death on Christmas Day, 2000. For much of his academic career and retirement, Quine was America's best known and most celebrated philosopher.[56] We are, therefore, well advised to look at some of the salient points of his mature philosophical thought.

To begin to understand Quine's concerns and orientation is to look, if only briefly, at his extraordinarily influential paper "Two Dogmas of Empiricism."[57] The paper is difficult going, and some of the arguments are hard to follow, but its central theses are clear. There are two flawed dogmas in modern empiricism, especially in the logical positivists' empiricism that Quine had studied as a young man and had rejected:

> One is a belief in some fundamental cleavage between truths which are *analytic*, or grounded in meanings independently of matters of fact, and truths which are *synthetic*, or grounded in fact. The other dogma is *reductionism*: the belief that each meaningful statement is equivalent to some logical construct upon terms which refer to immediate experience. Both dogmas, I shall argue, are ill-founded.[58]

The analytic-synthetic distinction had enjoyed a long and nearly canonical history among rationalists and empiricists alike. Quine traces the distinction as far back as Leibniz, Hume, and Kant, and we have just seen endorsements of it in C. I. Lewis.[59]

Kant's conception of an analytic statement is that "a statement is analytic when it is true by virtue of meanings and independently of facts."[60] The problem with this effort to define "analytic" in reference to statements is that "meaning" is itself far from clear and is not able to do the business that Kant asks it to do. For Quine there is a fundamental question that Kant needs to address before we can accept or reject his conception of analyticity: "what sort of things are meanings?"

At this point, however, one need not despair. We might claim that analytic statements belong to two classes. Class (1) includes those that are *"logically true,"* such as "No unmarried man is married." The characteristic of this kind of truth is that it "remains true under all reinterpretations of its components other than the logical particles."[61] Such particles might include "no," "un-," "not," "and." Class (2) includes statements like, "No bachelor is married." The salient characteristic of class (2) is that statements that fall within it can be converted into statements like those in class (1) by substituting synonyms for synonyms; "thus (2) can be turned into (1) by putting 'unmarried man' for its synonym 'bachelor'."

Nonetheless, there is a problem with class (2). We do not have an acceptable description of this class of analytic statements and, therefore, of analyticity itself, since "we have had . . . to lean on a notion of 'synonymy' which is no less in need of clarification than analyticity itself."[62] So if one is to make sense of the notion of analyticity and thereby preserve the analytic-synthetic distinction that Quine's antecedents and contemporaries valued so much, the problem is to clarify synonymy.

Attempts to clarify synonymy are not so straightforward as one might at first believe. One cannot say that two expressions are synonymous because one is defined in terms of the other. If, for example, we show that this is so by appealing to a dictionary, then we have not accomplished much. Those who compose dictionaries study usage and record in their dictionaries that, "bachelor" is defined as "unmarried man." This is a lexicographer's report, but it is also the result of empirical research, a report based upon the actual use of the word: "Certainly the 'definition' which is the lexicographer's report of an observed synonymy cannot be taken as the ground of the synonymy."[63]

The problem that Quine takes up persists. How can we provide a coherent account of the meaning of analyticity, an account that is compelling enough to sustain the analytic-synthetic distinction? Philosophers might appeal to cases in which a definition and what it defines are strictly synonymous because philosophers or scientists have themselves stipulated this synonymity. This is fine as far as it goes, but it does not go very far. Quine concedes but then cautions: "Here we have a really transparent case of synonymy created by definition; would that all species of synonymy were as intelligible. For the rest, definition rests on synonymy rather than explaining it."[64] Where, then, can one go from here if his concern is to deny Quine's insistence that the analytic-synthetic distinction is too hollow to stand as a dogma of empiricism and positivism?

One move, which Quine anticipates, is to the notion of interchangeability. Here the synonymy that analytic statements require comes to this: ". . . the synonymy of two linguistic forms consists simply in their interchangeability in all contexts without a change in truth value—interchangeability, in Leibniz's phrase *salve veritate*."[65] If, therefore, "bachelor" and "unmarried man" are interchangeable without any change in truth, we might say "Necessarily all and only bachelors are unmarried men." But Quine points out that in a sentence like this one, presumed to be analytic, the adverb "Necessarily" is used on the presumption that it applies only to an analytic statement, and this is the problem. Quine's concern is to see whether one can make sense of a class or kind of propositions that is analytic. If, however, we hold that an analytic statement is one that can be introduced by the adverb "Necessarily," then "we have already made satisfactory sense of 'analytic'."[66]

In more general and instructive terms, Quine wishes to make this point against those who believe that interchangeability in a given language is what we must recognize in order to arrive at a defensible concept of analyticity. He also wishes to show exactly why the point he makes is clinching: "If a language contains an intensional adverb "necessarily" in the sense lately noted, or other particles to the same effect, then interchangeability *salve veritate* in such a language does afford a sufficient condition of cognitive synonymy; but such a language is intelligible only in so far as the notion of analyticity is already understood in advance."[67] In still simpler terms, if we wish to get at analyticity first by appealing to interchangeability of terms *salve veritate* and thus to cognitive synonymy, we must already presume a notion of intelligible and serviceable analyticity. That presumption is, of course, problematic since one who holds fast to the analytic-synthetic distinction is just the person whom Quine's criticism puts on the defensive. Quine wants to know the meaning of "analytic," and those from whom he wishes to have an answer presume the thing in question, *viz.* that he and anyone else interested in the question already knows the answer.

As a last ditch effort to maintain the analytic-synthetic distinction, Quine addresses the position that he traces to the Viennese logical positivist Rudolph Carnap. We are to consider some artificial language **L** with a set of semantical rules. These rules tell us, among other things, certain statements, and no others, are analytic statements of **L**. But this will not do the intended job: "Now here the difficulty is simply that the rules contain the word 'analytic', which we do not understand! We understand what expressions the rules attribute analyticity to, but we do not understand what the rules attribute to these expressions."[68]

Once more, if Quine's analysis is correct, those who try in the most refined ways to maintain the analytic-synthetic distinction are frustrated. These semantical rules that are supposed to identify the analytic statements in some artificial language are useful only on the assumption that we understand what analyticity is, but they do not help us to come to the understanding that we seek: ". . . a model which takes analyticity merely as an irreducible character is unlikely to throw light on the problem of explicating analyticity."[69]

Quine's conclusion is that despite the fine genealogy of the distinction between analytic statements, which are factually barren, and synthetic statements, which report (or misreport) factual information, no one has managed successfully to draw an acceptable, illuminating line between the two kinds of statements. No such distinction has been established either by logical analysis or empirical investigation. *"That there is a distinction to be drawn at all is an unempirical dogma of empiricists, a metaphysical article of faith."*[70]

This quotation is not only a criticism of the empiricist-positivists whose work Quine knew. More than this, it is a knife in the back of what these positivists reject out of hand. Any "unempirical dogma" or "metaphysical article of faith" is anathema to positivists and empiricists who dismiss it as meaningless or as "literally insignificant." Quine's remark does not, therefore, simply conclude his well-tuned criticism of the analytic-synthetic distinction. It also calls attention to the sense in which those positivists he criticizes are subject to the identical complaints that they forcefully, often intolerantly, level at an assortment of theists and metaphysicians.[71]

Quine does not stop here. The second dogma about which he has reservations, the "dogma of reductionism," is the lingering notion that to "each synthetic statement, there is associated a unique range of possible sensory events such that the occurrence of any of them would add to the likelihood of the truth of the statement, and that there is associated also another unique range of possible sensory events whose occurrence would detract from that likelihood."[72] Now this dogma might sound modest, but it overlooks what Quine stresses, namely that these so-called synthetic statements answer to a totality of sense experience, "not individually but only as a corporate body." What does Quine mean?

Viewing the verification or disconfirmation of a statement in terms of an identifiable set of observations is to view that process in artificially insular terms. Here we find Quine is still another philosopher who looks over his shoulder at James. We cannot validate or invalidate a statement merely by looking to a very few different statements that support or deny its truth. Experience is not so narrowly drawn. For Quine, as for James, when a new observation—a "recalcitrant experience"—jars the balance of our previous experience, we may be called upon to adjust our previous beliefs. These beliefs may, in some rare cases, involve the totality of what we formerly believed and called "true." The need for a reformulation of our beliefs may call upon us to "take a pragmatic stand on the question of choosing between language forms, scientific frameworks; but . . . pragmatism leaves off at the imagined boundary between the analytic and the synthetic." In the end, therefore, Quine too takes his stand with pragmatism, not with the specious demands and suspect distinctions of diehard positivists.[73]

Because Quine is more than a critical epistemologist and logician, it is also worthwhile to say something about his approach to reality, to what there is. In his paper "Posits and Reality," Quine considers the familiar ways that analytic philosophers have dealt with the recurrent question: In what does reality consist?[74] Some philosophers, following or anticipating the lead of physicists, tell us that what is real at base are molecules in motion. This theory has proved useful on the grounds of its simplicity, compatibility with standing laws of motion, scope, fruitfulness and, in some cases, testability. Despite these benefits, which are what scientists so often seek in their theories, one can say that the reasons to value the molecular theory of reality provide no evidence to support its truth: "Might the molecular doctrine not be ever so useful in organizing and extending our knowledge of the behavior of observable things, and yet be factually false?"[75]

The answer to the question above is a qualified yes, but it is in some measure beside the point. The molecular doctrine is less suited to answering questions about the ultimately real than it is to pragmatic questions and objectives that physicists wish successfully to address. "The sentences which seem to propound molecules are just devices for organizing the significant sentences of physical theory. No matter if physics makes molecules or other insensible particles seem more fundamental than the objects of common sense; *the particles are posited for the sake of a simple physics*."[76]

Perhaps most of us might say that the bodies we confront daily and about which we share a common language are real. These include, among countless others, tables, chairs, stones, desks, trees, blankets, and bottles. Further, we might pronounce these "real" because, unlike molecules or atoms, we confront them in experience. But what about the sense data that, like Lewis's "given," are nearer still to the senses on which we must rely if we are to know what is real: "What are given in sensation are variformed and varicolored visual patches, varitextured and varitempered tactual feels; desks are no more to be found among these data than molecules. If we have evidence for the existence of the bodies of common sense, we have it only in the way in which we may be said to have evidence for the existence of molecules."[77]

Although, therefore, the language and theories of the physicists leave us a sophisticated account of what there is and the common sense account provides us a world in which easy discourse and identification are salient advantages, the proper verdict ought to be that what is actually real are sense data. But this is a verdict shot through with dissatisfaction and doubts. We are left to suppose that there may be no other people in the world and that the real world may itself be nothing more than the collection of one's own primitive data of sensation. To know that Quine is serious about this is to look at what he says in an oft-quoted passage near the close of "Two Dogmas of Empiricism":

> As an empiricist I continue to think of the conceptual scheme of sciences as a tool, ultimately, for predicting future experience in the light of past experience. Physical objects are conceptually imported into the situation as convenient intermediaries—not by definition in terms of experience, but simply as irreducible posits comparable, epistemologically to the gods of Homer. For my part I do . . . believe in physical objects and not in Homer's gods; and I consider it a scientific error to believe otherwise. . . . Both sorts of entities enter our conception only as cultural posits. The myth of physical objects is epistemologically superior to most in that it has proved more efficacious than other myths as a device for working a manageable structure into the flux of experience.[78]

There is no reason to doubt Quine's seriousness, but neither is there a need to cast him in the role of a skeptic or solipsist.

Rather than doubt the reality of objects or expect physicists to doubt the existence of invisible particles, Quine believes that the basis for granting the reality of objects and molecules is that they enable us to navigate and to organize our experience. If we are seeking evidence that what we posit is also real, the best we can do is look to its fruits: "The benefits of the molecular doctrine . . . , and the manifest benefits of the aboriginal posit of ordinary bodies, are the best evidence of reality we can ask. . . ."[79] So regarded, we can say that sense data, the objects of common sense, and the particles of molecular physicists are fundamental, but they are not fundamental in a single fashion.

Sense data are what Quine calls "*evidentially* fundamental" since each of us is indebted to his or her senses "for every hint of bodies." He calls the particles that concern physics "*naturally* fundamental" because they serve, as well as we can tell, to account for the behavior of all that occurs. And the bodies of common sense are "*conceptually* fundamental" insofar as "it is by reference to them that the very notions of reality and evidence are acquired, and that the concepts which have to do with physical particles or even with sense data tend to be framed and phrased."[80]

If we concentrate on the "processes of the physical world," we recognize that it presents itself to us through our senses. When we focus on the way we address each other through language and when what we encounter are objects whose positions, properties, and interactions we express to each other using the tools of language, we tend to regard these objects as primarily real. When scientists, pursuing their scientific interests, use the data of sense experience, as well as what characterizes the properties and behavior of familiar macroscopic objects, a particular scientific picture of reality takes pride of place.[81]

None of these cases provides firm and fixed principles that can be employed to demarcate just how we confront the world. I can directly validate sentences about my having eaten breakfast. No other sentences, themselves products of any inference, are necessary or useful to confirm this fact about my interaction with the world, but this immediacy is not always characteristic of my experience: "Many sentences even about common sense bodies rest wholly on indirect evidence; witness the statement that one of the pennies now in my pocket was in my pocket last week. Conversely, sentences even about electrons are sometimes directly conditioned to sensory stimulation, e.g., via the cloud chamber."[82] We cannot decide antecedently what is real in terms of what we might call epistemic priority or proximity. A context and diverse interests often dictate what we might call "real."

Furthermore, the statements that we make about bodies, those bodies that are familiar and those that are far too small to encounter directly, are part of a larger system. But this larger system is itself flexible and, as such, does not provide a guarantee that things are always as they seem to be or that statements about them are eternally true. What we say about molecular particles is different from what we say about the conceptually antecedent bodies we sense, and what we say about the latter will be different from what we say about sense data. But no matter how we frame sentences about the world and about our experience of and in it, we are to keep in view the values that Quine stressed at the beginning of his essay—simplicity, fecundity, scope, and verifiability—"we can hope for no surer touchstone of reality."[83] These benefits may not provide some final transcript of the "real," but they are the best we can hope for as criteria for judging what we are prepared to count as real. In the end, for Quine, the best that we can hope for also turns out to be the best that we can do.

Quine's distaste for dualisms like the analytic-synthetic distinction, as well as his "holistic" approach to the intersecting orders of common sense, science, and sensation, might make an easier task of understanding his thesis in "Epistemology Naturalized" (1968).[84] In spite of his own firm commitments to empiricism, Quine saw the limitations of empiricism or of any alternative "-ism" in generating a satisfactory theory of knowledge. Among other things, a theory of knowledge is satisfactory if it enables us to make reasonable claims about the existence and nature of an external world, that is, about a world of bodies that are supposed to be independent of perceivers. Unfortunately, the story line is about failure for all the approaches to knowledge that Quine knew.

Descartes, Locke, Hume, and the logical positivists of the twentieth century offered no way to know a world separate from our sense impressions, nor did any of them find a way to justify claims to strict knowledge of general or singular statements about the future.[85] The dilemma for Hume and for other doctrinaire empiricists was that so long as they insisted upon what Quine himself maintains, they had to confront the impossibility of "strictly deriving the science of the external world from sensory evidence." What they and Quine could not reject were the two unassailable principles of empiricism: "One is that whatever evidence there *is* for science *is* sensory evidence. The other . . . is that all inculcations of meanings of words must rest ultimately on sensory evidence."[86]

Granting these two principles and the incapacity to use them to get beyond the world that we confront directly with our senses, Quine presses a novel approach to epistemology itself: "The stimulation of his sensory receptors is all the evidence anyone has had to go on, ultimately, at arriving at his picture of the world. . . . *Why not settle for psychology*?"[87] This amounts to conceding that insofar as so many traditional questions in epistemology defy answers, we would do better to look for the causes of what we believe and sense just as scientists seek causes for phenomena that they wish better to understand and categorize. In Quine's view, we are better off to concede the epistemic limitations of empiricism and then to recognize that traditional epistemology, especially efforts to acquire knowledge, has no fruitful consequences. In place of this barren approach to "inaccessible and ineffable" knowledge of some trans-sensory external world, we turn to an epistemology that, as naturalized, is a branch of scientific inquiry.[88]

Quine is not denying the legitimacy of epistemological issues and problems, but he is emphatic that we must see epistemology in terms that are at odds with most philosophical traditions. In a very important text, he describes the appropriate niche for "doing" epistemology:

> Epistemology . . . simply falls into place as a chapter of psychology and hence of natural science. It studies a natural phenomenon, viz., a physical human subject. This human subject is accorded a certain experimental controlled input—certain patterns of irradiation in assorted frequencies, for instance—and in the fullness of time the subject delivers as output a description of the three-dimensional external world and its history.[89]

Quine adds that the "relation between the meager input and torrential output" is one we are inclined to study for about the same reasons that have led to philosophers' interest in epistemology. We are curious about the connections between evidence and about a theory of the natural world that falls beyond and outside all the evidence that we take in.

With epistemology naturalized, we concentrate on *how* "human subjects," confronted by sense data, come to believe there is a world of bodies that is separate from them and from their sensations. Our answers, if we can provide them, should meet the same criteria in terms of which we respond to and evaluate any other scientific question. In order not to leave his position so vague that we are at a loss to know what naturalized epistemology is like, Quine provides a case familiar to philosophers at least as far back as Descartes and Berkeley.

"Our retinas are irradiated in two dimensions, yet we see things as three-dimensional without conscious inference."[90] Now, we ask, what here counts as observation? Is it our two-dimensional sensory reception or "conscious three-dimensional apprehension?" Philosophers who approached epistemology nonscientifically treated three-dimensional apprehension as primary, but found themselves unable to understand it. As Quine sees it, the question is simplified and so too is the answer once we treat epistemology as a branch of psychology and nuerophysiology: "What to count as observation now can be settled in terms of the stimulation of sensory receptions, let consciousness fall where it may."[91]

Indeed, once we are willing to treat epistemology as scientists treat their respective sciences, many of the old, haunting epistemological problems drop from view. The question whether sense data ("sensory atoms") are prior to the complex objects that we notice, for example, what we call "tables" and "chairs," ceases to be a problem worth any sustained attention: "A is epistemologically prior to B if A is causally nearer than B to the sensory receptors." What was once insoluble to philosophers becomes a question for psychologists and physiologists. This question, unlike so many in philosophy, has a straightforward answer, which Quine provides in an uncomplicated admonition: "just talk explicitly in terms of causal proximity to sensory receptors and drop the talk of epistemological priority."[92]

"Causal proximity to sensory receptions" has in its turn indefeasible ties to what Quine and others call "observation sentences." An observation sentence for Quine "is one on which all speakers of the language give the same verdict when given the same concurrent stimulation." The traditional and haunting problem of the subjectivity of knowledge-claims is addressed and overcome when we think of epistemology in terms of verification that is so much a part of basic science: "Since the distinguishing trait of an observation sentence is intersubjective agreement under agreeing stimulation, a corporeal subject matter is likelier than not."[93]

Put directly, verifying that under stimulation **s** (some visual experience or observation), all observers—or nearly all observers—report that **p** ("There is a red pen on the desk") counts as empirical confirmation that "I know there is a red pen on the desk." This example has no shock value, nor does Quine claim that it has. It amounts to nothing more than an instance of naturalized epistemology at work. Scientific procedures and evidence validate epistemological claims that skeptics and others, who fret about our knowledge of an external world, deny we can validate. But they make their skeptical claims largely because they see epistemology as an area that is different and estranged from the empirical sciences. Quine obviously disagrees.

Alex Orenstein, reflecting on Quine's position and why he defends it, offers a helpful comment: "This argument for why epistemology must be naturalized . . . involves one of the most integral of themes in Quine's philosophy—that we cannot stand apart from our scientific world view and make philosophical judgements. The philosopher's view is inevitably an extension of the scientist's. There is continuity, if not an actual unity, of science and philosophy."[94]

The position of anyone who defends naturalized epistemology assumes, as James assumed in "Pragmatism's Theory of Truth," that we are necessarily circumscribed by our actual and possible experiences.[95] If this is so, then philosophers who talk seriously about an extra-experiential perspective are dreaming. Skepticism is born from demands that cannot possibly be satisfied. Quine's rendering of naturalized epistemology urges philosophers to abandon these empty dreams of a privileged perspective and to see what we can know of the world as we actually experience it.

Richard Rorty: Philosophical Analysis in Retreat and Pragmatism Rising

Richard Rorty (1931–) is the only philosopher we discuss in this essay, or in any earlier essay, who is still alive. Born in New York City and educated as an undergraduate at the University of Chicago and as a graduate student at Yale, Rorty taught at Princeton for twenty years before leaving first for the University of Virginia and then for Stanford. He continues to lecture at Stanford as a professor of comparative literature. In a sense Rorty speaks for the demise of the analytic tradition in philosophy, although this is not to say that contemporary analysts are in retreat and share his point of view. Making an effort to determine that point of view is our task.[96]

There is no direct point of departure for trying to sketch Rorty's post-analytic thought—the thought on which his reputation rests and is likely to rest for years to come. One must, however, begin somewhere, so possibly the best point of departure is with some of Rorty's observations and complaints in *Philosophy and the Mirror of Nature* (1979), a book ten years in the making and one that philosophers, literary critics, and linguists feel almost obligated to read.

Rorty gives us a clue to the principal thesis of *Philosophy and the Mirror of Nature* when he writes of the pragmatism and holism of the Viennese philosopher Ludwig Wittgenstein (1889–1951), Quine, and the University of Pittsburgh's Wilfred Sellars (1912–1989), ". . . let us see truth as, in James's phrase, 'what is better for us to believe' rather than as 'the accurate representation of reality'. Or, to put the points less provocatively, they show us that the notion of 'accurate representation' is simply an automatic and empty compliment which we pay to those beliefs which are successful in helping us do what we want to do."[97]

Having carefully worked through the writings of these philosophers, as well as Kant's *Critique of Pure Reason*, Rorty reached a conclusion closely related to that of Quine, namely that it is difficult to justify even the idea of a philosophical "theory of knowledge."[98] The problem for Rorty, as it has been for James, is that there is no way to defend the view that knowledge is a "Mirror of Nature," an accurate representation of something that we call "reality." His position is that when we recognize knowledge in terms of "the social justification of belief," we will no longer need to think of it, incorrectly, as representational of anything.

Despite some obvious similarities, it is a mistake to think that Rorty is simply restating the argument and conclusion of Quine's "Epistemology Naturalized." Rorty recognized his debts to Quine, among others, but he also saw that he was himself moving in an even more radical direction where the status of philosophy is concerned.[99] Rorty sees beyond the naturalization of epistemology and argues that philosophy, as it is practiced by strict analysts and earlier by seventeenth- and eighteenth-century rationalists and empiricists, effectively closes its own shop and puts itself out of business. Therein lies one of the chief differences between Quine and Rorty: "If we see philosophy as a matter of conversation and of social practice, rather than as an attempt to mirror nature, we will not be likely to envisage a metapractice which will be the critique of all possible forms of social practice. So holism produces, as Quine has argued in detail . . . , a conception of philosophy which has nothing to do with the quest for certainty."[100] But what view of philosophy takes the place of the analytic tradition, with its appeal to the analytic-synthetic distinction and the "given"?

Rorty answers this question in part by adopting something close to behaviorism whenever the assorted problems of knowledge arise. He agrees with Quine, as well as Sellars, that we cannot account for the nature of knowledge by maintaining the view that the knower has ideas or experiences that represent reality. Rather, we do better when we come to understand that "an 'account of the nature of knowledge' can be, at most, a description of human behavior."[101]

Although the terminology of *Philosophy and the Mirror of Nature* is more complicated than what we find in James's "Pragmatism's Conception of Truth," there is a congruence between these two works that is hard to exaggerate. Truth for James is, as we have already seen, what works *within* experience. It performs the celebrated "marriage function" that enables us to move comfortably about in the world of thought and action. Because James denies that there is any possibility of standing outside experience to see whether it corresponds to or mirrors something we call "reality," there is no use and no good in adopting a view that a true statement **s** is one that corresponds to an independent fact **f**.

Rorty, having called upon Quine and others who also reject different, but related, theories of correspondence, says about knowledge more or less what James says of truth. Philosophers need to acknowledge that the historical clutter of attempts to validate this or that theory of knowledge miscarries insofar as what we know is conceived as a sentence that mirrors a fact. What we have at our disposal is behavior, chiefly linguistic behavior, and social constructs, and these do not provide an epistemological platform or foundation that enables us to get beyond language and behavior. The search for such a platform, our demand for such a foundation, like the quest for a theory of knowledge as a mirror of nature, is futile. The problem is old and familiar. If to know something in the strict sense of "to know" requires escaping a lockstep with experience, we cannot know whatever it is we seek. The implications for philosophy are deep and, as far as Rorty is concerned, inescapable:

> If there are no privileged representations in this mirror, then it will no longer answer to the need for a touchstone for choice between justified and unjustified claims upon our belief. Unless some other such framework can be found, the abandonment of the image of the Mirror leads us to abandon the notion of philosophy as a discipline which adjudicates the claims of science and religion, mathematics and poetry, reason and sentiment, allocating an appropriate place to each.[102]

In other words, once philosophy loses its function, that is, to arbitrate the claims to knowledge in the empirical sciences, the exact sciences, the social sciences, religion, and ethics, there is little left for philosophy to do. Having lost its preeminent role, it may have lost its function as well. This is the peril for philosophy and philosophers who think that their job is to secure the truth and to arrive at knowledge that lies behind or beyond experience.

Rorty delivers something close to this same message in the essay "A World Well Lost" (1972).[103] Here he takes on the position of critics who maintain that, "although our only *test* of truth must be the coherence of our beliefs with one another, still the *nature* of truth must be 'correspondence to reality'."[104] These critics insist that the "real" world imposes itself upon us as perceivers and knowers, and that *the* truth is what correctly describes this world. This world, as ultimately real, is completely "independent of our knowledge" and might not be mirrored in any of our perceptions or conform to any of our beliefs. But as soon as one suggests this picture of what is real, he or she has admitted a troubling and now familiar consequence, namely that what is true of a reality may be, in fact and in principle, inaccessible to us. What, on this view of the real nature of things, comes of the traditional philosophical quest for truth and desire to know? ". . . [F]or purposes of developing a controversial and nontrivial doctrine of truth as correspondence, only an utterly vague characterization of some such terms as 'cause of the impacts upon our receptivity and goal of our faculty of spontaneity' will do. 'Truth' in the sense of 'truth taken apart from any theory' and 'world' taken as 'what determines such truth' are notions that were . . . made for each other."[105] The unrelenting skeptic is triumphant. How can we ever arrive at or know that we have arrived at the truth that we are after?

Rorty believes that there is no satisfactory answer to this question. We are left with either an inaccessible realm that is "the ineffable cause of sense and goal of intellect," or something far closer to the views of James and Dewey: the world we wish to know is simply that conceptual scheme or system of objects and occurrences that for the present conform to our beliefs and verify our expectations.[106] Correspondence *within* our experience and coherence as characteristic of the countless beliefs we hold about the whole of experience work for a philosopher like Dewey, who has no taste for the sterile "quest for certainty." But experiential correspondence and a coherent collection of beliefs about our present experience, and about what we can reasonably expect from experience to come, is not enough for stubborn realists. They continue to talk about and to hope for a glimpse of ultimate truth.

Rorty's preferences in this play of alternatives is pragmatic. He has no loyalties to the metaphysical attitudes of die-hard realists. A willingness to "confront the confusion and clutter" of experience with all of our available assets enables us to navigate, to anticipate and, occasionally, to rest. As a result, "We may reach a point at which . . . we are capable of stopping doing philosophy when we want to."[107]

Rorty amplifies his attitudes toward philosophy in an important, frequently cited essay, "Nineteenth-Century Idealism and Twentieth-Century Textualism" (1980).[108] He announces that his concern in this essay is to refine a specific "crude formula and to make it possible." The formula, actually a conjunction of two distinct but related points, is the nineteenth-century idealist desire "to substitute one sort of science (philosophy) for another (natural science) as the center of culture" and the twentieth-century textualist's wish "to place literature in the center, and to treat both science and philosophy as, at best, literary genres." What does Rorty have in mind?

First, a characteristic of any science is a vocabulary shared by scientists who participate in a specific endeavor, and a characteristic of literature is that it proceeds without arguments. "By 'literature', then I shall mean the areas of culture which . . . forego agreement on an encompassing critical vocabulary, and thus forego argumentation."[109] From the perspective of nineteenth-century idealists, who disparage the mission of the sciences, in favor of the wider and richer scope of philosophy, and of textualists, who ask whether a literary vocabulary or language is "good" rather than "true," the sciences and their technical vocabulary fall short of some higher interests and activities. "The scientist, they say, is discovering 'merely scientific' or 'merely empirical' or 'merely phenomenal' or 'merely positive' or 'merely technical' truths. Such dismissive epithets express the suspicion that the scientist merely goes through mechanical procedures, checking of the truth value of propositions. . . ."[110] Second, in a shared distaste for the mission and technical vocabulary of the sciences, both idealism and textualism are a kind of romanticism that prefigure pragmatism.[111]

But before pragmatism and before nineteenth-century idealism, the notion crystallized that philosophy was equipped to deal with questions that the individual sciences could not answer. Under the influence of Locke, Hume, and Kant (each of whom addressed the question how we can know the nature of ultimate reality if the sole and immediate objects of perception are our own ideas),[112] we encounter the notion that philosophy is a kind of "*super*-science." As such, philosophy alone is equipped, if any branch of inquiry is equipped, to take on questions about reality, truth, morality, and aesthetics. This conception of philosophy was, as Rorty describes it, short-lived. Before the end of the nineteenth century, it became clear that philosophy had become so extravagantly speculative that the stories it told, especially in the hands of idealists (including Royce), were nothing more than the exercises of professors in departments of philosophy. Philosophy became what it remains, a name, "like the words 'classics' and 'psychology', for an academic department where memories of youthful hope are cherished, and wistful yearnings for recapturing past glories survive."[113]

For Rorty, then, the end of philosophy, conceived as a privileged conduit to the actual nature of things, was Hegel's influential decision to treat philosophy as a speculative, not simply reflective, discipline. Once speculation, without argumentation, eclipses truth seeking, philosophy becomes the bedfellow of *literary* culture. It tells stories. Some of its stories are intriguing while others are uninspired and banal. "The romanticism which Hegel brought to philosophy reinforced the hope that literature might be the successor subject to philosophy. . . ."[114]

The story does not end with Hegel and those whom he influenced directly. Rorty says that there is another step in the process that militates against philosophy as it was once conceived. Here we look to Nietzsche and to James. This German romantic and this pioneering American pragmatist saw no sense in thinking of philosophy, past or present, as cutting through appearances in order to take us to reality. "They were content to take the halo off words like 'truth' and 'science' and 'knowledge' and 'reality', rather than offering a view about the nature of the things named by these words."[115] Neither Nietzsche nor James—and this they share with the textualist culture that refuses to see literary vocabularies as revealing anything beyond the text—could for a moment talk of getting to the essential nature of things. For them we are after ways of confronting and talking about the world that help "us get what we want."[116] For Rorty, pragmatism is the philosophical equivalent of the kind of modern or recent literature that does not judge itself in terms of veracity and that asks critics not to judge it in those terms. What counts far more is "its autonomy and novelty."[117] Pragmatism assists us to "get what we want" as long as what we want is not "Truth with a big T."[118]

In the end, Rorty is not quite announcing the death of philosophy and its replacement by a culture of textualists who see more clearly than philosophers what they are doing, although he comes close to this declaration. He is saying that as long as philosophers see their job as unmasking or penetrating the appearances in order to lay bare reality, they completely misunderstand their discipline and their task. No philosophy is able to take on and carry out this effort. The reason is not so much that the right philosophy for the job has not yet emerged; rather, it is that there is no "right" philosophy as Jacques Bouveresse puts it for this impossible, preposterous undertaking.[119]

Having rejected this tired and dated conception, Rorty argues in *Contingency, Irony, and Solidarity* that the American pragmatists saw better than other philosophers what philosophy as a tool can do. Like any other tool, it can handle some jobs but not all jobs.[120] We use a wrench to tighten and loosen bolts, not to remove stains, and one should use philosophy to get about more easily in the world we experience, not to reach a world that is supposed to lie beyond all possible experience.

If we are prepared to conceive of philosophy as helping us to address authentic problems and to dismiss pseudo-problems or empty and distracting debates, then we conceive philosophy as we should. On the other hand, if philosophers maintain that philosophy ought to open doors to allow us to glimpse what underpins the phenomena, they do a disservice to philosophy. There are, for Rorty and the classical pragmatists, no good reasons to think that there are any such doors; nor, as a consequence, are there good arguments that there is anything outside the phenomena to glimpse.

Rorty is persuaded that philosophers must cease to search for and venerate the "intrinsic nature" of the universe and the individual essential natures of its component parts. Instead, they must ". . . treat *everything*—our language, our conscience, our community—as a product of time and chance. To reach this point would be, in Freud's words, to 'treat chance as worthy of determining our fate."[121]

Time and chance obviously stand in opposition to eternity and necessity. This is a fact, not a failing. Contingency and mutability are threatening only to traditional philosophers, from Plato to Royce, whose guiding assumptions and misdirected efforts Dewey criticizes in *The Quest for Certainty* and *Experience and Nature*. For Rorty, the pragmatists, and Nietzsche, it turns out that contingency, time, and change are opportunities for adventure, novelty, and wisdom. To shun these opportunities and at the same time to see the world in counterfeit and metaphysically speculative terms is to miss out on the best that philosophy has to offer, namely the resources and resolve to reshape the world as we meet it head on. Given this view, the world that exists is the world that becomes. It is the world that we can in some measure mold to our own needs and desires. This is a view that leaves Platonists and their followers gasping, but it is the view that for Rorty and his pragmatic antecedents comes as close as we can ever come to that honorific *world as it really is*.

Epilogue

We have reached the end of this phase of our story. We have looked at philosophers, trends, and episodes over a period of three hundred years of philosophy in America. Readers who have made their way through the first nine essays are in position to look back and to judge for themselves the philosophical theology of Edwards, the revolutionary thought of the Founding Fathers, the metaphysics of Emerson and Royce, the naturalism of Santayana, the pragmatism of Peirce, James, and Dewey, and the later analytic pragmatism of Lewis, Quine, and Rorty.

Philosophy in America begins with religious thinkers and practical patriots who were less interested in originality than in saving our souls or in saving us from overlords and landlords across the Atlantic. It takes on new life when the voices in favor of philosophical independence try to reject the cultural past and to invent a truly American intellectual future. Their own transcendental invention is ephemeral, but their brief for a truly American philosophy is realized and ripened by pragmatists who were at work during and beyond the Gilded Age and into the present.

That philosophy in America is not always uniquely and exclusively American should not be surprising. Even as Emerson was demanding self-reliance from men and women who were accustomed to borrow from traditions and European antecedents, he was studying and paraphrasing Kant, Coleridge, and Thomas Carlyle. The French visitor Tocqueville (1805–1859), writing of America as an outsider, agreed with Emerson: "The Americans have no philosophic school which is their own. . . ."[122] But not everyone we have discussed saw this state of affairs as a failing. Wright and Dewey openly admired and granted the influence of Darwin on their philosophies, and James was pleased to dedicate *Pragmatism* "to the memory of John Stuart Mill. . . ."[123] Lewis, Quine, and Rorty acknowledge the importance and impact of Continental philosophy and Viennese logical positivism as they developed their own philosophies and philosophical reactions.

Again, the most obvious conclusion to draw from all of this is that, despite Emersonian impatience with imported thought and culture, American thinkers have always been open to provocative ideas, fruitful theories, and important insights. They need not come from America to thrive in America. Where, after all, was Santayana born, and where did he do some of his best philosophical work? Explicit in pragmatism, the one philosophy that comes closest to being American from the outset is the position that a good idea is one that works within its context. No first- or second-generation pragmatist ever thought that an idea which does its job must have an American pedigree. For Peirce, Dewey, and James, it makes as little sense to cultivate and praise philosophy in America, because it is American, as it does to praise any good idea or thesis on the basis of its national origin.

This pragmatic attitude still prevails. American philosophers do not test a thesis or assess a new point of view by asking whether it was generated and hatched at Harvard, Yale, or Princeton. Methodology, ontology, and epistemology have no need to show their papers or establish their ancestry. Fortunately, where the free flow of philosophical ideas is concerned, there was nothing like the American Protection Association (1887) or Immigration Restriction League (1894), whose missions were to exclude "intruders" into white, Protestant America.[124]

The tests that theories and novel ideas must pass are those that philosophical theories have had to pass since at least the time of Francis Bacon (1561–1626). These tests bear on their utility, coherence, consistency, and economy. A theory is accepted or rejected, ideally, based upon how well it survives thoughtful and penetrating criticism. These criticisms are advanced by those who have reservations about new theories, not about their country of origin. James's and Dewey's praise for pluralism is clearly at odds with the monism of Spinoza and Hegel, but their doubts about monism are not rooted in any distaste for the Dutch or the Germans.

The adjective "American" has no purchase when one raises serious philosophical objections to a world view or theory of knowledge. One can reasonably conjecture that the unfinished story of philosophy in America will resemble similar unfinished stories in any other country that comes to mind. New approaches to perennial philosophical problems will displace older approaches. New sets of philosophical interests will make their appearance, and older interests will recede for a time.

This cycle will continue as it always has. There is no end in sight, but why should there be? There is nothing stagnant or complete about the desire to know, whether that desire reveals itself in philosophy, the natural and social sciences, or the arts. Until and unless men and women abandon this desire to know, inquiry will continue in America just as it will almost everywhere else on the planet. Among philosophers, satisfying this desire is more like a hope than a result. Peirce and Dewey knew that "stopping points" are simply another phrase for "points of departure."

All that is likely to be specifically American in this unending quest is that sometimes American philosophers—recently Quine and Rorty—raise issues, ask questions, and proffer answers in ways that other philosophers had not quite conceived. This rendering of philosophy in America may be enough to establish that studying its history and thinking about its future are worth our time. But any such determination must wait until we have looked at ethical, social, and political thought that has shaped, and sometimes misshaped, America's history and values.

NOTES

1. See Bruce Kuklick's remarks in *A History of American Philosophy: 1720–2000* (Oxford, 2001), 257–8.
2. Ibid., 214, 215.
3. "The Pragmatic Element in Knowledge," *University of California Publications in Philosophy*, **6**, (1926), 205; emphasis added.
4. *The Structure of Empirical Knowledge* (Cambridge, Mass., 1985), 72.
5. *Mind and the World-Order* (New York, 1929), 57–8.
6. Ibid. 53. This insistence upon the ineffability of the given in sense, the given that Lewis sometimes calls "qualia," is not stressed in *An Analysis of Knowledge and Valuation*. For a possible explanation why this is so, see *The Structure of Empirical Knowledge*, 73–4.
7. Ibid. 54.
8. "The Pragmatic Element in Knowledge," 217.
9. *An Analysis of Knowledge and Valuation*, 171–72.
10. *Critique of Pure Reason*, tr. Norman Kemp Smith (London, 1929), 93; emphasis added. Compare *Mind and the World-Order*, 120–21.

11. *The Structure of Empirical Knowledge*, 73.
12. *An Analysis of Knowledge and Valuation*, 180.
13. Ibid., 179. Compare a similar remark in Descartes's *Meditations*: *The Philosophical Writings of Descartes*, trans. John Cottingham, Robert Stoothoff, and Dugold Murdoch (2 vols., Cambridge, 1985), II, 19.
14. *Mind and the World Order*, 118–21.
15. *An Analysis of Knowledge and Valuation*, 188–9.
16. *Mind and the World-Order*, 119.
17. Ibid. 120. See also page 133.
18. Ibid. 133–4.
19. See Kuklick's discussion of Lewis's position that empirical knowledge is at most probable. *A History of Philosophy in America: 1720–2000*, 217.
20. *An Analysis of Knowledge and Valuation*, 185. See also pages 333–6. Compare similar claims in *Mind and the World-Order*, 281, 319.
21. *Mind and the World-Order*, 283. This fact about empirical knowledge is not problematic except for those thinkers who insist that all knowledge must be certain. They will either have to maintain that "empirical knowledge" is oxymoronic or, against all odds, decide that they can settle for a more dilute conception of knowledge.
22. *Mind and the World-Order*, 38.
23. Ibid. 275.
24. Ibid. 277.
25. See Essay 6, note 30.
26. This kind of example is captured in more general terms by what Lewis writes in *Mind and the World-Order*, 318. See also what Lewis says about verification and knowledge in "The Pragmatic Element in Knowledge," 217.
27. *Mind and the World-Order*, 224.
28. Ibid. 264–5.
29. *Critique of Pure Reason*, 41–2.
30. *Mind and the World-Order*, 230–31; emphasis added.
31. Ibid. 231.
32. Morton White, *Pragmatism and the American Mind* (New York, 1973), 104.
33. *Mind and the World-Order*, 240.
34. Ibid. 245.
35. Ibid. 251.
36. *An Inquiry Concerning Human Understanding*, ed. Charles W. Hende (Indianapolis, 1955), 40.
37. "The Pragmatic Element in Knowledge," 206.
38. Ibid. 221; emphasis added.
39. Ibid. 219; emphasis added.
40. Ibid. 223, 224.
41. Ibid. 227.
42. Ibid. 226.
43. Ibid.
44. Ibid. 227.
45. Bonjour's critical discussion of Lewis's philosophy is incisive and a direct path to standard objections to Lewis's theory of knowledge, *The Structure of Empirical Knowledge*, 72–80. For an important analysis and criticism of Lewis and others on the ties between verification and knowledge, see Norman Malcolm, *Knowledge and Certainty* (Ithaca, 1963), 1–57. For a discussion of Lewis on ethics and value, which does not concern us here, see White's *Pragmatism and the American Mind*, 102–4, 129–30, 155–67.
46. "The Pragmatic Element in Knowledge," 216, 222.
47. *The Analysis of Knowledge and Valuation*, 188.
48. Aristotle, *Posterior Analytics*, trans and commentary by Jonathan Barnes (Oxford, 1975), 88, 248–50.
49. *Inquiry Concerning Human Understanding*, 51–3, 58–61, 86–9.

50. "The Pragmatic Element in Knowledge," 242.
51. *An Essay Concerning Human Understanding*, II, xxiii, 3, 4.
52. *A Treatise of Human Nature*, ed. L. A. Selby-Bigge, rev. P. H. Nidditch (Oxford, 1978), 166, 172.
53. "The Pragmatic Element in Knowledge," 205.
54. See, in addition to references earlier in this discussion, Kant's "Table of Categories" that includes, among others, the relational categories of cause and effect, as well as that of substance and its qualities. Kant says that these and other concepts exist a priori in the understanding. He adds, in what sounds very much like Lewis, "Indeed, it is because it contains these concepts that it is called pure understanding; for by them alone can it *understand* anything in the manifold of intuition, that is, think an object of intuition." *Critique of Pure Reason*, 113, 114.
55. Compare Berkeley's *ad hoc* treatment of relational knowledge and "notional" knowledge of oneself, in the second edition of his *Principles of Human Knowledge* (1734), section 89. Berkeley also, either *ad hoc* or by default, invents a new category for knowing what seems to him not to arise directly from unmediated experience.
56. For a useful sketch of Quine's life, see Alex Orenstein, *W.V. Quine* (Princeton, 2002), 1–10.
57. "Two Dogmas of Empiricism," in W. V. Quine, *From a Logical Point of View* (Cambridge, Mass., 1953), 20–46.
58. Ibid. 20.
59. *Mind and the World-Order*, 303–8, 312.
60. "Two Dogmas of Empiricism," 21.
61. Ibid. 22–3.
62. Ibid. 23.
63. Ibid. 24.
64. Ibid. 26.
65. Ibid. 27.
66. Ibid. 31.
67. Ibid.
68. Ibid. 33.
69. Ibid. 36.
70. Ibid. 37; emphasis added. For very brief critical remarks on Quine's position, see Roderick M. Chisholm, *Theory of Knowledge*, 2nd edition (Englewood Cliffs, 1977), 61.
71. See, for example, A. J. Ayer, *Language, Truth and Logic*, (London, 1946), 43–4, 114–20.
72. "Two Dogmas of Empiricism," 40–41.
73. Ibid. 46.
74. "Posits and Reality" (1955), in Quine, *The Ways of Paradox and Other Essays* (New York, 1966), 233–41.
75. Ibid. 235.
76. Ibid. 237; emphasis added.
77. Ibid.
78. "Two Dogmas of Empiricism," 44.
79. "Posits and Reality," 238–9.
80. Ibid. 239.
81. Ibid. 240.
82. Ibid.
83. Ibid. 241.
84. "Epistemology Naturalized," in *Ontological Relativity and Other Essays* (New York, 1969), 69–90.
85. Ibid. 71–2.
86. Ibid. 75.
87. Ibid.
88. Ibid. 78–9.
89. Ibid. 82–3.
90. Ibid. 84.

91. "Epistemology Naturalized," 84.
92. Ibid. 85.
93. Ibid. 86–87.
94. *W.V. O. Quine*, 177. See also Dirk Koppelberg's similar assessment of Quine's reasons for adopting and arguing for naturalized epistemology in "Why and How to Naturalize Epistemology," in *Perspectives on Quine*, ed. Robert B. Barrett and Roger F. Gibson (Cambridge, Mass., 1990), 203–4.
95. *Pragmatism and Other Writings*, ed. Giles Gunn (New York, 2000), 97–9.
96. Kuklick offers an abbreviated summary of Rorty's professional life and philosophy, in *A History of Philosophy in America: 1720–2000*, 275–80.
97. *Philosophy and the Mirror of Nature* (Princeton, 1979), 10.
98. Ibid. 169.
99. Ibid. 182. See also West's comments in *The American Evasion of Philosophy* (Madison, 1989), 201–3.
100. *Philosophy and the Mirror of Nature*, 171.
101. Ibid. 182.
102. Ibid. 212.
103. For one summary of the argument of this essay, see *The American Evasion of Philosophy*, 197–8.
104. Richard Rorty, *Consequences of Pragmatism (Essays: 1972–1980)* (Minneapolis, 1982), 12.
105. Ibid. 14–15.
106. Ibid. 15.
107. Ibid. 17.
108. This essay is included in *Consequences of Pragmatism*, 139–59.
109. Ibid. 141, 142.
110. Ibid.
111. Ibid. Rorty defines "romanticism" in the context that concerns him as "the thesis that what is most important for human life is not what propositions we believe but what vocabulary we use."
112. Rorty says that Berkeley crafted this philosophical problem when he insisted that the exclusive objects of perception and knowledge are ideas and that "nothing can be like an idea except an idea." Ibid. 146.
113. Ibid. 147.
114. Ibid. 149–50.
115. Ibid. 150.
116. Ibid. 152. The philosopher Jacques Derrida says, "there is nothing outside the text," 140.
117. Ibid. 153.
118. *Pragmatism and Other Essays*, 102. See also Rorty's more elaborate statement of what comes very close to James's position. *Contingency, Irony, and Solidarity* (Cambridge, 1989), 8.
119. Jacques Bouveresse, "Reading Rorty: Pragmatism and Its Consequences," in *Rorty and His Critics*, ed. Robert B. Brandom (Oxford, 2000), 138.
120. Ibid. 17, 19.
121. Ibid. 22.
122. Alexis deToqueville, *Democracy in America*, ed. Sanford Kessler, trans Stephen D. Grant (Indianapolis, 2000), 170.
123. *Pragmatism and Other Essays*, 3.
124. Steven M. Gillon and Cathy D. Matson, *The American Experiment: A History of the United States* (2 vols. Boston, 2002), II, 750–55.

PART II
American Ethics, Social and Political Philosophy

Essay 10
The Continuing Revolution: Abolitionism and American Women's Rights and Civil Rights

The task of this essay is to comment on abolitionism and the women's rights and civil rights movements in the United States, with principal attention to some early works. The prominent themes and elements of the works discussed here are the dignity and value of the human being, self-respect, and a spirit of optimism, individualism (whether to argue for or against it), and reform.

Like Essay 3, "Philosophies of Revolution and Resolution," this essay poses the difficulty that most of the works are not specifically philosophical and the majority of the thinkers involved are not philosophers. An early representative of the women's rights movement, Elizabeth Cady Stanton, stands out from most of the others in that she recognized her own work as philosophical and reformist—notwithstanding that she continues to be largely ignored as a philosopher, both in the history of American philosophy and in the Western philosophical tradition generally.[1] In the abolitionist movement Frederick Douglass's arguments reveal a clearly philosophical backdrop. Martin Luther King, Jr.'s *philosophy* of nonviolence and love depends heavily upon the influence of Socrates and Henry David Thoreau, among others. Marilyn Frye, a contemporary radical lesbian feminist, presents in *The Politics of Reality: Essays in Feminist Philosophy*,[2] a scathing description of the continuing subordination and subjection of women that reveals problems going well beyond a simple and straightforward solution like a recognition of the *legal* rights of women. Other thinkers represented in this essay are Thomas Jefferson, Sarah and Angelina Grimké, and William Lloyd Garrison.

The moral and political outlook upon which the themes of this essay are built appears to be primarily a sort of Kantian[3] deontological[4] model of individual and social responsibility emphasizing the primacy of duty over mere consequentialist concerns. Although it is tempting to speak of the necessity to recognize and defend the rights of African Americans and women from the point of view of utilitarian calculations,[5] the sort of view prevalent in the major works of the American civil rights and women's rights movements is primarily deontological. For these theorists and orators, arguing for what is right, and defending the rights of individual people, is their overriding emphasis. In holding this position, we do not deny that there is a consequentialist turn to moral and political theorizing in American thought. It is simply that a Kantian view seems to be a concern of most of the theorists in the abolitionist, women's rights, and civil rights movements. What makes their works primarily deontological in character is the affinity of their way of thinking to the second formulation of the categorical imperative that one is to treat humanity, whether considering ourselves or others, "always as an end and never merely as a means only."[6]

One of Kant's most often noted examples is the moral unacceptability of the lying promise. In this example, a person is to ask whether it would be right for her to lie to another person about her intent to repay when she needs to obtain money. In lying to the other person, one makes it impossible for that person to make an informed and rational decision whether to hand over the money that one wishes to "borrow." To lie is to treat another person like a thing, as though he or she has only *use-value* rather than inherent dignity as a rational, autonomous moral agent.

The abolitionists and thinkers in the women's rights and civil rights movements consistently used the dignity and value of the human being as a foundation for their arguments against oppression, slavery, unfairness, and exploitation. They refused to acquiesce in the poor reasoning of those who claimed that emancipating enslaved people or recognizing the rights of all women would in some way "rend" the fabric of society. Angelina Grimké argued that we ought not to withdraw from anti-slavery work for fear of negative consequences to ourselves. If we see her claim in this context as deontological, her manner of thinking might be subjected to the same brand of criticism lodged against Immanuel Kant by John Stuart Mill when Mill said that Kant's view was actually consequentialist.[7] But for these thinkers, there are some consequences that are simply immeasurable and incalculable. They are incalculable because they are harmful to the dignity of humanity, something that simply cannot be calculated, added up, subtracted, or multiplied by the temporary and contingent benefits of mere pecuniary profit or pretensions to fears of social upheaval. There is no mechanism by which we may begin to calculate the damage that slavery and the subjection of women and African Americans cause. The pretended benefits that slave owners claimed that they would retain by slavery's continued existence, and the fears of men that the very fabric of society would be rent by the recognition of the human rights of women,[8] are irrelevant to, and are overridden by, respect for humanity.

Similar to the way in which the New England Transcendentalists were intent upon completing the American Revolution by insisting upon independence from the influences of the past and European traditions, so too early and contemporary American feminists are concerned to revolt against the authoritarian chains of the past. For these activists, white women and all African Americans, no less than white men in power, must be situated so that the potential greatness of a young and upcoming nation may be realized.

It is well known that the American Declaration of Independence asserts that "all men are created equal" and "are endowed by their creator with certain inalienable rights," among them "life, liberty, and the pursuit of happiness." It is also far too well established that Thomas Jefferson and others of the founders of the new American republic left out of consideration African American slaves and American women in drafting the Declaration and in creating the United States Constitution.[9] Both white women and African American slaves were customarily denied the most basic legal and civil rights. Women were traditionally and legally subordinated to their husbands, losing the right to their property upon marriage. In the early United States, the legal subordination of women denied them the right to vote. A woman was considered not much more than a child, and upon the death of her husband, not she, but a male relative (or some other "responsible" adult male person) was generally appointed legal guardian of dependent children. Divorce was nearly impossible into the late 1800s, and divorced women tended to fare horribly both economically and socially. Women's opportunities for economic independence were severely limited as a result of corresponding limitations in educational opportunities and the simple fact that women were traditionally paid significantly less than men for equal or comparable work.

The conditions for African American slaves were certainly no better than for white women and were, in almost all cases, materially worse. In the American South there were many laws that, if broken by a slave, were punishable by death while the same "crimes," committed by a white person, were either not punishable at all (because they were not considered crimes) or were met with minimal punishment. As Frederick Douglass and women's rights activists were often careful to note, the condition of African American women was worst of all. They were not only subject to unfair and inhuman treatment in their condition as slaves, but they were also victims of injustices far exceeding the experience of their male counterparts.[10]

If there is to be equal justice, it is to the Declaration of Independence and the U.S. Constitution that women's rights activists and abolitionists (and later reformers for civil rights) found they must turn. They saw the potential in doing so to begin the transformation of American society from one guaranteeing life, liberty, and the pursuit of happiness only to a select few to guaranteeing these basic rights to all citizens and persons in its domain.

The Revolution is essentially incomplete when more than half of the American people are denied the most basic human rights and are thereby relegated to the status of things. Dignity and respect for the individual human being does not exist when he or she is without legal and political representation in being denied the right to vote. There is little or no chance for a human being to take advantage of the opportunities and rights provided by the U.S. Constitution, to develop fully as a moral being, when he or she is denied an education, freedom, the right to his or her own earnings, and even the right to determine what will happen to his or her own body.

The American writers, thinkers, and activists discussed in this essay hold that it is essential to a person to be recognized as a fully human, responsible being entitled to sovereignty over his or her own body. All human beings are subject to the same vicissitudes, calamities, pleasures, and sufferings and all ought to be afforded the same status as moral beings. They share the conviction that all women and all African Americans are rational beings and as such are to be afforded the same rights and responsibilities as any other human being, especially as citizens of a country founded on principles of right, equality, and justice.[11] There is a transformation of culture, society, attitudes, and actions that must be realized for injustice to be defeated and for humanity to achieve recognition of the rights of all.

The American women's rights and civil rights movements have historically run parallel to each other.[12] Agitators for women's rights have also tended to recognize and argue against the inhumane and unjustifiable treatment of African Americans, whether as slaves or in their unequal capacity in American society after emancipation. The reverse is also generally true. African Americans recognized, as Martin Luther King, Jr. said so forcefully, that "injustice anywhere is a threat to justice everywhere"[13] and that something must be done to combat it. But there is more to the creation and justification of ideas than simply to produce eloquent arguments and fine distinctions. There is much to be done in practice to transform an idea into a way of living, of being, and of doing.[14]

Thomas Jefferson on Slavery

Jefferson's commentary on the issue of slavery in "The administration of justice and the description of the laws?" in his *Notes on the State of Virginia* is testimony to the intractable problems of slavery that plagued the new American republic. We find in Jefferson's actions and in this work the tension between his thought regarding the moral unacceptability of slavery and his continuing to hold slaves. The same tensions also exist under some interpretations of the meaning of constitutional guarantees. Joseph J. Ellis points out that the discussions and debates about slavery affected and divided representatives to the Constitutional Convention. The problem came from disagreements between northern and southern states and their delegates' interpretations of the arguments of the Revolution. Ellis notes that "the delegates from New England and most of the Middle Atlantic states drew directly on the inspirational rhetoric of the revolutionary legacy to argue that slavery was inherently incompatible with the republican values on which the American Revolution had been based."[15] Much of the southern argument, however, revolved around the notion, also embodied in constitutional guarantees and derived from a Lockean understanding of property rights, that governments not only exist by the consent of the governed, but that they exist for "the regulation and preservation of property."[16] Since slaves were considered property by their owners, southern delegates were in no way moved by northerners' arguments.[17] Ultimately, as Ellis points out, the Constitution "contained no provisions that specifically sanctioned slavery as a permanent and protected institution south of the Potomac or anywhere else. The distinguishing feature of the document when it came to slavery was its evasiveness."[18]

Even in many cases in which people were moved toward accepting arguments for emancipation of slaves, the question what to do with former slaves when they were freed was problematic. Jefferson's well-known position was that emancipation carried with it the "danger" of miscegenation and the likelihood that the "deep rooted prejudices" of white people toward the slaves would lead to conflict. Jefferson's own prejudices are clear. He held that African Americans were neither so beautiful nor so intelligent as white people (in reason, Jefferson says, "they are much inferior" and, he adds, "I advance it, therefore, as a suspicion only, that the blacks . . . are inferior to the whites in the endowments both of body and mind").[19] Furthermore, he argued that they smell bad, are considerably different from white people in their "ardent" desires and affections, are lazy (Jefferson notes that it is surprising to him that slaves tend to avoid work whenever they can),[20] and are so thoroughly different from and inferior to white people that it would be impossible for freed slaves and whites to live together profitably or peacefully. Jefferson's solution was to provide freed slaves with a basic education, supplies sufficient to begin an independent life, and to move them from the United States altogether and establish their own country. Where to move or relocate them was itself a distinct problem, and the question of remuneration to slave owners remained unresolved.

There is much to be said about Jefferson's purported objections to miscegenation considering his well-established affair with Sally Hemings, and about relocation of freed slaves. These issues are beyond the scope of our discussion but Jefferson's comments about African Americans and the problems of slavery provide an ample place to start in the discussion of the anti-slavery and civil rights movements in the United States.

William Lloyd Garrison and the Declaration of Sentiments of the American Anti-Slavery Society

William Lloyd Garrison (1805–1879), leader of the American Anti-Slavery Society, founder and publisher of the abolitionist newspaper *The Liberator* and activist for women's rights, held the position that the work of the revolutionaries was incomplete. Just as the founders of the new American republic fought against their oppressors in order to be free, so too must a war be waged against the oppressors of the human spirit who would hold other human beings in bondage. In fact, according to Garrison, the cause of anti-slavery justifies a revolution against oppression[21] because "Our fathers were never slaves—never bought and sold like cattle—never shut out from the light of knowledge and religion—never subjected to the lash of brutal taskmasters."[22] Those people for whom Garrison was speaking and

> for whose emancipation we are striving . . . are recognized by the laws, and treated by their fellow-beings, as marketable commodities . . . , for the crime of having a dark complexion, (and they) suffer the pangs of hunger, the infliction of stripes, and the ignominy of brutal servitude. They are kept in heathenish darkness by laws expressly enacted to make their instruction a criminal offense.[23]

Garrison's arguments against slavery focus primarily on the humanity of the slave, not on any sort of benefits that might accrue to slave owners by their emancipation. Garrison was not concerned to try to assuage the condition of slaveholders. He was concerned to make it clear that slaves are human beings and have the right to be free.[24] Furthermore, in keeping with a spirit of duty to God, to human beings, and out of respect for humanity itself, it is the obligation of the American people to "deliver our land from its deadliest curse" and to secure to the African American "all the rights and privileges which belong to them as men and as Americans—come what may to our persons, our interests, or our reputations—whether we live to witness the triumph of LIBERTY, JUSTICE and HUMANITY, or perish ultimately as martyrs in this great, benevolent and holy cause."[25]

Garrison's arguments for emancipation of slaves rested on commitment to principles embodied in the Declaration of Independence, not on the Constitution.[26] Both Garrison and the Grimkés held the position that all human beings are created equal, and as such, they are all to be afforded the same rights as white men. The arguments of Angelina Grimké express effectively the ideas of Garrisonian abolitionism while at the same time building the case for women's rights, so it is to her works that we now turn.

Angelina Emily Grimké and the Appeal to the Christian Women of the South

The Grimké sisters (Angelina [1805–79] and Sarah [1792–1873]) were powerful, early voices in the anti-slavery and women's rights movements in the United States. Going against the tide of southern culture and sentiment,[27] the Grimké sisters spoke with eloquent conviction against both slavery and the subordination of women. Further, Sara Evans notes that the Grimké sisters also defied the attitude that it was "unnatural" for a woman to speak in public or otherwise act against her natural position as a being in need of protection by men.

> Neither Sarah nor Angelina Grimké, however, felt 'unnatural.' They spoke from deep moral conviction in the tradition of evangelical reform. And they sharpened the contradiction in the ideology of true womanhood: How could women discharge their moral duty while remaining silent on the fundamental moral dilemma of their time? In defense of their actions, the Grimké sisters asserted their kinship with female slaves, eloquently fusing the issues of race and gender. . . .[28]

Angelina Grimké's work against slavery in her "Appeal to the Christian Women of the South"[29] echoes the sort of sentiment found in the Garrisonian "Declaration of Sentiments," in that it is our *duty* to fight against slavery regardless of the consequences to ourselves.[30] Angelina Grimké addresses herself to southern women,[31] believing that their influence can and will make a difference. She recognizes that women may doubt the efficacy of their actions against slavery, claiming that since they have no political voice they cannot vote against slavery, nor do anything of any significance. Furthermore, some women might object that the personal cost will be too much to bear. They may be criticized, arrested, and ostracized. To these objections, Angelina Grimké answers that women have power in speaking to their husbands, brothers, and sons who can overthrow the system with their vote and with their influence. She emphasized that a woman's concern should be to do what is right, not to be sidetracked by temporary consequences, no matter how unpleasant.

Angelina Grimké tells her audience in "Appeal to the Christian Women of the South," that they can and must read the Scriptures to see that what she has said against the (supposed) Biblical justification of slavery is right; they must pray on the subject and, if they find slavery sinful, "do whatsoever your hands find to do, leaving the consequences entirely to him, who still says to us whenever we try to reason away duty from the fear of consequences, '*What is that to thee, follow thou me*'." Grimké insists that women must act by freeing their own slaves, paying wages to those who wish to remain as servants, and educating them. To those who reply that women engaged in education of slaves will be arrested, Grimké replies: "Be not surprised when I say such wicked laws *ought to be no barrier* in the way of your duty. . . ." And if anyone believes that freeing slaves is to no purpose because freed slaves will be taken up and sold again, Grimké's position is that it is just as wrong to reason this way as it would have been wrong for Peter and John to refuse to preach because they would be imprisoned. "*Consequences*," Grimké asserts, "belong no more to *you*, than they did to these apostles. Duty is ours and events are God's." To those who think that such a "course of conduct would inevitably expose us to great suffering," Grimké replies: "Yes! My Christian friends, I believe it would, but this will *not* excuse you or any one else for the neglect of *duty*. . . ." The anti-consequentialist, pro-deontological stance here is clear. When it comes to our duties, we must face the consequences as contingent and temporal inconveniences that cannot override the demands of moral duty.

Given the Grimké sisters' religious background, it is no surprise that Angelina's arguments against slavery, and that both sisters' arguments against the oppression of women, would have a particularly religious bent. In fact, in the "Appeal to the Christian Women of the South," Angelina Grimké runs through several arguments based on supposed scriptural justifications for slaveholding and defeats them all with clear, concise, and vehement counterarguments.

Her first argument is that Adam was given dominion over fish, fowl, and other *irrational* beings, but there is, she holds, no reference either in the creation of man or in the post-deluvian world to any power vested in mankind over anything but irrational animals. And since mankind is not irrational, man was never "put *under the feet of man*."[32]

Second, Grimké argues against those who believe that Genesis provides justification for slavery. Her position is that there is in that work no such justification for the institution of slavery from the fact that Canaan's posterity was to be consigned to servitude any more than because it is described in scripture that the Egyptians enslaved the Israelites that it *should* be so. And in any case, she says that those who see slavery as a fulfillment of prophecy ought to take care to note that "the fulfillment of prophecy will *not cover one sin* in the awful days of account. . . ."[33] In other words, that human actions may *fulfill* prophecy is no justification or excuse for immoral action. There are prophecies that are clearly contrary to morality and to goodness, and to act according to the realization of those prophecies does not excuse the guilty.

Others may argue that the patriarchs were slaveholders and so, by their example, slavery is right. Her reply is that the servants of Abraham were not equal in condition to the slaves of the American south. Abraham's slaves had access to weapons, the child of Abraham (Ishmail) and his servant woman was recognized to be the son of Abraham, just as Isaac was Abraham's son by his wife Sarah, and would have inherited Abraham's property. Given these facts and being careful to use the term "servant" with respect to the "slaves" of Abraham, Grimké points out that "if slaveholders are determined to hold slaves as long as they can, let them not dare say that the God of mercy and truth *ever* sanctioned such a system of cruelty and wrong. It is blasphemy against him."[34]

That the slave is a human being is, for Grimké, unquestionable. She points out the irony in the language of the southern master who wishes to justify the practice of holding slaves by referring to slaves as "chattels personal." Slaveholders do so because they recognize that a *human being* cannot be a slave. Thus, in calling African Americans "chattels personal," it is possible to rob them of wages, spouses, children, and friends. Turning again to her interpretation of Genesis, Grimké points out that for the slaveholder, "it is wise in them (slaveholders), to keep them (slaves) in abject ignorance, for the strong man armed must be bound before we can spoil his house—the powerful intellect of man must be bound down with the iron chains of nescience before we can rob him of his rights as a man; we must reduce him to a *thing* before we can claim the right to set our feet upon his neck,[35] because it was only *all things* which were originally *put under the feet of man* by the Almighty."

Others may attempt to justify slavery by pointing out that slaves have been in bondage so long that they are accustomed to it but that slavery is likewise unjustified for white people since they have not been in bondage. Grimké's reply is that this is a sorry justification for slavery because if it were to hold, we would have to ask ourselves whether we would be willing to subject our children to slavery (since they would know nothing different if they were in that condition all their lives). We would have to ask whether, if it is true that slaves are better off under the condition of slavery than free people because they are thereby "freed" from the problems of providing for themselves and their families, they would then be willing to put their children under the yoke of servitude. The answer is clear.[36] For Angelina Grimké, there are no arguments sufficient to justify slavery. The good and well-justified arguments are, instead, all on the other side. The same holds true for the Grimkés with respect to arguments justifying the subordination of women to men.

Sarah Grimké on the Equality of the Sexes

Just as Angelina Grimké argued against slavery and for the duty of Christian women to speak out against it, so too the Grimkés were opposed to the unjustified, immoral, and unfair treatment of women in American society. Their letters bear lively testimony to that conviction and provide arguments in favor of recognition of the equality of women with men in the moral, legal, political, and spiritual realms.

In "The Original Equality of Woman," Sarah Grimké writes that she will give her "views on the Province of Woman" by examining the subject from the point of view of the Bible. Her position is that "every thing that has been written on the subject, has been the result of a misconception of the simple truths revealed in the Scriptures, in consequences of the false translation of many passages of Holy Writ. . . ."[37] Grimké's position is that God created woman and man *both* in His image, and that both are equally to exercise dominion over other creatures, but *not* to exercise dominion over each other. Thus, Sarah Grimké rejects as a problem of translation the position that because Eve was purportedly created from the rib of Adam she is, therefore, in some way his inferior. But even in this case, there are those who would argue that woman is to be subservient, subjected, and inferior to man because it was Eve, the first woman, who was responsible for the fall from grace.

Sarah Grimké's argument in the "Original Equality of Woman" proceeds on the basis of the individualist evangelical belief that to fulfill one's duties, it is necessary to know what they are; and to know what they are, it is the duty of every person, first and foremost, to search the scriptures individually *without* being hindered by the views of others. Her argument that women are men's moral equals proceeds, generally, in the following way.[38]

In Genesis, man and woman were both given dominion over all other creatures.[39] Here, therefore, there is no moral difference between man and woman because both together were created to have dominion over "every other creature, *but not over each other*."[40] Further, in the recapitulation of creation, God created woman so that man would not be alone. But since "creation swarmed with animated beings capable of natural affection," God must have created woman for moral and intellectual companionship as one who is "*in all respects his equal*." As moral equals, the fall, too, must be equally the fault of both Adam and Eve because, although Eve sinned first, Adam was involved in the same sin through the "instrumentality of his equal,"[41] one, like himself, "who was liable to transgress the divine command."[42] It follows, then, that upon the commission of the first sin, they both fell from happiness, "*but not from equality*." Further, according to Grimké, as the result of their transgression, God pronounced *as a prophecy* that Eve would be subject to her husband, and that he would rule over her.[43] But since prophecy is *not identical* with God's commands, and Adam's being dominant over Eve is a prophecy, *not a command*, it follows ultimately that woman is bound in subjection only to God.

The argument continues in a much more fully philosophical light in her fourth letter, "Social Intercourse of the Sexes."[44] Grimké's position is that men and women are moral equals, and that their *social* dealings with each other are based on social custom and tradition and founded generally on the recognition of the difference between their sexes. This, however, does nothing to elevate their relations consistent with their status as immortal beings. The tendency to apprehend or understand each other with respect only to the difference in sex is "calculated to excite and keep alive the lowest propensities of our nature," and there is nothing that has "tended more to destroy the true *dignity* of woman, than the fact that she is approached by man in the character of a female"[45] and not as another immortal and moral being.

To live according to the commands of God, it is necessary, Grimké holds, for women to "rise from the station where *man*, not God, has placed her, and claim those sacred and inalienable rights, as a moral and responsible being, with which her Creator has invested her." It is, therefore, the *duty* of all human beings to fill their position as moral, rational beings.[46]

Men often object, however, that women ought not to talk about or engage themselves in affairs that are inappropriate to their sex.[47] Grimké disagrees. Her view is that it is part of the improvement of the human being to do what is morally required, and in doing so, woman will become more fully moral, more efficacious in her duties to her children and family, and thereby elevate herself to a level of moral and intellectual commitment consistent with her existence as a moral and rational being.

Sarah Grimké's argument concerning the necessity to recognize the equal moral status of women was primarily religious and focused on the notion that all moral beings have a duty to God to discharge their functions as moral and intellectual beings *because* they are obliged to do so by God. As such, her arguments are not so clearly aligned with the notion that women have an independent existence and an unquestionable right to equal status in the moral and intellectual realms, simply because they are human beings. In fact, Grimké's reasoning here is quite clearly circular. Nonetheless, the Grimké sisters' arguments for women's rights and abolition are the first of the voices of women to be heard clearly in the early American republic. Another voice was soon to be heard, and this woman would claim constitutional and moral authority for the rights of women *without* reference to scriptural justification. This woman turned the world of women's rights activism toward more fully secular arguments in focusing attention on legal issues, education, and employment for women. By doing so, Elizabeth Cady Stanton (and Lucretia Mott), in drafting the Seneca Falls Declaration of Sentiments, could appeal more broadly to human beings, not simply to Christian women and men.

Elizabeth Cady Stanton and the First (Ever) Woman's Rights Convention

Elizabeth Cady Stanton (1815–1902) married the abolitionist Henry Stanton and gave birth to seven children, but the demands of domestic life did not result in stifled intellectual and social activity. In fact, her association with Henry Stanton and her cousin Gerrit Smith (a friend of Frederick Douglass and John Brown), as well as meeting and befriending Lucretia Mott in London at an anti-slavery society meeting, provided intellectual stimulation and social activity influencing her social activism. Like the Grimkés, Elizabeth Cady Stanton saw close affinities between abolitionism and the question of women's rights. Although women's rights were her primary focus and her attention to and dealings with the question of the emancipation and rights of African Americans was at best uneven[48] and sometimes half-hearted, her work in both of these realms of reform of law and society are significant in their political and philosophical import.

The "Seneca Falls Declaration of Sentiments and Resolutions" adheres to principles embodied in the Declaration of Independence. It is so closely allied with the form and substance of the Declaration of Independence that the same rationale for revolution is utilized by Cady Stanton in stating the grievances of women against oppression and subordination. Where in the Declaration of Independence Thomas Jefferson listed injuries and injustices that led to the necessity for revolution, Elizabeth Cady Stanton lists the "repeated injuries and usurpations on the part of man toward woman" that have been designed to establish tyranny over her. Tyranny has been accomplished by depriving women of the right to vote, although their property is taxed, thus supporting a government in which they have no voice and no political representation. In marriage, women are "civilly dead." Women have been treated as morally irresponsible beings and in cases of custody of children, men were regularly granted custody based on the assumption of their superiority over women. The result is, as Cady Stanton put it in the "Declaration of Sentiments," that man "has endeavored, in every way that he could, to destroy her confidence in her own powers, to lessen her self-respect, and to make her willing to lead a dependent and abject life." Still, there were women who claimed that they had "all the rights they want(ed)."Some women actually argued against what was probably the most striking element of the Seneca Falls Declaration of Sentiments and Resolutions, the 9th resolution, calling for women to be granted the right to vote.[49]

The importance of gaining the right to vote for women is not to be underestimated.[50] Lacking political equality manifesting itself in ineligibility to vote, for Stanton, made it possible for men to perpetrate injustices on women. Stanton listed these injustices among the grievances that women have against the oppression and enslavement of women by men.[51] Stanton's position on the right of women to vote is that it is guaranteed by the U.S. Constitution.

Elizabeth Cady Stanton did not live long enough to see the passage of the 19th Amendment to the Constitution in 1920, but her work is a testament to woman's right to stand on an equal footing with man as a responsible human being, entitled to the same rights and privileges, and fully capable of exercising them. The philosophical impact of Cady Stanton's position regarding the rights of women is even more fully expressed in her works on the influence of religious beliefs on women's social, moral, political, and religious status and in "The Solitude of Self,"[52] her most celebrated speech.

Elizabeth Cady Stanton, "The Solitude of Self," and *The Woman's Bible*

In their fight for women's rights and the emancipation of slaves, Angelina and Sarah Grimké relied heavily on appeals to Christianity. But much of Stanton's commentary on the Bible focuses on the myriad ways in which it fails to characterize women fairly or completely and how it is an instrument in the hands of oppressors to continue to shove women into permanent positions of subservience and subordination. In much the same way that Emerson felt disillusionment with the remnants of Calvinism and its insistence on human sin and depravity, Stanton was disillusioned not only by the bonds of the society into which she was born, but found it exacerbated by the imposition of artificial constraints placed upon women by religious zealots and institutions.

Stanton's most clearly philosophical work, "Solitude of Self," gives us a compelling look at the value of individual solitude given the right conditions, but also the incredible and overarching feeling of nearly incomprehensible fear that accompanies solitude when a human being is not properly prepared to experience it. The New England Transcendentalist's celebration of self-reliance makes perfectly good sense for people who are prepared properly for the test of individual strength and will that living necessarily involves. But for a human being lacking the intellectual ammunition necessary to deal with the ultimate solitude that we all sometimes feel, there is nothing to celebrate and everything to lament for the dignity of the individual.

In "Solitude of Self," Stanton recounts the poignant story of a young servant girl who spends Christmas Eve carefully preparing and decorating her employer's family Christmas tree, delighting in the prospect of the coming joy and celebration of the holiday. But in the morning when the family members awaken and exchange gifts with each other, there is no gift for the servant girl and no acknowledgment even of her presence among them. Devastated, she runs from the house and spends the remainder of the day alone with her thoughts, banished to the stark and lonely solitude of the barren rock upon which she sits. The rock represents not only the abandonment of a human being by others, but also the intense poverty of the thoughts of the uneducated child who now drowns in desolate solitude. The society in which she lives does not feel her pain and provides her nothing with which to console herself. At the very least, an educated man in solitary confinement can occupy himself with literature he has read and the identification he can feel with characters in books. He can exercise his intellect with theories and principles, continuing to engage in the conversations of humanity through this acquaintance. The servant girl, however, is alone with her sorrow and is not afforded the opportunity to overcome hardship and sadness.

For Stanton, such neglect of a human being is unconscionable. A civilized, progressive society has an obligation to every human being to see to it that her individual life is acknowledged as largely solitary in its most difficult moments. In moments of painful solitude, the voice of reason and the power of knowledge can be with those who are otherwise alone. The condition of women in patriarchal society is much like the condition of the servant girl;[53] in fact she is perhaps the representative woman who lacks power and acknowledgment, whose dreams and aspirations are rendered empty and unrealizable by the coldness of others. According to Beth Waggenspack, Stanton's "tragically powerful case asserted that people had to be prepared to live with themselves, to fight for themselves, and to suffer for themselves. Women, she claimed, were poorly prepared to do so because of mistaken notions about the ability of others to share the burdens that life presented."[54]

The solitude of self to which Stanton refers is a recurring theme in her work. In fact, the meaning of "self-sovereignty" goes beyond Stanton's original claims in her speeches and writings on sex and marriage. Ellen Carol Dubois contends that Stanton's "central point was that women ought to be able to control their own sexual lives, a right which she called 'individual' or 'self' sovereignty."[55] Waggenspack, however, holds that Stanton's work on the whole is an expression of the need for women, indeed for all human beings, to be able to stand on their own, not to be dependent upon anyone.

According to Elizabeth Cady Stanton, the Bible is one of the single most oppressive tools in the hands of men to question the full humanity, the independence, and indeed the moral status of women. Stanton considered not only laws, but social conventions arising from religious doctrine, as the most significant barriers in the way of women's improvement.

Elizabeth Cady Stanton's *The Woman's Bible* is probably one of the most revolutionary and radical works in the history of American thought. Stanton and her co-authors[56] took on traditional interpretations and translations of the Bible, arguing that there are many passages in which women are depicted unfairly, and in which men, who have been the *only* translators and interpreters of the Bible, have interpreted and translated it to their own benefit. Stanton's reasoning concerning why women ought to provide commentary on the Old and New Testaments is that if men can do it, then women can, too.[57]

Stanton reasoned that if the Bible teaches that women are men's equals, it makes no sense that women are not invited to join revising committees. But just as Henry Stanton and Lucretia Mott said that adding the 9th Resolution to the Seneca Falls document would make the women's rights convention and its framers seem "ridiculous," so too did Stanton receive indications that it would be "ridiculous" for women to attempt any interpretive revision of or commentary on the Bible. Stanton asks whether "any man wrote to the late revising committee of the Divines to stop their work on the ground that it was ridiculous for men to revise the Bible. Why is it more ridiculous for women to protest against her present status in the Old and New Testaments . . . than in the statutes and constitution of the state?"[58] Women have managed to make legislators change statutes to improve the lot of women (actions that a few decades earlier also seemed ridiculous) and there is no reason that women cannot manage to make changes in the Bible or at least provide critical commentary on it.

Stanton's commitment to Enlightenment ideals of the use of individual reason, combined with late nineteenth-century optimism, could not be more apparent. A woman who refuses to attempt to improve her status in the religious realm is obviously not attending to the fact that her "political and social degradation are but an outgrowth of (her) status in the Bible" and that progressive people must "wipe the dew off (their) spectacles, and see that the world is moving". Women have an obligation to themselves, and to all other women, to take on all political, social, moral, or religious institutions that tend toward degradation. To those who object that they cannot do it, that it would not be "politic" to do so, Stanton replies that they are simply cowards. There are numerous women who are capable of being on the revising committee, but they refuse to offer their assistance. Stanton's assessment of their refusal is that they "are all suffering from the inherited ideas of their inferiority; they do not perceive it, yet such is the true explanation of their solicitude, lest they should seem to be too self-asserting".

For Stanton, however, women *must* be self-asserting because women's existence, like the existence of all human beings, is characterized by the solitude of self, and the self-assertive self-reliance that is required for a life of human dignity cannot be achieved when women acquiesce in the attitude of religions that degrade women. Women ought to engage in criticism, interpretation, and revision of the Bible to show clearly to all those who think that the Bible is a work glorifying the existence of women, that "in plain English it does not exalt and dignify woman" no matter what it may say in Greek or Hebrew.

For Stanton, the Bible was a source not of morality, but of *immorality* insofar as it is used to subjugate women. The purpose of *The Woman's Bible* was, simply, to be "a challenge to the meaning and authority of biblical scriptures and . . . an attempt to liberate women from the 'religious superstitions' that she believed blocked their emancipation."[59] Consider, again, the story of the fall of man.[60]

Who was at fault for the fall? Kathi Kern points out that Eve was not tempted by material things, but by *knowledge*.[61] A being tempted by *knowledge* is certainly a rational being, not one to be taken lightly, and, as Sarah Grimké pointed out, man would be much more acceptable as a moral exemplar and teacher to women if, instead of going along with Eve in committing sin, Adam had instead declined to do so. But Adam did not do so, and the moral and rational *equality* of men and women is established here, certainly not distinction or inequality, or *justification* for the subordination of women to men. Stanton's view of the behavior of Eve in the Garden of Eden is that she sought knowledge and *this*, it seems, makes her of better moral character than Adam. In fact, another commentator in *The Woman's Bible*, Lillie Blake, questions Adam's superiority on the basis of his behavior when God discovered his human creations' transgression. Adam blamed it all on Eve instead of taking responsibility for his own actions. For the commentators in Stanton's *Woman's Bible*, this behavior raises serious doubts about men's claims that *they* are superior to women. Adam is, it seems, *not* the person to whom men ought to look for a moral exemplar or their model of superiority over women.[62]

Kathi Kern explains that in Stanton's time, a common interpretation of the fall[63] was that Eve was inferior to Adam because she was created from his rib, and therefore she was both less knowledgeable about the world and more vulnerable to sin than Adam. Because Eve was not so experienced in the world as Adam, she was "imbecilic" compared with him, explaining why the serpent went to her rather than to him as a candidate for temptation.

This is certainly a creative way for women's detractors to explain why Eve was responsible for sin, but it is not the only way, or perhaps not even the best way to understand who is culpable. It is important to note here that some interpreters of the story of original sin are not moved to accept commonly held beliefs regarding it. Evelin Sullivan, in *The Concise Book of Lying*, contends that God may have told a *lie* to Adam and Eve, and that it was not the serpent who did so. God is reported to have told his human creations that if they ate the fruit of the tree of knowledge of good and evil, on the day they did so they would surely die. And of course they did *not* die on that day. Sullivan notes that God expelled Adam and Eve from the Garden of Eden *after* they gained knowledge but *before* they had the chance to eat of the fruit of the tree of *life*. Sullivan explains that apologists for traditional biblical interpretation of the story of the fall assert that the claim that Adam and Eve would die on the day of their transgression was meant only *metaphorically*. For Sullivan, however, this explanation "does not wash. Adam and Eve and their descendants die because the serpent either did not know, or did not get around to telling, or did not care to tell, Eve about the tree of life."[64] Sullivan's additional comments are of particular interest here:

> The blunt fact is that the first character to tell a manifest lie in the Bible is God himself, who plays the role of the father who does not want his children to do something and who scares them with a lie to keep them from doing it. Suppose he had told them the truth: there are two trees I don't want you to eat from because eating from one will make you godlike and eating from the other will make you immortal—and I don't want you to be godlike and immortal. Would that have kept his children away from the trees? Or would they have wondered all too soon why, if advancement to the rank of god is so easy, they are forbidden to take that step? Would they have gone further and asked themselves what odd insecurity on the part of their creator was to blame for his injunction, and what bad thing could possibly happen to them if they became godlike and immortal—not to mention why he put forbidden trees in the garden in the first place?[65]

Sullivan's questions are fascinating and lead to the question whether, if Adam and Eve had eaten from the tree of life, they would have become immortal. If they both would have become immortal, that is more fuel to add to the fire of women's equality with men. Furthermore, Sullivan's comment regarding the "lies" told by God are a way in which one may add to Stanton's reasons to be unconvinced that the Bible serves as a model of moral behavior.

Stanton's work in the cause of women's rights is unquestionably significant in its social, historical, and philosophical contexts. Stanton was one of the first American women to take on secular *and* ecclesiastical authority to find the causes for and proposed solutions to the subordination and subjection of women.[66] She did so in a particularly individualist and modernist fashion by framing her arguments with central focus on the rights of the individual, supported by the need for education for all people, and the particularly American (pre)occupation with attention to principles embedded in the Declaration of Independence and the Constitution.

Frederick Douglass, the Fourth of July, and Human Dignity

Frederick Douglass's harsh words on the nature of slavery provide a powerful description of the deplorable life of the slave and how the American penchant for respect for and protection of individual rights is only selectively applied and acknowledged.[67] Douglass describes the legal and social relation of master and slave:

> A master is one—to speak in the vocabulary of the southern states—who claims and exercises a right of property in the person of a fellow-man.

> This he does with the force of the law and the sanction of southern religion. The law gives the master absolute power over the slave. He may work him, flog him, hire him out, sell him, and, in certain contingencies, *kill* him, with perfect impunity. The slave is a human being, divested of all rights—reduced to the level of a brute—a mere "chattel" in the eye of the law—placed beyond the circle of human brotherhood—cut off from his kind—his name, which the "recording angel" may have enrolled in heaven, among the blest, is impiously inserted in a *master's ledger*, with horses, sheep, and swine.[68]

The slave was given no more consideration than a common farm animal and was often treated with less dignity and respect than a pig. But it is even worse than this, because the slave was denied basic consideration as a human being in the intellectual, moral, and religious realms. Douglass comments that "it is only when we contemplate the slave as a moral and intellectual being, that we can adequately comprehend the unparalleled enormity of slavery, and the intense criminality of the slaveholder."[69] The "first work of slavery," according to Douglass, "is to destroy all sense of high moral and religious responsibility. It reduces a man to a mere machine. It cuts him off from his Maker, it hides from him the laws of God, and leaves him to grope his way from time to eternity in the dark, under the arbitrary and despotic control of a frail, depraved, and sinful fellow-man."[70] Prior to emancipation, in almost all the southern slaveholding states, it was a crime to teach a slave to read. Douglass recounts that when told that Douglass could read, his master recoiled in horror, stating that next he would want to learn to write—and then he would run away. Douglass did, in fact, escape from the bonds of slavery.[71]

Douglass escaped to freedom in Massachusetts and shortly thereafter joined the Garrisonians in the cause of abolition. Douglass was originally committed to Garrison's position that the U.S. Constitution was a pro-slavery document, but reconsidered his position and in 1851 renounced adherence to the anticonstitutionalist Garrisonians' view.[72] Douglass, on the other hand, did not discount the use of constitutional claims to argue *against* slavery and show that it is *not* a pro-slavery document. For Douglass, if the Constitution is read and interpreted as it *ought* to be, it is plain to see that it is a "glorious liberty document."[73] A careful reading, he says, will show that nowhere will one see the words "slavery," "slaveholding," or "slave" in it.[74] According to Douglass, if the constitution was meant to be a proslavery document, never to mention the word "slave" would be an exceptionally ineffective way to get the point across.[75]

We now turn to the philosophical import of the constitutionalist distinction of the argument of "What to the Slave is the Fourth of July?" (1852).[76] Douglass begins by noting that the United States is a mere seventy-six years old, in its childhood as a nation. It is therefore still impressionable, and Douglass remains hopeful that the youthful character of the American nation will make it possible for changes for the better to take place. For Douglass, change will come about when Americans apply the principles of the Declaration of Independence to everyone and realize its inclusive meaning.

Douglass turns his attention to the resolution of the Declaration of Independence, asserting that "these united colonies are, and of right, ought to be free and

Independent States" and that the connection between Britain and the colonies *is* dissolved by the resolution. This resolution provides the American citizen with something about which to feel pride, patriotism, and gratitude. When it comes to the question of the celebration of independence of a people and nation from the bonds of slavery perpetrated by its mother country, Frederick Douglass notes that "This Fourth of July is *yours*, not *mine*. *You* may rejoice, *I* must mourn." It is certainly not the case here that Douglass is seeking sympathy or in any way demeaning himself in protesting the wrongs that he spends considerable time listing in the Fourth of July oration.[77]

Bernard Boxill argues that protest is necessary, that "persons have reason to protest their wrongs not only to stop injustice but also to show self-respect and to know themselves as self-respecting."[78] Booker T. Washington held the position that Americans did not mind "being accused of degradation" of their own moral character in allowing slavery just so "long as its affairs, its advancement, and its moral salvation remained the center of moral concern."[79] An argument against slavery, therefore, that does *not* include protests against the wrongs done to a person is an argument that does not point to the *rights* of the person who is *wronged*, but instead points to a very different sort of argument against slavery. The argument to which it points insists that the moral fabric of society is weakened by the existence of slavery, that it is the moral character of those who have rights and who allow slavery to exist that is being damaged.[80] The sort of protest against slavery used by Frederick Douglass is *not* that the protester wants pity, but that the protester is entitled to recognition of his rights. As Boxill puts it:

> The idea that the protester seeks sympathy is unlikely, since in claiming his rights he affirms that he is claiming what he can demand and exact, and sympathy cannot be demanded and exacted. The idea that the protester is self-pitying is likewise implausible, since a person who feels pity for himself typically believes that his condition is deplorable and unavoidable, and this is not (at) all what the protester affirms. On the contrary, he affirms that his condition is avoidable, he insists that what he protests is precisely the illegitimate, and hence avoidable, interference by others in the exercise of his rights, and he expresses the sentiment, not of self-pity, but of resentment.[81]

What the protester wants, Boxill claims, is to be left alone, not to be interfered with. This means that when a person protests wrongs against him, he is expressing "a righteous and self-respecting concern for himself."[82]

It is this understanding of the nature of the anti-slavery, civil rights, and women's rights movements that demands attention. There is no free person who can understand completely the plight and misery of the slave; there is no man who can fully understand the wrongs committed against women.[83] To demand one's rights is *not* to seek pity, or to ask someone for something as a *gift*, or to elicit sympathy—it is to *demand* what is already one's own. For that, no further argument is necessary. As Douglass noted, there were those who wished that he would argue more vehemently "to make a favorable impression on the public mind."[84] But Douglass needs no argument to prove that slavery is wrong, because if it is wrong to enslave a human being, it is wrong to enslave the African American.[85] No arguments are needed to prove that African Americans are human beings. It is admitted in the administration of laws in the south that hold the African American slave to very stringent punishments for violations of law. But there is in fact an argument in Douglass's speech that establishes his appeal to the intent of the framers of the Constitution. The argument is essentially this: "Natural law links law to morality; natural law upholds human equality and opposes slavery; the Founders were natural lawyers; therefore the Declaration and the Constitution that the Founders wrote must also have been intended to uphold human equality and oppose slavery. So any appearance that it does not must be illusory."[86]

Boxill considers what the protester wants from others—and what he wants is for others not to violate his rights. It is not necessary for the protester to convince other people that he has rights, because it is not mere consequences alone that are the point. If it were consequences accruing to the protester that mattered, then it might be best not to protest at all since protest often leads to violence from one's detractors. The point is that protest is *not* a way to prove that the victim of wrongs has rights. It is, instead, "an affirmation that a victim of injury has rights."[87]

Protest against the wrongs of slavery and other social injustices against African Americans are primarily arguments centered on the dignity and value of the human being, not on transient and temporal consequences to be experienced either by the protester or by his or her oppressor. It is consequences to humanity on the whole, and to the dignity of humanity, that are of the most import in these arguments.[88]

Martin Luther King, Jr. and the "Letter from the Birmingham Jail"

The work and life of Martin Luther King, Jr. embody in action a long history of commitment to American ideals. From Thoreau, King borrows and utilizes the concept and efficacy of civil disobedience. It is not possible to *do* anything about wrongs simply by acknowledging them; it is necessary to *act* and to *act decisively* for positive change to come about. It is also, in the style of Thoreau, necessary for the objector against injustice not to engage in injustice himself. This is why, for King, it is necessary to engage in nonviolent resistance. However, Thoreau refused allegiance to a government that was *the slave's government* and advocated distancing oneself from it. King, on the other hand, was an assimilationist like Frederick Douglass, who held the position that it is possible for all races to live together in peace and under conditions of justice. So to remove oneself from the problems, to claim that one is not supporting an injustice when not actively supporting a government perpetrating it, is simply not enough. It is necessary to do more than refuse to be part of the problem; it is necessary to become part of the solution. King's solution to the problems plaguing the races, to the problems brought on by racism, was to adhere to a philosophy of love.[89]

For King, we ought not to claim that protests are *causing* social problems. It is instead lamentable that there are conditions in society making it necessary for

African Americans to engage in protest in the first place, and King insists that we must not look "merely at effects," but must also "grapple with underlying causes."[90] The causes are the actions, opinions, and beliefs of those who refuse to acknowledge the civil rights of African Americans that are guaranteed in anti-segregation laws and in the Constitution. Mark E. Brandon contends that for King, the Constitution and the Declaration of Independence were "contracts, specifically (they are) promissory notes whose promises he insisted the nation was obliged to honor."[91] For King, according to Brandon, there are two elements to the constitutionalist arguments. The first is a "commitment to equality, dignity, and decency of treatment for African-Americans" and the second is that of assimilation of all racial communities.

The commitment to justice in King's position is a commitment to the community, a commitment to all of humanity, to help realize the creation of a society of fairness. King's arguments in the *Letter from the Birmingham Jail* are that segregation laws are unjust because they do not respect the dignity of the human being and that such laws are inflicted on a minority for the benefit of a majority. King says that he is in Birmingham because injustice is in Birmingham. This is exactly the sort of reasoning that Thoreau employed in refusing to pay the poll tax that would support the institution of slavery. He was jailed for not paying the tax, but preferred to be in jail where he could be free from injustice rather than to remain out of jail and do nothing to change prevailing social conditions.

There are those who think (just as women's rights activists were told) that it is best simply to wait, that time will provide the corrective to social wrongs. But King points out that in the history of the wrongs against African Americans, the word "wait" has always ultimately meant "never" and the time for waiting to realize "constitutional and god-given rights" is long past. It is time to act, to resist the injustices that racism has perpetrated against African Americans.

Opponents of King's position, however, believe that resisting and protesting result in lawlessness. King, again, is not moved. He contends in the *Letter from the Birmingham Jail* that there is a difference between just laws and unjust laws and that we have an obligation to abide by only those that are just. King's position is that one can tell the difference between a just law and an unjust law by considering that a

> just law is a man-made code that squares with the moral law or the law of God. An unjust law is a code that is out of harmony with the moral law. To put it in the terms of Saint Thomas Aquinas, an unjust law is a human law that is not rooted in eternal and natural law. Any law that uplifts human personality is just. Any law that degrades human personality is unjust. All segregation statutes are unjust because segregation distorts the soul and damages the personality. It gives the segregator a false sense of superiority, and the segregated a false sense of inferiority.

Segregation relegates some people to the status of things, so segregation is socially, politically, and most important, morally unjustified. It is perfectly acceptable, then, to persuade others to break laws that are *immoral*. We owe allegiance to laws that are consistent with the dignity of humanity, that recognize the value of the human being, and we have a moral obligation to act against any law that degrades the individual. Yet King's detractors believed that it was necessary to condemn nonviolent action because it precipitates violence. King asks: "Isn't this like condemning the robbed man because his possession of money precipitated the evil act of robbery?" He adds: "We must come to see, as federal courts have consistently affirmed, that it is immoral to urge an individual to withdraw his efforts to gain his basic constitutional rights because the quest precipitates violence. Society must protect the robbed and punish the robber."

King's constitutionalist claims are clearly linked to the view of Frederick Douglass in this respect. Douglass and King both held that "the Constitution challenged America to a higher destiny" and that the tension between theory embodied in American ideals and practices (such as segregation) revealed a "deep 'two-faced' character of American popular culture."[92]

To combat the immorality of segregation, King argues in the *Letter from the Birmingham Jail* that African Americans must practice a "philosophy of love" in civil disobedience such that "One who breaks an unjust law must do it *openly, lovingly* . . . and with a willingness to accept the penalty. I submit that an individual who breaks a law that conscience tells him is unjust, and willingly accepts the penalty by staying in jail to arouse the conscience of the community over its injustice, is in reality expressing the very highest respect for law. . . ." There is nothing extreme in this view, nothing indicative of a lack of respect for law, or advocacy of irrationalism and violence. King's position is a middle ground, an assimilationist position. He notes that he finds himself

> in the middle of two opposing forces in the Negro community. One is the force of complacency made up of Negroes who, as a result of long years of oppression, have been so completely drained of self-respect and a sense of "somebodiness" that they have adjusted to segregation and, of a few Negroes in the middle class who, because of a degree of academic and economic security, and because at points they profit by segregation, have unconsciously become insensitive to the problems of the masses. The other force is one of bitterness and hatred, and comes perilously close to advocating violence. It is expressed in the various black nationalist groups that are springing up over the nation, the largest and best known being Elijah Muhammad's Muslim movement. This movement is nourished by the contemporary frustration over the continued existence of racial discrimination. It is made up of people who have lost faith in America, who have absolutely repudiated Christianity, and who have concluded that the white man is an incurable "devil." I have tried to stand between these two forces, saying that we need not follow the "do-nothingism" of the complacent or the hatred and despair of the black nationalist. There is the more excellent way of love and nonviolent protest. . . .[93]

King characterizes the way of nonviolent protest in "Pilgrimage to Nonviolence":

> [W]hile the nonviolent resister is passive in the sense that he is not physically aggressive toward his opponent, his mind and emotions are always active,

> constantly seeking to persuade his opponent that he is wrong. The method is passive physically, but strongly active spiritually. It is not passive nonresistance to evil, it is active nonviolent resistance to evil.[94]

King explains that the purpose is not to humiliate an opponent, but to make a friend of him. King says that the methods of nonviolence are "not ends themselves; they are merely means to awaken a sense of moral shame in the opponent. The end is redemption and reconciliation."[95] Redemption and reconciliation appear to happen to both parties, both to the oppressed and to the oppressor. The oppressed has his rights realized; the oppressor brings himself back into the moral community. Hanes Walton argues that

> King firmly believed that as a method of civil disobedience, nonviolent resistance and direct action, is the most potent weapon available to oppressed people in their struggle for freedom and human dignity. It is a way of disarming the opponent, exposing his moral weaknesses, undermining his morale, and, at the same time, affecting his conscience. It paralyzes and confuses the power structure against which it is directed, while it endows its initiators with a new sense of self-respect, duty, strength, devotion, courage, and dignity. To employ the method of nonviolence, one must be very strong spiritually; spiritual strength is the opposite of the shirking passivity associated with cowardice. Strictly speaking, nonviolence does not defeat the opponent, but tries to win his friendship and understanding.[96]

The method of nonviolent resistance is not, as Greg Moses explains, a philosophy of weakness. Because Black terrorism in the civil rights era would have been suicidal, a method of social change had to be found that would be effective in achieving the goals of assimilation and integration, but that would not exacerbate alienation from the community. Traditional reasoning seems to tell us that nonviolence is a "glorified victimology" and that "strength finds its true meaning in violence."

"This is the requirement that King's logic of nonviolence rejects. For King, nonviolence is the high road to true power. . . . The logic of nonviolence seeks power within a disciplined framework that views violence as inevitably shortsighted."[97] In this respect, traditional reasoning regarding nonviolence is very much like the reasoning of patriarchy indicating that *justice* is superior to *care*. Carol Gilligan explained in her work that there appears to be a very clear distinction between distinctly male and female forms of reasoning about questions of justice.[98] Men tend to engage in moral reasoning closely associated with liberal thinking and requiring, at best, that our obligations to others are simply to leave them alone, to protect their negative rights. Note, for example, the way in which John Locke's law of nature is expressed. His view was that we have an obligation to ourselves to preserve our own lives, and "when (our own lives come) not in competition, ought (we), as much as (we) can, *to preserve the rest of mankind*, and may not, unless it be to do justice on an offender, take away, or impair the life, or what tends to the preservation of the life, the liberty, health, limb, or goods of another."[99]

On Locke's view, what we are obligated to do is simply to stay out of each other's way, not being required positively to *assist* anyone else. On the other hand, women's understanding of morality is much more relational in that it is *care* of self and others that takes precedence over leaving them alone, and essential to this notion is the contention that we are primarily *relational* beings who are affected by, and in turn affect, others and that our obligations are not satisfied simply by staying out of each other's way. For some reason, women's adherence to the distinction between moral voices or conceptions of justice has the tendency to lead traditionalists in philosophy to deny the claim that there is such a distinction. Greg Moses notes that "both feminism and nonviolence have a way of provoking angry denials. Men are flustered by critiques of patriarchy in much the same way that whites are perturbed by discussions of racism."[100]

There is more to this distinction in the reasoning embedded in King's nonviolent philosophy of love. It is attending to the fact that if we conceive of society as founded only on individual liberties, we can do so by thinking only or primarily in terms of liberal individualism, not taking into account the existence or needs, or the rights or dignity, of others. It is at the point that we begin to think in terms of equality as a social rather than an individual concept that we move from the realm of liberal individualist thinking to a more relational sort of moral and political outlook which takes into account that there is no such thing as understanding equality without noting that the concept necessitates consideration of others. As Moses puts it:

> With the conceptual move to equality (from liberty), we are prevented from conceiving liberation in individualistic terms. My equality depends upon your equality. Our equality becomes a collective problem that no longer admits of individual or unilateral solutions. There is no immediate theoretical conflict between my equality and yours. It is important, then, to note that King has made this conceptual move from freedom to equality as he frames a choice between a chaos of conflicting individuals and a community of harmonizing equals.[101] . . .

It is important also to realize that the method of nonviolent resistance is *not* an attack against people who do evil; it is an attack against evil itself. In that sense, the nonviolent protester seeks to defeat evil, "not the persons victimized by evil."[102] It is a statement eliciting action designed to show that the oppressed is morally superior to his oppressor. King states that "since the white man's personality is greatly distorted by segregation, and his soul is greatly scarred, he needs the love of the Negro. The Negro must love the white man, because the white man needs his love to remove his tensions, insecurities, and fears."[103] The love that informs King's philosophical position is *agape* which

> springs from the *need* of the other person—his need for belonging to the best in the human family. The Samaritan who helped the Jew on the Jericho Road was "good" because he responded to the human need that he was presented with. God's love is eternal and fails not because man needs his love. St. Paul assures us that the loving act of redemption was done "while we were yet sinners"—that is, at the point of our greatest need for love. "*Agape* is not a weak, passive love. It is love in action. *Agape* is love seeking to preserve and

create community. It is insistence on community even when one seeks to break it. *Agape* is a willingness to sacrifice in the interest of mutuality. *Agape* is a willingness to go to any length to restore community."[104]

Marilyn Frye and Radical Separatist Feminism

Marilyn Frye's work marks a distinct difference from most of the thinkers that have been considered so far. We have seen emphasis on the notion that *difference* is something that ought not to be considered in achieving justice or in developing a sense of it, that differences between the races and sexes are accidental properties of human beings and are morally and politically irrelevant. People argue on the basis of this sort of thinking that we ought not to make distinctions between men and women, or between black and white, or between any other contingent and temporal differences because there is some underlying rationality and moral value of each person and *that* is what ought to be considered in doling out rights (such as to vote) and determining a person's responsibilities. For thinkers of such optimistic character, like Frederick Douglass who believed that racism would disappear when slavery did, or like woman suffragists who thought that the problem of women's subordination would be solved by securing their right to vote, a rational approach to problems is the way to their solution. On this optimistic view, all we need to do is recognize our essential human (rational) nature, and we will see that there really are no relevant distinctions between people and that all ought to be treated and regarded as the same.

Such idealization of the solutions to moral and political problems is just that: It is too idealistic. The patterns and practices of oppression and enslavement are too subtle and too deeply ingrained in American culture (and perhaps the world over) to be obviated by hopes of assimilation. Marilyn Frye shows with vivid and powerful imagery what sorts of oppression and violence continue to be done to women and what ought to be done to eliminate these forms of despotic rule over others. Her position is hopeful, but she does not argue for a sort of *sameness* between men and women; in fact she is doubtful that any mechanism of equalization is even possible between them. She is, then, a separatist.[105]

In "In and Out of Harm's Way: Arrogance and Love,"[106] Frye presents a picture of the machinations invoked in patriarchal society that render women oppressed, exploited, and enslaved. She does so to make it possible for women to resist or escape such machinations and to create conditions in which we can realize, and not simply imagine, "the female human animal unharmed" by these processes. It is a vision of what it would be for women to be freed from the chains of patriarchy, from the coercion, exploitation, oppression—and ultimately from the slavery of women that is the result of masculinist thought and action in patriarchy. But this is not all, for Frye has a view of the transformation, of the reform, of women's condition such that women are no longer subject to these degrading practices.

Frye explains that women become slaves (or at least much like slaves) in patriarchal societies through a system of coercion and exploitation that makes them oddly complicit in their own oppression. As Frye explains, we can understand the distinction between coercion and freedom if we will but take the time to comprehend that there are cases in which a person is coerced *even* when the person *is* capable of doing something different from what he or she in fact does do. Making such a distinction is reminiscent of, but clearly different from, Jonathan Edwards's conception of determinism such that one is free when one is able to do what he or she *desires* to do, when he or she is not constrained physically. This conception of things is also employed by John Locke in his *Essay Concerning Human Understanding* in the example of the man who is locked in a room but does not know that this is the case. If he wishes to stay in the room and is unaware that it is locked, then he is free because *he is doing what he wants to do* and is not physically restrained. But what if he wished to leave the room and found it locked? The analysis of his condition is then perhaps quite different because he no longer wishes to do what he is doing (stay in the room) and instead wishes to leave but *cannot do so*. But again, we can return to the description of conditions in which he does not desire to leave and happily convince ourselves that he is not coerced.

This explanation may be problematic, however, because it depends on the assumption that what a person *wants* to do is a result of his or her own free choice.[107] Frye doubts that this is always the case, contrary to the position of Jean-Paul Sartre. Frye's attitude is anything but forgiving and understanding toward Sartre's claim that a person is responsible for all things he does since she sees his view (which is, in many ways, the view of those who believe that a woman *can, if she wants to,* leave abusive conditions) as a narrow-minded one in which the conception of coercion is itself distorted. As Frye explains, under this view, a person can be coerced into doing something only when she is physically overpowered and cannot act under her own power. This condition could be explained in a case of rape, for example, in which the rapist threatens to kill a woman, and she "agrees" to sexual activity with him to avoid death, and then is considered to have *consented* because she did not fight, run away, or otherwise resist. Frye sees such conditions as coercion in the same way that we understand that a robber who threatens to shoot a person if she does not hand over her money is not *literally* controlling the movements (or lack of movements) of the victim's body, but the coercer has arranged conditions so that the least unpleasant of available alternatives is the one on which the victim feels she *must* act. When this is the case, one has been coerced because, had conditions been different, the victim would not have given over her money to anyone, and would not have thought of doing so in the first place. But simple cases of coercion such as this are not all there is to the oppression and exploitation of women who *are also* coerced into occupying positions of subordination in patriarchal society. The simple version of coercion is efficient only in limited cases and for a limited time. But if a coercer desires that a person continue to perform or behave in a certain way for him, he has to engage in much more subtle forms of control.

More effective, long-lasting, and subtle forms of control can be explained by the coercion experienced by a person forced into white slavery, in which she is abducted, tortured, and effectively and ultimately alienated from all things familiar to her, and is at all times afraid for her life at the hands of her abductor. Such control and coercion take place, as Frye explains, in a three-stage process of abduction, seasoning, and criminalization.[108]

What has to happen to the human being who is coerced and exploited in such violent ways is that she must be manipulated so that what results is "detachment of the victim's will and intelligence from the victim's own interests and their attachment to the interest of the exploiter."[109] In sum, what needs to happen to achieve effective subordination of a woman is that she no longer sees herself as a being with self-respect, that she no longer (as would naturally or ordinarily be the case) sees her own interests as the center of her concerns. She needs to exist for *the other* and not *for herself*. She no longer thinks primarily of her own survival, of herself as an independent being, but sees herself as a being *made* to serve the interests of someone else. She has no other alternative.

The sort of coercion and slavery into which women are put in these extreme, but unfortunately real and even more unfortunately common, cases may seem too radical for belief. But Frye explains further what she calls the "metaphysics of this process" in which

> [b]rutality and radical helplessness create a fissure: the animal intelligence has no vehicle; the animal body misjudges and is inappropriately grateful (for not being beaten at the end of the "seasoning" stage of brutalization). The intelligent body ceases to be: intelligence and bodilyness are sundered, unable to ground or defeat each other or themselves. Mind and body, thus made separate, are then reconnected, but only indirectly: their interactions and communications now mediated by the man's will and interest. Mind and body can preserve themselves only by subordinating each other to him. The woman or girl now serves herself only by serving him, and can interpret herself only by reference to him. He has rent her in two and grafted the raw ends to himself so she can act, but only in his interest. She has been annexed and is his appendage.[110]

The imagery is vivid and Frye intends to produce discomfort in the reader. This is the case because the more violent and extreme examples she utilizes are no less than analogs to the sorts of processes and practices that are employed by men in patriarchal societies to control *all* women through the use of the male's "arrogant eye."

The arrogant eye is the point of view of the arrogant perceiver who holds that "the world and everything in it (with the occasional exception of other men) is in the nature of things there *for* him, that she is by her constitution and *telos* his servant."[111] This, according to Frye, is itself coercive. This is the case because men have traditionally had "the cultural and institutional power to make the misdefinition (of what is 'good' or 'healthy') stick"[112]—and men have traditionally had that power in patriarchy because they define the notions of normalcy, rightness, goodness, and so on.[113]

Frye explains what it means in philosophy and science to perceive with an arrogant eye. The arrogant perceiver (man) believes that he is dominant over the world and that this is the way the world is supposed to be. Whether we consider

Abrahamic religions and their story of creation in which women are responsible for sin and are subordinated to men, or whether we consider the philosophy of science in which we try to *control* nature (which is perceived traditionally as being "female"), there is a tradition of usurpation of power over women, over nature, over *things* that man sees as part of the good for himself, and that to which he appropriates and claims for himself a *right*. But what the arrogant perceiver does not realize is that, as Frye puts it, what is sauce for the goose is sauce for the gander, and *women* are constituted such that they see, too, that their own lives can be understood as created for *themselves* (or at least they could, under different circumstances, live their lives as if that were the case), and it is not so easy to claim that women are in some way behaving "badly" or that there is something "wrong" with them when they behave such that "*her* substance is organized primarily on principles which align it to *her* interests and welfare."[114] Nothing, it seems, could be more annoying to the arrogant perceiver.

But men are not the only arrogant perceivers. It is unfortunately the case that women may become arrogant perceivers as well. The woman who sacrifices herself for the good of others sees *through* the arrogant eye—not because she is seeing the world as organized and arranged simply for *her*, but she instead has a perverted perception of the world in which selflessness becomes living *for another* instead of for herself and in which she adopts the arrogant eye by assuming the interest of another instead of the interest of herself. To claim that a person who sacrifices herself for the interest of another is a selfless person is wrong, but for Frye, it is equally wrong to claim that this person *loves* the thing or being for whom she is sacrificing.

The loving eye, the contrary of the arrogant eye,[115] is a healthy look at the independence of *the other*. The loving eye can tell "one's own interests from those of others and (know) where one's self leaves off and another begins"; it is not arrogant. It recognizes the other as an independent being with value, with dignity, and behaves in such a way that those things are not stolen from the other nor are they, for the self, relegated to the interests of the other. To possess a loving eye would be to eschew the tendency of the arrogator to believe that all things exist for him, by him, and to be controlled for his interests. The loving eye, and living in a world in which women are freed by it, and freed *from* the arrogant eye, is one in which "what we are and how we are, or what we would be and how we would be if not molded by the arrogating eye, is: *not molded to man, not dependent*."[116]

What Frye has in mind is a world in which we would respond to each other's needs freely, not "*bound* by concepts or by terror in a dependence upon those of another."[117] Marilyn Frye is certainly not saying that there are no women who are independent or who live lives of some independent significance. What she does say is that women are presented by history (or even presented in our own experiences) as in some way obligated or indebted to men for their success. Frye contends that

> there is in the fabric of our lives, not always visible but always affecting its texture and strength, a mortal dread of being outside the field of vision of the arrogant eye. That eye gives all things meaning by connecting all things to each other by way of their references to one point—Man. We fear that if we

> are not in that web of meaning there will be no meaning: our work will be meaningless, our lives of no value, our accomplishments empty, our identities illusory.[118]

This, for Frye, is "a terrible disability." It arises because, in thinking of themselves as independent, but also as needing or wanting to form a community of others like themselves, women may become arrogators as well. This would happen when women think that one who does not behave consistently with a position like her own cannot be part of the community—that we must somehow ignore those who do not agree and who do not fit the mold or the conditions of an "imagined community of harmony." What happens then is that women adopt the arrogant eye and perpetrate on others exactly the conditions from which they are attempting to flee as it is imposed upon them by men. Adopting an arrogant eye in this way is the direct result of believing that to have a harmonious community of agreement means that all women have to be the *same* and that they have to agree with each other. But for Frye, the problem with this is that it is precisely the notion of community that is required for meaning to exist and community and meaning are created "*not* a monogenous herd, for without difference there can be no meaning."[119] And what we have then to do, as Frye sees it, is to wait and see what will happen if women can begin to know each other as independent, if we can exist under the gaze of the loving eye rather than the steely stare of the arrogant eye.

Just as Martin Luther King noted that American attitudes remained racist even after the civil rights victories were won, so also Marilyn Frye notices that even in the face of the progress women have made in fighting the chains of patriarchal and misogynist thinking, the remnants of the arrogant eye are never far away. Women's solidarity with each other against the dangers of arrogation is a way in which justice and fairness might begin to be achieved. To remove the bonds of racism and sexism and to combat the attitudes that make them possible can create a society in which human independence and dignity, not simply male or white independence and dignity, can be recognized, acted upon, and used as a vehicle by which our society can be made more inclusive, more just, and more fair.

What Frye is doing is very similar to what all the reformers in this essay have attempted to do. They have attempted to find a kind of binding force between individualism and community that will make both the individual and the community meaningful and in some way efficacious in making the world in which we live a better place. Although Frye and others in this essay are clearly different in many ways, they are all using love, solidarity, or understanding the place of the individual in the community as the means to heal the wrongs that we inflict on ourselves and each other. The separatism of Frye and the assimilationism of Martin Luther King, Jr., can then be understood as consistent with each other. They both work within a cultural framework expressing the tension that exists between our penchant for individuality and our need for community; they both work within a framework in which the cultural, historical, and philosophical norms have influenced their thought, and in which the claims of the individual distinct from the claims of the community are in conflict.

Conclusion

America's early tendency was to think in terms of negative rights and to center on individualism. This sort of thinking is dangerous if left to itself, if we do not take into consideration our relational nature. We may succumb to the tendency to think of ourselves in egoistic terms such that our obligations to others are simply to stay out of their way, not to interfere with them, and then to ignore the conditions that we create in thinking in that manner. At the same time, to focus too much on differences is perhaps to make an equally dangerous mistake, since attention to difference can lead to evaluations about those differences that again throw us back into modes of oppressive thought and action. The assimilationism of Douglass, King, and the Grimké sisters expresses the tendency to focus on our relational selves, on our equality, while ignoring important differences. On the other hand, the thought of Stanton and Frye seems centered on *dissimilarity* while insisting upon *equality* in some spheres but not in others. It is not clear which theoretical backdrop ought to be adopted. Perhaps it is both and neither at the same time. There are things to be said for both positions, ways in which either position can lead to benefits both socially in our relations with others and individually in our insistence upon respect for our equal rights.

Whether Frye's loving eye or King's philosophy of love, Cady Stanton's independent and self-reliant individualism, or Douglass's constitutionalist and rationalistic argumentation have provided or will provide solutions to the problems of oppression, enslavement, coercion, unfairness, injustice, and inequality remain unsolved. Those problems are addressed in the next essay on contemporary ethical and political thought as it manifests itself in the distinctions between the individual *and* the community and the individual *in* the community.

NOTES

1. Note, for example, that Linda Lopez McAlister's *Hypatia's Daughters* (Bloomington, 1996) has no chapter on Stanton. Further, perusal of the *Philosopher's Index* shows three articles on Elizabeth Cady Stanton as "subject." Refreshingly, Beth Waggenspack, in *The Search for Self-Sovereignty* (New York, 1999) specifically refers to Stanton as a philosopher in her own right, as did Stanton herself. There are other works recognizing Stanton's philosophical *contributions* to the women's rights movement, but as a *philosopher*, she is generally unrecognized.
2. Marilyn Frye, *The Politics of Reality: Essays in Feminist Theory* (Freedom, CA, 1983).
3. Immanuel Kant contended that all women and all nonwhite non-Europeans were socially, morally, and intellectually inferior to white European men. It might seem odd, then, to utilize Kantian moral theory as a moral orientation or focus for this essay. Fortunately, it is possible to separate Kant's sexist and racist attitudes from his moral theory as a whole.
4. A deontological ethical theory is distinct from a teleological theory at least in virtue of the distinction between the primacy of the right over the good (deontology) and the teleologist's adherence to the notion that the good is prior to the right. The deontologist holds that consequences are not to be considered in determining the moral worth of an action or of an individual while the teleologist holds that the production of some sort of *good* end determines the moral value of the action. For a brief, accessible discussion of the distinction between deontological, teleological (and other) theories of

morality, see Onora O'Neill's "Kantian Ethics" in Peter Singer, ed., *A Companion to Ethics* (Cambridge, 1993), 175–85; and Phillip Pettit's "Consequentialism" in the same volume, 230–40.

5. Utilitarianism's major exponent was John Stuart Mill. His work, *Utilitarianism*, ed. George Sher (Indianapolis, 2001) expresses the principal theses of utilitarian consequentialism. It is, generally, the philosophical position that what is morally right to do is to perform actions that produce the greatest happiness for the greatest number of people. The Principle of Utility is that "actions are right in proportion as they tend to promote happiness, wrong as they tend to produce the reverse of happiness. By happiness is intended pleasure, and the absence of pain; by unhappiness, pain, and the privation of pleasure" (7). In its social formulation, utilitarian moralists hold the position that if the happiness of one person is a good thing, then the happiness of many is even better.
6. Immanuel Kant, *Foundations of the Metaphysics of Morals*, trans. Lewis White Beck (Indianapolis, 1959), 47.
7. See *Utilitarianism*, 3. Here, Mill contends that "when he (Kant) begins to deduce from this precept any of the actual duties of morality, he fails, almost grotesquely, to show that there would be any contradiction, any logical (not to say physical) impossibility, in the adoption by all rational beings of the most outrageously immoral rules of conduct. All he shows is that the consequences of their universal adoption would be such as no one would choose to incur."
8. The contemporary feminist analysis of patriarchal and misogynist notions that society would be irreparably harmed by granting women the right to vote, or by their inclusion in domains other than the purely domestic, is discussed by innumerable feminist philosophers. One among the feminists whose work extends well beyond this sort of early feminist theorizing is Marilyn Frye in *The Politics of Reality*.
9. Note that the original formulation of the Constitution specifically counts African American slaves as three-fifths of a person, so as they count, they count as property, not citizens, and certainly not as human beings for whom *being* property is clearly and morally impossible and reprehensible.
10. Arguments for black male suffrage were not enough for Elizabeth Cady Stanton and for her partner in the women's rights movement, Susan B. Anthony. Frederick Douglass argued that there was not the sort of urgency for women to be granted the right to vote that there was for black men because women are not "hunted down" or "dragged from their houses and hung upon lampposts" among many other horrors suffered by the African American. When asked by Stanton whether these things were not also true of black women, Douglass replied that it was true, not because they were women, but because they were black. Susan B. Anthony, however, held the position that no woman wishes to be dependent upon any man. See Kathryn Kish Sklar's reprint of the "Equal Rights Association Proceedings" of May 1869, in *Women's Rights Emerges within the Antislavery Movement, 1830–1870: A Brief History with Documents* (Boston, 2000), 200–201. At least in their condition as slaves, African American men and women were equal with one another; upon granting the right to vote to African American men, former slave women would *still* be in a condition unequal to, and hence subordinate to, those with whom they had once been equals. Very closely related to this problem, and continuing the discussion, is another essential element to note regarding the distinction between male African American slaves and their female counterparts. bell hooks, in *Ain't I a Woman?* (Boston, 1981) explains the relationship between patriarchy and racism, pointing out that one of the early arguments against slavery was that black men lost their status as patriarchs given the prevailing social and legal conditions (marriages among slaves had no legal status, for example). Here, "Scholars have argued . . . that by not allowing black men to assume their traditional patriarchal status, white men effectively emasculated them, reducing them to an effeminate state. Implicit in this assertion is the assumption that the worst that can happen to a man is that he be made to assume the social status of a woman. To suggest that

black men were dehumanized solely as a result of not being able to be patriarchs implies that the subjugation of black women was essential to the black males' development of a positive self-concept, an idea that only served to support a sexist social order" (20–21).

11. Angelina Grimké's conclusions regarding work for the anti-slavery cause reflects this notion where she says that she has "found the Anti-Slavery cause to be the high school of morals in our land—the school in which *human rights* are more fully investigated, and better understood and taught, than in any other. Here a great fundamental principle is uplifted and illuminated, and from this central light, rays innumerable stream all around. Human beings have *rights*, because they are *moral* beings: the rights of *all* men grow out of their moral nature; and as all men have the same moral nature, they have essentially the same rights. These rights may be wrested from the slave, but they cannot be alienated: his title to himself . . . is stamped on his moral being, and is, like it, imperishable. Now if rights are founded in the nature of our moral being, then the *mere circumstance of sex* does not give to man higher rights and responsibilities, than to woman." See "Human Rights not Founded on Sex" in Wendy McElroy, ed., *Freedom, Feminism and the State* (New York, 1982), 29.
12. Sara M. Evans points out in discussing the influence of Angelina and Sarah Grimké in both the anti-slavery and women's rights movements that "the anti-slavery movement provided women with both an ideological and a practical training ground in political activism for democratic and egalitarian change." *Born for Liberty: A History of Women in America* (New York, 1989), 80. McGlen and O'Connor note, too, that "participation in the antislavery movement helped to spark women's recognition that they, as a *class*, were subjected to discrimination." See Nancy E. McGlen and Karen O'Connor, *Women, Politics, and American Society* (Upper Saddle River, 1995), 4. It was, incidentally, at an anti-slavery society meeting in London that Lucretia Mott and Elizabeth Cady Stanton first conceived of the notion to hold a women's rights convention when they returned to the United States. The women's rights convention took place in 1848 in Seneca Falls, New York.
13. Martin Luther King, Jr., *The Letter from the Birmingham Jail*, foreword by Rev. Bernice King (New York, 1963, 1994), 2–3.
14. Hartog contends that "As a people, Americans may be 'constitutionally' incapable of characterizing rights claims as moves in a zero-sum game. Lawyers know that a new, increased, or transformed public good must always be alleged as the necessary consequence of any recognition of previously unrecognized rights; there must be some net benefit to the public welfare. Americans have never simply righted wrongs; they have always been making things better." See Hendrik Hartog, "The Constitution of Aspiration and 'The Rights that Belong to Us All'" (In PART II: Rights Consciousness in American History), *Journal of American History*, Vol. 74, No. 3, December 1987 (1013–34) 1025. It is in an understanding of the nature of duty and a spirit of reform in American thought that the two elements of a deontologist's respect for persons, and the consequentialist's insistence upon a focus on good consequences, can take hold and exist side-by-side.
15. Joseph J. Ellis, *Founding Brothers* (New York, 2000), 91.
16. John Locke, *Second Treatise of Government*, ed. C. B. Macpherson (Indianapolis, 1980), 8.
17. In the following discussion of "Appeal to the Christian Women of the South," Angelina Grimké makes the claim that slaveholders were able to justify inhumane treatment and ownership of other human beings *by denying their humanity*. It would then follow that *if* they are not human, they are then *things* that may be owned by others.
18. *Founding Brothers*, 93. That evasiveness, of course, provided the possibility for constitutionalist arguments against the institution of slavery and for the recognition and protection of rights for white women and African Americans to proceed.
19. Thomas Jefferson, in *The Life and Selected Writings of Thomas Jefferson*, ed. Adrienne Koch and William Peden (New York, 1944).
20. The irony here would be almost humorous if it were not that so many white people believed Jefferson's characterizations to have basis in fact. Especially with respect to

work, it seems almost axiomatic that a person forced to work, and who does not receive appropriate (or any) payment, recognition, or benefit from that work, would avoid it whenever possible. There are affinities here, of course, to Marx's analysis of the condition of workers and the antagonistic struggle between labor and owners of the means of production.

21. Brandon recounts that Garrison argued in favor of anti-slavery secession and burned a copy of the Constitution in protest in 1854. Garrison even argued that the northern states ought to secede from the Union. On this point, Brandon discusses the distinction between Thoreau's position on the ultimate moral obligation of the citizen to civil disobedience and Garrison's northern secessionist views. See Mark E. Brandon, *Free in the World: American Slavery and Constitutional Failure* (Princeton, 1998) pp. 184ff.
22. William Lloyd Garrison, "Declaration of the National Anti-Slavery Convention" (1833), ed. William E. Cain, *William Lloyd Garrison and the Fight Against Slavery* (Boston, 1995), 91.
23. Ibid. 91.
24. Garrison does say that emancipation of slaves, "by infusing motives into their breasts, would make them doubly valuable to the masters as free laborers," but even given this statement, the point is that it is wrong to believe that masters should be compensated for the loss of slaves after emancipation because (1) man cannot hold property in man, (2) "slavery is a crime" in and of itself so that "freeing the slave is not depriving them (slaveholders) of property, but restoring it to its rightful owner; it is not wronging the master, but righting the slave—restoring him to himself." Ibid. 92.
25. Ibid. 94.
26. Garrison and Frederick Douglass clashed and ultimately parted company in the abolitionist movement over the interpretation of the U.S. Constitution as an anti-slavery document. Garrison held that it was certainly not an anti-slavery document, and although Douglass originally agreed with the Garrisonian interpretation of the Constitution, he ultimately repudiated that view.
27. Angelina Grimké had reason to fear for her life after the publication of the "Appeal to the Christian Women of the South." Reaction in the south to her writings was so extreme that postmasters burned copies of the work. See Sklar, *Women's Rights*, 19.
28. *Born for Liberty*, 80. See also Angelina Grimké's letter to Theodore Weld and John Greenleaf Whittier in which she notes that their urging her not to speak on the issue of women's rights while working for abolition is inconsistent on their part. She points out that "*this invasion of our rights* was just such an attack upon *us*, as that made upon Abolitionists generally, when they were told a few years ago that *they had no right* to discuss the subject of Slavery. Did *you* take notice of this assertion? Why no!" (reprinted in *Women's Rights*, 131, emphasis in original). She adds that "*The time* to assert a right is *the* time when *that* right is denied. *We must establish this right*, for if we do not, it will be impossible for *us* to go on *with the work of Emancipation. . . .*" (131, emphasis in original). It is apparent here how hard was the fight for women's rights when the very woman who was urged by William Lloyd Garrison to speak on the subject of slavery, and who later married Theodore Weld, was told point blank that she might hurt the cause of abolition if she were to speak on the issue of women's rights.
29. Gerda Lerner, in *The Grimké Sisters from South Carolina*, (New York, 1967), points out that there is "nothing novel in the antislavery Bible argument or the defense of abolitionism Angelina Grimké offered. Yet her *Appeal* is unique in abolitionist literature because it is the only appeal by a Southern abolitionist woman to Southern women. It is remarkable also for its simple and direct tone, the absence of fashionable rhetoric and its bold logic which in the name of righteousness advises even lawbreaking with Garrisonian unconcern" (141). It is important to note here that "lawbreaking with Garrisonian unconcern" is consistent with Thoreau's conception of civil disobedience in the fight against slavery and Martin Luther King's willingness to suffer the consequences of his brand of civil disobedience for the advancement of civil rights for African Americans.

30. Lerner notes that Angelina Grimké's arguments against slavery revolve around the notions that "slavery was contrary to human law, contrary to the teachings of Jesus, contrary to the Declaration of Independence" and that "the core of her argument was her belief in the manhood and equality of the slave and in his *natural* right to freedom" (138). See also Angelina Grimké's letter to William Lloyd Garrison (reprinted in part in *Women's Rights,* 15) in which she contends that abolition is a duty and the consequences in the loss of property or suffering that must be endured to do that duty are not important compared to the duty to do what is right.
31. It makes good sense that Angelina Grimké would write specifically to *southern* women on the issue of slavery given that southern women had axes to grind against conditions of their own that were exacerbated by the problem of slavery. See, for example, Anne Firor Scott's "Women's Perspective on the Patriarchy in the 1850s" in *The Journal of American History*, Vol. 61, No. 1 (June 1974), 52–64 for her analysis of the problem of patriarchy in the antebellum American south and indications of women's dissatisfaction, both morally and socially, with slavery. bell hooks (*Ain't I a Woman*) makes reference to the "dissatisfaction" of southern women with the institution of slavery and the uncomfortable tension arising from it. Southern women were aware that their husbands regularly had sexual relations with female slaves and that the brutal treatment of female slaves also in other ways was recognized by southern women as possibly their own lot if it were not for the fact that men's violence was directed more at slaves than at white women.
32. Angelina Grimké, *Appeal to the Christian Women of the South* (New York, 1969), 3.
33. Ibid.
34. See also Frederick Douglass's "What to the Slave is the Fourth of July?" where he argues that American churches are in agreement with the passage of the Fugitive Slave Law and generally are not opposed to the institution of slavery. For Douglass, better to be an atheist, better to be anything, than one who subscribes to such a horrendous doctrine as that God would justify slavery. See "What to the Slave is the Fourth of July?" in David B. Chesebrough, *Frederick Douglass: Oratory from Slavery* (Westport, 1998), 122–4.
35. Sarah Grimké, in a letter of July 7, 1837, uses the same metaphor to describe the subordination of women to men. Here she expresses the notion that women are equal to men as moral and intellectual beings and that: "All I ask of our brethren is, that they will take their feet from off our necks and permit us to stand upright on that ground which God designed us to occupy." See letter II in *Letters on the Equality of the Sexes and the Condition of Woman* (New York, 1970 [reprint of the 1838 original]), 10.
36. See also Douglass's "What to the Slave is the Fourth of July?" where he asserts that there is no reason for him to argue that slavery is not established by God. "There is blasphemy in the thought. That which is inhuman, cannot be divine! *Who* can reason on such a proposition? They that can, may; I cannot." See Chesebrough's reprint of Douglass's oration, 117.
37. Sarah Grimké, "Letter I: The Original Equality of Woman," in *Letters on the Equality of the Sexes and the Condition of Woman*, 4.
38. These propositions are derived from Ibid. 3–8.
39. Here, Sarah Grimké is making reference to the first account of creation in Genesis in which man and woman are created at the same time. She quotes Scripture: "And God said, Let us make man in our own image, after our likeness; . . . So God created man in his own image, in the image of God created he him, *male and female created he them*" (emphasis added). See also Nancy Tuana's discussion of the creation myths in the Old Testament in *The Less Noble Sex* (Bloomington, 1993), esp. 7–10.
40. Emphasis added.
41. It is interesting to note here that Sarah Grimké at least hints that Eve, having come into the world recently and having experience only with Adam, a person like herself, must have been "beguiled" by a "being with whom she was unacquainted" and "of satanic intelligence, she was in all probability entirely ignorant"; she ought not, then, be so harshly criticized as *solely* responsible for the fall.

42. Grimké argues that man is shown clearly *not* to be superior to woman. If, she says, Adam had "reproved his wife, and endeavored to lead her to repentance instead of sharing in her guilt," it would make sense then to say that man is superior to woman; but the facts show that he exhibited as much (moral) weakness as Eve.
43. At this point, Sarah Grimké goes into some detail regarding the distinction between a command of God and a prophecy. She claims that the same "mode of expression" was used in speaking to Cain about Abel. And it is not the case that Cain was to be *subject* by command to his brother, but that God foresaw that this would be the case. Grimké explains that the problem here is with the understanding of the words "will" and "shall." She notes that God made this proclamation to Eve, not to Adam, and if it were a command, it would have been made to him, and not to her. Instead God's words are meant to indicate that Eve will become subservient to Adam, not that God has *commanded* that it be so. Note, too, that in Angelina Grimké's "Appeal to the Christian Women of the South," an argument identical in form and very similar in content is put forth against those who claim that the Bible justifies slavery. There, Grimké claims that God foresaw that slavery would exist, but the simple fact that God knows or foresees a fact or an event does not justify it *morally*.
44. "Letter IV: Social Intercourse of the Sexes," in *Letters on the Equality of the Sexes and the Condition of Women*, 22–6.
45. Sarah Grimké's notion that men thinking of women *as women* (by referring to their sex or gender and not thinking of them simply as *human beings*) is in some way demeaning to women is, perhaps, the result of her assimilationist view—that all human beings ought to be understood as *the same*. But it is also possible that this view is dominated by the patriarchal view that the "ideal human being" is a male—rational, powerful, acquisitive, and domineering. See, for example, Virginia Held's view of this sort of phenomenon in her "Feminist Transformations of Moral Theory" and the related discussion in this volume in Essay 11.
46. On this point, Sklar comments on the Grimkés' concept of "moral beings" such that it was in their time "a concept that recognized women's circumstances as historically and socially constructed. This view helped them recognize women's claim on society as a group. The Grimké's view of women's rights did not prompt her to see women as interchangeable units shorn of social context, but as collective beings with moral voices capable of expressing their collective experience" (37). Sklar notes, too, that Sarah Grimké's 12th letter ("The Legal Disabilities of Women"), shows the "parallels between the legal status of married women and that of slaves" (146), showing again the close affinity that existed between women's rights and anti-slavery argumentation.
47. Grimké refers to woman's role in stemming the tide of "iniquity and misery," evidently an allusion to relations between the sexes, to disease, prostitution, and other "miseries" befalling the human species.
48. Lois W. Banner (74) notes that "In later years she (Cady Stanton) demanded educational qualifications for voting and categorized Irish and black males according to ethnic stereotypes. In the last decade of her life she supported American imperialism on the grounds of Anglo-Saxon superiority." See *Elizabeth Cady Stanton: A Radical for Women's Rights* (Boston, 1980). Ellen Carol DuBois, in *Elizabeth Cady Stanton and Susan B. Anthony: Correspondence, Writings, Speeches* (New York, 1981), hereafter abbreviated as *Correspondence*, adds that "political forces beyond their (Cady Stanton and Susan B. Anthony) control had made it impossible to unite the demands of women and the freedmen, but Stanton and Anthony took the further step of opposing feminism to Black suffrage. On the one hand, they argued that white women, educated and virtuous, were more deserving of the vote than the ex-slaves. On the other hand, they attempted to build feminism on the basis of white women's racism" (92).
49. Henry Stanton and Lucretia Mott told Elizabeth that adding this resolution would make them all seem "ridiculous." See *The Search for Self-Sovereignty*, 20. Elizabeth Cady Stanton persisted (along with Frederick Douglass) on this matter, and ultimately the resolution passed. The affinity here to the prevailing social attitude is interesting. William L. O'Neill, in *Feminism in America: A History* (New Brunswick, 1989), asks why,

if the "anti's" argued that suffrage for women wasn't important, did they spend so much time and energy arguing against it? If women did not *need* the right to vote, then where is the harm in granting the right? Stanton answers this question in her speech, "Home Life" (1875), referring to the groundbreaking work of John Stuart Mill and Harriett Taylor in *The Subjection of Women*. Stanton notes that Mill "says the generality of the male sex cannot yet tolerate the idea of living with an equal at the fireside; and here is the secret of the opposition to woman's equality in the state and the church—men are not ready to recognize it in the home. This is the real danger apprehended in giving woman the ballot, for as long as man makes, interprets, and executes the laws for himself, he holds the power under any system. Hence when he expresses the fear that liberty for woman would upset the family relation, he acknowledges that her present condition of subjection is not of her own choosing, and that if she had the power the whole relation would be essentially changed." See *Correspondence*, 132.

50. Neither, of course, should the importance of the notion of individual rights and the meaning of such claims in constitutional interpretation. Hendrik Hartog points out that "the long contest over slavery did more than any other cause to stimulate the development of an alternate, rights conscious, interpretation of the federal constitution." He adds that "all the varying meanings that have been derived from the phrase 'equal protection of the laws' are rooted in contending visions of what it was that was overthrown by the end of slavery" (*Journal of American History*, 1017).
51. Banner notes (71) that "Theodore Tilton, a friend and fellow reformer, realized the interdependent role of suffrage in her thought, and put it well in an 1895 tribute. To Cady Stanton, Tilton wrote, suffrage had been more a means than an end; its lack more a symbol of woman's degradation than its major cause. Indeed, as Tilton realized, woman's suffrage had never been more important to her than such concerns as divorce, coeducation, or changing basic attitudes about men and women." Whether woman suffrage was a means to an end or an end in itself is probably irrelevant to the overall importance of granting the right to vote to women. If granting women the right to vote will help to change social conditions or whether changing social conditions will lead to the right to vote, the importance of the right is found in the recognition of the dignity of the individual, and to deny that right is to put women in the position of slaves to men.
52. Waggenspack notes that Elizabeth Cady Stanton's speech "The Solitude of Self" did not repeat Stanton's "well-known arguments for women's rights," but instead, "Cady Stanton chose to argue that such rights were due because of one unfailing cause: all people have responsibilities for themselves" (83). The issue of the right to vote is more than simply granting to women a legal right. It is part of the recognition of the dignity and value of a human being that has consequences far beyond mere political concerns.
53. Stanton elaborates on this notion in her speech "Our Girls" (1872) where she notes that for girls, their lot is "simply to revolve around some man, to live only for him, in him, with him, to be fed, clothed, housed, guarded and controlled by him, today by Father or Brother, tomorrow by Husband or Son, no matter how wise or mature they are, never to know the freedom and dignity that are secured in self-dependence and self-support" See *Correspondence*, 141.
54. *The Search for Self-Sovereignty*, 86–7.
55. *Correspondence*, 95.
56. Stanton explains in the "Introduction" to *The Woman's Bible* that female Hebrew and Greek scholars refused to take part in revising the Bible because they feared for their reputations. Other women hesitated to participate because they feared that association with more "liberal" women would compromise their religious views. Stanton expresses her impatience with such people by pointing out that the Bible is "like any other book, to be judged on its merits." This is not simply a particularly American attitude toward authority, but the attitude of the Enlightenment in general, expressed, for example, in Kant's "What is Enlightenment?" See Lewis White Beck, trans., "What is Enlightenment?" in *Foundations of the Metaphysics of Morals* (Indianapolis, 1959), 85–92.

57. Ultimately, Stanton and her associates did not *revise* the Bible but wrote extensive commentary on it, providing their views of the elements of the Bible that were translated or interpreted to express the inferiority of women and to justify their subordination to men.
58. Elizabeth Cady Stanton, "Introduction" to *The Woman's Bible*, repr. in Alice S. Rossi, ed., *The Feminist Papers* (Boston, 1973), 401–406.
59. Kathi Kern, "Rereading Eve," *Elizabeth Cady Stanton and The Woman's Bible*, 1885–1896, in *Women's Studies* 19: 371–83, 374.
60. It is not possible here to comment on or explicate more than some general elements of the argumentation contained in *The Woman's Bible*, so we are constraining ourselves to a brief discussion only of one particularly telling element of the Bible to which the commentators and authors of *The Woman's Bible* directed their attention.
61. "Rereading Eve," 375.
62. For a more complete account of the story of Genesis and other elements of *The Woman's Bible*, see Kathi Kern, *Mrs. Stanton's Bible* (Ithaca, 2001).
63. Ibid. 79.
64. Evelin Sullivan, *The Concise Book of Lying* (New York, 2001), 8.
65. Ibid. 8–9.
66. For a detailed analysis of the attitude of women's inferiority in the Western philosophical tradition, see Nancy Tuana, *The Less Noble Sex* and, for analysis of particular philosophers' views on this issue, Tuana's *Woman and the History of Philosophy* (New York, 1992). A valuable anthology of sources focused on philosophical arguments concerning the inferiority and subordination of women is Rosemary Agonito's *History of Ideas on Woman* (New York, 1977).
67. See Frederick Douglass, "The Nature of Slavery," in *My Bondage and My Freedom* (New York, 1969), 430–31.
68. Ibid. 429.
69. Ibid. 431.
70. Ibid.
71. See Douglass's recounting of this event, his description of the conditions under which he lived, and his subsequent escape from slavery in Part I of *My Bondage and My Freedom* and for the account of his escape, see the University of Virginia Electronic Text Center Document, "My Escape from Slavery" at http://etext.lib.virginia.edu/etcbin/browse-mixed-new?id=DouEsca&images=images/modeng&data=/texts/english/modeng/parsed&tag=public. Douglass did not specify the means of his escape in *My Bondage and My Freedom* for fear that the method he used would no longer be effective for others and that those who had assisted him to escape would suffer as a result.
72. See, for a brief description and analysis of Frederick Douglass's political involvement and disagreement with the Garrisonian arguments concerning the U.S. Constitution as a proslavery document, Chesebrough's *Frederick Douglass*, 39–49.
73. "What to the Slave is the Fourth of July?" 126.
74. Douglass's claim here is true insofar as those words are not used in the Constitution, but there are numerous *references* to slavery in the Constitution, among them the notorious "three-fifths clause." Charles W. Mills, in "Whose Fourth of July? Frederick Douglass and 'Original Intent'" in *Frederick Douglass: A Critical Reader* (Malden, 1999), 100–142, notes that it "should be obvious that these claims are at best problematic, and at worst obviously false. . . . Constitutional scholars . . . have pointed out that there was a deliberate decision on the part of the Framers to use circuitous and euphemistic language so as to avoid formal reference to slavery, but that in practice everybody knew what was being talked about" (114). Mills goes into detail explaining why Douglass would adopt such a bizarre and obviously false position, but the important point is the reasoning that if the framers of the Constitution recognized African Americans as *men* and that it is wrong to enslave men, then there is an obvious contradiction, and the framers of the constitution could not have intended something so obviously wrong.

75. See "What to the Slave is the Fourth of July?" 126.
76. Mills, in "Whose Fourth of July? Frederick Douglass and 'Original Intent'," notes that in Douglass's Fourth of July speech, "the central themes of Douglass's mature thought are all present: the scornful exposure of the gap between the noble ideals and the actual reality of the American polity; the insistence on black personhood and the (supposed) fact of slavery's violation of natural law morality; the corresponding appeal to his audience's moral sense; and above all the optimistic faith in the original Constitution and the original intent of the Framers as a vehicle of eventual change" (100). Note too that for Mills, Douglass's argument, had it included a ". . . *strategic* use of the Constitution would have brought him closer to twentieth-century African-American legal activism, where the question of original intent is subordinated to the notion of a living and evolving document whose meaning alters over time" (113).
77. For the aspect of Douglass's work pointing to a conception of self-respect in protesting wrongs, see Bernard Boxill, "Self-Respect and Protest," *Philosophy and Public Affairs*, 6:1 (Autumn 1976): 58–69.
78. Ibid. 59.
79. Ibid. 60.
80. See the next section on Martin Luther King, Jr., and his philosophy of nonviolence for a very similar position regarding the moral character of perpetrators of injustice. King's contention was that African Americans have an obligation to argue for recognition of the rights of African Americans not only for the benefit of the African American people, but also because the moral character of those who denied such rights was being hurt by their actions and beliefs.
81. "Self-Respect and Protest," 61.
82. Ibid.
83. Elizabeth Cady Stanton, however, held that white women could more fully understand the plight of the slave than white men. She asserts: "a privileged class can never conceive the feelings of those who are born to contempt, to inferiority, to degradation. Herein is woman more fully identified with the slave than man can possibly be, for she can take the subjective view." See Stanton's "Speech to the Anniversary of the American Anti-Slavery Society" in *Correspondence*, 83.
84. "What to the Slave is the Fourth of July?" 116.
85. Mills notes that Douglass wanted to put the audience in "a moral and conceptual bind," forcing them to grant that the cause of the Revolutionaries and the cause of the abolitionists are on an equal footing. For Douglass, all the arguments of the Revolution can "be applied equally well to the abolitionists in their struggle against slavery. So if one believes in 'natural justice,' if one agrees with Locke that 'man is entitled to liberty' and 'that he is the rightful owner of his own body,' then—since blacks are equally 'men' who should be self-owning—there must be an end to the 'dividing' and 'subdividing' of the 'discourse' of liberty that the countenancing of slavery requires." (103–104).
86. "Whose Fourth of July?," 108. Mills argues in this article and in *The Racial Contract* (Ithaca, 1997) that contractarian thinking informing the American republic is actually a *racial* contract upholding white supremacy.
87. "Self-Respect and Protest," 63.
88. Frank M. Kirkland, in "Enslavement, Moral Suasion, and Struggles" in Bill E. Lawson and Frank M. Kirkland, *Frederick Douglass: A Critical Reader* (Malden, 1999) argues that there is a serious problem with the notion that there is a *duty* to end the practice of slavery. Garrison held the position that it was our duty to abolish slavery, that it is part of our moral nature to do so, and we are therefore morally obliged by God to do so. Kirkland notes that "God as the source of the obligation enables the abolition of slavery to get a grip on us, to be prescribed for us, to bind us. But . . . this would make the obligation *extrinsic* to the act of (or even claim for) abolition, and the obligation's source (God's benevolence), reflected in our moral sense to do good, (not in the rightness intrinsic to the act or claim itself), would be what motivates us, not obligates us, to abolish slavery. Hence moral suasion could not persuade us of the claim that the abolition

of slavery is morally right *necessarily*; it could only convince us of the moral benevolence that would be both the source of and the incentive for abolishing slavery" (260–61). If Kirkland is right, then perhaps it is also the case that employing constitutionalist arguments to end slavery is *not* arguing that slavery is wrong in and of itself.

89. In this, King was influenced by the work of Mohandas Gandhi (1869–1948).
90. Martin Luther King, Jr., *Letter from the Birmingham Jail* (New York, 1963). All references to King's *Letter* are from this edition.
91. *Free in the World*, 218–19.
92. Greg Moses, *Revolution of Conscience* (New York, 1997), 23.
93. Hanes Walton, Jr., explains that King's position can be understood such that "the antagonism between the position of black power advocates and King lies in their divergent visions of what, ultimately, is socially desirable for the black community: black separatism or an integrated state wherein all races would be as brothers. Rather than shun the white man for his fallen state, King saw his redemption to be the particular province of the black mission. On this score he saw black militants as having given up on one of the crucial tasks, of having forsaken one of their duties toward God. For only through complete integration could the unity and essence of the beloved community be expressed, and that was the final vision toward which all other activity aimed." Hanes Walton, Jr., *The Political Philosophy of Martin Luther King, Jr.* (New York, 1971), 92–3.
94. Martin Luther King, Jr., "Pilgrimage to Nonviolence," in Herbert J. Storing, ed., *What Country Have I?* (New York, 1970), 113.
95. Ibid.
96. *The Political Philosophy of Martin Luther King, Jr.*, 62.
97. *Revolution of Conscience*, x.
98. See Carol Gilligan's research on this issue in *In a Different Voice: Psychological Theory and Woman's Development* (Cambridge, 1994).
99. *Second Treatise of Government*, 9.
100. *Revolution of Conscience*, xii.
101. Ibid. 34.
102. "Pilgrimage to Nonviolence," 113. It is *not* the oppressed person who is victimized by evil—it is the person who perpetrates injustice, who is the oppressor, who is most affected morally by the *doing* of evil. The notion here is very clearly associated with Socrates' position that it is better to be the victim of injustice than to be its perpetrator. See Plato, *The Republic*, Book I.
103. "Pilgrimage to Nonviolence," 115.
104. Ibid.
105. It is important here to note that the history of American moral and political thought in the abolition, women's rights, and civil rights movement is *not* characterized solely by assimilationist thinking. A significant number of thinkers and reformers thought instead in terms of separation and distinctions and differences that are incommensurable. One notable case is Malcolm X, affiliated with *Nation of Islam* and a radical in his own right, but a radical separatist in his early work and development. In "The Ballot or the Bullet," Malcolm X argues that America is not his country, it is not the African American's country at all, and that gaining and keeping the rights to which African Americans are entitled requires violent direct action against oppressors.
106. *Politics of Reality*, 52–83.
107. See Ibid. 54–57 on "Coercision."
108. Ibid. 62–3.
109. Ibid. 60.
110. Ibid. 64–5.
111. Ibid. 69. The term "arrogant" expresses the notion of "arrogation" in which a person believes himself to be the center of the universe, that all things exist for him—and that anything not fitting this description is in some way different, malformed—that there is something wrong with a thing that does not fit his picture of the world. It does not seem to dawn on the arrogant perceiver that there is something wrong with *him*.

112. Ibid. 70.
113. The history of Western philosophy, up until very recent times, rarely, if ever, mentions the contributions of women to philosophy. Feminist thinkers have noted for many years that the history of philosophy is primarily (and perhaps exclusively) a male domain in which the conceptions of reality, of knowledge, of right and wrong, are defined exclusively from a male point of view. In fact, even language often reflects patriarchal, male-dominant attitudes in referring to things to be used, and for which males tend to have emotional attachment, as "she." Note, for example, that men's cars, boats, and airplanes are "her." They are things men enter, things they control, things they "drive" or steer to destinations they wish to reach, and for their own purposes.
114. *Politics of Reality*, 70. See also Jean Hampton's explanation of the tradition and problems associated with believing that "selflessness" is morally praiseworthy. Her contention is that "selflessness" is not a good thing, and that concern for others is only healthy and morally acceptable when a human being does not, at the same time, subordinate his or her own interests to others, as though the sacrificer has no individual value. Jean Hampton, "Selflessness and the Loss of Self" in *Social Philosophy and Policy* 10 (1): 135–65.
115. *Politics of Reality*, 75.
116. Ibid. 77.
117. Ibid.
118. Ibid. 80.
119. Ibid. 81.

Essay 11
Contemporary American Ethics and Politics: The Individual and the Community

Tensions between the tenets of political liberalism, communitarianism, and feminist thought characterize contemporary American ethics and political theory. Political liberalism centers on abstract procedures for the constitution of justice with respect primarily to the protection of individual rights. Political liberalism conceives of human beings as largely self-interested, isolated individuals in competition with others for scarce or valuable resources. Communitarians hold the position that political liberalism is an incomplete, inaccurate account of our political condition and that putting it into practice exacerbates problems associated with liberal democratic institutions. For the communitarian, we need to understand ourselves as relational beings, morally tied to the communities of which we are members. Feminist theorizing about the nature of morality and political institutions tends toward clarification of the meaning of justice and rights in traditional theories. It is also a critique of theory and practice in male-centered conceptions of ethics and politics that discount or ignore the experience of women and fail to consider fully our relational nature as human beings.

Four American moral and political theorists whose work exemplifies and clarifies these approaches to the nature of ethics and politics and whose positions stand in clear contrast to each other are John Rawls (1921–2002), Robert Nozick (1938–2002), Michael Sandel, and Virginia Held. Rawls's position in "Justice as Fairness" (1958) and in his groundbreaking 1971 book *A Theory of Justice* is that to achieve a sense of the meaning of justice and to see fairness as the basis for an appropriate conception of it, we must formulate, understand, and implement procedures and practices that are fair in the basic institutions of society. To do so will ensure that individual liberty is secured and protected and that differences in wealth and opportunity are justified only when those differences are to the advantage of all (or to the least advantaged members of society). Nozick, in his *Anarchy, State and Utopia* (1974), takes issue with Rawls's position, adopting a Lockean conception of the nature of entitlements and arguing that the Rawlsian principles of justice are *patterned* principles constituting *unfairness* and *injustice* in the distribution of social resources. In his 1984 article, "The Procedural Republic and the Unencumbered Self," and in his *Democracy's Discontent* (1986), Michael

Sandel takes on rationalistic political theories like those of Rawls and Nozick, arguing that although there have been important practical and social advances in the procedures set up in traditional political liberalism, we are at a point at which "democracy's discontent" arises from (1) the fear that we are no longer in control of the political process governing our lives and (2) that the "moral fabric of community is unraveling around us."[1] Sandel proposes an alternative, communitarian solution to alleviate this discontent and thereby enrich and improve our conceptions and practices of justice and social morality. Finally, Virginia Held argues in her 1990 "Feminist Transformations of Moral Theory" that there is much further to go in understanding and creating moral (and political) theories than what male-centered theorists have presented. Fundamental changes in methods and goals of theorizing must be made and new conceptions of the nature of ethics and politics must be developed to create the possibility of a more inclusive and encompassing manner of theorizing about the moral and the political than we currently have developed.

Rawls: Justice as Fairness

John Rawls argues that to understand the nature of justice, we must conceive of it based on fairness. The simple fact that people occupy different positions in society, and that there are differences in the distribution of wealth, is not an indication of injustice or of unfairness. We recognize, for example, that there are benefits to be gained for all members of a practice or institution when different people occupy different positions and when some positions are attended with greater benefits than others. What we recognize as unfair and unjust are cases in which those who occupy different, privileged positions occupy them as the result of the application of principles and procedures that disadvantage others. In other words, if a person occupies a position in society that was not open to others to acquire in a fair, objective, and unbiased competition, then the position occupied by that person was obtained unjustly, and there is then sufficient reason for those who did not have the opportunity to win the position in a fair competition to complain that they have been treated unjustly.

Rawls's theory of justice is Kantian, not utilitarian or intuitionist. This is important to note as the continuation of a trend in American ethical and political thought. Recall that in Essay 10, we argued that a prominent form of argumentation for abolitionism and the movements for women's rights and civil rights had a particularly Kantian emphasis. This tendency in American ethical and political theorizing continues with the work of Rawls. Rawls explains why justice as fairness cannot be formulated on the basis of either a utilitarian or intuitionist ethical foundation, and why it is important for transforming theory into practice that the Kantian model of moral and political theorizing about the nature of the human subject must be adopted.

For Rawls, utilitarian argumentation for the creation of a just society and just institutions is doomed to failure. This is the case because utilitarian thinking makes it possible that some people may be *used* for the benefit of others. Rawls says that "[o]ffhand it hardly seems likely that persons who view themselves as equals, entitled to press their claims upon one another, would agree to a principle which may require lesser life prospects for some simply for the sake of a greater sum of advantages enjoyed by others."[2] Although advancing the common good is important for Rawls, it is not more important than securing the rights of individuals. The common good cannot be advanced, in fact, if individuals are not secure in the integrity of their persons and in the protection of rights. Intuitionism as a foundation for justice is also unacceptable because there is "a plurality of first principles which may conflict to give contrary directives in particular types of cases; and . . . they include no explicit method . . . for weighing these principles against one another."[3] In other words, moral intuitionism cannot stand as the foundation of justice as fairness because its principles are not universally established (anyone's intuitions may be different from those of anyone or everyone else) and in cases in which there is more than one intuited principle to which a person may appeal for direction in moral and political matters, it is not clear which principle is to take priority. Rawls's argument regarding this issue is itself Kantian, in fact, since Kant contends that there is one and only one categorical imperative, and therefore there can be no problem of the priority of rules or conflict between them.

Rawls's position is that his two principles of justice are categorical imperatives and that *not* to theorize about politics from a deontological point of view makes fairness impossible. The principles of justice that Rawls puts forth as forming the basis for justice as fairness are categorical imperatives because "to act from the principles of justice is to act from categorical imperatives in the sense that they apply to us whatever in particular our aims are."[4] Understanding political theory in this way makes it possible for Rawls to accommodate the simple fact that individual people conceive of the good in various ways,[5] and accommodating variations on ideas of the good renders his theory all-inclusive. It does not put limitations on the ends or goals that particular individuals wish to achieve, and it is consistent with the Kantian emphasis on individual autonomy. Since a person acts heteronomously when constrained by desire rather than reason, developing the "argument for the two principles of justice does not assume that the parties have particular ends, but only that they desire certain primary goods. These are things that it is rational to want whatever else one wants."[6] So Rawls's theory does not depend on the particular, temporal, and changeable elements of human life, but provides a framework from which rational ends may be attained no matter what they are. It is not, for Rawls, that we must argue for or advocate any particular goal for any person or group, but that our theory of justice makes it possible for diverse people to strive for any particular goals that are consistent with respect for persons. To assume in advance some particular conception of the good, some goal for which everyone must strive, is to limit the autonomy of individuals who, as rational beings, have the capacity to determine such things for themselves.

Rawls assumes we should understand that human beings are self-interested, that their primary concern is to gain for themselves the best possible position that they can obtain. For Rawls, this means that people engaged in deliberations about the rules that should be implemented to provide procedures for a just society must be *maximin* rules. Maximin rules are those which, when applied, make the best out of the worst case. Alternately, one could say that utilizing a maximin strategy is consistent with the goals of rationally self-interested people concerned to further their own interests. We realize that people occupy different social positions, and no one wishes to be at the bottom of the hierarchy of positions; however, we also realize that there are people who will be there. Realizing that they will be there does *not*, however, imply that they deserve to be there, or that they should live under conditions in which their dignity as human beings is compromised. It is therefore the case that whatever rules are created to govern the basic structure of society must maximize the minimum position.

Further, since Rawls builds the notion of differing conceptions of the good into the development of his theory of justice, he does not understand justice requiring that all human beings conceive of morality in the same way, or even that they agree on a particular system of government. The purpose of Rawls's theory is not to create new governments and societies, but to provide principles of justice upon which governments may be based. Rawls's theory therefore applies to existing institutions and centers on applying principles to them consistent with the stated purpose of his theory, that is, to ensure that justice exists in those institutions. It is to be used as a test and corrective for systems that are already in place.

Since Rawls's position on the creation of justice in institutions applies to preexisting states of affairs, and because conditions that already have been obtained may be unjust, there must be a procedure by which rationally self-interested people, concerned to further their own interests, will judge and appropriately alter the procedures by which institutions function and choose principles of justice to order those institutions properly. To achieve the goal of ensuring justice, Rawls explains that people will recognize two specific principles of justice and will choose to govern the functioning of social institutions according to them. Those two principles are "The Equal Liberty Principle" and "The Difference Principle." The Equal Liberty Principle is that

> [E]ach person is to have an equal right to the most extensive basic liberty compatible with a similar liberty for others.[7]

The equal liberty principle is understood to be lexically prior to the second principle.[8] The second principle is

> [S]ocial and economic inequalities are to be arranged so that they are both (a) reasonably expected to be to everyone's advantage, and (b) attached to positions and offices open to all.[9]

The Difference Principle establishes the conditions under which disparities in wealth, status, or opportunities are acceptable and requires that such disparities are consistent with the requirements of the equal liberty principle. The equal liberty principle puts restrictions on the difference principle such that liberty may be limited only for the sake of liberty, and that whatever liberty is limited is agreeable or acceptable to those whose liberty has been limited. It is only when the two principles are followed and their requirements met that justice as fairness can be obtained in our social interactions. There is, for Rawls, no way in which we can justify the claim that a rational person would *want* to give up liberty for economic security or in any other way become socially disadvantaged (to have limited and unequal liberty) for the limited, contingent, and insecure benefits to be obtained by higher social or economic status.

To explain how people concerned to establish just procedures will reach the conclusion that the two principles of justice are to be accepted as the foundation of their institutions, Rawls proposes a framework called the "original position" characterized by the "veil of ignorance." The "original position" is a hypothetical condition in which people imagine themselves to be situated and in which they have not yet decided on the procedures to govern institutions and systems. In the original position, people recognize and acknowledge distinctions between and among themselves such that not all have the same life plans or goals, but all recognize that they have both plans and goals and wish to live under conditions in which they may be furthered and realized. Rawls says that the original position therefore "insures that the fundamental agreements reached in it are fair."[10]

Rawls's original position is the rough analog to the traditional contractarian's state of nature in which people come together to form cooperative groups to render themselves better off than they would be in an isolated, nonsocial condition. The classical contractarian model of the state of nature is a hypothetical condition in which people live without governments or accepted moral, social, and political institutions or agreements in effect. Some contractarians, like Thomas Hobbes, argue that conditions in the state of nature would be unbearable because the nature of human beings is to be acquisitive, uncooperative, and self-interested. In Hobbes's state of nature, people would be at constant war with each other, forced to attempt to preserve their lives by any means available, and thus live a life that is "solitary, poor, nasty, brutish and short." Since rational human beings wish not to live and die in harsh and unbearable conditions, they will, according to Hobbes, join together and institute a government that will solve the problems of the state of nature by creating and maintaining social order, including the establishment of rules, principles, and procedures for the conduct of our associated lives.[11]

John Locke, following Hobbes, conceives of the state of nature in a roughly similar way. Locke, however, does not describe human beings living in the state of nature in entirely nonmoral, nonassociative conditions. In his view, human beings are basically rational, adhere to a moral system, and can and do form peaceful and fruitful associations with each other. The problem, however, and one to which Rawls's argument has clear affinities, and to which Robert Nozick turns his attention, is that the associations we have with each other may be arranged such that injustice exists. In Locke's view, it is not institutions that are unjust. It is instead that there are people who are not willing or able to engage with others in socially cooperative ways who will violate the law of nature requiring that we may not interfere with the rights of others. For Locke, social cooperation and institutions that we have already established require government for regulation and preservation of property. For Locke, in short, "noxious" people, who will not or cannot abide by the rules in place, make government necessary at the outset, and government therefore exists to protect already existent property and social institutions.

Rawls conceives of the original position as hypothetical, as a mind experiment. In this way, Rawls's argument avoids the charge that there never was an historical period to which we can point, in which people existed "naturally," without social organization. Although Rawls's view is purely procedural, not constructive of governments, it is not clear either for classical social contract theories such as those of Hobbes and Locke—or for Rawls—why the agreement established in the state of nature or in the original position will or should continue to govern future generations. This critique is prefigured in Thomas Paine's thought where he argues for the necessity to break away from British rule by noting one of the peculiar problems of monarchy. That problem is that even if people at one point decided to establish monarchy as a preferred system of government, every human being at birth is new to the world, so to speak, and has just as much right to forge new political relationships as did their parents. Rawls's position, however, may avoid this criticism if we hold that the principles of justice are applicable to all political organization and therefore need be established only once. The assumption here is, like the assumption for acceptance of the Kantian categorical imperative, that the principles of justice are creatures of reason and are therefore not limited by time, preference, or any other contingency.

Notwithstanding these potential limitations of Rawls's theory, it is important to note that simply imagining oneself in a condition in which new principles of justice are to be formulated and accepted is not enough in itself. It requires the addition of a mechanism by which *fairness* is guaranteed to characterize deliberations about the formulation and acceptance of principles and that fairness will remain in the application of the principles resulting from deliberations. That mechanism is Rawls's "veil of ignorance."

The veil of ignorance is part of the original position. Its purpose is to ensure that the principles of justice framed and adopted by the original contractors are acceptable to all. To be acceptable to all, they must be neutral with respect to individuals in establishing procedures. The veil of ignorance is a prerequisite to the choice of principles such that deliberators imagine themselves to be ignorant of particular facts about their existence that might lead them to choose principles that advantage some and disadvantage others. The veil of ignorance requires, then, that the original contractors choose principles of justice in a condition in which they deliberate as if they were unaware of nonessential or accidental facts about their own cases. The veil requires that the contractors not consider temporary and contingent facts about persons such as sex, income, level of intelligence, race, or religious preference. This is an important element of Rawls's argumentation for the principles of justice because allowing temporary, accidental, and extraneous factors characterizing a person to taint deliberations may lead an original contractor to prefer to set up a system in which advantages are given to him or her based on those factors. Instead, what the contractors must do in the Rawlsian original position is consider and choose principles of justice that are neutral with respect to such contingencies. This does not mean that the original contractors will not know that they are intelligent, that they are gendered beings, or that they may subscribe to some religious orientation. It is instead that they will assume that they do not *know* which particular religion they prefer (if any). They will not know whether they are exceptionally well endowed with intellectual capacity, or whether they are members of a presently oppressed or an advantaged class. The main idea for Rawls is that if people do not know these particular facts about themselves, then they will not, upon lifting the veil of ignorance, find themselves in a position in which they have chosen principles that end in oppression of themselves. If, for example, an original contractor does not know whether he or she is Catholic or Jewish, among many other possibilities, that contractor will not agree to principles of justice that create disadvantageous conditions for Catholics or Jews. Furthermore, since the contractors do not know their place in society with respect to these sorts of characteristics, they will not choose principles that unfairly create conditions of *advantage* for any particular person or group, again, because they make their choices based on the assumption that they do not know whether they are or are not members of such a group.

Since Rawls's position depends heavily on the notion that it must be merit that gains benefits for a person, it is *unfair* to set up procedures for social institutions such that contingencies like the wealth of one's family determine the ability to gain access to social goods. So, for example, the original contractors would be careful not to set up a system in which only children of wealthy parents may obtain an education. Since education is one of the primary social goods that leads to the opportunity to gain further goods and thereby advance one's own interests, the contractors will choose to arrange conditions so that, consistent with the Difference Principle, any inequalities in wealth and opportunity that do exist are arranged to be to the benefit of all (in Rawls's early formulation of the difference principle) or (in his later formulation in *A Theory of Justice*) to the benefit of society's least well-off members.[12]

Rawls's theory leads, then, to a welfare-state in which distribution and redistribution of wealth and property are necessary to ensure that all people are able to live within the conditions set up with the Equal Liberty Principle. Remember that the Equal Liberty Principle requires that every person has access to and is able to enjoy the most extensive liberty possible that is consistent with a similar liberty for everyone else. This means, for example, that no person will be required, or will want, to give up his or her liberty for economic security or the ability to achieve other, non-qualitative social goods. That is, Rawls's first principle is qualitative while the second is quantitative. The first principle makes clear that our relations with each other must not manifest themselves in ways in which anyone is oppressed.[13] The second principle requires that we all recognize and accept that some people will be in social positions that are more lucrative or more desirable than others, but that if they occupy such positions, their occupation of the positions does not undermine either the free exercise of the liberties of others or their access to basic necessities.[14] Understanding this aspect of Rawls's theory also makes it possible to understand what it is that Robert Nozick finds so problematic with Rawls's theory of justice. It is, therefore, to Nozick's theory that we now turn.

Nozick: The Minimal State and Distributive Justice

Robert Nozick holds the position that Rawls's theory of justice utilizing the Difference Principle is anything but a theory of *justice*. Nozick conceives of the nature of justice with respect to distributional principles and procedures on the model of Locke's *The Second Treatise of Government*. Here, Locke holds the position that every person is entitled to possess, distribute, and otherwise "dispose" of his (or her, for our purposes) property as he (or she) sees fit and, as Locke is careful to specify, do so within the bounds of the law of nature. The Lockean law of nature distinctly provides that every person is free to do with his property anything he wishes to do *just so long as* he does not violate the law of nature in doing so. What this means for Locke is that we rationally recognize our obligation to preserve our own lives, and that we do nothing to others in their attempts to preserve their lives, exercise their liberties, or handle their property as they wish. The exception, for Locke, occurs only when one's life comes "in competition." In that case, all bets are off and one may and must do what is required for survival. Otherwise, for Locke, we have an obligation to "preserve the rest of mankind" by not interfering with them in the exercise of their rights. There is nothing in Locke's law of nature that includes anything but obligations *not to interfere* with others.[15]

Nozick centers his attention squarely upon this Lockean view of the nature of our rights to property in formulating his own conception of principles of justice with respect to the transfer and acquisition of property. His principles, in contrast to those of Rawls, are minimalist principles having to do with the right of all people to utilize whatever advantages they may naturally possess or socially acquire to further their own interests *without* interference from others, or from government, in the way in which they go about their business. In essence, Nozick argues against Rawlsian *patterned* principles of justice that are bound to fail of their own accord because they are inconsistent with any reasonable conception of human motivation or desire, and which are unjust if applied because they deprive people of that which they have acquired under fair conditions.

For Nozick, to begin to explain the necessity for the existence of the state, and in turn to make it clear what the limits of the power and reach of government are, and this so that we can *justify* the existence of the state, we should consider state of nature theory, a condition of anarchy. We need not, for Nozick, consider the state of nature to be as Hobbes described it. For Hobbes, the state of nature is a condition of deteriorating, intolerable conditions among people, resulting ultimately in a rationale for the state's existence, but not in a justification for it.[16] Neither, however, must we take a pollyanic view and believe that everyone in a natural condition would do everything exactly as it should be done and that no one would ever clash with or disagree with anyone else. Instead, Nozick takes the view that we can utilize the concept of the state of nature in which people *generally* behave as they ought to behave to provide a rationale for the existence of a political state. And since it is possible for a state to violate the rights that people would possess without a state, it is important to note that Nozick's position is a *moral* one leading to a political one in the sense that, for him, "what persons may and may not do to one another limits what they may do through the apparatus of a state, or do to establish such an apparatus. The moral prohibitions it is permissible to enforce are the source of whatever legitimacy the state's fundamental coercive power has."[17]

If we reason that a state, to operate consistently with the dignity and independence of persons, must be neutral with respect to persons, then a state consisting of redistributional principles of justice, such as Rawls's Difference Principle, is neither a respecter of persons nor is it neutral. As Nozick puts the case, "side constraints upon action reflect the underlying Kantian principle that individuals are ends and not merely means; they may not be sacrificed or used for the achieving of other ends without their consent,"[18] so cases in which one person is made to bear the costs for a greater overall good are not justified. To clarify, Nozick explains that there are cases in which people sometimes sacrifice one thing to gain some benefit in some other way. So, for example, we sometimes diet or exercise to look or feel better. Denying oneself food (or certain types of food) or restful leisure time results in a benefit of some other kind either immediately or later. The question, however, is whether there are conditions under which some person or people must sacrifice or bear costs for the benefit of others, or for some more general social good. Nozick's answer is unmistakably that it is not the case that such sacrifices are justified:

> [T]here is no *social entity* with a good that undergoes some sacrifice for its own good. There are only individual people, different individual people, with their own individual lives. Using one of these people for the benefit of others, uses him and benefits the others. Nothing more. What happens is that something is done to him for the sake of others. Talk of an overall social good covers this up. (Intentionally?) To use a person in this way does not sufficiently respect and take account of the fact that he is a separate person, that his is the only life he has. *He* does not get some overbalancing good from his sacrifice, and no one is entitled to force this upon him—least of all a state or government that claims allegiance (as other individuals do not) and that therefore scrupulously must be *neutral* between its citizens.[19]

In other words, it is possible and justifiable for a person to sacrifice something of his own for his own benefit now or in the future because the person who is doing so is doing so *for himself*. But to claim that one person must sacrifice for others is to use that person as a thing and thereby violate the person's autonomy and rights. Nozick's view is that using a person is unjustified because "moral side constraints upon what we may do . . . reflect the fact of our separate existences" and "there is no moral outweighing of one of our lives by others so as to lead to a greater overall *social* good. There is no justified sacrifice of some of us for others."[20]

We should note, too, that requiring that we must in some way pay for the benefits we receive from society is unjust or objectionable. Nozick uses the example of giving a book to another person. If person A gives a book to person B, it is wrong to suppose that if person B did not ask for the book or in some way agree with A to pay for it, that A has a right to take money from B in exchange for the book.[21] Nozick's position is that

> one cannot, whatever one's purposes, just act so as to give people benefits and then demand (or seize) payment. Nor can a group of persons do this. If you may not charge and collect for benefits you bestow without prior agreement, you certainly may not do so for benefits whose bestowal costs you nothing, and most certainly people need not repay you for costless-to-provide benefits which yet *others* provided them. So the fact that we partially are "social products" in that we benefit from current patterns and forms created by the multitudinous actions of a long string of long-forgotten people . . . does not create in us a general floating debt which the current society can collect and use as it will.[22]

This conception of the processes taking place in the use of a theory of justice requiring that people pay in some way for benefits they receive, even when the benefits are the result of processes long forgotten and not under the individual's control, is the sort of theory of justice to which Nozick takes exception. It is, in short, the kind of theory of justice advanced by Rawls.

Nozick explains that questions of distribution with respect to the term "distributive justice" are not neutral for the plain and simple reason that it is an individual person who, in a redistributional scheme, is being used as an instrument to improve or benefit others or society on the whole. For Nozick, there is "no *central* distribution, no person or group entitled to control all the resources, jointly deciding how they are to be doled out. What each person gets, he gets from others who give to him in exchange for something, or as a gift."[23] To show even more clearly what is wrong with a principle of justice requiring redistribution of wealth from one person to another, Nozick considers the case of Wilt Chamberlain and the extra money he might earn or gain above and beyond his regular salary and the salaries of his fellow players.[24]

Suppose that Wilt Chamberlain is in such great demand as a basketball player that many spectators come to games primarily or solely to see him play. Suppose, further, that a million people are voluntarily willing to pay an extra fee to see him play, so they drop an extra twenty-five cents into a box marked with Chamberlain's name as they buy their tickets. Once they do so, those one million people have created a condition in which Chamberlain now has $250,000 that the other players do not receive. Is this fair? Is Wilt Chamberlain entitled to possess, use, distribute, and otherwise determine what to do with the money he has now in his possession?

Nozick's answer is that it certainly is fair, that there is no one who can rightfully claim any portion of the money from Chamberlain, nor may anyone distribute Chamberlain's money without his consent, and that this is the case because the transfer procedure by which the money was procured was itself fair. To justify this position, consider Nozick's explanation of the fact that "things come into the world already attached to people having entitlements over them."[25]

Nozick's entitlement theory operates on the basis of "the principle of justice in acquisition" and "the principle of justice in transfer."[26] These two principles constitute a justification of distribution of goods under any system such that "a distribution is just if everyone is entitled to the holdings they possess under the distribution."[27] When people obtain things fairly, they obtain them either through fair procedures of acquisition or through fair and just procedures of transfer. Nozick's view regarding what is fair and what is not is included in his definition of the subject of justice in holdings:

1. A person who acquires a holding in accordance with the principle of justice in acquisition is entitled to that holding.
2. A person who acquires a holding in accordance with the principle of justice in transfer, from someone else entitled to the holding, is entitled to the holding.
3. No one is entitled to a holding except by (repeated) applications of 1 and 2.[28]

The substance of Nozick's position here is that a person is entitled to what he has if he acquired it consistent with these principles. So, for example, Wilt Chamberlain is entitled to the extra income he receives because, we will assume, those who gave him the money received their money in accordance with the principle of justice in acquisition. Since a person has a right to do with what is his own as he sees fit, and if a person sees fit to give that money to Wilt Chamberlain for whatever purpose, then Chamberlain has received the funds in accordance with the principle of justice in transfer *and no one has a right to determine what will be done with that money, how it will be spent or not spent, except Wilt Chamberlain.* This is the case because "whatever arises from a just situation by just steps is itself just,"[29] and it is unjust to take from a person what is rightfully his own. And if it is true that no one has a right to interfere with others in doing with their legitimately gained property as they see fit, and so no individual or government has a right to redistribute that property, anything obtained through just means is obtained justly and what is to be done with things acquired in this way is no one's affair but that of its rightful owner. Furthermore, Chamberlain's *liberty* allows him to choose to do with his earnings as he wishes, just as those who pay extra to watch him play are free to do with justly acquired income as they see fit. The liberty of the individuals in the case of Wilt Chamberlain shows how liberty upsets patterns. Patterned principles of justice are, therefore, both logically inconsistent with the minimal state and they are practically unrealizable in their incompatibility with individual liberty.

There are those such as Rawls who hold the position that inequalities in wealth and opportunity are unjust unless they are to the benefit of everyone or to the least advantaged (worst off) members of society. Holding this kind of position is, for Nozick, nothing less than not respecting persons and so is not appropriately Kantian. Furthermore, the procedure from which a Rawlsian conception of distribution arises is inappropriate to an accurate conception of the way in which holdings are actually obtained.

To explain, Nozick makes a distinction between end-state and historical principles. "The entitlement theory of justice in distribution is *historical*; whether a distribution is just depends upon how it came about,"[30] not how it turns out. Nozick's theory is unlike end-result, current time-slice principles (such as those of Rawls) in which one holds "that the justice of a distribution is determined by how things are distributed (who has what) as judged by some *structural* principle(s) of just distribution."[31] In sum, for Nozick, Rawls's theory is an end-result, patterned and structured theory consisting of the redistribution of property to which no one but the rightful possessor is entitled.[32] Because Rawls's theory violates the Lockean conception of the right of the individual to do with his property and possessions as he sees fit, Nozick's arguments indicate that Rawls's theory is not a theory of justice, but is a theory of injustice because "no end-state principle or distributional patterned principle of justice can be continuously realized without continuous interference with people's lives."[33] And since Nozick's conception of the minimal state is that its purpose is to uphold the right of the individual to be left alone, Rawlsian liberalism goes too far.

If Rawls's theory of justice goes too far in allowing and requiring government to meddle in the affairs of the individual in exceeding the right, function, and purpose of government as a protective association, it may also be the case that Nozick's theory fails to go far enough in conceiving our relations with each other on his minimalist moral and political model. This is at the center of Michael Sandel's complaint against political liberalism in systems of thought like those of Rawls and Nozick. For Rawls and Nozick, the function of government is not to tell us what is good, or to lead us to some preconceived notion of what is good, but to create conditions in which we may search for the good for ourselves, where ideas of the good will and do differ between individuals. Understanding our political associations on minimalist liberal models like this is, for Sandel, a large part of the problems plaguing contemporary liberal societies. The solution, for Sandel, may depend on a reassessment of our social institutions and the moral foundations upon which they rest.

Sandel: The Procedural Republic and the Unencumbered Self

Michael Sandel's communitarian political thought rests on the notion that there must be a moral foundation for a complete rendering of political theory. For Sandel, it seems, creating and living by a political theory without a moral underpinning is like sailing in a ship with holes in the bottom. One spends too much time and energy bailing out water and not enough time sailing to one's destination. It is impossible to reach a destination when no one knows what it is, and political liberalism as political rationalism does not provide a clear conception of a destination and therefore cannot provide an adequate map for reaching one.[34] With its focus away from setting up or reflecting actual political institutions and its failure to specify a conception of the good, political liberalism gives us procedures to follow but no clearly defined goals, and it provides nothing for which a community may strive and nothing for it to do except be constrained by rules and procedures. Political systems not founded on well-formed moral conceptions and ships with leaky hulls ultimately sink and thereby fail to perform the function for which they are intended. The solution is, then, to find some other conception of our moral and political relations that specifies a goal and provides practical, not procedural, guidance in achieving it.

Unlike Rawls, who will not specify a particular conception of the good to which political thought and action might lead, Sandel recognizes the importance of moral theory providing a conception of the good that informs political theory and practice. Unlike Nozick, who adopts a Lockean moral viewpoint for the production of a politically minimalist conception of justice, Sandel's position is a maximalist political theory incorporating and recognizing moral theory as providing a rich concept of the human being. Regarding the paucity of much contemporary moral and political theorizing, Sandel puts the point succinctly: "[p]olitical philosophy seems often to reside at a distance from the world. Principles are one thing, politics another, and even our best efforts to 'live up' to our ideals typically founder on the gap between theory and practice."[35] For Sandel, what is wrong with liberal societies' conceptions of the nature of our political associations, and what is at the heart of the discontent of democracy, is that "notwithstanding the extension of the franchise (to women and African Americans) and the expansion of individual rights and entitlements in recent decades, there is a widespread sense that, individually and collectively, our control over the forces that govern our lives is receding rather than increasing. This sense is deepened by what appear simultaneously as the power and the powerlessness of the nation-state."[36] We are caught in the paradoxical feeling that the state is too intrusive because it might frustrate our purposes, and at the same time the state is "disempowered, unable effectively to control the domestic economy, to respond to persisting social ills, or to work America's will in the world."[37]

Both Rawls and Nozick admit that their theories of justice are not meant, and are not able, to incorporate complete ethical theories. Rawls makes it apparent that his purpose is not to do so when he writes:

> Justice as fairness is not a complete contract theory. For it is clear that the contractarian idea can be extended to the choice of more or less an entire ethical system, that is, to a system including principles for all the virtues and not only for justice. Now for the most part I shall consider only principles of justice and others closely related to them; I make no attempt to discuss the virtues in a systematic way. Obviously if justice as fairness succeeds reasonably well, a next step would be to study the more general view. . . .[38]

In essence, Rawls's position is that a theory of ethics, a moral view, comes *after* a consideration of justice. This, of course, is contrary to Sandel's view—that a theory and conception of morality ought to precede an understanding of the conception of justice *because* justice is a virtue, and virtue is and ought to be the subject matter of ethics. For Sandel, ethics must inform our political institutions, not stand in an incidental relation to them.

Lack of moral guidance for political theory and practice also exists in the justification of Nozick's minimalist entitlement theory. Introducing a Lockean account of the nature of justice with respect to distributional principles, Nozick says:

> Only when some divergence between our conception and Locke's is relevant to *political* philosophy, to our argument about the state, will it [Locke's state of nature] be mentioned. The completely accurate statement of the moral

> background, including the precise statement of the moral theory and its underlying basis, would require a full-scale presentation and is a task for another time. (A lifetime?) That task is so crucial, the gap left without its accomplishment so yawning, that it is only a minor comfort to note that we here are following the respectable tradition of Locke, who does not provide anything remotely resembling a satisfactory explanation of the status and basis of the law of nature in his *Second Treatise*.[39]

For Nozick, just as for Rawls, a theory of the virtues, or a conception of morality, does not precede political theorizing or the creation of political institutions. Nozick at least admits that not having an adequate theory of ethics to ground politics is unfortunate, but he proceeds nonetheless to create a political theory without a moral base. This is a mistake, according to Sandel, and is part and parcel of "democracy's discontent."

According to Sandel, the core theses of political liberalism are that "a just society seeks not to promote any particular ends, but enables its citizens to pursue their own ends, consistent with a similar liberty for all; it therefore must govern by principles that do not presuppose any particular conception of the good."[40] What this means is that in liberal societies, no conception of the good is preferred over any other. We recognize that there are many conceptions of the good that any person might choose to adopt, and therefore to require that some particular conception of the good inform the principles governing a society and its institutions is to limit the liberty or autonomy of individuals. For political liberalism, we claim, in Kantian fashion, the priority of the right over the good in this way, thereby empowering people to enable them to live unencumbered, not oppressed by the moral requirements that others may prefer that a person adopt.

In fact, it is precisely the (problematic) conception of a *person* that is at the heart of the liberal notion of the unencumbered self. That notion of the person is derived from Rawls's Kantian conception of the autonomy of the human being and recognition of a plurality of ends. For Kant, since different people have different visions of the good and various views of how they ought to live their lives to achieve the good life, there is no particular principle that we may derive *based on ends* that will provide a categorical, universal guide for morality. That is why Kant rejects ends as a basis for morality—ends are different and changeable, so they are contingent. For Kant, if we wish to establish a firm foundation for morality, it must not be contingent and changeable, but instead universal and immutable. The only principle, therefore, that will satisfy the universality requirement is a *categorical* imperative. The Kantian categorical imperative requires that we recognize each person's rationality and autonomy in giving the moral law to himself, and therefore we acknowledge each person's being able to understand also the requirement of morality to respect persons and to be bound to the imperative of morality that will apply all the time, to all cases, under all circumstances.

Understanding the nature of Kantian morality leads to its connection to political theory. Sandel describes the relationship such that on this Kantian model, "As the subject is prior to its ends, so the right is prior to the good. Society is best arranged when it is governed by principles that do not presuppose any particular conception of the good, for any other arrangement would fail to respect persons as being capable of choice; it would treat them as objects rather than subjects, as means rather than ends in themselves."[41]

Rawls uses this Kantian conception of the rational human subject in the original position to explain that it is *not* necessary or desirable that we know our particular circumstances in the world, but instead that we choose principles by which to govern our society that are formulated *in advance* of the particularity of our persons and of the particularities of our society. What this means, as Sandel puts it, is that in a Rawlsian scheme of things, "what is most essential to our personhood, are not the ends we choose but our capacity to choose them."[42] In other words, the unencumbered self sees itself as separated from and independent of any community at all. It is a subject that is sovereign over itself. It is a social being without a society and a moral being without a moral theory.

To say that the Rawlsian or liberal unencumbered self is a social being without a society is to hold that the unencumbered self is both undesirable and impossible. Liberal thinking separates the self from the society that largely informs it, rendering our selves artificial, rather than naturally social, beings. For the Rawlsian or Nozickian liberal, the individual is, like the Hobbesian individual who springs from the earth like a mushroom, having no associations with others,[43] or like the Cartesian thinker—an isolated, atomistic mind having no association with others, not even *knowing* that others exist, but endowed nonetheless with full rational capacity. For the communitarian, we are *not* like that. We come into the world with attachments, as members of families and communities, as participants in societies and governments, and to think of ourselves as unassociated, or disassociated, is simply to think of ourselves as abstractions, not as real human beings with aspirations, desires, and goals that are largely informed by our social dealings with others. As Sandel sees it, it is not *possible* to understand ourselves as "independent selves, independent in the sense that our identity is never tied to our aims and attachments."[44] Because we wish not simply to deliberate about ends, but to "deliberate well about the common good," it requires "more than the capacity to choose one's ends and to respect others' rights to do the same. It requires a knowledge of public affairs and also a sense of belonging, a concern for the whole, a moral bond with the community whose fate is at stake."[45]

What is wrong with the liberal thinking of Rawls and Nozick is, in short, that they do not see the human person as a member of a family, a community, a nation, or as having a history that is inseparably tied to the community of which the person is a member. "To imagine a person incapable of constitutive attachments such as these is not to conceive an ideally free and rational agent, but to imagine a person wholly without character, without moral depth."[46] This is part of Michael Stocker's complaint that modern moral theories "lack the person," having their central focus on moral rules rather than persons and their relationships that are central to moral theory.[47] In its political manifestations, for Sandel, it is "a striking feature of the welfare state that it offers a powerful promise of individual rights, and also demands of its citizens a high measure of mutual engagement. But the self-image that attends the rights cannot sustain the engagement."[48] In essence, there is something dramatically wrong with liberal societies' views of the relationship between the individual and the community, and we see it unfolding historically in the failure of liberalism to achieve its goals. Sandel puts it this way in his outline of the history of the decline of the philosophy of common purposes:

> By the mid- or late twentieth century, the national republic had run its course. Except for extraordinary moments, such as war, the nation proved too vast a scale across which to cultivate the shared self-understandings necessary to community in the formative, or constitutive sense. And so the gradual shift, in our practices and institutions, from a public philosophy of common purposes to one of fair procedures, from a politics of good to a politics of right, from the national republic to the procedural republic.[49]

Sandel describes the decline of the liberal state with its precarious adherence to moral theory, when it adheres at all, leading to the decline or erasure of community, leaving the individual with empty goals and aspirations because the individual is characterless, living in a society suffering the same moral disability. The sad moral of the story may just be that the character of political liberalism is to have no character, that the liberal human being has lost its humanity because both the individual and society have given way to abstract rules and procedures in their failure to recognize ourselves as relational beings.[50] In the liberal's march toward liberty, what he has lost is "some way of defining the relevant community of sharing, some way of seeing the participants as mutually indebted and morally engaged to begin with."[51]

What does Sandel offer as the corrective to the anomie, the isolation and extreme individualism created by liberalism in politics and moral theory? It is not clear, except that for the communitarian, we must understand ourselves leading lives as embedded, not unencumbered, selves. This is the case in the sense that we do not choose our social roles, but are born into them, or simply live in them, as members of families, societies, and groups. So the communitarian's view is that our morality is shaped by the community of which we are a part and that we find and form our identities in that community.

The problems here are obvious. Will Kymlicka points out in his essay on communitarianism that theorists like Sandel

> say that there are shared ends that can serve as the basis for a politics of the common good which will be legitimate to all groups in society. But they give no examples of such ends; perhaps because there are none. They say that these shared ends are to be found in our historical practices, but they do not mention that those practices were defined by a small section of society—propertied white men—to serve the interests of propertied, white men. Attempts to promote these kinds of ends reduce legitimacy and further exclude marginalized groups.[52]

What this means, of course, is that for the communitarian, the right or moral thing to do is to adopt "conceptions of the good that conform to the community's way of life, while discouraging conceptions of the good that conflict with it."[53]

The problem here is that we then return to suppression of doctrines, ideas, and ways of life that are contrary to the reigning community view. We may return to acceptance of oppression and exploitation of minorities, who are not necessarily part of the "shared" history of the community in power, and thereby sacrifice the gains in individual freedoms that liberal thinking has secured.

There are, then, serious problems with communitarianism that are commensurate with the problems associated with liberal individualism. Perhaps there is some other way of conceiving our moral and political lives that is more satisfying than either liberals or communitarians can provide.

Virginia Held: Feminist Transformations of Moral Theory

Virginia Held adheres to the position in "Feminist Transformations of Moral Theory" that there is much work to be done by feminists to correct the biases of traditional moral theories and build a feminist conception of morality. She does not offer a complete, fully formed moral theory of her own, nor does she hold that it would necessarily be desirable for anyone to do so. In fact, she notes that it is doubtful that there will be a fully worked out feminist moral theory, or any feminist "stars" like Rawls or Nozick because there are too many conversations being held to build a feminist ethical theory and because feminist theorists avoid the tendency of traditional theories to search for and find a dominant or primary theory. They do not seek such a theory because to do so goes against the feminists' belief that the search for a moral theory is something that people do as a community, not as isolated individuals.[54]

Making note of the relational character of feminist ethics and political theories and seeing their project as a shared community of interests reflects a tendency in feminist moral theorizing to insist that traditional moral theories fail to see human beings as relational beings. In this respect, feminist thinking is like communitarian theorizing in that it questions the value, veracity, and usefulness of conceptions of the human being as an isolated, individualistic, atomistic self. But it is not enough simply to see that the traditional moral theorist's conception of the person is inadequate because it does not take into account our relational nature. For the feminist theorist, what is also missing in traditional theorizing is that it does not take "adequate account of the experience of women" in moral theory[55] or, for that matter, in political theory.[56]

One of the important and influential distinctions made in traditional moral theories is the distinction between reason and emotion. Generally speaking, the history of philosophy is alive with references and intimations about the association of rationality with masculinity and power, and femininity with emotion and dependency. One might think that the corrective here is simply to include the experience of women in moral theorizing. Held, however, points out that this is not the solution because

> Moral theory as so far developed is incapable of correcting itself without an almost total transformation. It cannot simply absorb the gender that has been "left behind," even if both genders would want it to. To continue to

> build morality on rational principles opposed to the emotions and to include women among the rational will leave no one to reflect the promptings of the heart, which promptings can be moral rather than merely instinctive.[57]

In other words, Held's position is that simply to concern ourselves with "inclusiveness" by allowing others to share in a theory is to ignore the possibility that there may be very distinct differences between male and female conceptions of the nature of morality. What this entails is that true "inclusiveness" would manifest itself not simply in allowing women into the calculations and theoretical underpinnings of traditional moral theory, but to transform moral theories so that they include also the theories and experiences *of* women.

For Held, although there is no particular programme to which we may look that is *the* feminist ethical theory, it is still possible, important, and instructive to consider three major points of focus informing "feminist attempts to transform ethics into a theoretical and practical activity that could be acceptable from a feminist point of view."[58] Those three points are the traditional moral theories' distinction between reason and emotion, their distinction between public and private spheres, and their creation of a concept of self.[59]

In the history of philosophy and the history of ethics in particular, there has been a tendency to make a clear and value-laden distinction between reason and emotion. In Plato's work, especially in *The Republic*, we see diminution of the importance of emotion or desire in the relegation of these aspects of the human soul to the third and lowest level (below rationality and self-control) and associated with producers (artisans) rather than with "protectors" and "rulers."[60] We see it in Kant's almost complete discounting of emotion in the moral realm when he describes desires and goals as particular and contingent and therefore unfit for inclusion in a universally applicable moral theory. The best we might find in the history of traditional ethics is Mill, where he admits that our goal is happiness (an emotional state), but that we must find the most rational way to achieve it.[61]

As Held points out, what we find in the actual experience of women in the realm of the moral is a "salient (set of moral concerns) that differs from those of traditional or standard moral theory. Women's experience of moral problems seems to lead us to be especially concerned with actual relationships between embodied persons, and with what these relationships seem to require."[62] The sort of thing Held has in mind here is exemplified in the work of Sara Ruddick and Caroline Whitbeck on maternal ethics as well as Held's own work on the issue of mothering as a moral relation[63] in which the process of mothering as a moral activity has center stage.[64] Held shows that it is not only in this context that we see the distinction between the traditional conception of moral theory as properly focused on rationality rather than emotion (in ignoring mothering as a moral activity, for example),[65] but the example of relational ethics informed by the activity of mothering also leads us to her discussion of the distinction between the public and private realms. It further takes us to the affinity that exists between feminist and communitarian theorizing.

Held takes notice of the tendency in the history of philosophy relegating women to the private realm and men to the public.[66] Women's experiences have been traditionally assigned to the realm of the home while men's experiences are traditionally understood in the "public" realm as conquerors, heroes, and as business and political leaders. The tendency in the history of western thought has been to see the realms of men as of much more import and much more influential than the role of women in the home.

Seeing a woman's role in the realm of private human association as a purely biological process, but not as social or moral, is also common. To understand woman's place in human life in this way, however, is a mistake since the private realm is as much a moral realm as the public because "human mothering shapes language and culture, it forms human social personhood, it develops morality."[67] It is therefore inappropriate to think that the activity of mothering, or any kind of caring relationship, is outside the moral realm, having nothing to do with the development of human personhood or a society's moral outlook. People in caring roles *create* more than mere biological human beings; they create moral human beings. We are not, then, as the communitarian also points out (but without reference to the experience of women) isolated and alone in the world. We are very clearly relational beings, constructed by the society and the close, personal bonds that we share with others.

The third common element of feminist moral thinking to be contrasted with that of traditional moral theory is the concept of self. As Held notes, most traditional moral theories have barely noticed the significance of the moral realm of families, friendships, groups, and neighborhood concerns.[68] Held's point in this respect is much like that of Sandel on the same issue. The liberal conception of the person is incomplete because in conceiving of "others" as abstractions, traditional liberal moral theories have ignored the fact that "others" are "characteristically, actual flesh and blood other human beings for whom we have actual feelings and with whom we have real ties."[69] To think of people as isolated from others is not only unrealistic, it is not a picture of what it is to be a human being. It also ignores the fact that our relationships with others are part of what and who we are as human beings.

But it is a mistake to think that the feminist view that we are relational selves is identical to communitarianism. This is the case because, as Held points out, communitarians "pay no more attention than liberalism and standard moral theory to the experience of women, to the context of mothering, or to friendship as women experience it."[70] There are dangers of which to be wary in communitarianism. There are traditions that have oppressed and continued to oppress women, but contemporary communitarians have an "impoverished account of how women are to break with (those traditions)."[71] Furthermore, where Sandel criticizes individualism, he does so by focusing his attention on persons and their ends. So where Sandel criticizes the liberal conception of morality and political thought, Held finds a related critique of communitarianism. Held puts it this way:

> [T]he relational self of feminist theory is not only oriented toward purposive action. What we *are* is already a self related to other selves, regardless of our ends. For a relation between persons to make sense, we must be able to refer to the persons in the relation as well as to the relation. But we can reject the claims of individualism that the value of the relation must be reducible to values to the individuals in the relation; relations themselves can have value.

> We can also reject the claim that persons have value insofar as they contribute to the value of communal relations. Both persons and relations can have value. . . .[72]

The feminist view of our relations therefore might be understood to include relevant aspects of individualism as well as those of community, without preferring either as a dominant paradigm of moral thinking.[73]

To see the feminist ethicist or political theorist as willing and able to move with ease between conceptions of the self, of individualism and community, and between the reason/emotion distinction might subject feminists to the charge of relativism. This is perhaps a "danger" of feminist thinking, but it is not a necessary feature of it, especially if we are aware that emotion can be just as universal as reason.[74]

In the long run, what Held sees as the vision of a feminist future includes the following features.[75] A feminist society would be very different from a society of individuals pursuing only their own interests; it would include a cultural life designed to enrich people's lives, not to serve commercial interests. It would be a society in which government would be founded on the consent of the governed, but it would not take the traditional contractarian view that government should be formulated on the basis of a hypothetical contract. Relationships between real people pursuing real projects would instead be the key. And a feminist society "might understand the future of children to be its highest priority" because then it might be that fewer children would "grow up to be lawbreakers or irresponsible agents in need of ever more detailed legal restraints" and thus create a society in which our traditional concept of the state as a power-wielding construct might diminish. Held's view is thus a conception of human morality and society that tries to transcend the limitations and constraints of traditional moral and political theories, that recognizes the dangers of habit and tradition from the communitarian theorist's vision of encumbered selves, and that takes seriously the importance of the moral and political experience of women in transforming theory from something abstract and unapproachable to something concrete and applicable to real human lives.

Conclusion

The jury is still out, and probably will be for a long time to come, on whether it is possible to repair the problems of political liberalism caused by its obsession with individual rights and its impoverished conception of the human being. Neither, however, are communitarianism and feminist theorizing necessarily solutions to the problems that plague our moral and political associations. Their views, along with the views of the political liberal, may some day be meshed into a satisfying and human-centered, practical and theoretical project, or they may be superseded by a completely different sort of theory. For the present, however, we cannot determine which view of our moral and political lives will serve to solve the perennial problems of human association. But in American ethical and political thought today, just as in the theoretical projects of the founders of the American republic, satisfaction with just "good enough" will never do. The American penchant for living better and for doing better involves a persistent critical project that will, we suspect, continue to transform theories and practices to reflect the changing conditions that a complex society creates and embraces.

NOTES

1. Michael Sandel, *Democracy's Discontent* (Cambridge, 1996), 3.
2. John Rawls, *A Theory of Justice* (Cambridge, 1971), 15.
3. Ibid. 34.
4. Ibid. 253.
5. The inclusion of the notion that there are differing conceptions of the good is part of Michael Sandel's arguments against rationalistic and procedural accounts of justice to be discussed later in this essay.
6. Ibid. 253.
7. *A Theory of Justice*, 60.
8. It is necessary, according to Rawls, that the first principle be understood as existing and applying prior to the second because "a departure from the institutions of equal liberty required by the first principle cannot be justified by, or compensated for, by greater social and economic advantages" (ibid. 61). In short, no rational person would give up liberty for economic security. To do so would be self-defeating.
9. Ibid. 60. The more complete statement of the Difference Principle specifies that "social and economic inequalities are to be arranged so that they are both: (a) to the greatest benefit of the least advantaged . . . , and (b) attached to offices and positions open to all under conditions of fair equality of opportunity" (ibid. 302).
10. Ibid. 17.
11. The procedures and rules of associated living set up by the Hobbesian original contractors include everything from the distribution of property once government is established to what doctrines are to be taught in educational institutions. See Hobbes, *Leviathan*, ed. Michael Oakeshott (New York, 1962), chapters 18 and 21 on the "Rights of Sovereigns by Institution" and "The Liberty of Subjects."
12. Perhaps the formulation of Rawls's Difference Principle would not be so problematic if Rawls had left the principle in its original (1958) formulation specifying that differences in wealth and opportunity must be to the advantage of all rather than the final (1971) formulation in which differences must be to the advantage of society's worst-off members. This leaves open the possibility that those who are better off are made *worse off* so that the *worst off* are to benefit from redistribution. If this is the case, it is not clear that rational human beings, concerned to further their own interests, would be wise to agree to principles that would strip them of the benefits they might otherwise receive.
13. Jean Hampton, *Political Philosophy* (Boulder, 1997) argues that Rawls's contractarian method can be used to test our relationships for the presence of personal or political domination by considering "ties to friends or spouses or fellow citizens, when they are to people who are able to reciprocate what we give to them . . . , are morally acceptable only insofar as they do not involve, on either side, the infliction of costs or the confiscation of benefits over a significant period of time that implicitly reveal disregard rather than respect for that person. Someone who persistently takes more from you than you get from this person is using you by treating you as a source of benefits for which he or she need not reciprocate, as if you were some kind of servant. . . ." Doing this indicates disrespect of the person, "and it is this disrespect that . . . is at the heart of injustice . . ." (163).
14. David Conway notes that Rawls's reasoning with respect to the implications of the difference principle "seems clearly invalid" since Rawls holds that if a person does

not "deserve to enjoy better life-prospects than others, then that person deserves *not* to enjoy better life-prospects than these others." See David Conway, *Classical Liberalism* (New York, 1995), 32. It is paradoxical and wrong to think that if a person is in possession of characteristics that he does not deserve, that for the Rawlsian, it follows that someone else deserves the benefits. In other words, if I have a natural endowment that in some way benefits me but I do not *deserve* the benefit because I did not merit having it, then *you* are entitled to the benefit instead. But *you* did nothing to deserve the benefit, either.

15. This provision of the Lockean law of nature expresses the classic distinction between negative and positive rights. See, for one of the most celebrated discussions of this distinction, Sir Isaiah Berlin's *Four Essays on Liberty* (New York, 1970).
16. Robert Nozick, *Anarchy, State, and Utopia* (New York, 1974), 5.
17. Ibid. 6.
18. Ibid. 31.
19. Ibid. 33.
20. Ibid.
21. Ibid. 95.
22. Ibid.
23. Ibid. 149.
24. Wilt Chamberlain was a basketball player in the NBA in the 1960s and 1970s whose professional stature and skill are commensurate with those of Michael Jordan or Shaquille O'Neal in the 1990s.
25. *Anarchy, State, and Utopia*, 160.
26. Ibid. 150.
27. Ibid. 151.
28. Ibid.
29. Ibid.
30. Ibid. 153.
31. Ibid.
32. Nozick's explanation of a patterned principle of distribution is that "it specifies that a distribution is to vary along with some natural dimension, weighted sum of natural dimensions, or lexicographic ordering of natural dimensions" (156). Jean Hampton provides an interesting critique of Nozick's rejection of patterned principles and his belief that his own theory is not so constrained. Hampton points out that "Nozick explicitly says that a Lockean proviso (the notion contained in the law of nature that it is unjust for a person to take more than he needs from nature, and that there are cases in which some acquisitions will adversely affect the interests or lives of others) could involve the state in negating certain transfers that although in accord with the rules regulating just transfer, nonetheless result in a distribution of holdings that does not leave as much and as good for others in the community" and so Nozick "has given the state moral license to interfere in property holdings insofar as the state must enforce that proviso" and this is "an implicit admission that the state *is* under a moral obligation to enforce a certain 'pattern' in its implementation of a system of distributive justice. . . ." See *Political Philosophy*, 152.
33. *Anarchy, State, and Utopia*, 163.
34. Michael Oakeshott in "Rationalism in Politics," in *Rationalism in Politics and Other Essays* (Indianapolis, 1962) calls rationalistic politics "the politics of the felt need; for the Rationalist, politics are always charged with the feeling of the moment. He waits upon circumstance to provide him with his problems, but rejects its aid in their solution" (9). Oakeshott's explanation of rationalist politics (political liberalism) is one of the clearest and most complete accounts of the general problems with procedural accounts of justice and political activity. For example, Oakeshott points out that the liberal (rationalist) shuns experience and believes that "political machinery can take the place of moral and political education" (11). It is important also to note that not all versions of political liberalism are the same. There are important distinctions between classical and

modern or contemporary liberalism. See Alan Ryan, "Liberalism" in *A Companion to Contemporary Political Philosophy*, ed. Robert E. Goodin and Phillip Pettit (Cambridge, 1995), 291–311.

35. Sandel, "The Procedural Republic and the Unencumbered Self," *Political Theory* 12.1 (1984): 81.
36. Ibid. 92.
37. Ibid.
38. *A Theory of Justice*, 17.
39. *Anarchy State and Utopia*, 9. Simon Hailwood (*Exploring Nozick*, Aldershot, 1996, 50–51) explains that Nozick's characterization of Locke's theory is unfair and incomplete. Locke does, in fact, provide a foundation for his laws of nature in his acceptance of a Biblical account of property rights. Locke's position is that we are all endowed by God with property from the beginning of our existence. For Locke, we have a "property in our own person" and, by extension, a property in all that for which we have labored since our labor is just as much ours as the physical being with which we have been naturally endowed. See Locke's *Second Treatise of Government*, ed. C. B. Macpherson (Indianapolis, 1980), chapter 5, "Of Property."
40. "The Procedural Republic and the Unencumbered Self," 82.
41. Ibid. 85.
42. Ibid. 86.
43. See Thomas Hobbes, *De Cive*, ed. Howard Warrender (Oxford, 1983), 117, where Hobbes, explaining the origin of dominion of one person over another, suggests that we ought to "return again to the state of nature, and consider men as if but now sprung out of the earth, and suddenly (like mushrooms), come to full maturity, without all kind of engagement to each other."
44. "The Procedural Republic and the Unencumbered Self," 90. Jean Hampton notes that the communitarian complaint about the concept of the person in liberal theory is misguided because it is the value of human autonomy that is "driving the liberals' concern for the individual, and not some sort of implausible theory of the person as a socially naked atom" and that "the liberal is convinced that the best way to ensure that an individual can flourish within her community is to give her the freedom she needs to live (what will surely be) a highly social life in the way that she chooses." *Political Philosophy*, 186.
45. *Democracy's Discontent*, 5.
46. "The Procedural Republic and the Unencumbered Self," 90.
47. See Michael Stocker, "The Schizophrenia of Modern Ethical Theories," *Journal of Philosophy*, 12 AG 76; 73: 453–66.
48. "The Procedural Republic and the Unencumbered Self," 94.
49. Ibid. 93.
50. One might also charge that the unencumbered self of political liberalism is concerned primarily with justice, with protection of negative rights, but not with the community in which those rights are defended. Will Kymlicka takes exception to this claim, charging that a communitarian critique of liberalism based on the notion that there is a dichotomy between justice and community is mistaken. He says that "justice does not displace love or solidarity, and nothing in the idea of justice precludes people from choosing to forgo their rightful claims in order to help others. Justice simply ensures that these decisions are genuinely voluntary and that no one can force others to accept a subordinate position. Justice enables loving relationships, but ensures that they are not corrupted by domination or subordination" (368). See Kymlicka, "Communitarianism," *A Companion to Contemporary Political Philosophy*, ed. Robert E. Goodin and Phillip Pettit (Cambridge, 1995), 366–78. It is possible, then, that the communitarian critique of liberalism is based on straw-man formulations of the liberal's arguments.
51. *Democracy's Discontent*, 17.
52. "Communitarianism," 375.
53. Ibid. 370.

54. Virginia Held, "Feminist Transformations of Moral Theory," *Philosophy and Phenomenological Research*, Vol. I, Supplement, Fall 1990, 321–44, 328. Held quotes Kathryn Morgan's "Women and Moral Madness" in *Science, Morality and Feminist Theory*, ed. Marsha Hanen and Kai Nielsen (Calgary, 1987), 223.
55. "Feminist Transformations of Moral Theory," 321.
56. See, for example, the essays in Mary Lyndon Shanley and Carole Pateman, eds., *Feminist Interpretations and Political Theory* (University Park, 1991) and Judith Butler and Joan W. Scott, eds., *Feminists Theorize the Political* (New York, 1992).
57. "Feminist Transformations of Moral Theory," 327.
58. Ibid. 328.
59. For an important discussion of the gender specificity of Rawls's *A Theory of Justice*, and hence an example of the reason/emotion and public/private dichotomy, see Susan Moller Okin, "Reason and Feeling in Thinking About Justice," *Ethics*, 99: 2 (1989), 229–49.
60. See Plato, *Republic*, Bk. IV, ch. xiii, 434d–441c and ch. xiv, 441c–445b, trans. F. M. Cornford (London, 1980).
61. "Feminist Transformations of Moral Theory," 330.
62. Ibid. See also her "Feminist Inquiry and the Future" in Virginia Held, ed., *Justice and Care: Essential Readings in Feminist Ethics* (Boulder, 1995), 153–76, esp. 156–7, in which she argues that "an adequate moral theory should be built on appropriate feelings as well as on appropriate reasoning" (157).
63. See Virginia Held, "The Obligations of Mothers and Fathers," in Joyce Trebilcot, ed., *Mothering: Essays in Feminist Theory* (Totowa, 1984).
64. For an accessible and clear overview of maternal ethics, see Rosemarie Tong, *Feminine and Feminist Ethics* (Belmont, 1993), chapter 7. For a general summary of feminist ethics, see Jean Grimshaw, "The Idea of a Female Ethics," in *A Companion to Ethics*, ed. Peter Singer (Cambridge, 1993), 491–9.
65. Held is aware that not all feminist theorists believe that it is desirable to think of a distinctively female conception of ethics based on emotion since equating "tendencies women in fact display with feminist views" is dangerous since women's tendencies "may well be the result of the sexist, oppressive conditions in which women's lives have been lived" ("Feminist Transformations of Moral Theory," 331).
66. See also Essay 10 for indications of this tendency of thought against which Angelina and Sarah Grimke had to fight to be accepted as orators and writers in the abolitionist and women's rights movements, and Elizabeth Cady Stanton's battle against a related tendency in her comments regarding the appropriateness of women commenting on or interpreting the Bible.
67. "Feminist Transformations of Moral Theory," 335.
68. Ibid. 337.
69. Ibid. 338.
70. Ibid. 339.
71. Held, *Feminist Morality* (Chicago, 1993), 188.
72. Ibid. 190.
73. For a discussion of feminist communitarianism, see Maria Lugones, "Community," in *A Companion to Feminist Philosophy*, ed. Allison Jaggar and Iris Marion Young (Malden, 1998), 466–74 and Marilyn Friedman's "Feminism and Modern Friendship: Dislocating the Community" *Ethics*, Vol. 99, No. 2 (Jan., 1989), 275–90.
74. "Feminist Transformations of Moral Theory," 332. Communitarian thinking in general is also subject to this charge, insofar as there is a multitude of communities that exist and of which people may become members. Furthermore, there is the problem of membership in overlapping communities. What does one do when the values of two or more communities conflict with each other? Which of them is to take precedence?
75. "Feminist Inquiry and the Future," 169–72.

Index